Jane Welsh Carlyle, Geraldine Endsor Jewsbury

Selections from the Letters of Geraldine Endsor Jewsbury

to Jane Welsh Carlyle

Jane Welsh Carlyle, Geraldine Endsor Jewsbury

Selections from the Letters of Geraldine Endsor Jewsbury
to *Jane Welsh Carlyle*

ISBN/EAN: 9783337019174

Printed in Europe, USA, Canada, Australia, Japan

Cover: Foto ©ninafisch / pixelio.de

More available books at **www.hansebooks.com**

MISS JEWSBURY'S LETTERS

PRINTED BY
SPOTTISWOODE AND CO., NEW-STREET SQUARE
LONDON

SELECTIONS FROM THE LETTERS

OF

GERALDINE ENDSOR JEWSBURY

TO

JANE WELSH CARLYLE

EDITED BY

MRS. ALEXANDER IRELAND

AUTHOR OF 'THE LIFE OF JANE WELSH CARLYLE'

PREFACED BY

A MONOGRAPH ON MISS JEWSBURY, BY THE EDITOR

LONDON

LONGMANS, GREEN, AND CO.

AND NEW YORK: 15 EAST 16th STREET

1892

All rights reserved

INTRODUCTION

FRIENDSHIPS between women have occasionally furnished material for ignorant sneers. 'A sudden thought strikes me. Let us swear an eternal friendship!' was not a kind hit, though it bore within it a grain of truth. Women are impulsive, and must have some object for their love. Even school-girls conceive almost a passion one for another, until 'deep calls unto deep,' and they learn life's truest need. The memorable and touching friendships of mature women for each other are too well known to need proof of their existence. If they are, in a sense, a compromise, what then ? In these undying, clinging attachments, it may sometimes be noted that one of the women is masculine in her very womanhood, dominating in intellect or will, or possessed of some subtle force of which we know nothing, and the other is 'a woman indeed'— defenceless, tender, instinctively craving after that 'shadow of the substance' for which she was made to long. At times, two women, each isolated as to the natural relation with the other sex, will turn blindly to each other, and fling their lavish and uncared-for wealth of love into each other's hearts. The bosom where no child ever nestled will draw unto itself some nature where a heart-hunger has been left unfed, and clasp it close. Again, the woman who has loved, and has drawn back with a sick dissatisfaction from the scanty fare man's love has meted out to her, will turn desperately to one of her own sex, and pour out the unappreciated treasure of her heart. And again, the woman who knows man's love, and must forego to bask in its warm, glowing beams, will rest on another woman's love as on something safe—something that shall not wound, nor cut, nor pierce, nor leave her stranded. She may even find an avenue for a confidence the craving for which is eating into her heart, and, in trust and sympathy, she may heal her own wounds while she pours oil and balm into those of another. Such was the friendship between Miss Jewsbury and Mrs. Carlyle. If it did not 'pass the love of woman,' it certainly reached the utmost boundary of which that sacred 'relationship of the spirit' is capable. Each woman bore with her, as a birthright, love itself; but the one was married and lonely, the other was *un*married and lonely. Over each had the 'car of Juggernaut' passed with searing bruise. Each knew the meaning of the words 'Thou shalt not have'! Each knew precisely what each wanted, but had not. The one was masculine in many ways, and she it was who bore the yoke of marriage, and the deeper cross of wedded loneliness. The other, feminine to the heart's core, seemed to have the full cup of love ever at her lips, yet by some irony of fate was left lonely—died lonely, in one sense; and the two women loved each other passionately. Their correspondence, so glowing with life that it is still warm to the touch of the spirit, breathes no ordinary friendship and needs no comment. That it is fragmentary is inevitable; but it is carved out of the living rock, and tells more of Jane Welsh Carlyle than of Geraldine Jewsbury. Of the latter I subjoin a few biographical particulars. I knew her well, and loved her much. It was not then given me to understand over what tragic depths the bright ever-changing ripples of her lively and witty manifestations played with such inextinguishable archness. But she is at rest; her beloved friend is at rest; and these letters, which I edit with a pain at my heart, tell their own tale, and confirm the words of him who said, 'Wise judges are we one of another!'

Geraldine Endsor Jewsbury was born at Measham, in Derbyshire, in the year 1812. Her father, Thomas Jewsbury, left Derbyshire, where business had not prospered well with him, about 1818, and settled in Manchester as a merchant, uniting with this business the duties of agent to the West of England Insurance Company. The family was rather large, the means rather narrow. One infant was born after the removal from Derbyshire. This was Sydney, who afterwards went to sea. The oldest of the family was Maria, afterwards Mrs. Fletcher, and she was nearly nineteen years of age when the heavy cares of the orphaned family devolved upon her. The latest born, Sydney, was but a month old at the time; Geraldine, about six years of age; and there were three other sons—Henry, Tom, and Frank. It was not until 1832 that Geraldine—the bright, fairy-like girl—was placed in the position which her sister vacated on her marriage with Mr. Fletcher; and in 1840, when Mr. Thomas Jewsbury died, and the household was broken up, Geraldine became housekeeper to her brother Frank, remaining with him until his marriage, which took place in 1853.

There was always a strong bond between the brother and sister—one that neither marriage, nor separation, nor death could alter. There had been a terrible shock to Geraldine's affections in the death of Mrs. Fletcher, her dear and only sister, who had acted a mother's part to her, and who had died in India when the sensitive Geraldine was only in her twenty-first year. So there was all the more love for Frank, and he had it! Geraldine's nature was rich in affection, sparkling with light, rapid in forming conclusions, which were not always of the wisest. Intellectually she was a man, but the heart within her was as womanly as ever daughter of Eve could boast. This combination of keen intellect and truly feminine heart—this being, defenceless and tender on the one hand, and strong enough to cleave the very rocks on the other—could never, in truth, grow old, never become hardened by the world's coarse realities. She was generous to a fault, and noble-hearted, yet mentally searching and sounding depths which it were happier for the average woman to leave unsounded.

It was in 1841 that Miss Jewsbury first met the Carlyles, when the 'sage of Chelsea' pronounced her to be 'one of the most interesting young women he had seen for years—clear, delicate sense and courage looking out of her small sylph-like figure.'

He could not know how intently he was to be regarded, in time, by the 'clear, delicate sense' which animated that small frame, nor could he then be aware of the links of iron that were forged on the instant between the hearts of the two women—the sparkling, sometimes stern, Jane Welsh Carlyle, and the brilliant, but ever tender, Geraldine Jewsbury. Nor could he know how the one was to uphold the other and turn to her, nor how the two were to exchange letters that were almost love-letters through the long years that were to come. He knew not of the passionate thirst that was unsatisfied in these two fiery natures, nor how each would, at times, look to the other for a straw to hold on to in the tempest of Life. For Miss Jewsbury had cast off ancient anchors, and was drifting wildly about in search of some safe mooring, and Mrs. Carlyle had long tossed on a dark and stormy sea, and knew not peace. A friendship of nearly half a century ended—or, shall I say, only fully *began* —with Mrs. Carlyle's death. Miss Jewsbury stood by the narrow bed in St. George's Hospital where the friend of her heart lay, struck down by death. On that very night they were to have met in bright and congenial society. 'The book was closed, when she had read but a page.' It was in 1854 that Miss Jewsbury removed to Chelsea, to be near her friend, and the letters show that the two were never apart in spirit. When Mrs. Carlyle died, in April, 1866, it was to Geraldine Jewsbury that the stricken man turned for sympathy. She, amongst all women, he felt, could and would give it. And though he characterised some of her dear remembrances of her lost friend as 'apocryphal,' he well knew that the love that had bound the two women together was one in which he had been unable to share, by reason of the lesser quantity of lovableness in himself, or its superabundance in them, or his faulty and mistaken estimate of many things—all silent when the stern lips of Jane Welsh Carlyle had closed in majestic repose upon the secrets of a woman's heart.

Miss Jewsbury had most fascinating conversational powers, a fine sense of humour, the most winning of manners, and a generous heart, which often led her straight on until, metaphorically, she dashed her head against a wall. Her sojourn with her brother Frank, before his marriage, was marked by the most delicious little parties, where literary men, and women too, felt at ease in the genial warmth, and, as Carlyle says, 'The burden was rolled from every heart.' But, with all these charming qualities, Miss Jewsbury was distinctly a literary woman, and did much hard work. Amongst her friends was W. E. Forster, with whom she visited Paris during the revolutionary excitement in May, 1848. She was a favourite with Sydney, Lady Morgan, with the late Lady Llanover, with Vicountess Combermere, and with many women of literary and artistic taste, who revelled in her bright presence. It was at her suggestion that Lady Martin (Helen Faucit) published her 'Female Characters of Shakespeare,' for which all students are so grateful. She assisted Lady Morgan in the arrangement of her 'Memoirs,' which, later on—namely, in 1868—were edited and published by William Hepworth Dixon.

But this original nature of hers could not for ever find satisfaction in 'arranging' other people's brain-products. Her own brain teemed with half-formed plots and novels. In 1845 she published her first novel, 'Zoe, the History of Two Lives,' and gave a presentment of Mirabeau as a lover of her heroine. The work was immature in parts, startling and unique here and there. In 1848 came the publication of 'The Half-Sisters,' which Miss Jewsbury wanted to dedicate to Jane Welsh Carlyle. The readers of Carlyle literature will remember how this wish on her part was received. Her next tale was written for the *Manchester Examiner and Times* in 1851, and afterwards appeared in book-form. It was called 'Marian Withers,' and dealt ably with much that bears on life in the Lancashire manufacturing districts. There are crudities in the book, strange 'solutions of continuity,' but much that goes to the heart, and much promise of greater things. Her next novel (a little disappointing), dated 1855, was 'Constance Herbert,' and the following year saw the publication of a truly well-told tale, 'The Sorrows of Gentility,' which may be read and re-read with advantage. Her last novel was 'Right or Wrong,' published in 1859. This list, however, does not nearly represent the extent of her literary labours. She had done other work; had brought out two stories for children: 'The History of an Adopted Child' in 1852, and 'Angelo, or the Pine Forest in the Alps' in 1855; many contributions she had sent to Mr. S. C. Hall's 'Juvenile Budget'; and, what was more significant, she had come into relations with the editor of 'Household Words.' The following letter, of which the original has been in my hands, will show in what very high esteem Miss Jewsbury stood with Charles Dickens:—

Copy of Letter from Charles Dickens to Miss Jewsbury.

'Devonshire Terrace, London: Feb. 1850.

'Dear Miss Jewsbury,—I make no apology for addressing you thus, for I am a reader of yours, and I hope I have that knowledge of you which may justify a frank approach.

'I don't know whether you know that I am about to commence, at the end of next month, a new, cheap, weekly literary journal, intended to displace some of the offensive matter in that form now afloat. Be this as it may, I am steadily and actively engaged in such a design, and if I could induce you to write any papers or short stories for it I should, I sincerely assure you, set great store by your help, and be much gratified in having it.

'I purpose publishing none of the writers' names— neither my own nor any others—in the periodical itself, but to give to these parents, in such a case as yours, the power of reclaiming their own children, after a certain time, if they should desire to do so. The payment, of course, is prompt and good. In no respect, I trust, would you have to regret forming the connection, and in all respects I should be truly earnest in my desire to make it most agreeable to you.

'If I were to write a whole book on the subject I hardly know that I could do more than impress you with a sense of my being in want of your aid, because I estimate its value highly. I have a kind of confidence that I cannot mean to do that so steadfastly without doing it *somehow*, even in this short note. Therefore I leave it here.

'Believe me, faithfully yours,
'CHARLES DICKENS.

'Miss Jewsbury.'

It was little to be wondered at that these two quick and ardent natures understood each other; but the tribute here paid by Dickens to Miss Jewsbury as a writer stands quite apart from the fascination of her womanly nature, which shed a 'glamour' over men and women alike, and bore with it a sort of enchanted atmosphere—not valuable to the caterer for a weekly journal, though delightful in social life. Miss Jewsbury had an ambition—it was to become a journalist, to move in the world of letters as a man, a good comrade, 'one of the craft.' Except in the case of her close friendship with Jane Welsh Carlyle, the tie of friendship with women did not fetter her, whilst the easy triumph of having a man always in love with her—or, more correctly speaking, several men at a time—did not fill up the wants of a nature which had wings and wished to fly. But she was heavily handicapped in the race. For, added to the fact that she was a woman and not a man—a fact by no means to be overlooked, since woman cannot have, and almost ought not to have, what sportsmen call the 'staying' qualities—she was of a most delicately-balanced nervous constitution, and entirely unfitted to do her 'tale of bricks' in the ordinary 'hack'-fashion of the work so regularly and automatically done by male workers. Her slender frame, vibrating with every breeze that blew, was absolutely incapable of the drudgery demanded of a professional literary woman the moment she pretends to enter the lists on an equal footing with man. All her bright abilities failed her at times. And no wonder! As a well-known writer has said, 'what is woman, regarded as a literary worker? Simply an inferior animal, educated by an inferior animal. And what is man? He is a superior being, educated by a superior being. So how can they ever be equal on that particular line?' The theory meets with a constant and crushing contradiction in exceptional cases;

but so much of it is true, that a woman, though she may in certain circumstances understand better, go more rapidly to work, achieve faster, in mental labour of a high order than can her fellow man, is yet liable to collapses, eclipses, failures of power, sad to behold, unfitting her for the steady strain of ever-recurring work, which to the average man is the very 'breath of his nostrils,' and which holds him up while his gentler companion must sink by the wayside, overpowered by some nervous trouble or other complication, which reminds her that, after all, she is a woman. Journalism is rather a stern occupation; its demands are of the character of the celebrated 'laws of the Medes and Persians,' and their fulfilment is wholly incompatible with a *migraine* or a 'day off,' unless officially permitted. Yet did this delicate woman for many years contribute constantly to the 'Athenæum'—reviewing in its pages, and wielding her strong and subtle pen in various directions, independently of her own books. So she worked, she loved, and cast a colour of rose over other and sadder lives; she wept, and dried her tears, and she arose again, to work and love once more— and what further fulfilment of a woman's true calling can be looked for in one for whom the closer, more real calling—that of wife and mother—seemed out of reach? The strong sympathy Miss Jewsbury had with her brother Frank was touching in its undisguised reality. While he was yet unmarried that bright home at Greenheys, Manchester, attracted many shining spirits—many who could shine there, and not elsewhere. Many an overladen heart laid down its 'carking care' on that genial threshold, and, later on, when Miss Jewsbury had left Manchester and gone to reside in London—near that friend of her heart, Jane Welsh Carlyle—she would still come to visit Frank, and the brother and sister seemed, even to the outer world, to forget the years and the circumstances which had placed their lots in different counties. Geraldine Jewsbury had a pretty and harmless pleasure in shocking the feelings of 'Mrs. Grundy,' and when her married brother, who was somewhat precise in his expressions and modes of thinking, met her on neutral ground—dining, perhaps, in the house of some common friend—the lively lady would deliberately give rein to her sparkling wit in remarks addressed either directly to her brother, and calculated to make his hair stand on end, or with a graceful *naïveté* make them audibly to her hostess, for the benefit of the whole company, and display the most impenetrable unconsciousness of what she had done!

Here was a nature with which Mrs. Carlyle, endowed by heredity with a decided strain of 'Bohemianism,' could sympathise keenly enough. The small conventionalities and meaningless proprieties of daily life were as nothing in the eyes of these two. They could laugh together, they could utter to each other the scathing judgments on men and things which neither really felt; but, what is more, they could weep together, quarrel like lovers, make peace like lovers, despair together when all was dark to both, smile when the smallest ray of sun shone on either; and show each to the other the wounds which each was too proud to show to the world—those terrible hurts which a woman instinctively hides, and most anxiously from those of her own sex. Each was isolated in many ways, and the stronger one suffered more, needed more, and received more, was less able to bear sympathy, while more utterly incapable of admitting pity—that cruel would-be healer of wounds. Jane Welsh Carlyle, in a fragment of a journal kept by her, under date of March 26, 1856, says:—

'To-day it has blown knives and files—a cold, rasping, savage day: excruciating for sick nerves. Dear Geraldine, as though she could contend with the very elements on my behalf, brought me a bunch of violets, and a bouquet of the loveliest, most fragrant flowers. Talking with her all I have done, or could do. Have mercy upon me, O Lord, for I am weak. . . . O Lord, heal me! . . .'

The significant expression, 'Talking with her all I have done, or could do,' tells the tale of that dear friendship. The strangely-assorted friends could minister each to the heart-pain of the other, and on that day it may fairly be concluded that talking with Mrs. Carlyle was probably all Miss Jewsbury had done or could do!

So the matter lies in a nutshell. They could not help each other very much, in some senses, but in the highest sense of all they undoubtedly did succour each other. It was the stronger who leaned on the weaker, as we so often see in life. Mrs. Carlyle had iron and steel where Miss Jewsbury had softer substances, yet it was on Geraldine Jewsbury that the reserved woman poured some of her agony, some of her rare joy; and the attachment was no one-sided affair, if, indeed, that which deserves the name of attachment ever is so!

There are some beautiful plants which cannot grow unless trained *en espalier*, and such was the nature of Miss Jewsbury. Her strength lay largely in her weakness, and *vice-versâ*. That it should have been a woman who gave the needed support was a mere accident of fate, life, Providence—what you will!

But this was the fact, and without the feminine sympathy of Geraldine Jewsbury it may be doubted if the brave, brilliant, unhappy Mrs. Carlyle would have held on to her cross, would have stilled the beating of those restless wings which always beat against the bars, would have survived the awful moment, which comes at times to the strong, not so often to the weak—I mean the moment in which the

a

spirit seems to ask the question of itself, 'Shall I go on or not?' The answer to this query is by no means to be found in encyclopædias, philosophy, or reason. It must come in a heart-to-heart communion of some kind, and to Mrs. Carlyle it certainly did come in the warm, faithful, undying love of Miss Jewsbury.

There is a certain armour which proud natures are apt to rivet on themselves, from some motive or other, and which, once assumed, becomes difficult, almost impossible, to lay down, though under it a human heart may all the while be panting for relief. The struggle may or may not be apparent, but it is a desperate matter when there is felt to be no possibility of laying aside the iron links. The longed-for relaxation Mrs. Carlyle found in Miss Jewsbury, in whose intimate presence she could be herself. It was, in some sense, as though the Tragic Muse rested her head on the fairy-like bosom of an 'Ariel,' but this 'Ariel' had also depths of her own.

And the two were comforted!

It was in 1866, after Mrs. Carlyle's death, that Miss Jewsbury removed to Sevenoaks, Kent. Life had lost one of its greatest charms for her. A violent shock had been given to those mysterious links which bind men and women to life. The short time spent by that bedside in St. George's Hospital had shorn away much of what remained of the buoyancy of her keen and ardent spirit. The colour had faded from the everlasting rose, and though Miss Jewsbury still wrote at times, still retained the honouring friendship of such men as Carlyle, J. A. Froude, Huxley, and a host of other men and women who loved her, she began that slow process of ceasing to live which is one penalty brilliant natures have to pay, at times, for the superabundance of vitality granted them at an earlier period. She must have longed 'for the touch of a vanished hand, and the sound of a voice that is still.' But she said little on the subject.

Quietly she succumbed to a disease now believed by those most skilled in medical diagnosis to trace its first start very frequently to mental causes—I mean cancer. Thus smitten, she removed to a private hospital in Burwood Place, Edgware Road, London, and there went through her martyrdom—a hard, almost cruel, ending to a life with such sunny proclivities.

But care and kindness never deserted her; and among her last acts was one of loyalty, for, propped up on her bed of pain, she manfully destroyed, day by day, all the letters from Mrs. Carlyle which were in her possession, having promised that she would do so. Death stopped the process, and the dying hand left *one* letter, which I printed in my 'Life of Mrs. Carlyle.' In Shakespeare's words, 'The rest is silence.'

But the beloved friend had not destroyed the letters of Miss Jewsbury. She probably meant to do so, some day. She felt, perhaps, that it was hard to destroy so much love and warmth, and she had no warning given her. Hers was a summons of the sudden kind, which leaves no time for the carrying out of fixed determinations. So the letters survived, and the 'other side' can only be filled in by the heart.

During Miss Jewsbury's last illness she often asked me to tell her the little speeches of my children, any little thing about them. And I wrote, receiving and expecting no reply, in the vain hope that these innocent trivialities might beguile her of an hour of her painful change from Life to Death. For she knew the children, and had always a heart for young things. I never knew if these small chronicles of mine did her any good. I knew she had brave and noble spirits about her, who watched her last struggle with pain, and could alleviate where I could not. It was on September 23, 1880, that she folded the bright wings so sadly weighted with mortal conflict, closed her once dancing eyes, and slept in peace.

She was sixty-eight years of age at the time of her death, and was buried in Brompton Cemetery, in Lady Morgan's vault. A fitting epitaph for her would have been, 'Qui multum amavit,' for truly she loved much and well.

It is Dickens who says, 'What the poor are to the poor, only God knows.'

I would say, 'What a woman is to a woman, only a woman knows.'

And with these words I close my imperfect record of a woman whom I, too, loved, and whose letters tell what she was to one of the most remarkable women the world has known—or, rather, has not known.

ANNIE E. IRELAND.

September, 1892.

SELECTIONS OF LETTERS

FROM

MISS JEWSBURY TO JANE WELSH CARLYLE

1841.

LETTER 1.

Saturday, April 15, 1841.

DEAREST JANE,—You will think I am possessed by as great a mania for letter-writing as any of Richardson's heroines, but the fact is, I continue unable to see to do anything but what I feel specially inclined for, and I profit by it to write to you, for the time is coming when I must attend to many things which have only their necessity to recommend them. I think of you very often; indeed, you are scarcely ever out of mind. But I wish I could think of you as strong and well, though then you would no longer be the same person. But I want sadly to know how you are—do write a line, and fill your letter about yourself—I am growing really anxious to know how you are going on in every way—mind, body, and estate. I did a foolish thing yesterday, but it was so pleasant I can't find in my heart to repent of it. I went to spend the day with a lady who has been very kind to me since I was shut up; who has nearly read me through your husband's lectures on Hero Worship. She lives at a large pleasant old-fashioned house in a garden with plenty of trees in it (by the way, De Quincey was born there). There was a party in the evening, and a sort of 'Masque' acted: it was got up for the holidays last Christmas, but as many of her friends had not seen it they repeated it last night. It would have done credit in all respects to Macready himself. She had provided a pair of queer spectacles for me, but I obstinately refused to look through such a destroying medium. I have only recently formed a personal acquaintance with her, though I have long known her by reputation for all manner of goodness: she is one you would like, and says things which constantly remind me of you. She was left a widow about five years since with a family of boys, and it is quite beautiful to see the way in which she has brought them up. She is a most ardent admirer of your husband, though not just what I should call a disciple; but she has taken great pains to influence the minds and habits of all the young men who come to her house and who are her sons' companions, and she doses them with your husband's books—by way of giving them right feelings and so forth. She is a Christian by way of belief, and I dare not say a great deal to her that lies in my heart, but she has a fine mind and fine feelings, and she is an acquisition to be very thankful for. She said something the other day that struck me. We were talking of women, and I said ' the sufferings of any individual woman, however great, seem to be absorbed in that of her sex, and the sufferings of women seem not to be recognised as altogether the legitimate evils of life. Providence does not seem to count them as items in the troubles it imposes on the world, to take no account of them.' She said, ' all must be made perfect through suffering, and a woman's trials are appointed through her affections : it is only through them that she is capable of suffering, at least I think so '—but you will be tired of hearing so much of one you do not know. (Monday morning.) I was half in hopes of a letter from you yesterday, but instead there came one from an estimable young damsel of my acquaintance, who sends me word that by way of a winter occupation she has been reading half a dozen of the stiffest Greek plays in the original ! besides getting through any number of volumes of tough Puritan divinity !! and several other items equally ponderous. Well, my dear, it is certainly a great credit to one to have such virtue exemplified by one's acquaintances, and I have a great notion that old orthodox doctrine of ' imputed virtues ' is correct. I can't help feeling as if I had deserved a good child's reward myself when any of my friends do right! Is there any hope of seeing Carlyle on his way home? or is there any prospect of your coming through Liverpool this year? I am not going to fill my letter with what I think about those glorious lectures, because I have some questions to ask him, and I can say it then—you would smile if you knew what is at the end of my pen to say, but it would not be in mirth, and I ought to have learned, by this time, that we know not what we do when we envy ; but to tell you the truth, I did for a few minutes feel there was something very dazzling in bearing the name you do! Now don't misunderstand—and think what I should not wish you to think! Walking in a triumph must needs be dazzling. It is well for a woman to be, as it were, absorbed, just in proportion to the intenseness of her passion, though every thought, feeling, and power of intellect is called into perfection, in order that it may be an offering to the one she has made her idol ! A woman cannot, in her turn, be to the man all that he is to her—she cannot (except in rare cases) be the first and last object of life to him. All the great business affairs of the world must get themselves transacted by men, and only occupation that comes by necessity—and not, as a woman's occupation does, from a voluntary setting about something to avoid idleness—will prevent the most desperate devotion and the most sublime affection from being other than secondary to the daily grand business affairs which keep society in shape and going. Added to which, a man does not, in a general way, understand our refinements in the matter of love; owing to our having little real occupation, our own female branch of the subject has been much more highly cultivated and comes to greater perfection than with men; we love with a desire to give them pleasure—they love us to please themselves. A man who has had *le plus grand succès* among women, and who was the most passionate and poetically refined lover in his manners and conversation you could wish to find, once said to me in a fit of truth (he was in a fit of remorse for circumstances I well knew, so he had no reason to pretend, and keep up appearances to me—I will tell you the tale some day) : ' But I can form no idea of what women mean by those refined notions of theirs. I like a woman to love me in that way, but I do not in the least understand it. There is nothing but passion, more or less refined, in a man's love for a woman, let him talk as he will, and don't you be ready to believe any man who says the contrary.'

So, my dear, let us look our lot boldly in the face at once; if it has been given us to love—for it is not every woman who receives that terrible gift—let us submit without vain struggling as to the conditions. It brings suffering as surely as life brings death! We shall have no reward except what our own soul gives us. We can never be for a continuance to the one we love what they are to us, and it is very uncertain that we may die when all that has made our life worth living is gone. It takes a great deal of misery to kill; in all this we fulfil our destiny, and we form no unimportant link in the economy of life. It may be that we women are made as we are in order that they may in some sort fertilise the world; their passionate affection, and their devotedness, though it brings no good to themselves, yet goes far towards making the world at large a better and more supportable place, and prevents its being altogether a 'den of cruelty and fierce habitations.' Do not all religions seem to shadow forth an occult law of nature in the notion (common to all) of vicarious sacrifices—the few suffering, undeservedly, to benefit the many? We shall go on loving blindly, and making our very souls as the ground for them we love. And yet, after all, let us not forget that they who cause this suffering are only acting according to their nature, and are not altogether to be blamed; they take and make use of what we give, and bring forth the effects in some other shape; we centre in them, they centre in what is exterior and lies without them, and those things of the world which they consider of importance, and for which they weary and waste themselves, likewise bring no return to them, but work on to some end which we do not yet discern. We shall go on loving, they will go on struggling and toiling, and we are alike mercifully allowed to die—after a while.

I don't know whether you will agree with this, and I cannot see to argue, for my eyes are very bad and painful. Do write, please. Did you receive a long letter, and a little picture I sent you soon after I got home? Poor dear —— is rather better, I am thankful to say. Take care of yourself. How is Mr. Carlyle? Will you give my love to him, and believe me, dearest, your most faithful and affectionate,

G. E. JEWSBURY.

You will be just blinded in trying to make this out. Kind regards to ——.

LETTER 2.

Friday—Monday (Postmark, April 19), 1841.

Dearest Jane,—I don't know that I have anything to tell you, specially worth writing down. But my eyes are still too weak to allow me to read; writing does not try them so much, and you are the only person I feel tempted to talk to just now! What would I have given to be with you this last week! though, after all, quietness and rest were the best things for you. Still, I would have liked to join my rest to yours, for I also have attained to the 'Giaour's' beatitude, and feel just now uncertain whether I am alive or dead! Lying on a sofa as I am, half dreaming, half dozing, in a light that is neither light nor darkness—except for occasional twinges of recollection I should have altogether attained to a highly pacified and vegetative state, which will be changed, perhaps not for the better, so soon as I can bear the light of day. This was to have been a gay week. I was engaged to two grand parties—not fine, stilted 'conversation affairs,' but regular unsophisticated dances!—and I was obliged to send back-word to both. I had rather set my heart on one of them, at the house of one of the nicest women I know down here. It is a German family; and she is such a charming, natural, kind-hearted creature, just cultivated up (to) the most agreeable point, and stops short of any pretensions! Only to think what harlequinade tricks fate sometimes plays one! The other day Mr. ―― sent up word by my brother that he was in town, and should come up to see me. He has not been since our memorable conversation; and whilst I was rather wondering what turn things would take this time, there arrived, not him, but a most sober and reputable matron of my acquaintance, who came, she said, 'just to teach me how to net,' thinking that it would be a nice amusement for me now that I could not see to read or work! and she stayed all afternoon. ―― did not come at all for some reason or another, and on the whole I was not sorry, for seeing him now is like the meeting of two ghosts on the other side Styx. Each has been connected so strangely with the history of so many feelings and incidents, which at the time seemed as if their memory could never pass away. And what has been the end of so much passionate suffering, so much love which all the parties thought would endure for ever? The woman he loved so madly—of whom he declared (to one he trusted) that he would rather obtain her friendship even, than have possession of her whole sex—died of a broken heart, or, rather, of a cancer, which Sir Astley Cooper said had been brought on by grief and anxiety of mind. She was a fine creature. I never saw her but once; but I heard of her from many quarters, and from those who knew her best. She was married to a man who did not care for her, and she, till she met ——, did not know what affection meant. His own testimony, and the way he spoke of her to me (that time we had our conversation), was enough to absolve her from all censure except the deepest commiseration. Her sister (who knew nothing of the matter) said, after her death, that she used to sit for hours gazing on the wall without seeing anything or speaking a word. When asked, What are you thinking about?—' Oh, many things; don't talk to me!' He, for whom she had risked everything—very soon after he had obtained everything—began to grow, not indifferent exactly, but satisfied. Unfortunately for her, she and her husband were obliged to leave this country; in absence she lost her influence over him. In a very short time he forced her to break with him; he married for *convenance,* and is now the father of a family, is a respectable man, and in prosperous circumstances. Since her death he professes, to those who knew the facts, bitterly to regret the past; but it is somewhat dubious whether these brave sentiments are real, or assumed as a piece of his respectability.

I, who was a bystander, have the recollection of the faith I then had in his good qualities, and the strong feeling I had for him, and the firm belief in his chivalrous, honourable dealing towards her, and the undoubting trust in her submission to duty, honour, and so forth. I did believe, then, in many fine things, and even now I only doubt their durability, or rather it now seems unreasonable to expect high-pressure efforts except from a steam-engine, and even that wears out; and why should we regret that things are so constituted? The fact of all that is worth having, and even life itself, being precarious, gives it a value beyond its own, and those who have an eternity to trust to, little know the desperate tenacity of those who have to make the most of Time! I cannot explain to you the superstitious value I set on those I ever love, and the sort of religious feeling with which I try to guard every word or thought which might raise a shade between us.

No, my dear, you must first have no hope of anything beyond this world, before you can know how very precious is a friend we really love. This letter has been written à *plusieurs reprises,* for my eyes are rather worse, if anything, to-day than they were this day week, so that now I can hardly write, and what is to become of me I don't know!

I have more time for thinking than is at all agreeable. All this while I have never thanked you for your letter—it made me feel very sad. Those efforts after strength are weary things, and I doubt whether they do much good. They go to exhaust what strength we may possess. On the whole, I cannot help thinking it is the wisest to let ourselves be drifted along. Time brings quiet and strength naturally; in fact, the very change he works in us and in our feelings is equivalent to strength. There are two lines in Coleridge's translation of 'Wallenstein' that haunt me from morning to night, and have done so ever since I began to know what endurance meant. 'What pang is permanent with man? From the highest as from the vilest things he learns to wean himself, and the strong hours conquer him!'

If you will, from time to time, send me word how you go on, it will be a great favour. Just now I am especially anxious to hear from you; if you cannot guess why, I won't tell you. Do not plague yourself to write long letters, but say how you are in every way; patronise the pronoun 'I' as much as I do myself! Never mind telling me anything, except inasmuch as it affects or interests you! I have not said a tithe of what I have thought of when lying on the sofa. You little know the comfort it is to me to have you to think of, nor how much I think of you. If you take an interest in my friend ———, she is rather better, at least was last Tuesday. She had a scheme in her head which had quite roused her. Heaven only knows whether it will prove wise and feasible, but even the power of hoping is no small blessing to her!

She did talk of going to the seaside in a few weeks, and it was settled that I should go with her when she went, but all is yet in a state of uncertainty.

Is your husband returned from his excursion?

I heartily hope he will be the better for it.

Will you give my love to him? He has had splendid weather. So soon as I have eyes to see to write a reputable letter, there are several knotty points I want him to solve for me, but I cannot venture to send him the sort of scrawl I bestow on you. 'Les sept cordes' are waiting for me at the bookseller's, I expect, but they will not get touched yet awhile, hélas! I am too cross this morning to write any more. I am in an ill humour with my doctor, too, which is almost as bad in a patient as it would be for a hungry man to quarrel with his bread and butter! Offer my respects to your brother-in-law, and you may tell him that I have about as little to contend with as a young woman of 'my sort' could hope to find anywhere. To the immortal credit of all the people here be it spoken, they take me as I am, which is a great virtue in my eyes of course; and then they hang up Nymphs, and Cupids, and Psyches, &c., &c., in their dining-rooms, so that, 'sans peur et sans reproche,' as I told you before, I have said ten thousand things to you in my own mind which are not written in this letter. I wish you were here to-day. An individual I once named to you is coming here this evening. It is well for us that we cannot solve all the problems presented to us in this world; for my own part, I am quite reconciled that my heart should be deceitful sometimes. I don't want to know the truth of what it means, and if 'Job' had been a wise man he would never have asked the question. Give my remembrances to ——, your damsel, and believe me, most affectionately yours,

G. E. J.

P.S.—I began a little tale called the 'Lune de

Lait' in one of your French newspapers. Could you spare me some of the succeeding numbers to finish it? for I took great interest in it. I will return them by post—if it is not convenient, never mind, however.

LETTER 3.

Tuesday (Date of Postmark, May 6, 1841).

Dearest Jane,—You must take up with scraps till I can see to indite a regular reputably written letter. I have been doing something, and I half fear that, like most busybodies, I have been doing wrong. Some friends of mine are gone up to London this week— Mrs. ―― and her father. This father is a great collector of pictures, and is considered one of the first judges in the county; he has a valuable collection of works of art. It struck me that he would be a most likely person to do something if he could see Count Peppoli's pictures, even if he did not buy; his word and judgment would do good (down here, at least). I wrote a line to ―― to tell him to get him to see them if possible, but as I recollected that ―― has not the *entrée*, will you (if you think the thing worth the trouble) send any sort of a talisman to him which may open the door; understand that I do not want you to be plagued with the people in any shape or way, but Mr. ――, great, rough, and sooty-looking man as he is, has done the work of two generations towards civilising the town he lives in, is always buying pictures himself, and making other people buy them too. Do not think me taking a liberty, and don't plague yourself in any way. How are you? are you going on getting strong? Heaven knows when I shall see again fairly! Is Carlyle come back? A friend has been good enough to come and read to me all day in 'Hero-Worship'; but I cannot write any more now.

Ever yours,
G. E. J.

LETTER 4.

Monday, June 15, 1841.

Dearest Jane,—There is a great deal I want to say to you, but when I begin to write to you it seems difficult, almost impossible, to put it down as it really is.

I would give the world—that is, all my expectations in it—for the space between four walls where I might talk to you in peace for an hour, so many things occur every day which I should like you to know at the time, but I cannot patronise 'small beer' so far as to chronicle them, and besides, they are only interesting for the minute—like newspapers. But there is not a day that I do not most sadly want you. Your letters tell me little or nothing about yourself, and, besides, you don't like writing, and I cannot find the heart to plague you to write, and then there is so little connection between the world you live in and that which I live in, every day seems to separate us more, and these stiff documents are the only substitute for speech and sight; I want to see you more than I can tell you. I cannot write half I want to say, and I dare not write even a quarter of what could be written, so these letters are very unsatisfactory all ways. One thing you may do, however—tell me how you are, and how you go on; never mind other people or news of any sort, it is you I want to hear about. I think of you a great deal, and with an anxiety I cannot account for. I can't express my feelings even to myself, only by tears; but I am no good to you, and I, who wish to be and do anything that might be a comfort to you, can give you nothing but vague, undefined yearnings to be yours in some way. I can use no expressions of affection. I don't like using them. I am jealous of giving you what I have ever offered to another, and, besides, talk as much as I will, it's the same thing said over and over; you will let me be yours, and think of me as such, will you not? How are you? Do you sleep well still? That is my *summum bonum* of felicity. I can get through any given amount of plague if I may sleep all night without dreaming. I am come home again ten days since, and, after all, I am best here, though it is not much

I do. My eyes are, I suppose, well, but I cannot use them for long together, and the green spectacles are still in requisition. They are weak, my dear, and weakness in all things is the worst sort of ailment; *au reste* I am well and have nothing to plague me just now, but I suppose that is a beatific state which never lasts long.

My friend —— is much better, and I am relieved from much anxiety about her. I have begun to do something, and I have a strong notion that it will have to be undone again. I think we are both of us mad; but there is a sort of instinct sometimes which leads one to do things that seem to have no profit in them beyond the fact that they ought not to be done! What I am after now is something of the kind you once suggested. One day, as we were walking in the grounds, Mrs. —— exclaimed, looking at the house, 'If we could but make those walls tell all they have ever seen or heard for the last seven years, they would teach (to women especially) more than they have ever been taught yet.' This had no reference to anything previous, but we began settling all the various affairs that had been transacted there, and the fierce passages of life and suffering we had seen pass, and our philosophy on the same! Well, we agreed to make it into a history in letters. The actual letters that were written from time to time have been destroyed; but now that some of the persons are

c

dead, and others married or removed far away, there is a strange sort of pleasure in working out one's own peculiar notions on certain subjects. I should like you to see it, but I much fear that it would be objected to if I asked leave. I wonder whether you would agree with us! Do you remember in one of your letters you tell me that 'I am clever, but wrong on certain points'? How much I wish that you would give me some of your own philosophy some time! One day, whilst at Seaforth, a youth I have known a long time took it into his head to be very confidential, and preached his own gospel for the space of a whole afternoon! He had been thrown on the world very young to shift for himself, and a real little youth of the world he had become. He looked so young—though he is twenty-five—that one could not call him a man! The mere facts that he told me were not disguised and beautified, yet the *morale* that stood out clear was to the effect that men cannot afford to be very long or very much in earnest in their intercourse with women; that when a woman got thoroughly earnest and engrossed, a man who had any regard for himself or her would break off at once! That *une grande passion* ' was an embarrassing affair, and was very dangerous to people who had to get a living,' and that he had always ' broken off' as soon as he came to his senses; that women seemed to think it was the only object of interest in life, and it was a desperate thing to let them go too far. One thing specially struck me—though this was not said to me, only repeated to me—viz., that all men who have received an English education hate a woman in proportion as she commits herself for them, though a woman cares for a man exactly in the proportion in which she has made sacrifices for him, evidently thinking and showing, he thought, that all that was in the world—business and riches and success and so forth—were the only realities, and the only things worth making objects! He is neither better nor worse, but an average specimen of the generality of men. He once did me a material piece of kindness, and he was not in love with me; he had taken a fit of kindness to a friend of mine, and he raised himself in my opinion, and showed more real feeling than I had supposed in him. To be sure, the fact that my friend did not care about him would account for his good behaviour; it was not put in his power to behave ill! This will seem stupid to you, not knowing the people and the circumstances; but it had a great interest for me, and it set me moralising to think how much more miserable we should be than we are if we had our eyes opened to discern always true from make-believe. I have great sympathy with that prayer of the Ancient Mariner, 'O let me be awake, my God, or let me sleep alway!' There is something else I long very much to tell you, but I dare not in a letter.

I wish there were some photographic process by which one's mind could be struck off and transferred to that of the friend we wish to know it, without the medium of this confounded letter-writing!

I want your counsel, and I cannot even ask for it! Well, my dear, I must not omit to tell you that, by way of natural female occupation, I am engaged in preparing a 'baby basket' for my sister-in-law, who is expecting her first little one next month. This is the ' ha'penny worth of bread to so much sack.'

I am going to drink tea and take my work to a very nice lady, one who interests me much—a real specimen of an English woman. She is married, and devoted to her husband, who is also a real specimen of an English *mari*. I am sure she is not happy, by several little observations she has dropped, though she would start to think she had given such an impression; but there is a great deal that wants saying about matrimony. Who dare say it? I have read the 'Sept Cordes' at last, and full of genius it is—more so, I think, than any other of the writer's works. No one but herself could have written it; but what a pity that such splendid truths should be buried in the earth! She might do so much more than she has done.

Why will she do nothing but write novels? I

am also deep in a very different book, and am equally chained to it, though I had to begin by an odd volume. It is altogether fascinating, and there is such a fine, healthy feeling through it all, and so much human sympathy, and wit enough to endow all the libraries of useful (?) knowledge 'ever inflicted on the world.'

It was a volume of 'Rabelais' I got hold of the other day, and shall not rest till I have got the beginning of him. I cannot give you an idea of the delight it has given me. The Old French is a great bore; but it is well worth the plague of it.

A poor lady of my acquaintance is in great trouble; she has just lost a daughter, of whom I was very fond, under most painful circumstances, and I must go and see her. It makes my heart sick to see her. Her husband is a great scoundrel; he left his family, after tormenting them to death, and now he increases their trouble by all sorts of vexations, and it makes me mad to hear people coolly say, 'I understand Mrs. ―― has a violent temper,' as if a woman was to be steel and marble under the most unprovoked outrages! I wish I might say my say about matrimony. This is a tremendously long letter.

God bless you, dear love. Take care of yourself, and write as soon as you can.

Ever yours,
G. E. J.

LETTER 5.

Addressed to Mrs. Carlyle when she was at Templand, on her last visit to her mother, Mrs. Welsh.

Thursday (Postmark, July, 1841).

Carissima mia,—I am not going to write you a long letter; I only want to tell you that I hope all your perils and annoyances are over. Your cousins promised to send me word when they received tidings of your safe arrival. You will have plenty to do, so do not, my darling, plague yourself to write to me just yet. To have seen you has given me enough to think about, and you are never out of either my head or my heart. After you left on Tuesday I felt so horribly wretched, too miserable even to cry, and what could be done? I was obliged to go back into the drawing-room, and listen to that doctor talk about the transmigration of souls across me to that sedate-looking young damsel, who replied, like Mrs. Chapone and Hannah More 'rolled into one,' and I had taken up Mrs. Ellis's 'Women of England,' which made the oddest running commentary you can imagine, till the whole thing became so exquisitely absurd that, in spite of everything, I began to laugh, and so immoderately that neither the lady nor gentleman considered me worth speaking to for the rest of the evening. When your cousins returned, it gave me great comfort to hear that the Captain was such a respectable man, and your cousin Alick quite won my heart by the judicious things he said to satisfy me that, on the whole, you would have had more annoyances by land, in changing carriages, &c., than even by sea. I don't know whether it really would have been so, but I felt glad for anyone to say so, and to try to make me believe it. He is a very nice youth indeed, and seems so fond of you. Your cousins were exceedingly kind to me, and the eldest, with the young lady who had stayed all night, escorted me to the railway next morning. I found a letter from 'my papa' waiting for me, saying that he was to be in Liverpool yesterday, and giving his address, so I suppose I am restored to favour again. I felt very vexed that I should have just missed seeing him; however, I suppose he will come over. Take care of yourself, dear love. Write to me when you are settled, and tell me how all goes with you, and whether you are materially worse for being in the open air all night, and whether it rained, &c.— tell me everything about you. This is not intended for a letter, but I could not rest without writing to ask you how you did, though I cannot have the answer for a long time.

I have no time to say more just now, except that I am ever and always yours,

G. E. J.

P.S.—You will offer my respects to your husband,

and tell him that I tried to remember one of the young lady's speeches, thinking it would be a good epigraph for his article on 'George Sandism,' only I despair of doing it justice—the manner in which it was *debité*—'I think decidedly that all novels— modern ones especially—ought to be burnt.' 'What!' said I, 'all of them?' 'Yes, let them all go together. People would do far better to study history, and if they were properly trained to it they would find it quite as amusing. I could not read a novel for half an hour!' It reads flat, but as she said it, it was *impayable*. Good-bye, dear one!

LETTER 6.

(Postmark, July 6, 1841.)

Dearest Jane,—Your note, which by some extraordinary chance has come to hand to-day, has almost driven me crazy with delight at the idea of seeing you so soon; but why are you obliged to go straight to Liverpool? Why can you not come and spend a few days here?

I have plenty of accommodation for you, for ——, the baggage and all. I will go on with you to Liverpool, if you like, afterwards; but come to me first. It will make scarcely any difference in the expense; or, if you will not bring —— and the baggage, bring yourself and send her on to announce your arrival.

Come; I can discern no reason why you should not. You do not like anyone in your room, I know, so you shall have one all to yourself. I am just wild to see you. There is so much for you to tell me. Don't plague yourself to write a letter. Just write 'Yes' on a piece of paper, and I shall know that I may expect you—that all is well with you. I can guess: your happiness will be no dream; you have earned it by doing and suffering like no other woman, and I have great faith in the doctrine of recompense or retribution. I never knew it fail, and I have seen scores of instances. You have not yet gathered the harvest of your self-sacrifices, but it will come, and be worth the long patience you have had for it. Mine is not a vain theory. It is as true as cause and effect can make it. We cannot avoid or avert the consequences of our actions, whether they be good or bad. But I am too happy to philosophise. I shall see you in a few days. Till I do see you, I cannot believe the fact. In a parenthesis—your husband's taking himself off round by Newcastle will sadly damage the plans of our Royal Institution directors. Now that they are clear of the election they were purposing to invite him to visit us in March, and to give us a lecture, and they would have made all sorts of fuss with him. I had told Mrs. ——, who is the mother of one of the directors, and she had told them that you would be at Liverpool on your way to Scotland, and they intended to try to catch him *en route*. But they must be disappointed this time; but, so that you come, I care for nothing and no one else. It is only yourself I want to see.

Ever, dear love, your most affectionate

GERALDINE.

(In tremendous haste.)

LETTER 7.

Tuesday (Postmark, August 4, 1841).

My darling Jane,—I thank God that you are safe on dry ground once more, and if ever you go on board a steamer again you shall have a strait-waistcoat and a commission of lunacy shall be issued against you! Your long letter left me rather uneasy about you, and I was very glad of your cousin's little note; pray thank her for it! How very kind of you to get her to write it! I am as busy as any old fairy godmother; whether I am doing good or harm heaven and the event only know, or whether I shall prove a most magnanimous and devoted friend or a great rascal I am sure I can't predict. But have you never noticed that when one has been trying to do something really good one is much nearer committing some special sin than when one keeps on in the selfish, matter-of-fact prudence of minding one's own business, and that alone? I would give a great deal to see you just now.

My own affairs have now, I think, come to a crisis. I was first driven half-mad, what between real emotion and rage and indignation, and now I have, I think, subsided into a calm which, it is to be hoped, will be final on this point at least. Last Monday I was invited to a christening, and requested to stand proxy for a relative who lives at a distance; my friend was one of the sponsors, and by some chance we were left *tête-à-tête* for more than an hour. Well, my dear, nothing heroic passed; when he entered the drawing-room of the house where the christening was, I was lying on the sofa in that state of weariness when one feels as if one were sinking into it. (I had been walking a great deal.) In a few minutes the only other person in the room left to dress.

I did not rise—I could not, and because it was easier to lie still. At first he tried to make a sort of general common-place conversation about the pretty houses that are building in the neighbourhood, and some compliments on my improved appearance, made exactly in the sort of half-gallant manner in which the most ordinary acquaintance could be addressed—one in the habit of being seen every day —for there was no strangership in the tone. I could have stood anything but civility, and I am afraid I uttered an ejaculation much stronger than became the lips of a young lady.

I was much more astonished at myself than he seemed to be, for he continued for a minute in the most composed and gentle strain, and then, professing to think that I seemed fatigued, took up a book. I kept my eyes shut, and lay as still as if I had been dead, instead of feeling every vein beating within me like a sledge-hammer; after a while other people came into the room, and he said, 'You have been asleep, I think!!!' I said, 'you know that I have not.' I was sorry I said anything, afterwards. As if Fate had determined to mock us with opportunities which would have made a pair of lovers happy for a month, it was fixed that we were to walk home in the evening, and after we had all started some change in the procession made it necessary for him to offer me his arm. There was no possibility of avoiding it, and we walked more than a mile together. He still seemed as unconscious as ever, but this time he began to tell me of some of his affairs, and especially of the prosperity of a scheme he has been long engaged in, and from his anxiety about which I know dates the beginning of his indifference to myself. He calmly went on to tell me of all the hindrances and disappointments and difficulties of all sorts he had had to encounter, that he wondered he had been able to persevere, but that now he thought things would go on well. No more notice, interest, or reference shown or made towards myself than if I had not existed! I never felt till then how utterly useless and valueless I was to him, and how unintelligible to him is all I have suffered for the last three years; and yet he is a man, walking about and looking like other men, and seems on excellent terms with himself besides!

I was too oppressed and too helpless to cry, and besides, now I know that what my lot has been is, in the main, that of every woman who does as I have done—for those who try to make their lot contrary to custom, are always broken in the attempt.

I might have been spared many aggravating circumstances, but the end must soon come. I have been made more melancholy by a speech last Saturday my papa made at random, which seemed to shew the end that must needs come to all these things. I cannot tell you how good and kind he was—he is a man worth calling a man, he is strong enough to be trusted—and yet, if one knew the secrets of his life, how much misery he may have caused! It seems as if when one loved another thoroughly, it only gives them the power of making us suffer. I have just received two letters which have quite bewildered me, one from poor —— and the other from Betsy. I fear much that —— will not live long, and I could find in my heart to wish her dead; she wants that element of resistance which is indispensable if people are to get through the world—she is a weed, drifted by the current—and yet how gloriously well she has been treated.

—— has been spending a couple of days with her. He called on me as he passed through, but I was not at home. I wish I could send you her real letter about what passed; however, the one she has written for —— is quite to the life. I like it much; what do you think of it? Some of the doctrine I should have wished insisted on more; however, it is all as true as a copy from the life can be! She has written a great deal more of the tale, and I think she improves. I am not allowed to do anything just now, my eyes are so very weak.

This letter is not half what I intended it to be when I sat down. I have said little or nothing that I wanted to say. How are you? Do write me a good account of yourself. I think of you as Catholics think of their saints, to keep them out of evil; as regards me, the odds are in the devil's favour, for I am obliged to be idle, and, though a sober matron told me this morning that it was very beneficial to retire within ourselves and meditate, *c'est selon*, and it does not agree with me just now!! Does —— take care of you? Thank Heaven you are within reach of your mother! I have a most superstitious faith in a mother, and I feel glad every day to think that you are not far from yours.

Do you know, my love, that I have actually been resolving to try to be conformable and more proper-behaved in my manners and conversation, in order to be more of a credit to you! If I am to be your friend I must, and ought to, be a more responsible and less whimsical person than I am!!

I would wish to be worth something for you. Thank Carlyle for the French newspaper, and give my best respects to him. I am anxiously looking for his 'George Sand' article, in the hope of a word in season. I will write to you again—I am too harassed just now, and I have been besides much annoyed by something since I began this letter. . . .

LETTER 8.

Seaforth House (Date probably August, 1841).

Dearest Jane,—Your most welcome letter was forwarded me here when I came last week.

I made up my mind to start suddenly at the last, having made the brilliant discovery that I might as well transact my idleness in company as in solitude. And there was another reason too. I feared being alone any longer: it is no fancy one can be stronger and braver when with others. Do you remember the story of Blue Beard's key—how, when the stain was scoured out on one side it reappeared on the other? Well, it is true of many things besides. This is a most beautiful place close by the sea, and I am with the friend you have so often heard me name, and I have the respectable comfort of feeling *sans gêne* in every respect. We are something like that piece of science which says that 'two substances made perfectly smooth by grinding together will adhere without any cement.' She was the first intimate friend I ever made, and we have been gradually grinding together for the last seven years. She takes as much interest in all that interests me as if it were herself, and *vice versâ*. She is a splendid creature in every way, except that she cannot keep counsel.

Of course, I never trust her except with what concerns myself; and I run the risk, for she is so true and generous that her sympathy quite outbalances the inconvenience. She comes nearer to my notion of a woman of genius than any other I have yet seen. She has a fine creative faculty, which is my notion of genius, and she is strong, can live without either the affection or sympathy of others—live on her own resources in a way I cannot understand; but when she does care for anyone it is an affection that is as strong and enduring as a rock.

She is wild after your husband's books, and I have been saving up my eyes to read the lectures. Her sister, a most fine character also, is here too, so we are quite a party, and you would laugh to see us getting half crazy about the book. I have contrived to get the 'Sept Cordes' at last, but all my eyesight has so far been spent on the lectures. They are all gone to Liverpool this morning, but I begged to be left behind. I cannot tell you how glad I am to hear that you keep well. Don't plague yourself about anything. Your letter has made me quite happy, for I was beginning to feel the want of hearing from you. Nevertheless, I like better to think of you as well and keeping quiet, than that you should exert yourself to indite letters and tell me what you are about, and so interrupt the process.

My eyes you ask after. *Hélas!* they are weak, very weak still, and I am become a connoisseur in the different shades of green spectacles. I can do nothing without them, and have no less than three pairs at this minute. Give my kind regards to ——, and tell her that the garment is actually in my drawer at home, that its appearance here has caused me as much speculation as its disappearance did her; but I, being a philosopher, concluded that some inquiry would in time be made after it, when the owner discovered the loss. I send you some German newspapers. I don't know whether you care about those things, but the people here tell me it is a very fine article. I, having only had an account of it in broken English, don't know much about the matter, but the writer seems to have some notion of proper reverence; only, on the whole, I have a great deal of the Catholic in me, and I don't approve of people sitting in judgment on my popes, even to admire them. They ought to 'hear and obey,' and 'anathematise those who do not.' This paper is too thin, so that I dare not write on each side of it, and I can't see to read over what is written, and the governess is going to the post and will take this. So good-bye, my dear love. Take care of yourself. How is Carlyle after his journey? Write when you have nothing better to do and are up to it. Remember that I love you always.

Ever yours,
G. E. J.

LETTER 9.

Addressed to Mrs. Carlyle, under cover to Mrs. Welsh, Templand.

[Fragment.]

(Date, September.)

. . . Whether it will ever subside, I don't know. I think not. He has wearied me out, and I feel almost to despise him ; he has destroyed all interest in himself. So, my dear, your counsel is very easy to practise just now ; and yet, up to that day, a word, a look, or even less, would have made me more his than ever.

There is but a point between 'too late' and 'there is yet time'—that once passed, it is for ever after nothing but too late ! I have been in this place —a beautiful sea-bathing place—about a fortnight. I am staying with a very old friend, who has been ordered here for her health ; but I hope now that the danger is in great measure over. You have heard me speak of her as being such a sweet specimen of an English lady, and also as being so desperate about a disagreeable un-English husband, who did not understand anything desperate ; however, he has found great favour in my eyes of late for his real, thoughtful kindness, and the thorough healthy affection he has shown through all her illness. I quite repent sundry disagreeable speeches I have made about him, so this is a sort of *amende* to satisfy my conscience !

——, I am glad to say, was getting better in every way the last letter I had from her. It is a great relief to me, for I was getting really uneasy. Do write, dear love, soon. I am more anxious than you can tell to know all prospers with you. I am glad you are at Templand. May I send love to your mother ? I cannot help loving all that belongs to you. Respects to your husband. In tremendous haste,

Your most affectionate
G.

Direct to me, under cover, to
  Mrs. JOHN HARGREAVES,
   Lytham, near Preston,
    Lancashire.

LETTER 10.

Wednesday morning (Postmark, October 29, 1841).

Dearest Jane,—Your letter arrived yesterday. I don't know that I am glad of it, for it has created a painful yearning to see you and talk to you.

I have such a thousand things I want to say to you, it has made me very melancholy.

Do not, my love, speak of yourself in such tones. You are not a judge of yourself, or your own case. You have neither failed nor fallen short in anything you have proposed to yourself. You are only worn by the daily struggle of life. It is the weight of life that at times presses on us too grievously to be borne, and then one asks oneself, Why must we go on enduring? to what purpose is all this waste? and one feels tempted to throw up the game altogether. Even I (who have had comparatively little to endure) have known what it is to feel all the motives, which had once seemed as imperative as necessity, suddenly begin to look like mere fancies, which I had imposed on myself; and when I have looked round there has seemed no real cause why I should go on doing and enduring, when my own suffering seemed the only reality left. At such times one feels almost mad, for there is none to appeal to, and none to answer when one calls. If one begins to stand still in one's course to question, it is like trying to stop in a crowd when all are hurrying the same way—we are only thrown off our balance, and trampled on and bruised. We must allow ourselves to be carried along; the impulse of one day carries us through the next. So long as we live we must go on struggling, according to the strength that is in us, against the forces that would overwhelm us. It is no voluntary thing: it is the instinct of life. Everything in the world has a tendency to run into dissolution, and life is a fighting against it. So long as we are alive must we go on without resting : the only comfort I know is that, eventually, we must die. There are times when we are more than usually oppressed and wearied, and then there is no word that can be spoken to refresh us : it passes partially away of itself. Nothing remains in the same form long together; but if we are to begin to doubt the course we have pursued—the reasons which induced us to take it—there is nothing but madness for it. What we *call* madness, that is ; for whether it is the most mad to do or to abstain from doing I know not, nor can tell; but go on we must while we live. You, my love, have been true to your own self in all you have done, and that, as a mere matter of cause and effect, must bring good. I feel more and more how little it is that the most devoted love can do towards giving comfort or doing any real good. Suffering is suffering, and affection is but 'a vainly precious thing.'

I love you, my darling, more than I can express, more than I am conscious of myself, and yet I can do nothing for you, not even help you to sew up one of your interminable seams!

A good evangelical once said to me that the great comfort of going to Heaven would be the unruffled self-complacency in which we might then indulge! and it seems, in truth, a great element of comfort. So I counsel you, my dearest, to cultivate a complacent view of yourself, and do not run down your own character by accusing it of vanity and all sorts of hard things! I feel to love you more and more every day, and you will laugh, but I feel towards you much more like a lover than a female friend! What would I give to see you for an hour! for in writing it is vain to attempt giving you anything like a true account of myself. As to my confounded eyes, they are not well, but advancing by slow degrees. I myself have subsided into a sort of chronic laziness, and achieve nothing beyond a stray row of my Turkish stitch ; in fact, I cannot yet see to do much, and I have begun to find out the superior pleasure of doing nothing! Even writing a common note requires a greater effort than I feel inclined to make!! I am grown dreadfully stupid, and altogether am in a sort of 'dead thaw,' which I try to represent to my conscience as a step achieved towards repose and equanimity!!

Mr. —— has been painting here and in Liverpool for the last three months. I have seen a great deal of him. He is returning to London next week. I have told him to call on you. He can tell you more about me than anybody else ; will you let me commend him to you? Will you allow him to call on you from time to time? Till I see you I can tell you nothing ; all my drama seems winding up. Though the *dénouement* has been neither matrimony nor death, everything has settled itself in the best possible way as regards everybody with whom I have been connected.

I have not done being astonished at the comfort and order which have resulted from what at one time seemed a very chaos.

I told you in my last that it was well with me, and I can say so still. I think my laziness arises in part from the perfect state of contentment in which I am. An odd circumstance I must tell you—my *ci-devant* friend has taken it into his head to fall in love afresh! There was no previous notice; he called suddenly (he had not been to see me since our breach), and as quietly as if we had parted the day before wished to put things on their old footing, to take matters up from where we left off. At first he offered no explanation, or attempt at explanation, himself, but seemed quite to think that my affection had been kept at boiling point for his benefit; but I suppose I am a woman, for all the tears and sighs I had bestowed on him seemed to have become so many petrifactions!!

My heart was hardened; I told him that no one but himself could have estranged me, but that now it was too late. I could feel neither pain nor pleasure on his account; his behaviour all through was of a piece with the last two years and a half. He shewed a little emotion, but very little, and was only earnest in entreating that I would leave off making such bitter speeches to him, which I promised to do, and he also asked leave to come and see me occasionally, which I also agreed to. . . . He still calls, but seldom. Well, my dear, what do you say to this? I hope you don't think me very fickle. Will you offer my best regards to Mr. Carlyle? An 'Athenæum,' directed by him, has just been delivered to me; pray thank him for remembering me. I shall read the article with great interest. A French lady of my acquaintance has just lent me Mme. Lafaye's Memoires.

I cannot say that I have been taken with them, amusing as they are. She was not half genuine enough to commit crimes à la Medea, and that is the only reason I fancy she may be innocent; *au reste*, there is such a Mme. de Genlis flavour through it all, that I have no patience. I cannot write any more just now; this is hardly worth your reading. *En attendant mieux*, it will tell you that I love you, that I think of you, that I try to imitate you. Write to me, dear love, when you can find time from sitting on a cushion and sewing up a seam! I know the full amount of virtue it requires, yet half-a-day's sewing would give me such a fit of depression and *ennui* as a week's idleness would not repair. In my eyes you well deserve a niche in the Calendar. I had rather wear a hair shirt than make a linen one, or alter a 'winter shawl.' By the way, I contemplate achieving a tippet for you to wear under that said shawl, but when it will be finished I am not rash enough to guess. Mrs. ——— has been having a grand dinner-party; I was invited over to it, but I could not well leave home for one or two reasons. ——— is come to stay with her own family in Manchester, which rejoices me much. Mrs. ——— inquires after you in every letter; she has been in a sort of domestic disquietude—her cook, who has lived with her since her marriage, has thought fit suddenly to get married herself.

Good bye, dear love.

Ever your own
G. E. J.

1842.

LETTER 11.

January 1, 1841, or 1842.[1]

Dearest Jane,—A happy new year to you, and no more of them than you desire! I don't like having time measured by such set horizons so that we cannot help knowing how it goes, or seeing how very little worth anything fills the space between. This last year has been the best I ever have had; it has brought me much good, on the strength of which I feel able to go on many days. I have found you, and now I wonder how I ever lived without you, and it is strange, but you are of infinitely more worth and importance in my eyes than ' my new friend.'

You come nearer to me; I don't feel towards you as if you were a woman. What will to-day bring you? Comfort that you had not last year—and yet, dear love, there seems to me a want of security in your lot, as if the thing you loved never stood still beside you. You seem to live in a sort of a passionate kaleidoscope, never able either to know, or to control, the next change, but obliged to endure what-

[1] I am inclined to date this letter January 1, 1842, from close reference and internal evidence alike.—A. E. I.

ever comes. It would not suit me, whatever fun you may make of my present way of going on. There is a relief in the entire absence of all strong emotion ' et l'un vaut bien l'autre.' I would not exchange with you. Nay! if I could transmigrate into a duckpond, I would sell my hopes of a reversionary paradise for a very small consideration!

I cannot feel up to anything very desperate—and if ' my new friend ' took to tormenting me I should actually dissolve under it ! I could not oppose even the resistance of endurance. So you see, my darling, matters are better arranged for me than you imagine, on the whole. You say one thing which is true, to a degree—but more witty than true, nevertheless. You say 'the sentimental is always a got-up thing,' a ' do at the bottom of it.' Now, *selon moi*, the sentiment is an instinct with us women. It is religion to us. It is what chemists would call the 'menstruum' in which all our qualities are worked and made manifest, which holds them together. There is nothing got-up in the real sentiment which lies within us, but *hélas*! the real ' do ' begins when we have to try to be satisfied with the very pitiful gods and shrines at which, *faute de mieux*, we have to worship. It is when we have to shut our eyes and pray that they may not be opened for us—that is the unreal, make-believe part of the business! We know, at the bottom of our hearts, the exalted qualities we fancy we are yielding to are not inherent in our idols, and we do like poor Don Quixote, who first expected that his helmet would turn the blow of a sword—and, trying the experiment honestly, he demolished it altogether. After repairing the damage he tried it again, but this time he took care not to hit it so hard! Well, my dear, but let me tell you this much about myself—I really and truly care a great deal more about ' my new friend' than you seem to fancy. I could at one time have been yet more attached to him if he would have let me, but somehow he has always seemed to put himself between us. All you say of him and his way of speaking of me is true enough, but I explain it differently. He does not love me thoroughly, he does not care for me, as he did, as he does for ——, separated as they are, and though of necessity all is at an end between them, yet she is deified in his eyes!

He loves her as if she were dead; that was a genuine passion, and I don't think it is in man to feel the same twice! I know that he is capable of loving as I never believed a man could before. Our relation is made up of other things as well as love. I have begun, and I must go on! I feel almost as much bound to him as if I were his wife. At present I am necessary to him. As long as I continue to be so, nothing would tempt me to break with him. As a friend, when I see you I can tell you many circumstances which placed us in our present position with each other, but which I cannot well write down. Whether my affection for him will cool down into a mere friendship, or will increase till it comes to a specimen of 'la grande passion,' I do not know. It must take its chance! Magnanimity is not my vocation, and I am beginning to feel dreadfully annoyed at being so completely degraded to a second place by the 'souvenir de Julie.' It cools me down! I cannot be desperately in love on such meagre fare: but I should as soon think of leaving a husband if I were married, as of contemplating the idea of finding a more convenable friend. It will be he who dissolves the friendship if it is ever done, not me, and he behaved really well when I went into such a rage about that letter I told you of, and he is coming again into this part of the world very soon, and I never feel any of his faults when he is with me!

I have been practical with a vengeance all this week. I could face Rhadamanthus himself with boldness. Listen! When I got home from Leeds I found my servant ill, and I had to find a substitute in an instant! Well, this unlucky substitute left me at a minute's notice on Christmas Day, and there was I, left with a servant ill in bed and eight people to provide a dinner for, nothing but myself to stand between them and starvation! Well, I made the plum-pudding and stuffed the turkey, and got them to begin to cook, and I borrowed my sister-in-law's servant for an hour as soon as she came from church, and the dinner was handsomely achieved, and an old 'gourmand' who was here to dinner declared that the sauces were all excellent, and my pudding was every morsel eaten! So there was *un grand succès* for you! But the next day was Sunday, and I could not go out to look for another servant, and I could not borrow one either, so I was obliged to light the fires and work till Monday morning, at one o'clock, a beneficent angel in the shape of my sister's old servant came to see how I was getting on, so I was able to get out, and find a help on my own account, and I have made a vow never to work again when I can be lazy! for I never knew the comfort of laziness till now—and, to make matters better, it was a bitter frost all the time! Well, my love, I have since then knitted you the enclosed ruff as a specimen of my Turkish stitch! It is not very nice, but will do, however, at night, when you go out in the cold; and pray consider its imperfections as so many autograph proofs that it is really and truly my own work! I have a dreadful headache, and I cannot see any more, except to tell you that I love you, and should much like to see you in your 'piquante' costume. I have set up a lovely embroidered merino, which people tell me looks well; I can only hope so. How is Mr. Carlyle? Give him my best regards, and all sorts of good Christmas wishes! Your own

G——.

P.S.—Mrs. ——! I have heard of her books. I have not seen any. From what I have been told I am not much inclined to fall in love with her; she seems one of those didactic women, and she expresses a great disapprobation of Unitarians! as to 'hiding under a bushel,' though any light worth lighting up the world with will burn up or shine through the bushel stupid enough to stand over it; but if you are disposed to be actively benevolent, God forbid *I* should hinder you! So you know 'Paracelsus'! I have been more pleased with that book than any for a long time, and have read it over and over again. There is an inarticulate power in it—a something greater than the man himself could comprehend struggling to get itself said! —— lent it to me, and I have not found in my heart to return it yet. Once more, good-bye. Write very soon!

LETTER 12.

Monday (Date on Postmark, January 25, 1842).

My darling Jane,—A thousand thanks for your kindness in writing so soon! Your letter made me happy, for I could not help almost fearing that you would be out of all patience with me.

I had half written a long letter to you two days

ago, but by some accident it got burned by mistake with some other papers, and I am sorry for it, because I said many things I am not in a humour to say this morning.

I had a letter from my friend; he will be here, I expect, in the course of a week or ten days. There was a something through it all which would have cost me many tears had you not given me the courage to look and see how matters really stand with me, though he evidently intended to be most affectionate and so forth. . . . The process of being harried out of a charming delusion with beautiful blue in it is painful, and no wonder we try to make it hold round us as long as possible; and, besides, as far as certain peculiarly charming delusions are concerned, there are many feelings which induce a woman to cling to the one she has chosen long after she begins to suspect his unsuitability. We always want to persuade ourselves that one we love is the very first we have felt for. We regret every word and look of kindness which has been bestowed on another. We would wish to be perfect and entire in all our thoughts for him we choose, and flatter ourselves that he will be the only one, and then when it comes to be seen that the friendship must cease— that we have fancied a reality when it was none— no woman can help feeling degraded in her own eyes, and less worthy of finding one who will love as she desires, for she has given her first feelings already! A man may make it a source of complacency to have had the love of many women, but a woman must feel painfully humbled at having to alter her choice once. As to my actual position with my friend, that must be guided by circumstances. So long as I can be of any comfort or service to him, I will. I must abide by the step I have taken; he is now what he was then, and I have no right to punish him for my own want of penetration. And besides, I have great faith in things settling themselves naturally. I am free (thanks to you), and the rest must take its chance!

I have had a small adventure since I wrote last to you. Fate seems raining adventures on me just now, and is giving me a parody on the wishes and hopes of the very best four years of my life.

I told you of the sort of explanation come to about a year ago. I have hardly seen him since, and never once alone. He neglected to come many times when he might have done, and I began to think all that passed then was a mere piece of acting to make himself interesting, but on Wednesday night last he came up. I was alone (he had ascertained that I should be), and at first we talked about natural things, but gradually he led back the conversation to that night, and spoke bitterly of the regret and shame he felt at what he was and what he might have been, and what he had thrown away, and then he dashed at once *in medias res*, saying that he once cared for me, and if he could only have believed he had had a chance of success, he should never have loved anyone else ; and then he rushed from the other side of the room, and fell down, *selon les règles*, at my feet, begging that I would try to care for him again, as I had once done. And all this time I was as cold and calm as marble! I could not even feel agitated, or embarrassed, and yet he was the very first I ever cared for, and though he never said, in so many words, that he had any regard for me, there were a hundred things which made me hope it; but I was so really engrossed by caring for him that I did not much trouble myself about what he thought of me. I felt content to wait, but when he married, there was so much that was pitiful and bad, that it gave me a real disgust. If he had married for real reasons, I could have forgiven him, but . . . since that period he has been out of the pale of all those who used to be his best friends, and now he is bitterly feeling the consequences of his own deeds. He might have been such a glorious creature. Even now, knowing him as I do, I cannot help having a degree of interest in him I never suspected. If he is sincere, and really desirous to come back to us, and be one of us, as he used to be, I can be a friend for him, out of whom he may get good. Surely such passionate sensibility was never given for nothing ; and he must have some good left; all his gifts can never have been utterly wasted. I have felt more since he went than I did at the time. I shall not choose ever to see much of him. I don't think it is in him to care for a woman except as she would wish, and no woman ever stood a chance with him yet, and I have thought since that there was mere presumptive goodness in my offer to be his friend; he is more likely to do me harm than I to do him good. I am afraid of having much to do with him. If it had come six years ago, we might both have been better worth than we are. Well, my dear, to talk of something else. . . .

I am hoping to go to Seaforth next Monday to stay as long as I can, and I shall only be too glad to call on your cousins; would that you were in Liverpool, or any hope of getting you there! You must think of Seaforth as your natural home when you visit that region. I have had a parcel of callers and a bad headache since beginning this, so excuse all imperfections and write very soon, please. By the way, I had Emerson's 'Essays' lent me on Saturday, and I have read nearly half through them.

I like the one on 'Spiritual Laws' much, but I don't take to the man—he is a dry, cold, sententious Yankee; he spiritualises profit and loss, and strikes a very fair balance, and says many true and many sensible things, but he owes himself to your husband, I think, and has not a grain of his passionate eloquence, which makes one's heart burn within one.

I can profit by him now, but I might have read him till doomsday before I knew your husband, and been neither better nor worse. I don't take to the man at all; he is sober, honest, and so forth, because he clearly sees he gets more by it. It is the most profitable and safe investment he can make of his faculties.

Your husband would be rather aghast if he suspected what I do—viz., that the opening of his eyes to my manifold perfections has happened to ——, from the fact that your husband has honoured me enough to take any notice of me; he is a great admirer of his, and I feel pretty certain that his having taken any interest in me has been the means of quickening my friends' perceptions.

Mrs. —— has determined to have a repetition of our play to-morrow night, as it went so well before, and Mrs. —— has lent me a dress so beautiful that no lover or love could enter my heart when I had the prospect of wearing it, and I have got a cap as pretty as your Greek one, and I intend to have a brilliant evening to-morrow, and forget everything else; if ever I get my eyesight well I will try if I cannot work you a dress like mine—it is an invention of Mrs. ——'s own. Now I must go out, so good-bye, dear love. Write very soon, please, and tell me what you think of all I have told you

Ever your own
G. E. J.

LETTER 13.

Thursday night (Postmark, February 19, 1842).

My dearest Jane,—I have begun one or two notes to you and accomplished none, for, though I want to write to you, I don't too well know what to say, or, rather, how to say it. Your last came just as the car came to the door to take me to the railway—I wish it had been to take me within reach of you. I cannot tell you how your letter made me feel; you have not been out of my mind many minutes together since I read it. I am very anxious about you, but do not either plague yourself to write or to make any detail or explanations. There are times certainly when it is a comfort to talk, but more often it is a nuisance, and you know that it needs no interesting particulars to rouse my sympathy then (that is a 'Minerva Press' word I don't like, but I know no other). Those headaches of yours are real nasty things, and God knows what they may end in! I wish you had not received my two last letters when you did; how selfish and egotistic those pitiful details must have seemed, but yet I have no instinct to know that you were 'all right.' I see how it will be; you and your kaleidoscope will be both shattered together some of these days, and then there will come passionate regrets and useless endeavours to make you what you were before, and then the astonishing discovery will come that the past cannot be undone, though sought earnestly with tears. Do not write till you quite feel inclined; no fear that I shall set it down to a fit of anything. You know I love you as nobody else can, and everything you do is right in my eyes. I went to town yesterday for the first time since I came here. Among others I called on your cousins, but none of them were at home. I shall call again before I leave. Mrs. —— is as handsome and kind as ever; she often talks and wishes either fit or chance would send you here again. I think it would make her perfectly happy. I have had a visit from my friend since I wrote. I really repent of all the ill-natured things I have said about him. He behaved so really well. As to Mrs. ——'s brother ——, he has turned out a very promising scoundrel. I have thought out the mischief he was nearly doing. I am not clear of him yet, but I hope in a fair way of being so; he did all he could to make a break between his sister and me by saying the most shameful things to each of us. He was horrified lest I should tell her our last interview, for fear of our comparing notes, but the first thing I did was to tell her everything, for the more I reflected on what had passed I felt he was not to be trusted. And, my word! the pitiful spectacle he made, when we came to talk him over, was enough to put one out of conceit with mankind now and evermore. I wrote to tell him what I had done in a most civil and, indeed, kind letter, if he will but take it so ; I don't want to vex him, because he has not the gift of telling anything but lies, as I and his sister know to our cost. So this is the state of my affairs at present. I am taking German lessons again from Mrs. ⸻'s tutor. I shall remain here I daresay for three weeks longer. I wish you were here to have splendid air and perfect quiet, and to join us in our walks on the top of the house, and to lie on the sofa 'in the little dim room.' This is a most stupid letter, but I had not the heart to write about anything. Mrs. ⸻ has gone to a singing lecture, and I have stayed at home to finish this. She told me to send her love. Once more—do not plague yourself in any way about me. I would give the world to see you, if only for an hour. Do take care of yourself as well as you can.

Ever, dear love, your own
G.

P.S.—What do you try for your headaches ? Cold water to the top of my head does me good always. If they are very acute, hot turpentine. It 'does not injure the most delicate fabric,' as they say of marking-ink, and I have seen it perform wonderful cures. Put it on the head, not the forehead. The next time you write let me hear a better account of you.

I fear my visit to town is put off for good and all.

The lady I was to have visited has had several domestic troubles; how can people sell their souls for the sake of furniture and respectability? She has made me register a vow against keeping up appearances.

Mr. —— has just come in, and desires his kind regards.

LETTER 14.

Written when Mrs. Carlyle was suffering from the death of her mother.[1]

Sunday Afternoon (Dated May, 1842).

Dear Love,—I am become very anxious to hear something about you; it does not seem natural to have you silent so long. Even your cousin has not written to me, and I miss tidings of you more than I can tell you. I feel as if I were separated from you. I want to know what you are doing, how you are. There are so many things I want to know about you, and yet I don't want to plague you. I reproach myself for even wishing you to write or exert yourself, and yet I cannot help hoping every day at post-time. I don't think you are ever absolutely out of my mind. You are there as a sort of under-current; other things are like visitors to be attended to, and

[1] Mrs. Welsh, Mrs. Carlyle's beautiful mother, had died on February 26, 1842—too suddenly to allow of her daughter's being with her at the last. The blow was a severe one, and Mrs. Carlyle was still smarting under her sorrow when Miss Jewsbury wrote the letter.—A. E. I.

dismissed. If you were happy I don't think I should care for you half so much. I am very anxious about you, and I can do nothing to help you. I love you more than anything else I have in the world, and what must I do if you are to go on suffering in this way? Take some pity on yourself, and don't spend all your strength on misery!

I wish I could see you, if but for an hour. Letters are very good-for-nothing, and never arrive at the right time. I love you, my darling; it may do you no good now, but it may be a comfort some time, it will be always there for you. I thought I had a great deal to tell you, but, somehow, I have not the heart to say anything. All my own affairs are much as usual, neither good nor bad; but I had a visit from —— on Sunday, and he was here again yesterday. I can't make him out, nor feel to believe what he says—which is all the better, perhaps. His children are here with his mother, he is to bring them to see me. He is coming to London shortly. He must feel very anxious with such a large family, in these bad times. I had a letter from 'my friend' about three weeks since, written in very low spirits. I have been much worried, and am getting out of all manner of patience, and yet I can't find in my heart to say or do anything unkind just now, being of 'Mr. Mantalini's' opinion, that we 'should not scratch or claw, but pet and comfort' when our friends are not happy. But I was a great fool to set up for being quixotic, and taking the *rôle* I did. One's conscience reproaches one much more stingingly for one's follies than one's crimes. I am sadly out of countenance when I think of myself. Mrs. —— was over here last week for the Association. She inquired very affectionately after you. I am trying to indite wisdom, if I cannot act it. I am hard at work on the said tale I told you of, and when you are well enough I should like you to see what is done, for you have been the imaginary 'chair' I have addressed myself to. The first sheet of this letter was written on Sunday afternoon, and I could not finish it yesterday. This is Tuesday night. Do, dear love, try to let me know how you go on! I have no spirit to write to you; it seems such cold-blooded egotism to tell you my own matters, and to think of you makes me sad any minute. What can I tell you that will do you any good? If tears would comfort you, you would have felt it long since, for I cannot think of you without them! You and your lot are a riddle to me. If men reap the things they sow, why are you not happier than you are? Do, dear love, let me hear something about you! I will not be long before I write to you again, though it is painful to call and not be heard. Dear, dear love, good-bye!

Your very own

G.

P.S.—Will you give my best regards to Mr. Carlyle? I hope he keeps well. How does his book prosper? My little niece, the other day, offered to make me a book-mark, and asked me what name she should put on it. I told her Jane. So there it is for you, my darling!

I like bringing your name in, and yet I cannot talk about you to anyone, except just a short word now and then, and that never seems what I meant to have said. Can you understand that? (Tuesday.)

LETTER 15.[1]

Monday Afternoon, May 20, 1842.

My darling Love,—Your letter came this morning, and has made me more sad than I care to express.

I am not surprised at anything you say. I should only wonder if it were not so. I know full well that giddy, uprooted feeling that leaves one wondering why one is left on the earth, or why one was ever sent here. Your loss is now what it was five months ago, when it first occurred: the strange thing is, not that we are so long in getting reconciled to our bereavement, but that we [are] able to find life tolerable after the 'desire of our eyes has been taken away by a stroke.' I have often wondered how this could be; but it is so. I suppose we have, with

[1] Again, the subject of the letter is Mrs. Carlyle's grief at her mother's death.—A. E. I.

trees, the property of growing over the deepest incisions made in the bark. The only thing that gives me any hope for you is, that I have seen women get cheerful—I mean regain an average degree of pleasure in life—after the death of a child, even when that child has been an only one. There is a woman in this neighbourhood who lost her whole family, consisting of three daughters, one after another, under most distressing circumstances, and yet she has recovered; and she was a widow, which made her situation still more desolate. If I had not seen such strange power in life to overcome affliction in every imaginable shape I should indeed tremble about you. I cannot think that it will be thus with you always, and yet at times it seems 'hoping against hope,' for why should you take comfort hereafter more than now? A friend of mine once said to me, after having had to endure intense bodily agony, 'it seemed suddenly to open my eyes to all the misery there was in the world, and of which mine was only a fragment.' Those words have grown on me. Everything suffers—man and beast, and creeping thing, and the suffering of each is to the full amount of what they can endure. I don't think there is one living who has not felt at some period that their sufferings were intolerable, too grievous to be borne. You recollect that expression of terrible agony in the Revelation, 'they gnawed their tongues for pain.' But it is of no use talking about the sufferings allotted to others, for our own portion has an individuality and fits close to us, eating into our souls like fire. We could find some ease under the worst troubles of others if they fell to us. It is only our own that press down upon us on all sides, and from which there is no escape. Still, I don't think, either from what I know myself or have seen in others, that this season lasts very long; either the sufferers die under it, and so escape themselves, or else they live through it and find calmer days. For there is a better time, if we can only hold out till it comes. But the worst of it is, that in such afflictions as yours is, the idea of ever becoming comforted is altogether loathsome, and so, my darling, I can do you no good. I can but see you struggling in the dark waters, ready to be swallowed up in them, and can help you in no wise. You must 'exploiter' your sorrow in its length and breadth. It's no use trying to stay you by words without meaning. I never heard of anybody but 'Job' who could look within himself and find a fair catalogue of virtues when he was in affliction, and that, I fancy, is why nobody feels much sympathy with him. Are you, do you think, the only one who feels utterly worthless? It is in such times as these that one seems made aware of all the unutterable vanity of one's own heart. It is always there, but we do not feel our real worthlessness till we are brought face to face with such great realities.

I have often thought that the grand thing in religion is that we stand naked and open in the eyes of Him with whom we have to do. Neither appearances nor make-believes are of any avail. There is no deceit before Him. I can give you no idea of the relief that thought is to me. What shall be hereafter we neither know nor can know, but we shall be in the hands of Him who placed us here, then as now. I have wished so often since you have been in affliction that I could speak to you a single word of all that Christian people comfort themselves with, and find strong consolation in it, too; but I neither know anything nor believe in anything. But one thing I am quite sure of having proved, that so long as we are in this place 'whatsoever our hand finds to do we must do it with all our might.' We must work whilst it is called to-day, for the night cometh. To what our work tends, God knows, and why we must work I cannot give you any reason that would sound logical; but so long as we do what lies before us to do, so long it is well with us. If we grow weary and faint by the way, the night cometh, and it will not be long in coming. We must just have faith enough to strive honestly till then, even though the reason and the motive cannot be spoken in intelligible words. You are broken just now, but if your task be not ended fresh strength will come to you; but, remember, that if you are to be taken away from us, it will make the way of those who remain behind very dismal indeed. Therefore, do not regret staying with us a little longer.

Do you know that I have found myself more soothed when in trouble by going to the Mass in a Catholic chapel, than by anything else in the world. The doctrines 'may all go hang,' as you once said, but you will find every thought and feeling which you cannot utter even to yourself drawn out, as [it] were, and uttered in aspirations to the same unknown and unseen Power that afflicts us. I can only speak to the effect their Litany has on myself. Only think of the many millions of sufferers that same Catholic Church has given comfort to. There is a Catholic chapel very near you, and, when you feel in the humour, go in by yourself! I cannot endure having any companion with me at such times. Their talk, whether wise or foolish, spoils all; and, don't think me cracked for proposing such a thing to you: that 'Agnus Dei'—'miserere nobis'—is the only prayer that ever sounds like the utterance of necessity. Now, dear love, farewell! So long as you are thus wretched I suffer too, not metaphorically, but in sad earnest. Give my dear love to your husband.

Ever your own
G. E. J.

Tuesday Morning.

LETTER 16.

Seaforth: Friday (Postmark, May 30, 1842).

My Darling,—Your note has made me very sad. There is nothing to be said to it, as you cannot be comforted, but time—time, that is the only hope and refuge for all of us! I know full well what it is to cease to see the necessity of struggling; it would puzzle the wisest of us to point it out at the best of times, but the inscrutableness does not always press upon us so heavily—it does not come till we see into some deep trouble, and then are like to go mad. To all of us life is a riddle put more or less unintelligibly, and death is the only end we can see—for we may die, and that is a strong consolation, of which nothing can defraud us. We cannot well be more dark or miserable than we are; we shall all die—no exception, no fear of exemption. Every morning I say this to myself. When I am in sorrow, it is the only comfort that has strength in it. Why, indeed, must we go on struggling, rising up early and late and taking rest? 'Behold, He giveth His beloved sleep!' And yet it is not well that you feel this so constantly that it swallows up all other feelings. Life is not strong in you when you are thus—it will not be so always. There is a strength in life to make us endure it. I am astonished sometimes to find that I am glad to be alive—that the instinct of feeling that 'it is

F

a pleasant thing to behold the sun, and that light is good.' And this is a feeling that will spring up in your heart after a while, crushed and dead as it seems now. When my father died I cannot tell you the horrible sense of desolateness and insecurity that struck through me. I had friends to love me, who would do anything for me, but I had no right to count on their endurance. I had lost the one on whose love I could depend as on the earth itself —the one whose relationship seemed to revoke the law of change pronounced against all other things in this world. Our parents and relations are given us by the same unknown Power which sent us into this world, given to us like our own bodies, without our knowing how or where, and when they are taken from us our ties to this life are loosened, and all seems tottering—nothing can supply their place. But yet even this gets blunted after a while; we can and do live, when we are put to it, on wonderfully little, without all we at first fancied indispensable, and then for ever after the love of such friends as are left or raised up to us becomes strangely precious in a way no one else can understand. We strain them to us with all our force, to try to supply the place of that natural necessity which united us without effort on our part to those who are gone! We have always a fear that the friends we have made for ourselves will leave us; we were only afraid for the others that they would be taken away. Dear love, this present strange, stunned state you will recover from. No fear of your sinking down into apathy—there is too much for you to do. You are necessary to the welfare of too many; your life will take shape again, though now it seems nothing but confused hopelessness. The thought of you brings tears to my eyes any moment it comes. Do not be so very wretched. I can give you no comfort—there is none—but from time to time write when you can, but don't plague yourself. I also will write without waiting. I am most thankful the dear little cousin still stays with you. Give my love to her. I am glad that your husband is well, and that he has his book to busy himself in. It is like a child to him. I am here since a week. I go home in a few days. Mrs. —— sends her love to you. I wish you could be within reach of her; she would be a comfort to you, as she has been to me. Good bye, dear love; take care of yourself for the sake of others besides yourself!

LETTER 17.

Sunday (Postmark, June 14, 1842).

My dear Love,—I am beginning to want to hear something about you again. Has your cousin cut my acquaintance, as she never writes now? Don't plague yourself to write, for I don't think it is a very good

employment for you. If I could be in the place of
Providence to you for a few months, I know what
you should do; but you are not likely to realise my
castle-building in your behalf, nor are you more
likely to guess my schemes for rendering you all
that you were meant to be—all that you even now
might be. But 'God is great,' as the poor Mussulman
says, and it may be that He intends you better and
more than either you or I dare hope; at least, I will
not believe that you will be left altogether comfort-
less! Is it not Job who says that 'trouble springeth
out of the ground'? And if so, may not consolation
also arise when we see least signs of its coming? But
this is idle talking: what will come must come, and
hoping seems a waste of energy. I am really unhappy
about you, and I would willingly have some evil laid
on myself if so I might hear that you were lightened
of your suffering. I am, as you said, very free from
anything like trouble at present, but I feel as if I had
no right to be so when you are as you are; and
besides, my present exemption seems to throw me
beyond your pale, as it were. However, as our
intervals of ease are only given to get strength for the
next trouble, it will not divide us long. If I had
had many claims of what you call natural affection
on me I could not have cared for you as I do. At
least, those of my friends in whom they are fully filled
up are not those who are able to care for any beyond

them. Their friends are unnecessary, they are never more than 'the stranger that is within the gate,' and this must account to you for what may seem like exaggeration in me. The grand meeting of wise men begins next week; I suppose the only thing that interests me about it is that it will bring over Mrs. ———. I do not purpose going to any of the lectures. but if any companion turns up for the *Soirée* I will not gainsay him. But I shall not let ——— commit the extravagance of subscribing. I wish so often you could see Mrs. ——— sometimes. She has the art of saying comforting things in a way that looks like sorcery, for she somehow makes one feel the better for what she has said. Our 'joint tale' is getting on, but I fear we have neither of us the genius of hard work or making haste. Whilst I was at Seaforth the weather was too fine for anything but walking in the grounds, and here I have many calls on me that eat up time and yet tell for nothing in the way of work. You will laugh when you hear of one employment that has fallen to me—helping three women who are in spiritual difficulties, and anxious to inquire their way into the Catholic Church? How they got the first start that way I don't know, but they came to me to borrow books, knowing that I am connected with several Catholics. So how they will settle it Heaven knows! Never draw people to doubts, when they have them not.

Talking of Catholics, I met a man the other day you must have heard of, for his reputation as a scholar especially is great. I mean Dr. Wiseman. He is a bishop now, and the President of Upcott. He is quite desperate about the Church. He was the beginning of the Oxford Tract disturbance, and the one object he seems to live for is the bringing back the Supremacy of the Catholic Church in England. He is the very realisation of all you could imagine the Hildebrands and Gregories to have been, who built up the Church in the beginning. I heard him preach from the Altar, or rather I saw him, for though it was a most able and eloquent harangue, he was the more remarkable of the two. There was nothing in the least degree theatrical or savouring of the elocution master; it was like looking at statuary. Mrs. —— whispered to me 'It's like seeing Pasta.' He could not come out to Seaforth as he intended, so we were engaged to meet him after service at a friend's house where we were staying. He loses nothing in a room, though he is an ugly fat man wearing spectacles. He is a man of downright genius for ruling, and bends and breaks everybody who comes to his own will, and I don't think he would stand at a trifle. I met with a book the other day I should like you to see. You would even now take more interest in it than you would imagine. It was a volume of sermons, of all things, by Newman, of

Oxford. I wished for you more than I can tell you; they are full of the most exquisite things, quite independent of the doctrine he holds. One expression struck me much. He is speaking of the grave as the point at which we seem most sensibly to touch most on the unseen world. He says: 'We lay our brother in that dwelling which is all glorious within, and full of odours, which are the prayers of the saints and holy voices crying, How long, O Lord?' I have not the book at hand, or I would copy you the whole passage; it is too beautiful to trust to memory for. I have made this a long letter about many things you will not care about, but, my darling, let me hear of you soon—that is all I want to know about. Give my kind regards to your cousin, if she is still with you. I hope Mr. Carlyle is well. There are a good many things I want to ask him, especially about a book I have got hold of. I have no patience about letter-writing, it takes time and tells nothing; five minutes' speech is worth a ream of Bath-post paper crossed. Good-bye, dear Love. Ever your own

G. E. J.

1843.

LETTER 18.

Probably written in July, 1843, when Mrs. Carlyle had just been undergoing house-cleaning at Cheyne Row, with fear of thieves.—A. E. I.

Wednesday Night (Undated).

Dearest Jane,—When Mr. Carlyle wrote he said you had a cold, and were not well. Now, if he says you are not well, I know you must be really ill, and this, together with not hearing of you for so long, makes me uneasy. I have heard nothing about yourself for many weeks now; your last letter was all about your house and the thieves, not a word about yourself in it. I always grudge your writing about news (or) witty letters like the last. I want to hear about you, and there is nothing else you can tell me that I care to hear. If you are not in the humour, don't plague yourself to write a long letter, but just send me a few lines to say how you are going on, for the more I think about you the more I fear that all is not well. Do write directly, there's a darling, for I am more anxious than you think—getting really fidgety, according to my nature! I have not been well since I came home from Bowdon, though I suppose it is fancy, for I should be puzzled to say what is the matter—*au reste*, I am singularly free from discomfort of any other kind. Mrs. —— wishes me to go over to Seaforth, and I think of doing so. —— is much better than she was. On Sunday an old monk of an Order of Trappists came here—a most reputable old man. He took to a monastery from the wish 'to make a happy death,' as he told us. He entered when quite a young man, for he was haunted by a fear of death, and he went into the most rigid Order he could find in France, and he was eloquent about the satisfaction he found in the austerities and privations. He is now Prior of a monastery in Leicestershire, for they were turned out of France in 1830 for some reason or another. I was very much interested in him, though he is of a ' simplicité sans pareil,' and has a look of genuine meekness— the very first time I ever saw that virtue except in print. I have nothing else to tell you about. My life ought to be singularly prosperous, for just now it is of one even texture, and has no events to pull it to pieces. Will you tell Mr. Carlyle, with my love, that I am highly delighted at his receiving the tobacco so graciously, and that I have had a monomania about illicit tobacco ever since the fact of its superiority was revealed to me? and, by the blessing of Providence, I hope to be enabled to send him a more satisfactory quantity before long, so that he shall have the means of smoking genuine tobacco without stint. I rather expect to hear tidings of it to-night—nevertheless, Destiny sometimes interferes even about such trifles as these. Resignation is a grand thing when we can get nothing better: 'The bridge broke down, and they all tumbled in, "We'll find ground at the bottom," said Brian O'Lynn.' Now, dear Love, do send me a line, and that without delay, and believe me

Ever your own
G. E. J.

I have got my brother home again, raving about Glencoe and the Highlands.

LETTER 19.

(Postmark, October 17, 1843.)

Dearest Jane,—As you know of old, I generally contrive to get done all I feel disposed to do. You will have decided that I am a most shameful and unfeeling person, but you will be wrong. I shall say nothing of the 'kicks over kicks' to which we have fallen victims since I wrote last, and especially since your letter came, because those ought not to count for preventive checks. But, to say nothing of my fits of nervous sleeplessness, which have kept me in a sort of mesmeric state when ordinary mortals are alive and brisk, we have had company in the house, who, however, might all (with one exception) have gone and hanged themselves before they should have hindered me. All these have been hindrances and snares of the Evil One, to keep me from writing to you, and to make you expect and get disappointed, but the real cause has been that poor —— has been very ill, and two or three times when I have sat down and fairly begun to write to you she has been so ill and in so much pain that I could not find in my heart to do anything but sit beside her— for, as my father used to say when he was suffering, ' It is a comfort if you will look at one as if you were sorry !' And she has taken a fancy that rubbing her feet and hands soothes the nervous feeling that torments her, and it often gives her ease when nothing else does, and as, from practice, I do not feel tired, I am rather in request. But all this time I have been horribly uneasy about you, for though you laugh and make witty speeches, I know the state you are in. I fear still more the state you will be in, my poor darling. I could have sworn, I was so provoked on reading your letter. You have no one who has any sort of consideration for you, and then, forsooth, you and your comfort are to be sacrificed to getting things made as comfortable as Heaven, and at small outlay of anything besides. My dear child, you ought to know your value better, and not to allow your life to be worried away for no earthly good—it is a sort of quixotism you have for sacrificing yourself, never thinking that when you are at last fairly used up the state of ruin and desolation to which all will be reduced that you have most wished to benefit, as 'Faust' says, will come all the same, and 'cursed be patience!' You have had patience and endurance till I am sick of the virtues, and what have they done for you? Half-killed you! I can do you no good, but I am very unhappy about you. I will not plague you to write to me, but if you can get anybody to be scribe enough to indite two lines to say whether you are dead or alive, or quite mad, I shall be very glad and thankful. I had a note from —— yesterday, which I cannot too well read, but she talks of getting home this week, so I shall see her before I leave here. We are rather expecting Dr. Wiseman this week: this you feel no sympathy with, though I can assure you that the Catholic Church goes for nothing in the matter. But I shall make you laugh if I were with you to tell you all our plots, and schemes, and wickednesses— for it is a sort of historical style of wickedness that peculiarly takes my fancy. Also, on my own account I have indulged in a matrimonial scheme, but the gentleman is so dreadfully in love with himself that I have not patience, energy, hope, or inclination enough to persevere. Indeed, those things are not much in my way; it was only the eligibility that put it into my head. Sheridan

Knowles is down here trying to pick up a few pounds by lecturing on oratory. We went to hear him last night, and I brought back a stiff neck. We have met him several times, and he is by far the most lamentable tragedy I have seen either on or off the stage. He is very good and affectionate in his nature, but so dismally merry. Such deep depression and anxiety under all sorts of puns and jokes! This letter is written in haste, and is good for nothing, but you shall have another soon. —— has asked me at least half a dozen times 'whether I have done yet?' and now the man is waiting to take it to the post, and I am only too lucky to get the chance of its going in time. Mrs. —— is in Liverpool shopping, or would send love.

God bless you!

Ever your own

G. E. J.

LETTER 20.

Thursday (Date Uncertain, probably Whit-week, 1843).

Dear Jane,—I seem to have lost sight of everybody I care about. The postman has not brought me a single letter for nearly a fortnight; the last time he knocked it was only to bring a letter for the damsel who officiates as 'help' till —— comes back, which was an aggravation after the 'Griselda' fashion. I want to know how you are, both body and soul—whether you have yet fixed any place for your summer proceedings; whether you are finally delivered from your 'incubus'; whether—but, in short, it is like talking in a soliloquy. There is no voice, neither any who answereth! The weather is atrociously rough, and you may be thankful you have not set out on any summer excursion. It is the race-week here, when all the poor children have a holiday, and walk into the country, and expeditions to Dunham Park—in fact, a whole week's amusement to keep them out of mischief and away from the race-course, and, poor things, if they do not catch everlasting colds it will be a miracle. Yesterday I saw the clergyman of our church, who had just been to see his Sunday scholars, who were playing in a perfect swamp. The rain had soaked the meadow beyond the power of east wind and a short allowance of sun to dry it. And it makes one quite grieve for the nice white frocks and decent best clothes—for all make it a point of honour to be in their bettermost best—and they go pattering in procession through the streets singing with all their might. It is a sight I should like you to see, for I don't think it is anywhere to be seen except in Manchester and the immediately neighbouring towns. I am pretty decently dull; nothing happens that would in the least interest you to hear about, which is a sign of moral prosperity. Yesterday I heard an account of a great phreno-magnetic *soirée*, which is altogether beyond my comprehension. The lady who told me was present, and saw what she related. A young girl, a dressmaker, was a subject, and her brother was the operator. There seems to be no suspicion of collusion. The girl, poor thing, was in her normal state, a niminy-piminy, affected milliner, and nothing more, only seeming very much overcome by being in company with so many fine people. Her brother put her to sleep, and then pressed the organs of veneration and imitation at the same time. She is a great admirer of McNeil—and instantly she began to preach in his manner, and to imitate his style and action, everything, ... She delivered a most furious anathema against the Catholics, devoting them all to perdition very eloquently. Then she gave several other manifestations: philoprogenitiveness and veneration, when she devoted a baby, made of two pocket handkerchiefs, to a holy life, in a style that my informant declared was perfectly affecting. Then it was combined with combativeness, when she punished her child severely to keep it from evil; in fact, she was a puppet, moved every way and any way. She retained no consciousness of what had taken place when she awoke, which was fortunate, for I think it was abominable cruelty to try experiments of that sort on a human creature. But a poor cook excites my sympathy the most. It seems that if the magnetiser gives them a command during their magnetic state to be performed when they awake, they feel under an irresistible impulse to perform it, though they know not why—a sort of instinct. The master of this said cook told her that he was going to wake her, and then she was to go down stairs and get her supper, but first she must bring him into the drawing-room some bread and water! She went downstairs accordingly, and, as one of the other servants testified, she sat down to her supper as usual, and suddenly she seemed to recollect that she had something to do first, asked for the bread and water, saying her master would want it, carried it up where he was, amid a room full of people. He asked her why she brought it. She could not give any account of the reason: she only said, 'You want it: I am sure it will do you good,' looking all the time dreadfully perplexed. He, to try her, said: 'No; you see I have wine here.' She insisted, however, on leaving it, to the great edification of the company, who had heard the order given. The gentleman is very well known in Liverpool, a man of sober reputation, and in a general way of reasonable humanity. When people are in love, they are in a magnetic state, and are very much astonished at themselves when they come to their senses. The other night the man who caused me more good and evil feeling than I ever knew before or since the three years his influence lasted, ——, called here. I am frightened when I think of the last year, and yet even that one is now like a tale I have read—has no more to do with me, my present me, than the woes of Dido! Well, as I said, that very man came in the other evening, and stayed some time; he is really the most prosy, wearisome, commonplace person Nature ever created. Once, and not so long ago, that hour would have gilded a week; and now it required an effort of politeness not to give an intelligible hint to shorten his visit! . . .

No more at present. Take care of yourself, and believe me,

Ever yours,

G. E. J.

LETTER 21.

Monday Morning (Undated Fragment of 1843).

Dearest Jane,—I began a letter to you yesterday, but was so much interrupted that I got out of patience, and preferred beginning a fresh one this morning. I hope this brilliant weather is bringing you to life, as well as the trees and the flowers! Are you coming to Liverpool this spring? If so, of course, I count on you for a visit, both here and at Seaforth; anyway, I hope you have something better in store for yourself than to look at the sunshine on the glaring flags. Mrs. —— was here last week, and says that Seaforth looks lovely, so do, my dear, begin to think about rural life and getting pure air, at least, for it takes some indefinite quantity of thinking before anything gets done. I am beginning to feel better than I have done, and really I hope to be up to doing something. You must have thought my letter strangely cold and indifferent, and that I made but a poor return for all the pains and trouble you had bestowed on my concerns. But, indeed, my dear, I could not help it. I could not feel any 'appropriate sentiment' whatever; there was such a complete bankruptcy of vitality that I had not energy to wish myself dead, and out of this 'coil.' My strongest emotion was a resigned inclination for the rites of Christian burial —if anybody would have bestowed them without asking questions! So, my dear, I can only hope you have had just faith enough in me not to set me down as irredeemedly unthankful; for all along during the nervous attacks which alternated with the weakness I was tormented with the idea that I must seem so to you. Have you (of course you have) felt in dreams that odd sensation of doing the most foolish, unwise things in some critical emergency, conscious all the while that they were foolish, but not able to help yourself? That has been my state for the last month, till sometimes I have hoped I should awake to my natural senses and find I had been dreaming. I am quite sure of one thing, and that is, that rational conduct must be formed on the basis of good beef and mutton; nothing energetic or any way good can come from a diet of boiled rice and batter-pudding. That is a physical conclusion I have settled by my own experience, though abstinence from animal food might do for the intellect in a hot climate! . . .

[Fragment.]

LETTER 22.

Thursday (Undated Fragment, 1843).

Dearest Jane,—I must seem to you very stupid-hearted to keep sending you so often the accounts of the little odds and ends which make up my life down here, expecting you to feel an interest in them. It is not that I do not feel that they are altogether of another world, and another complexion, from what occupies you, but if I were with you and beside you all day long I doubt whether I could come nearer to you. I think I know in my heart what is in yours. I feel that I know what you are feeling and thinking; but there it must stay, for I can say nothing that will not be altogether foolish, utterly unprofitable, and unlike what is only dimly known at best. If it were not that you are now, even more than ever you were, the first thought on waking (as if you had been in my dreams) and the last at night, I should fancy that some separation had come between us, that we had fallen asunder in some way, for, as far as letters go, at any rate, those you get from me would fit anybody else as well. And yet it is a comfort to write to you, to be occupied with you anyway, though the thing done has so little in it that it would require more than a Hebrew imagination to see the resemblance between the type and the thing signified. Even when I am with you, I can never tell you an intelligible word of what is in my heart about you. I have often thought since that I must have seemed to you either very indifferent, or else altogether taken up with myself—very unsatisfactory, in short; but you must have patience with me. I do so love you, and that you know; but it is not in me to do you any good, though I would put my hands under your feet to keep you from a minute's pain. I cannot give you a stroke of gladness. But you have seen on a dull November day, when there is neither fog nor rain, but a quiet day without sun, and the sky all one cloud, and no change all the day, just before night there is always a bright gleam, the sky is lit with light. It is true of other things besides those lead-coloured, monotonous skies.

Do not vex yourself about not being in a writing humour. When you have anything to say, the humour will come too, and I shall know almost without your telling me. I have found an outline Mrs. —— once copied for me—one of Thorwaldsen's outlines. It is not so much finished as I thought it had been, and will give you but a faint idea. . . .

[Fragment.]

LETTER 23.

[Undated Fragment, 1843.]

I sat awake last night for nearly three hours, and I thought of you. How do you manage to keep up anything like a sound judgment in your unblessed sleeplessness? I might as soon live in a magic-lanthorn—everything I think about assumes such fantastic colours, and slips so from side to side, that, whether I am in my senses I cannot tell, or whether I am out of my senses I cannot tell, but all the next day, after a sleepless night, I go like 'one that has been stunned and is of sense forlorn.' I gave you a deal of sympathy last night; you have the length of two lives to live in one, which is more than one bargains for. Poor Mrs. —— once said to me, 'It is no use talking; in those sort of affairs woman must go the wall. And we cannot help it.' In Sir Astley Cooper's life there is an account of an operation he performed of taking up the aorta (the great artery that conveys the blood from the heart), knowing, as he said, that the compensating powers of Nature were such that she would supply its office by some other channel, and accommodate the system to it in a short time. In fact, there was no organ so absolutely indispensable but that its functions might be carried on by some other part of the machinery. I positively shivered to think of the *morale* that lay in that law of *physique*. ——'s wife, poor thing, is still in the asylum, and very little chance she will ever be well enough to come out. I have bestowed a great deal of comfort and sympathy upon him, but he is one of those 'who, with the best intentions, are always unfortunate,' and I am got to the fag-end of my powers of commiseration. He seems to run a neck-and-neck race with Fortune, and lose it by a fraction of an inch. It goes through everything. He has had some of his patent pumps (which another would make a fortune out of) made without seeing to his patent-right, and has so ingeniously contrived it as not to be able to obtain legal redress. The other day we invited him to dinner, and I had gone down to the kitchen and skinned and cut up the fowl for the curry with my own imperial hands, and helped to concoct the lemon pudding besides. Well, though he had ample notice, he contrived to get involved in another dinner engagement, and so spoiled both! He hammers, blundering, against a stone wall and never hits the point. My Christian sympathy is quite worn out, and if he ever comes to me again with his lament against Fortune, I shall certainly stare at him for a fool instead of condoling with him for a martyr.

There is a wholesome instinct at the bottom of our dislike to unfortunate people. I am still in a stupid and virtuous state. I cannot do two things at once. All my wits are gone wool-gathering for the benefit of my book, and I have none to spare for other things; so, my dear, if my letters to you fall off in both quantity and quality, don't go beating your brains for a more abstruse theory than Cuvier set up for the Deluge—viz., that as there is not water enough to cover all the earth at one time, when it flows over one place it ebbs from the opposite. A lady said to me the other day, 'Mrs. So-and-So is grown delightful. The last time she was here she was as quiet as you are!!!' That reminds me not to forget something. A man who has been here to tea to-night told me a person he knows well, and who is a great, stupid fellow, was asked what he intended to make of his son, as he was old enough to follow some calling. He said: 'Why, I have some thoughts of sending him to Mr. Brittle, the Calvinist minister, to make him a poet.' A fact, upon my honour! I have been scribbling this because I could not well go to bed till the man who told me this tale has taken his departure! He is just gone, so I will say goodnight too, having to make up for lost time! Do take care of yourself. If —— leaves you a desultory 'widow' whilst he goes into Wales, can you not come down here—*i.e.* if you like to leave London at all?

For I have what he would call a most wholesome desire to see you established in my pretty drawing-room, which you shall have all to yourself; and Frank has just been buying a most *recherché* bed of an original design, and that shall be made over to you! In short, if I could see you and speak to you, I should have no tragic mood for a year to come, I think, and really that is saying no little, for I have had a strong inclination to hang myself oftener than once within the last month. God bless you, and ever take care of you!

Ever your own
G. E. J.

Tuesday Night, 1843.

LETTER 24.

Tuesday Morning (Incomplete, Date doubtful), 1843-4.

Dearest Jane,—What will you have thought of me for being able to abstain so long from writing to you? And yet, my darling, if it had not been for a piece of conscientiousness you would have had a letter a fortnight ago, for there was a long one actually written. It had taken several days to do. Part of it was occupied in abusing a visitor who had come to torment us and destroy all our pleasant *dolce far niente* days, and my impatience was at the height, and I had relieved my heart by telling you my grievances. But before the letter was finished she had done one or two really good-natured things, and though I should have felt more at my ease under the civilities of a she tiger, I burnt my letter with a sort of compunction, and a letter to me now is a piece of work not to be lightly thought of. So, my dear, you have had to wait till another opportunity sprang up to replace what was so untimely destroyed. I am very anxious to hear and know how you have been prospering since you wrote last. Are you well settled again in London? I feel to rejoice that one can think of you as in a civilised region that requires no knowledge of geography to know whereabouts it is. But how are you, body and mind? Have you any near sources of annoyance? for one grows an 'amateur' in endurance, and able to distinguish nice shades in better and worse. I don't want you to be plagued, but if you would write soon it would be a great comfort. Tell me as much about yourself as can be said in a letter. I never keep very private letters, but destroy them at once, having the fear of a coroner's inquest before my eyes, and a great horror of all executors who can pry into secrets from a sense of duty! So you have a fancy for wishing to see Algiers? The *Morning Chronicle* spoiled all rose-coloured imaginings when it spoke of long rows of showy shops and abundance of second-rate French jewellery as being the principal features in it, and I never could get up any sentiment for that part of the world again! And yet, though a place may be nothing *per se*, yet I can understand how

Botany Bay might become a point of interest! I am come home again. I left Lytham last week after a stay of five weeks. It took my fancy exceedingly. I felt at the end as if awaking from a long, placid sleep. It is a very small, quiet place, not at all fashionable—has not even a circulating library, and only two donkeys; but it is a great place for boat-building, and the vessels and the sea and the mountains beyond used to look like some of Turner's pictures, and at times I was reminded, I don't know why, of some of the scenes in the 'Mysteries of Udolpho.'[1] If complete idleness can make people tranquil, I have achieved the supreme bliss of 'Buddhism,' or perhaps a duckpond would be a more graphic comparison. I have learned to knit—to the everlasting honour of the lady who achieved the teaching! I am even becoming aspiring enough to contemplate a Turkish cushion; if it is ever realised you shall have it. Somehow, it is soothing to me to contemplate myself as more efficient in such matters than you, my dear. You will not grudge me such a small solace? My eyes are much better than they were, only I cannot see yet to any purpose, and am consoled by hearing that these chronic inflammations are to continue *ad infinitum*, and that there is no knowing when my eyes will be available for every-day use. But I am now trying something that has

[1] Mrs. Radcliffe's.

been highly recommended, and as there is no real disease in the organ itself, no doubt it will get stronger by time, which seems to do and undo everything. Meanwhile, I have got frightened enough to be prudent. I cannot bear to write with pen and ink yet, so you must excuse pencil. The black and white dazzles. By the way, I have a State letter on the stocks to your husband, which is only waiting till it can be properly indited (for I dare not send him a scrawl)! I have been applied to for counsel on a matter far beyond my reach, and I must submit it to him, for I really dare say nothing. It is a nice point to settle. As you will have the benefit of the whole affair, there is no need to state it now. I had a letter from Mrs. —— yesterday. She has been in Wales for the last month, and she is now settled at home for the winter. She seems very inclined to go on with the book now that she is set at ease about you. By the way, I never thanked you for your patience in reading and criticising, but both were gratefully appreciated, and the criticism comforted us all; but I have lost my taste for writing, everything like desperation has faded away. What shall I say for myself? Even philosophising has departed from me . . . .

[Fragment.]

LETTER 25.

Thursday (Date doubtful, 1843-4).

Dearest Jane,—When your letter was brought me I was in the act of looking for a sheet of paper to write to you. I am very thankful to know what it is you are really doing, for you are never out of my head an hour together. It is not your breaking down, I fear—so long as you have anything to do you will never fail—but what is to be left of you in the end? But God made you to be the stay and help of everybody you love! It is your destiny, and you must do it! However, you seem to have had strength in a miraculous manner, and it will not fail you to the end. If you are to die in the end, you will have filled up your life, and filled it thoroughly; from neither the living nor the dying will you need any pity, but all honour and reverence instead. I am at this moment much more inclined to cry than to write this letter, when I feel and know that you are suffering; and still more when I think of the reaction that is to come, when all the active doing is taken into other hands, and you are left to be quiet. It is no use saying anything, I am as miserable about you as I can be; but there is no healing either wounds or sorrow by power of sympathy in these days—the more one loves, the more helpless one feels, for one's love is the best thing one has to give, and one sees of how very little use it is for all the practical purposes of lightening sorrow; and a great deal of what I suffer for you is at bottom for myself, for if you fell down dead or worn-out, what is to become of me? What am I to do without you; so you see the beautiful disinterestedness of human nature! By nature, at any rate, we are always unable to share our sorrows with the world in general. Carlyle is magnificent, and you are not wasted upon him, and that will be a consolation to feel some day.

He is much too grand for everyday life. A sphinx does not fit in comfortably to our parlour-life arrangements, but seen from a proper point of view it is a supernaturally grand thing! You must feel proud of belonging to him, after all, and he deserves to have you! Mortal praise can go no higher! I humbly beg to make an offering of a morsel of 'Cavendish' which I had given me yesterday, and which I have cut and prepared my own self! I must tell you an anecdote I heard the other day, and which is Gospel true. A man not far from here, who is very rich, took a fancy to fit up a little chapel in his parish church, in order that he and his family might worship with an imposing appearance. He went to a clever stonemason at Sadleworth, and told him to sculpture him some 'ancestors' to put on some monuments he was going to build in his chapel, and to cross their legs, that they might look as if they had been to the Crusades; he bought a quantity of banners at the same time!! This is the last absurd thing I have heard. Will you forgive me for trying to make you laugh, which, God knows why, one's friends seem to consider it a point of honour to attempt whenever we feel the most disinclined for such a performance! I have nothing to tell you about myself. My life is prosaic enough—ingrained prose, in fact (I wish yours were more like it)—but it is the only point in which I can offer it for your admiration. I am taking lessons in being good-humoured, and even placid, in temper, under the discipline of the worst-tempered and most irritable man in Christendom, who resents the concatenations of vexations and annoyances of a residence in Manchester, down to the very smoke and dust and rain, as offences committed by me! I have the comfort of being a compendious and tangible type of all his woes, an epitome of all the vexations that exist for him under the sun! As there is no appeal—except to the justice of Heaven, which is both vague and uncertain in its administration—I am learning to take it quietly without any protest, and have actually began to doubt whether, after all, I may not be an annoyance! 'He that is down need fear no fall, he that is low no pride,' as old John Bunyan says! And one may as well begin one's stage through the 'valley of humiliation' soon as late, and I have a theory that 'the patient Griselda' was *me*, in a previous existence. Write to me, dear love, when it is not a weariness, and the more minute you can be the more you will satisfy me! You cannot tell me too much. Now God bless you. I can only love you, but that you know I do, and always will. Good bye! and believe your own

G. E. J.

Mrs. —— leaves Liverpool to-day. She said she feared she could not get to see you till she returned.

1844.

LETTER 26.

Tuesday Night (Postmark, January 10, 1844).

Dearest Jane,—I am very much disturbed to have excited so much of your sympathy, though I am at this moment suffering all the fright I should have endured had I known the appearance things were presenting. Would you believe it! That inestimable parcel was sent off on Wednesday last, and a receipt for it given and taken! And how it contrived to be so long on its journey, the saints above only know! It was actually sealed up when that note to you was indited, and I suppose the fact was so vividly impressed upon me that all words to explain to others stayed away from the sense of not being required. But I am very vexed that you have been kept in any sort of discomfort. However, let it mollify you to know that if I could have suspected the state of things I should have been in the extremity of despair. But I have such a Mohammedan faith in the unerring decrees of post-offices and railways, that I never for a moment should have suspected them of overlooking any mortal mixture of sealing-wax and brown paper committed to their care, but, for the future, all my despatches shall be sent per post, even if it cost a sheet full of stamps! However, 'all's well that ends well!' and even of the sympathy there has been none lost, or altogether thrown away, for it has made me love you even better than I did before, though I wish it could have been given without any sort of worry to you. But then it would not have been sympathy, and I am too much obliged and needy of it altogether to have the grace to wish it undone! Only don't let there come a reaction! I always feel inclined to revenge myself when I have felt too much— by rushing an equal distance in the opposite extreme. So don't have to pay a fine for my 'treasure-trove,' as lawyers call it. I always chronicle my goings-on —for your edification! And where do you think I went to on Monday night? To the circus!! And I am afraid that a person of your refinement will for evermore consider me unworthy of sympathy, or delicate sensibility of any sort, when I own to have been decidedly amused and pleased to a degree approaching the superlative! I am half-ashamed of myself, or rather have a sneaking consciousness that I ought to be. There was Van Amburgh and all his beasts for one thing, but I did not care about them. They came quite at the last and were the least part of the entertainment; only I could not help feeling very sorry that such aristocratic animals as lions and tigers should so far forget their dignity as to act pretty-behaved ferocity for the amusement of a rabble; there was an elephant turned loose into the circle, a good-natured, peaceable creature, but I did really feel nervous lest, without any ill intention, he should go a few feet too far either to the right or left, and so get amongst the indulgent public! For there was only two feet in height of a deal board between him and it! However, he behaved exceedingly well. He lay down and stretched himself, and trotted, and carried his keeper, and opened his mouth, and finally disappeared—to my great relief. Then there was the poor pretty giraffe, looking like a captive princess; there was something quite pathetic in her appearance, and I wished her well dead, with all my heart! But she was apparently in the enjoyment of excellent health and resignation. Did you ever see a giraffe? If not, pray be on the watch for an opportunity; it is well worth some pains to accomplish! It is like seeing something from between the regions of truth and fiction: and now I have great hope to behold both a 'phœnix' and a 'griffin' before I die, for I am sure they all come from the same debatable land!

Lions and tigers and elephants one can understand without much stretch of imagination. One can fancy their ways of living, their manners and customs, and morality! But giraffes are from an unknown region! One does not know anything of their associations, one cannot imagine what they do 'in their own country,' but it must have been a stray stroke of fortune to bring one of them to tread the sawdust of a circus. But the attraction of the evening was the vaulting, and 'horsemanship,' and very impossible and incomprehensible it looked. But all my sympathies would wander behind a certain embroidered pink silk curtain, behind which men and horses vanished. I like to know the processes of things, and I was curious to know how the Apollo-like appearance we beheld had been produced, and still more curious to know what sort of souls resided in bodies of men who spent their whole lives in turning forty-four somersaults in succession. I would have given anything to go behind the scenes. All those riders and tumblers 'were men once,' and there was a darling little boy, not more than six years old—who stimulated my benevolent sensibility. If one could only take him away from such a life! If I were a Sultan, all children in his situation should be killed mercifully out of harm's way. You will be tired to death hearing all this, but it is the last and newest thing I have to amuse you! Let me see— yes! there is something else that will amuse you, too, as our sympathies run so well together. 'Men and Women,' by the author of 'Susan Hopley,' is a capital book with abundance of plots in it, and it kept even a hard-hearted novel-reader like me in a state of high excitement from the beginning to the end. It is quite a Godsend, for if you begin it you cannot put it down! At least I could not, and I neither skipped, nor yet looked on, to see what was coming, but went step by step, cutting my leaves as I went on!—and if that is not a compliment, what is? So do you get it, while this horrid thaw continues! This is a long letter all about nothing, but nothings make the sum of female life! I only hope the prospect from your window is pleasanter than it is from mine at this moment. Dirty, half-melted snow and fog, a swampy meadow, set off by a creeping cold damp, which gets into one's bones and nerves, and freezes there, utterly impossible to stir out, and no book in the house! So when this letter is sealed up I shall have to set to work in sheer despair, and perhaps if I can get another chapter finished, it may please my restless conscience to glow with virtuous complacency. Anyway, I must not stay making this epistle any longer. It was half written last night, after my return home, and the rest has got itself 'shiveringly' done this morning since breakfast. How is Mr. Carlyle? and how is 'Oliver Cromwell'? I am inclined to wish that worthy had never been born, for your sake. Take care of yourself! If I had a wishing-cap at this moment, I would wish for an eider-down coverlet to keep your feet warm. I saw one yesterday, and the comfort is indescribable,

and I thought how nice it would be for you ! I am
sure it is something like an angel's wing, so light and
soft. There ! after that stroke of imagination I shall
enter on nothing more prosaic, so good bye ! and God
bless you, dear love !

Ever your own
G. E. J.

[Wednesday morning. Begun on Tuesday, and finished the following day.—A. E. I.]

LETTER 27.

[Postmark, February 12, 1844.]

Dearest Jane,—What *is* the matter with you?
What *has been*? Thank God that there is a ' has been '
in the case ! But what have you been doing? I hope
the cruel cold weather goes for something in it—for
I have felt it most sympathetically. However, I am
manufacturing a small piece of comfort for you,
which you would have received along with this if I
had not been obliged to go to a concert last night.
It is an eider-down quilt for your feet. I have had a
floating vision of it for some time, but your letter of
yesterday fired me up to go out in search of the means
of realising it. I have sacrificed a rose-coloured
imagination for fear you should fancy it too delicate
for daily wear and tear, and have substituted a sober
brown covering without the least touch of ' charming
delusion ' about it—for which piece of virtue I exact

that you shall use it every day whilst winter lasts. I expect you will receive it on Wednesday, and I trust it will prove emblematic, 'significant of much,' as Carlyle has it. My dear child, have you had a medical man, or have you been consigned to the attentive care of John Carlyle?[1] Do try to take care of yourself. I am thankful to hear of all —— has done in the way of virtue, and I hope it will continue. After all, there is always a sort of excellence that discovers itself when, to ordinary lookers-on, the character seems worn to the bone. Certainly, if the doctrine of consequence has any truth in it, you ought to reap the good effects of your long-suffering and tender mercy towards her—and as the sailor contrived to make very decent soup from stones by adding good ingredients to them, it is possible that a good result may be obtained out of —— by a similar process. The tenderness you have heaped upon her must tell somewhere.

So my store of philosophy surprises you? My dear child, if I had enamelled myself with my own wisdom, the pores of my character would have been so effectually stopped that I could neither have taken anything in nor thrown anything out. Do not you recollect what St. Paul says, 'endure fools gladly: seeing you yourself are wise'? but I do not claim the benefit of the latter part of the Apostle's

---

[1] Dr. John Carlyle, brother of Thomas Carlyle.—A. E. I.

axiom, for I have a great notion that I really am a great fool, without any mitigating features—and so I can judge of wisdom like a disinterested spectator who is not a shareholder. As to 'that scene,' my dear—I came to the requisite knowledge very honestly, if you will but believe it—indeed I could not help it. I took a fit of studying metaphysics before I was 16, and would not have given a straw to read any book whose meaning did not lay at an unfathomable depth; and when I had gone through a course of those, I was fired with a glorious ambition to say my say on the much-vexed question of 'matter and spirit,' and, save the mark! the nature of life, and I accordingly set to work on physiology, and for nearly two years I read nothing else. There is at this moment a box upstairs full of extracts, and abstracts, and conclusions. I have a more than feminine ignorance of anatomy—I don't feel too sure on which side the heart lies—but, *en revanche*, I have physical philosophy enough now to stock the College of Surgeons. I have forgotten a great deal of it, and the taste for that sort of reading has gone by me— but out of such a decoction of Blumenbach-Magendie-Tiedemann-Cabanis, and ever so many more, it would be hard indeed if I had not gathered a few theories. And without any detriment to my fair fame, either, for I assure you I did not get the said books surreptitiously, but borrowed them from responsible persons, and read them before men and angels, and by way of climax, when I got into my desperate condition, from which I was barely emerging when you first saw me, I endeavoured to drown my pain, not by inditing a 'diary of an *ennuyée*,' but by writing an essay on materialism, which is or was in Mrs. ——'s hands. I fagged through Cudworth's folio before I finally abandoned myself to despair and hysterics; from all which it may be seen, that when people have cause for unhappiness, it is no good for them to try and cheat themselves. It must come on and be regularly worn out—'exploited,' as you call it. So you see there is nothing marvellous in my philosophy! I learnt the best part of it when I was very miserable, more miserable than one human being can be twice in one lifetime. As to the 'scene,' if it really is too bad it must be exchanged for something more placid. But I am sure I have read things far fiercer in Miss Porter's novels. The practical matter of getting the book printed drives me to despair. I don't in the least know how to do, or what to do. I will inquire about Wesley, the man who was Mrs. Hall's publisher, but I have an idea he may have died or transmigrated into some other form, and be no longer a serviceable publisher. However, to-day is Sunday, on which no manner of work can be done, so it is of no use bothering now. Tell Mazzini, however, that if he reviews it (no matter whether his article gets accepted or not) I shall consider it an ample harvest of reputation—in fact, quite worth writing the book to obtain. I wish he would write another article and let me translate it, for I am just in the humour for such work. I was at a party the other night when a man came in with a most peculiar physiognomy, an expression I could not comprehend at all. I asked the master of the house, 'who is that?' 'Oh, that is Mr. ——, the most proper man I knew in my life.' He never committed an indiscretion or got into a scrape of any sort, and never will.' I insisted on being introduced, and I studied him during the quadrille (for I could not make him talk), and I watched him all night (everybody gives him the same character)! There was a grave, Chinese look about him—*au reste*, he is a sort of cross between a Methodist parson and the genius of a white cravat. He came in a cab, and went away in a cab, and he always spoke in a low, even tone of voice. In short, he was like nothing else I ever saw. Last night I was at such a glorious concert. It was an amateur affair, given by a set of young Germans in this town. They sang quartets and duets, but I never knew what music was before. It was mostly German, one felt it to mean so much! It was like standing on the edge of another world and looking into it—you might have fancied you were listening to the 'Psalms of Heaven.' As you liked the notice of the 'Sphinx,' I have got two other

passages which have taken my fancy. Always out
of my dearly beloved—who is the most practical old
soul you can imagine, and in such a grave, unconscious way, though it must be owned that he is a
sad infidel, and explains the mysteries of the old gods
in a way to raise on end the hair of a devout believer
in them, like myself. He tells us in one place quite
coolly that 'Bacchus was a very spruce young
man'!!! But to make amends, listen to the following
account of Arabia, and figure to yourself getting
hold of such a book for the first time in this year of
our Lord: 'Next to these inhabit the Homeritæ, and
next to them the Sabæans. They possess "Arabia the
Happy," and are exceeding rich in all those things
which we esteem most precious, for the whole country
is naturally perfumed all over, everything almost growing there, and sending forth continually most excellent odours; on the sea coast grow balsam and cassia.
Higher in the heart of the country are shady woods
and forests, graced and beautified with stately trees
of frankincense and myrrh, palm trees, cinnamon and
such-like odoriferous plants; for none can enumerate
the several natures and properties of so great a
multitude, or the excellency of those sweet odours
that breathe out of every one of them, for their
excellency is such that it even ravishes the senses
with delight, as a thing divine and unutterable, and
these spices have nothing of a faint and languishing

smell, as those that come to our hands, but a strong and vigorous odour that strongly pierces all the senses to the utmost of their capacity. So they that have the advantage of these sweet odours are fit for that feigned meat of the gods called "Ambrosia," since those excellent perfumes cannot have a name assigned to them transcending their worth and dignity. Yet fortune has not imparted to men an entire and unmixed felicity in these things, but has joined some inconveniences to correct them, who, through a constant confluence of earthly blessings, have despised and slighted the gods, for these fragrant forests abound with red serpents of a span long, whose bite is deadly and incurable.' Then he goes on to another and less favoured part of Arabia, and says that in the desert a strange and wonderful thing often happens—'for sometimes, commonly in calm weather, there appear in the air shapes of divers living creatures, some standing still, others moving, some flying, others pursuing, and these are of a monstrous bigness, so that they greatly terrify such as are ignorant of the nature of them. Some of them pursue men, and when they take hold of them a trembling and a chilliness seizes upon all parts of their bodies, and therefore strangers unaccustomed to such things are ready to fall down dead with fear; but the natural inhabitants, being used to them, regard them not.' Now, my dear, you need not read all this; indeed it is an MS., and not a letter. I have been writing all afternoon, partly because I am in a humour to talk to you, and partly because when I am ill reading letters is a sort of gentle, lazy dulness, in which my soul takes delight. But recollect, my child, that though I write I am not so unconscionable as to expect you to read it all. That is quite optional, and not an article of obligation! I hope Mrs. —— is coming this week. So God bless you, my dear child! and let the next account of you be better, and believe me ever your own

G. E. J.

Sunday Afternoon.

LETTER 28.

Friday, March 2, 1844.

Dearest Jane,—Thank you, thank you, for all the plague you have taken about that MS. I could not have done it for myself! I well know the nuisance of it, so, my dear, pray believe that your labour of love is appreciated, and thank Carlyle for his letter of recommendation, which I don't value the less because I laughed at your account of it. If you could get me the original out of the hands of Messrs. Chapman and Hall, I would treasure it up and put it safe into my solitary drawer that rejoices in a lock and key. Whether your efforts in my behalf succeed or not, your goodness has been all the same, and I recollect my metaphysics too well not to know that success is an accident. I did read that dreadful trial, and I cannot tell you how sick at heart it made me. —— had been reading a newspaper at breakfast with vehement expressions of indignation, and finally gave it to me, with, 'There, Geraldine! read that! It is the most abominable thing I ever heard of'—and if it be any sort of consolation to poor Mrs. ——, she may know that the small portion of the public I have heard mention the matter are unanimous in declaring that it is a got-up case by her husband. Her guilt or innocence never comes to question. I read the whole, and the possibility of her being guilty never occurred to me; and I was ready to scratch the stupid old judge for his qualifying assertions about her. Nothing came out to injure her more than might be asserted of three-fourths of the innocent, respectable women in the world, and I feel quite thankful to you for your generous sympathy towards her. It was what I would have done myself, and if the sympathy of a stranger can do her any good, pray tell her that one woman at least both sympathises with and believes in her, though at the same time I would have heartily forgiven her if she had revenged herself. But I feel convinced that she has been faithful, as the phrase goes, and perhaps this is the most comforting assertion the poor woman could receive; but, my dear, I could not help feeling sorry for the two poor heedless girls mixed up in the matter. What a scene of horror was disclosed! I have not got rid of the effect it had on me yet. What unmitigated misery for so many persons, and what an irredeemable poltroon and scoundrel the man is to bring such things to the light of day, and involve so many. If his wife had a hundred lovers he ought to have been silent. I shall try to believe in the day of judgment, if it is only for his special benefit! One consolation is, that there is no escape from the consequences of our actions, and so he is provided for. I feel, my dear, quite as if I were personally obliged for what you have done for that poor woman. This is not intended for a letter, only just a word to save Sunday's post. I can't bear yours to wait so long for an answer of some sort. I fear you will not be better till the weather changes. The influenza hangs over one like an evil conscience! Nothing tangible, only a general sense of something wrong. Take care of yourself is all I can say. As to my household, ———, the servant, is able to crawl about her work, coughing as if within an inch of strangulation. ———'s throat very little better, but he too goes about his work without eating anything but mutton broth. For me, I suppose there is nothing the matter with me; but I am so weak and languid I can hardly walk, and to do anything is far beyond my capability.

I am thoroughly uncomfortable. I can hardly scrawl this without feeling sick to death. By the way, I hope I made it clear that we went out to dine on the strength of a solemn invitation, given, however, as an act of Christian consideration. Anyway, the idea of either going without dinner—of buying myself a quarter of a pound of cold meat—would never have occurred to me! I certainly am destitute of what the Margravine of Anspach calls 'negative virtues, which redeemed her from many mischiefs.' I wish in my heart you had less patience, it would be better for you! Only imagine that the horrid Goths are making preparations to build eighteen houses in the meadows before our house! and they have dug a pump! You don't imagine that I am going to put up with eighteen opposite neighbours, not a bit of it! Though it is provoking that we are just painted and papered so beautifully. Now, my darling, good-bye and God bless you; take care of yourself, and put up with nothing, but apply as many positive remedies as may be worth while. I shall write again on Sunday; meanwhile, believe me

Ever your own

G. E. J.

LETTER 29.

Sunday and Monday, March 2 and 3, 1844.

Dearest Jane,—Will you condescend to look on this cheesemonger-like note? But the truth is I have no other sort of paper, and I fear I have not ink enough to see me to the end of my letter. So I have just taken the precaution to direct my envelope first. How are you by this time? I have had a very bad week, being in bed nearly all the day, but Mr. —— promises me that I shall be better soon, so be hanged to complainings! I am just tired to death, and only wish matters were settled one way or other. It is terrible to be so good for nothing. Mrs. —— is coming here to-morrow, and I quite am looking forward to seeing her. She is very far from well. I am sure the race of doctors must be thriving apace. Whilst lying in bed I thought of a great many things to tell you, and now that I want to write them down, they are all gone. Do you recollect my telling you of the dreadful bore that a small youth had thought proper to become? Well, my dear, by a little thought and some good luck, I have transformed this bore into a blessing—not to myself but to a neighbour. I introduced him to a lady who wanted an eligible companion for her only son, and as I could give the youth a capital character, he is received with open arms, and I have watered the budding friendship, or rather—tea'd and coffee'd it. And he has taken root there in the most promising fashion, and he has removed his lodgings to a greater distance from here, so that now I am restored to my pristine amiability, and I feel as if I had done a very good deed to all parties. I have been revelling in the most queer old book ! I had read it before, some years ago, but it is better than when new. It is 'The History of John Buncle.'

Full, as the title-page says, of the most wonderful revelations, it is very curious to read it parallel with Horace Walpole's or George Selwyn's Letters. The country is England in both, and I must copy you a passage—written, recollect, not a hundred and twenty years ago—'And now, reader, as to Stonemoor country. If ever it should come into your head to wander over this wide and romantic part of our world at the Hazard of your neck, and the danger of being starved to death, your road is . . . . This is one way into the heart of Stonemoor in Richmondshire, and will bring you by the way among the dreadful northern fells of Westmorland, a frightful country, and a fatiguing march.' Then he goes on to describe a 'sandy valley, where cliffs are rising from the ground, a grand and amazing scene.' Then he is constantly falling in with more wonderful damsels than ever the Arabian Nights furnished (Zobeide and the Porter were nothing to him). He

I

travelled for a whole day through a hole which led to some wonderful cavern, and through the said cavern, 'full of beautiful concretions on the rising way, which formed the most beautiful pillars, walls, and figures of the finest carved work.' And they work their way out at the top of an exceeding high mountain, and have to clamber down a precipice, and instead of breaking their necks (he and his servant), as they ought in reason to have done, he discovers a fine country house and gardens in a delightful valley that extended with all the beauties of wood, and lawn, meadow and water from the foot of the mountain, and he is met by an elderly gentleman—'and a most beautiful young lady, whose eyes were vastly fine, large and long, black as night and had a sparkling brightness, as great as appears from the refraction of diamonds, and her whole behaviour was in the highest degree charming.'

She could talk Latin and any other tongue, and was a miracle of genius—but the entertainments are the best part of the business. There is something so hearty and rich in his pictures of the inside of these houses—the 'shady walks, playing fountains, and flowing tide' is quite as grand as anything in the 'Decameron.' There is a fresh air and pure, breezy feeling about the book that makes you feel as if you had been a journey into the country on a spring day yourself! There are disquisitions about every subject under Heaven. He once gets into a grand park, and finds a young lady in a romantic arbour writing from a Hebrew Bible! He is always on all occasions well received, and he is invited into the house to have some breakfast, 'and the lovely Harriott made tea for me, and had such plenty of fine cream and extraordinary bread and butter set before me that I breakfasted with uncommon pleasure.' Then he makes a declaration to the said Harriott, who considers it premature, as he had only been two hours in her company, and turns the conversation on to the probable language Adam and Eve spoke in Paradise, which they discuss as gravely as if nothing had happened. It was Hazlitt who first put me up to reading it; he mentions John Buncle in one of his essays; and certainly it ought to be counted to him for a good deed. Yesterday a man—who is—never mind what—brought me a curious treatise on alchemy. The book itself was printed in 1671, and professes to be, and there is no reason to doubt is, the last will and testament of Basil Valentine, monk of the Order of St. Benedict, 'which being alone, he hid under a table of marble behind the High Altar of the Cathedral Church, in the Imperial City of Erford, leaving it there to be found by him whom God's Providence should make worthy of it.' I have not had time to read much of it yet, but I daresay I shall find some very choice morsels for you before I have done. That is, if you care about hearing about such things, for as I don't go out, the different books I get hold of are all the worldly things I can give account of. By the way, did you ever write a book called 'Wedlock'? 'It is a novel in three volumes—and it is so like your conversation sometimes, that you have been in my mind from the beginning to the end, and I actually sat down to ask you the question one day last week, only had not energy to write a note. . . .

[Fragment.]

LETTER 30.

Sunday (Postmark, March 5, 1844).

Dearest Jane,—If there is one thing more than another that I specially ought not to do, it is writing a letter to-day. So of course I feel a particular call to do it, but whether it will be long or short, or in any wise worth reading, is entirely unknown to me. The fact is, that my influenza, or whatever the thing may be, has settled in my eyes, which at this moment are no more like eyes than they are like angels, being swelled and inflamed till they won't open, except just set themselves ajar, as one may say. Really, another time before I begin to complain I will wait a little, and ascertain how far the grievances are likely to extend, and so not waste all my eloquent complainings on the beginning.

The doctor has given me some medicine which is seemingly an importation from the bottomless pit— for it tastes like fire, and leaves a taste and smell as if a whole legion of devils had evaporated. Now, how are you? For the worse I get, the more I think of you and your ailments—a fellow-feeling, my dear— for I have the grace to believe that you are far worse off than I am. But as I am tired already of people asking me how I do, I won't torment you in the same way. Only recollect that you will confer a real comfort on me when you send word : ' I am better, on the road to be well.' When I wrote the other day I don't think I told you, or rather made you understand, how really grateful I am for all the trouble you have taken about me. I never can return thanks, and the more cause there is for thankfulness the more ungracious do I seem. I know so thoroughly all the disagreeableness of what you have just been doing— to say nothing of the danger, for it is a quicksand that has swallowed up more friendships than any Slough of Despond ever did—and I am so anxious you should understand that whether the thing succeeds ultimately or not is now quite beyond your care. You have done all and more than I could have expected in reason and conscience, even from the categories of love and friendship: so, my dear love, if the serious consideration 'of Messrs. Chapman and Hall' prove to be a rejection of the MSS., do not torment yourself by fancying that I shall attribute it to this, that, or the other cause—to anything, in short, beyond the simple fact that the said MSS. will not suit! which is a highly reasonable probability. The other week, at a concert, I heard a dissertation on the failure of many singers of decided talent. It came from a professional man, and had much practical meaning for decided talent in other things, and I laid it to heart. Anyway, this is only to beg you not to make, as you phrase it, 'a tether of hair to hang yourself,' and it is to get this said—that I am writing to-day! If 'Chapman and Hall' won't have it, give me as much sympathy as you will—but don't worry yourself by thinking you might have done anything more or different than you have done. I have got a confounded steel pen, which will hardly mark, and makes me fit to swear. I hate inflexible things of all sorts. By the way, I must tell you something that tickled my fancy in a novel the other day. Speaking of the hero, who is in some grievous distress, it says— 'The tears of anguish coursed each other *gracefully* down his cheeks!!!' Beat that in the course of your reading if you can! I have been reading Isaak Walton's 'Lives,' and in the life of George

Herbert there are a few lines that in case the MSS. ever gets printed I should like on the title-page :—

> Now I am here, what wilt thou do with me?
> None of my books will show.
> I read, and sigh, and wish I were a tree,
> For then I sure should grow
> To fruit or shade; at least
> Some bird would trust
> Her household with me, and
> I would be just.

Can you make it out? Is there not something very quaint and beautiful in it? How is poor Mrs. ——? If women would stand by each other, on the strength of sisterhood, as you have done by her, how much happier would it be in the world for all of them. I feel as if you had done me a favour. My wrath had been raised against the cruelty women show so often to each other very much of late, and I have very nearly broken off an acquaintance with one woman, for no other reason than that she said bitter things of a poor young creature who has no relations to stand up for her. I don't care whether they were true or false. They were what one woman has no business to say of another. I cannot send you any flowers, but I found this little book in my drawer the other day, and send it with all its imperfections. So good-bye, my dear love, and God bless you!

I cannot write any longer. Ever your

G. E. J.

LETTER 31.

Friday (Postmark, April 20, 1844).

Dearest Jane,—Many thanks for your very kind letter, which is just come. I lose no time in setting your sensitive soul to rest as to the annoyance I have sustained. Of course one always feels a little sheepish at finding one has failed, but I feel so perfectly convinced that in this instance I deserved to do so that ―― himself would be charmed with my perfect acquiescence in his rejection. I have a great deal too much virtue to be amused with what he says, but I have every intention of profiting by it, and I have a great idea that he will have done me a world of good. Only please explain to him that the books in question are not immoral, but only absurd. However, I will indite him a respectable article, and take great pains with it in every way. You soften down the sharp edges most tenderly, and your letter is quite worth my writing an article and having it refused, for you are more than good, my dear, and the quantity of this disagreeable trouble you have taken for me is 'deep in my heart.' Really, I was more touched by your trying to comfort me by talking of ―― than I can tell you. As to the article itself, it is of no value, and the public will be no better or worse whether the thing is bestowed upon it or not; but as I know definitely the objections it lies open to, and especially after Carlyle has taken the trouble of listening to it, I will re-write it, and try to make it as good as my capability will allow. It will be good practice at any rate, but don't consider yourself bound to plague yourself with it in any way. A long time ago a friend said ' that an artist who set great store by his work never came to anything good,' and I am sure it is true!

Dear me! one does not write with diamond dust that one should gather up all one's fragments so frugally! Well, my dear, and I have got to tell you that your representations about ' stops ' and ' capital letters ' is telling upon me slowly. I have borrowed Blair's lectures, and I expect my sentences will soon be on more creditable principles of composition, and I have already felt respectability dawning on my soul from this contemplation of the Doctor's immaculate wig and well-balanced visage. I was interrupted by dinner, and during dinner I have had a bright thought—viz., to go to school for my composition. A lady I know, no less than ——'s Mrs. ——, has had a monomania for teaching all her life. She set up a school for the real love of the thing, and English composition—*i.e.* grammar and syntax—was what she specially shone in. Well, she has written several little books for children, the English style of which is really beautiful, and I will go to her, and get her to teach me. She is a fierce evangelical, but we get on together notwithstanding, for she has a great deal of sense. She will not help me either to thoughts or opinions, but she can teach me what I want a great deal more—viz., the common rules of writing—for, however I may make a joke of the matter, I really know nothing at all about the commonest rules of English syntax, and always thought they came by nature, and the Devil is in it if I do not contrive to mend my faults. Whether what I write gets printed or not, it shall be done, and properly done too, or—hem! My dear, before I quit my egotism, will you tell me what egotism really is? —— says I have a tendency that way. It is an 'asses-bridge' of a problem I cannot be expected to pass. I am rattling on under the inspiration of your letter, and yet I am dished to a degree that is not marked in a moral thermometer. I am suffering from Mudieism, but it is the result of successful labours. I told you the place I had got for —— had fallen through, and a horrid woman would make me go to a tea-drinking there to show that I understood her conduct in nothing but a Pickwickian sense. Well, it was a good miss, and Providential as she says, but last Monday I heard of a lady's maid's place for her and went after it, and was asked to sit down in the hall 'par parenthèse.' However, I saw the old lady, and a very stiff old lady she was, and the place seemed a very eligible one, the only bugbear being that —— would have to clear-starch the collars, but Mrs. —— promised to teach her that, from the first principles. Yesterday —— was to go and speak to the lady (for there are two—the mother and daughter). Well, the place seemed highly advantageous, for I sent my servant —— with her, who told me that —— might manage everything but the clear-starching (the Devil take it!). There were petticoats, besides, to wash and iron, and ——'s heart failed, but there were too many advantages, and it was altogether too good to be lost, so after six o'clock last night I sallied out and paid them a visit. The daughter is a very reasonable and considerate person, and both are ladies, and I talked, and the result is they will 'put out' the petticoats, leaving only the collars and frills and her own clothes for ——, and they will bear with her shortcomings at first, and not expect perfection of clearness to begin with. She will have a parlour to herself, which she will not have to clean, and she will have to dress these two ladies, and do the plain sewing, according to her capacity, of which I spoke eloquently. She is to go in a fortnight from next Wednesday, and she is to have a week for herself to learn this said clear-starching, and my own milliner has promised to give her a few lessons in quilling and trimming, and cap-making. She is to begin at ten guineas, and to be 'raised.' If you will indite a letter to ——, putting spirit into her, and telling her that this horrid ironing and starching is very possible, you will do a great good, for, as —— said, 'Poor thing, she is not spiritful, and is easily frightened.' Mrs. —— has been like a mother to her. To be sure, she gives more good advice than enough, but she is a friend —— may kneel down and thank God for finding. So, my dear, will you put pen to paper, and tell —— she has capacity for sewing, and can learn everything else that is needed? The result is that what with walking and talking, and the anxiety, I am in a mesmeric sleep to-day. I did not get up till twelve o'clock, and if it had not been for your packet I should have lain on the sofa and slept till night. I hope Mr. —— is out of danger now. I have a tale for you, but it is too long to write now. Perhaps I will write on Sunday—anyway, you shall hear soon. By the way, many, many thanks for your sense about ——. I had half a mind to burn that nonsense about the shawl, for fear you might mistake it, but on second thoughts I had faith in you, and believed that you would have faith enough in me to see that I referred to —— as the source I was thinking of getting it from. I wish to Heaven he would not think it needful to pay me at all. He does good with his money. I am only a woman, and spend it, and the thought of being paid by —— goes against the grain terribly. I got more good in translating the article than he is aware of—anyway, I see that he only sends me part of the identical money he receives. The fancy for the shawl is gone by, and I have bought a sober and dowager-like black mantle, which, as an evangelical dressmaker insisted, was 'just in my style.' Now good-bye, and God bless you! Take care of yourself, and get as happy and amused as the devoted affection of your friends can make you, and pray accept my contribution to such a good purpose. Seriously, my darling, be a good child, and take care of yourself for my sake if nothing else.

Your own
G. E. J.

LETTER 32.

Sunday Afternoon (Postmark, June 5, 1844).

Dearest Jane,—You will never guess the cause that hindered your having a letter last week. A lady about whom, on her own account, it would be in vain to attempt to interest you; there never was a person with whom it was so unlikely you should have anything to do. This said lady came to dinner last Sunday, remained the afternoon (which is the time I take for writing to you), and the letter, of course, did not get written, and the Devil has been in it ever since. I began on Thursday, but in an access of toothache, and between the pain and the laudanum, I was fairly conquered and sent off to bed—the half-written page remaining as a monument of my helplessness. So you see the concatenation of events is very subtle, and there is 'more than is dreamed of in our philosophy.' At least, a great deal more than is to be explained! First, let me thank you for your last. You little know how glad I was to get it. As to your aunt, you may depend upon my turning every stone that lies within my reach. For some days after your letter came the weather was too bad for anything. The streets were impassable, even with the aid of all the virtues of the street-sweeping machine. Like other pieces of perfection, it depends for success upon not being too much tried! However, I have interested several worthy people, who are very likely to hear of something. I entertain no doubt of ultimate success, but there seems in these days a certain portion of waiting and searching that must be gone through and then something turns up. I never knew an ultimate failure, and I have watched a good many similar affairs ; so don't worry yourself. If old ——— has gone back to the 'Times,' he has as much patronage as a Prime Minister—viz., there are nearly as many persons who would be thankful to oblige him anyway he wishes, and if old ——— wore my chains, I would make the boasting, vainglorious old soul be of some use in this matter. .... The wit of man is 'indite,' so do not fancy I shall fidget myself or think this, that, or the other disagreeable thing about it if I don't hear any tidings for the next six months of its fate. Mrs. —— is chained to 'Consuelo' and can look off for no sublunary things. With difficulty I have roused her, and she says that 'she hopes your "substitute servant" and your ever-staying visitor will make your house so intolerable that, what between one thing and another, you will be obliged to accept her invitation in self-defence!'

LETTER 33.

Monday (Postmark, June 11, 1844).

Dearest Jane,—How are you and all your worries? I have no time to indite a Christian-like note, but I am not going to let ——'s packet go without my having at least a word in the business. I hope the flowers will bear their journey well, especially the yellow rose, which —— has been watching with quiet anxiety to see when it would be in fit state to travel. I am leaving here on Thursday, but as I have another fortnight to look forward to before summer is over, I shall make it fall when you come this way, which we are all counting upon as sure as on sunrise and sunset. Don't you go and be a tiresome 'Joshua,' and disappoint us by 'standing still.' My brother has set his heart on going to Spain the second week in July, and if you can manage your journey then, why the house will be as quiet as the Sleeping Beauty's Palace, and you can stay with me as long as you can find in your heart to do so, and then we will come on together to Liverpool. I want to see you very much; more than I have any chance of making you understand. I am tired to death of writing letters into space; the best of letters are fractions of fragments, and deceive one by pretending to do away with the inconveniences of absence—whereas one only writes, after a long separation, to oneself, instead of one's friend. Letters between people who have not seen each other for so long as we have, too, never are the exact signs of the things signified. One gets into a 'falsetto,' and altogether I am in a very bad humour, and don't feel at all inclined to write another letter this side Doomsday, except to people with whom there is some chance of getting the speech of in ordinary course of human probability! that is, chances that are likely to fall due within the mystical 'threescore-and-ten years.' I want to see you so much that I can write about nothing, tell you nothing, for what on earth do I know about you at this blessed moment? Nothing! I might just as well be writing a supposititious letter for a new edition of the 'Complete Letter-writer' from a lady to her female friend whom she has not seen for a long time! Do, my dear love, come! Leave the things at home to find their own level! That confounded ———! I have suppressed a very energetic curse that was at the tip of my pen, but it is in my heart for her all the same! ——— has gone catching cold over cold all through the winter, and has now a severe attack of what learned men call 'bronchitis': she is not at all in a good state of health, and she won't take any care of herself. Did you ever hear of Miss ———? Of course you have, because you once sent me an anecdote about her being left sitting by herself in the theatre because nobody came to carry her away! Well, she is now living in Liverpool in a state of wretched desolation; the brute she married treated her infamously, spent all her money, beat her, and actually when he was in a worse temper than usual used to put her at the top of the stairs and roll her down all the way to the bottom. She got separated from him at last, and the Devil knows what has become of him. But she, poor thing, is trying to keep herself from starving by painting miniatures at two guineas apiece. And she also gives lessons. A friend of ours, hearing of her quite by chance, went straight away to sit to her, and the servant who takes care of Miss ——— said, 'Eh! ma'am, I am so thankful a sitter has come, for we had not bread in the house!' Miss ———, however, in spite of all her troubles, is

K

strong and active, I was going to say—but she would be so if she had the wherewith! She converses very intelligently, and has a great love for music, sings well herself, with a fine contralto voice, starting from G—which, I suppose, is somewhere in the musical depths—and, would you believe it, she has had more than forty offers of marriage! Certainly the baseness of man is inscrutable. Mrs. —— only heard about her on Saturday, and she is not up to the magnanimity of sitting to her, but she is interesting herself about her very much, and she sent her a splendid bunch of flowers, which would be a little bit of sunshine for her. I have no time to say more now, except God bless you, and do come soon! Write, anyway, and say how you are, mind and body, and also how the flowers are. How does —— go on? and have you seen —— lately? In short, tell me a great deal, and believe me,

Ever your own,

G. E. JEWSBURY.

LETTER 34.

Friday, June 14, 1844.

Dearest Jane,—I came in from Liverpool only an hour ago, and was sitting very disconsolate, refreshing my exhausted nature with the *débris* of a grand dinner my brother thought proper to give yesterday, when your note was brought in, and it has given

me an actual indigestion with joy. My dear, is it a
real, sober fact that you will be here next week?
Never mind your gown; we have milliners here
endowed with an average of taste and imagination
equal to constructing one for you. So let me have
every minute of you that is possible. I am really
just stunned, and can hardly get my breath! If you
do disappoint me, and don't come, I shall do some
deed of dreadful note! All the house has just been
cleaned down for the summer, so you will have the
benefit of it. Nobody worth a house of ten pounds
is insensible to the pleasure of having it in order for a
'distinguished guest,' and actually it was the second
thought that came into my head; so you see you
have the very purest human nature undiluted with
the faintest tinge of propriety. I can't write to you
to-day, I am in too great a flutter. Perhaps by
Sunday I shall be more composed, and I will try to
write to you then. My dear, 'Chapman and Hall'
may just go to their own 'devils' and carry MSS. and
all with them, before I will bother myself with anything belonging to prosperity whilst you are in this
part of the world. And so. . . . My dear child, are
you quite sure that you are coming? I fear something will happen to the railway, or the house, or
'Oliver Cromwell,' and when there is anything good
before me at a distance of a few days I always get
afraid that I shall die before it comes close to me.

Now do make haste! I am in a fever already, so what shall I be if you delay long? I am very glad about Mrs. ——'s flowers. You may thank me you got them at last, for she turned modest, as she always does, and would have it that you would think them silly, and I had to swear and better swear that you were sillier than even myself, for that you would care for them even more than I should. This morning, before I came away, that good Mrs. —— had sent me a bunch of such geraniums I was in a great mind to pack them up and send them to you, but human nature carried it. I cannot find in my heart to send them, but you will be here before they are dead. I can hardly persuade myself that I am hoping for a sober fact, and not 'a castle in the air.' By the way, I feel strongly tempted to take a fit to ——, on the strength of his letter, there is something so very—*good*—about it. The sort of good that takes my fancy. Thanks for your good deed about ——, and pray tell Carlyle how very sensible I am of his note. It is no use trying to write more just now. God bless you dear, dear love, and send you safe here!

Ever your own
G. E. J.

LETTER 35.

Thursday (Postmark, June 21, 1844).

Dearest Jane,—Thank heaven! the day for your coming into this quarter of this world is finally settled. You are quite right in what you say about going first to Liverpool, which shows a degree of openness to conviction which I find very praiseworthy, especially as I had made the programme of your visitings very smooth to my own notions. However, as I shall get no good out of you whatever, when surrounded, as you will be there, you need not expect to see me come over to you. I shall wait in pure confidence of seeing you here when you can achieve it, and, provided I get my fair share of you, I will promise not to torment you, which is promising a great deal, for I am as jealous as a Turk, and don't, besides, care half a straw for seeing my friends except *tête-à-tête*, when I feel strongly disposed to assassinate everybody who does not keep out of reach! Really, if it were not that I am much humanised by the lessons which have so painfully been instilled into me, I fear I should be a great savage; anyway, I am sure that when one loves either man or woman it rouses all the ferocity that was calmly slumbering till then in the profound depths of indifference. So there's a piece of philosophy for you, if you have leisure to examine it. You may believe it, for it is Gospel true! I am just at this instant undergoing the torture of having my hair dressed, and I can hardly form my letters, besides every now and then having a lug enough to tear one's hair and ideas up by the roots. What is this about ——? I had not seen a newspaper for weeks till the other day, and then the first thing that caught my eye was Mr. ——'s application to Sir J. Graham and his reply, which roused me. What possible excuse can they make? However, all that when you come. I am just at my wits' end about that horrid MS.; the seven chapters are far heavier to me than they can be to a reader with the privilege of skipping. I cannot materially alter, but I am cutting short, which will do just as well. Next Monday! I shall be thinking of you all the day. Heaven send you safe without accident! When one has anything precious, either in the post or coming like a Christian, one always fears a suspension of the course of Nature not in their favour! Do take care of yourself, and send me word as soon as you get in, and say how you bore the journey. Don't bother yourself about sending a calm word before then; I don't want your journey delayed a minute—even to write to me. God bless you, my dear love. Do try to take care of yourself, and don't get worried by any considerations of either love or benevolence. I am not disposed to let anybody plague you but—myself! I shall feel easier when you are fairly in Liverpool—

you will be within reach. But recollect, not a step will I stir more than the wooden image of a saint out of its niche! Come to me, for I want you sadly in peace and quiet all to myself; so good-bye to Cheyne Row for the present.

Your own
G. E. J.

This ink will hardly mark; it is thick copying ink, and the pen is worse.

LETTER 86.

Sunday (Postmark, June 24, 1844).

Dearest Jane,—This is only a hasty kiss on your safe arrival, for you will be too tired for more, dear love; how glad I feel to know that you are so near! I wish I were with you to welcome you, but you are with those who love you. I hope you will have a bright day for your journey. Do write me a line when you are up to it to say how you are, bodily and spiritually! I think much of you; if you are not able to write, tell —— to send me a line to say how you are. I shall feel very anxious till I get it. Poor unfortunate Mrs. ——! Go and see her as soon as you can, for she will not be able to come to you. Her doctor—(may he be condemned to the first circle of Inferno for it!) has salivated her in a mistake!!! She entreated he would not give her mercury—he said he would not—that there was none in the

medicine she was taking four times a day, and when
the symptoms could not be mistaken he instituted an
inquiry, and found that the surgery-boy had made up
the wrong prescription and given calomel instead of
ipecacuanha! Did you ever? —— came last
night, and told me all this. He saw her on
Friday, and he says she is in a dismal state, quite
pulled down and altered already. I am in such a
fury about it! If she had been an ugly woman, one
would not have cared so much, though it would have
been provoking; but for a handsome creature like
her to have her beauty put in peril by such an
atrocious piece of carelessness is something to make
one's blood boil! Do, my dear love, comfort her as
much as you can. I have no other news of any
sort—and if I had, I have not patience to write. I
don't know the length of time you intend to be away
from home, so can make no definite petition; I trust
to your honour to give me a fair proportion of your
time. I don't want to worry you, but if you don't
stay to the utmost moment with me it will take more
magnanimity than I possess to forgive you, and so I
feel as jealous as a tiger, and not at all friendly or
amiable. God bless you, my dear love! and believe
me your own

G. E. J.

LETTER 37.

Date doubtful (Probably July 4, 1844).

Dearest Jane,—This is Sunday, and though I have nothing to say I have got in the habit of writing to you on this day. Real habit is as mysterious and magnetic as example! How are you? Have you enjoyed your holidays? I am looking forward to having you here so much, but it seems fated we are to meet in a crowd first! —— will be put out of the way if I don't go to Seaforth, so I shall be there with you for all or part of the time. I don't want to leave home before —— goes, and then, you know, you come back with me for as long as you can contrive. I have so many things to tell you, and having you there at Liverpool is tantalising to death! How do they go on without you at home? Don't worry yourself to write me notes to Liverpool; nothing is such a bore when one is visiting, and, besides, I am too desperate to see you to be able to stay my heart—with letters! They are only good starvation diet, at best! How is ——? I want to know whether any mischief has followed the opening of his letters. Actually, the other day I heard a man defending the practice!! It was in company, but I got into a fit of inexpressible rage, and if words and looks and thoughts would do a man 'grievous bodily harm,' or harm of any sort, this man did not escape scathless, and I have had my cheeks tinged with a chronic blush ever since, to think that the wretch who uttered such base and cringing words was the identical man I once . . . . the man I almost worshipped as a god!!! Merciful Heaven! Does one get wise as time passes on, or is it only that one's old folly goes out of fashion and looks as unbecoming as an antiquated ball-dress? I had such a beautiful Greek drinking tea here last night. Poor fellow! he has roused my sympathy most painfully. He is only twenty-two, and has just had two paralytic strokes within the last month, and it is grievous to see such a glorious creature hardly able to move. He is going to France to recruit, but I don't think he will live, and I would much rather die at once than live in fear of such a fate. I will write and tell you when I come to Liverpool, but it will depend on you and Mrs. ——. Take care and allow plenty of time for me. We shall have the house all to ourselves, and I think the winding up with perfect quiet will be a good finale to your visit.

Ever your own
G. E. J.

LETTER 38.

[Dated July, 1844, probably the 1st or 2nd instant, after a visit to Seaforth.—A. E. I.]

Dearest Jane,—I don't like sending on your letter without a word from myself, and yet what have I to say to you? I did not reach home last night till half-past eight. Three mortal hours on the road! I felt quite pleased you had escaped a horrible sickness and headache which fell even on me, who am by no means a susceptible traveller. The house was looking so nice, and tea all set out, like a wedding-breakfast with the principal character absent. I have been very lonely all day, but, thanks to a salutary fright at the prospect of the work lying before me, I have been too busy to be melancholy. But, my dear, it is all a pack of 'Unitarian stuff' when people say that when you are occupied you are happy, for I am not happy in the least, and though my very back aches keeping my heart company—my conscience is as sulky as a mule, and does not say a word of a civil thing to me. So, my dear, don't you be beguiled into working hard under false pretences! I could not help being diverted by my travelling companions yesterday. There was a Saracen's head in one corner looking so ridiculously like a sign-board, and dressed, like Hamlet, in inky black! It turned its eyes on me from time to time till I got half-mesmerised. I think the head must have belonged to some heathen—a Christian could not have looked so; then there was the editor of the 'Liverpool Times,' who read the 'Athenæum' with a grim, 'tomahawk look,' and there was a small specimen of Young England who talked incessantly in a way altogether 'impayable' till his uncle, a mild, elderly man, said : 'All peas grow above their sticks'—which set me off laughing till I had the comfort to see the Young England fairly out of countenance. The uncle in question was cousin to good Mrs. ——. I am going to drink tea with her this afternoon, though I don't feel half-tempted to turn out.

The instant I got in I fell foul of my cigars, and I never felt the want of them or the good of them so much. I am sure Providence itself put it into my head to smoke. 'It soothes our sorrows, heals our wounds, and wipes away our tears,' as one of Dr. Watts's hymns says. I send you a few of them to comfort you. I was just interrupted here by Mrs. ——'s son, who called to say tea was waiting, so what the sentence begun was to have been I don't know, and perhaps it will be lost for ever—unless it is thrown back like the spoiled glass into the furnace to be melted over again. I had a very pleasant evening; we talked over Seaforth and you. Mrs. —— told me that she would send her love if she dared, and that she often thought of the kiss you used to give her at night. You would like her if you could only be surrounded by her sons. The more I think of it, the more thankful I am for the friendship you feel for ———. You will get a great deal of good out of it. I feel much more inclined to be jealous of the impression you have made on her than of that she has made on you, because I know how slow she is to care for anyone, especially a woman, and she loves you already; but I think you can stand a great deal of love. Yesterday, when I left you, I did not realise that I was really saying a final good-bye. The sudden surprise of not taking you with me prevented my feeling anything else, and it was not till I got home that it struck me, and I did not just then need anything to make me more melancholy. Write to me as soon as you can, and tell me that you love me, for that is a word one cannot hear too often repeated, and I don't get feeling any remorse or evil fancies about you—circumstanced as you are. I would not have you with me on any consideration. If anything were to happen to your uncle before you see him again you would never have forgiven yourself for grieving him by coming to me, and I would do more to save you from five minutes' remorse than I would to keep you off any other pain. There is no armour for the soul against it, and Harriet Martineau herself could not reason you out of it.

You have a horribly tender conscience, and I fear you will, in some of your sleepless nights, go and torment yourself by fancying me pained or grieved in my mind. —— knows me better in some things than even you do; believe what she tells you in this matter rather than your own fancy; and besides, when I saw poor old Mr. Welsh's brightened-up face I was quite contented you should remain with him instead of me. Can I say more or think more? I am interrupted again. It is no use to try to get more said. God bless you, dear love!

Ever you own,
G. E. J.

I have kept Mr. Carlyle's letter separate.

July, 1844.

[Written after Mrs. Carlyle's stay with her uncle, in Maryland Street, and after her visit to Seaforth.—A. E. I.]

LETTER 89.

Sunday Morning, September 17, 1844.

Dear Jane,—This week is at an end, and how has it left you? I have thought of you every day, and I am much more anxious about you now that I suppose all is over, than when matters were going on! One always seems to fall into dissolution when one has come to a stand, and there is nothing more to do. I suppose one must be a sort of god before one can

rest with safety, or even satisfaction. I had a letter from Mrs. —— the other day; she is enjoying herself much—she has made ——, she says, 'swear that she will spend two days in London as they return,' that she may get to see you, and I fancy that will be before long, as they were only to remain three weeks or thereabouts in Paris. She will be so pleased with that introduction to G. Sand, for her letter was full of schemings how it would be possible to contrive it. Mrs. ——, it seems, knows a person who knows G. S., but then there were doubts whether she was get-at-able for everybody, and so many had left town; so I am thankful she will go now properly accredited, even if it should bore G. Sand to be visited. It will only be for half an hour, and the pleasure to —— will last for life; so, on the whole, you may set it down as one of the best good deeds you ever did—quite a 'Sunday best.' She (Mrs. ——) had been to see 'Rachel,' and had not got struck! She likes ——'s acting better than any she has seen; there's a delicate conjugal compliment—to which, of course, he will feel sensible, especially as he is kept on a short allowance of them!
—— is much astonished at the killing looks given by everybody to everybody, even by the veriest old hags of fish-women to equally old and ugly *hommes du peuple*. In short, love-making and eating seem the grave occupations of life; but the eating comes first.

In fact, she seems singularly struck with the Land of Goshen, with the abundance of 'dainty dishes' that are always in progress of being either cooked or eaten. The cooking is evidently the great mystery that has impressed her. I have written to —— for her letters, and when they come I will send them if there is anything very amusing in them. I must now go and get ready for my ill-advised expedition, *que diable allait il faire dans cette galère*! I had little to do to be beguiled with rural notions of a farm in Cheshire; but really I am so tired and worried with work that I jumped at the idea, and how I shall jump to find myself safe back again, and my feet on my fender; it is a lovely day, that is one comfort. This letter is not intrinsically worth the stamp that carries it, but there is always an excitement in opening a letter, and you will go on hoping for something till you get to the end, when it will be too much trouble to feel disappointed. How is Mazzini? If you are disinclined to write, do not worry yourself, it is an angelic infirmity I can sympathise with, but recollect that I am really in a bad way about you, and I think of you much more than if you were my lover. So God bless you, my dear love, and take care of you!

Ever your own
G. E. J.

P.S.—I am a great deal better than when I wrote last.

LETTER 40.

[Without date, referring to the novel of 'Zoe,' which was
published in 1845.]

Tuesday Night.

Dearest Jane,—And you have actually, with all your pain in your side, and pain all over, read through our manuscript! I could find in my heart to scold you, if it were not that I am so much obliged to you. I wrote last night, and you will get it all in good time, if the Fates have not moved my brother to forgetfulness and he brings it back in his pocket; and pray, profit by as many of the injunctions as yet remain possible. A thousand thanks for your real kindness! Your criticism made me laugh till I was half-dead, for you little know all our strivings after decency. If you had seen the work as it was first schemed, you would have had something to complain of; indeed, it struck us that people might get scandalised. So there have we been softening it down, and doing our very best to make it proper-behaved, and fancied we had succeeded to a miracle. You don't know the trouble we have taken to see what would look decent at a distance. It is a clear case we have no vocation for propriety, as such. As I heard to-day of an old doctor who said to a very delicate fragile young thing, an acquaintance of mine, 'My dear Miss ——, I will order you some strengthening medicine, I will order you anything, but it is of no

L

use; I can't put in what Nature has left out,' and so, my dear, I say we will try to be pretty-behaved, but it will be of no use. It will be like Sir E. L. Bulwer's morality: we want the natural perception for it! In the scene which I fancy is the one in which the objection is most tangible, you don't know how I begged that you might have on the 'velvet cloak lined with fur,' but Betsy said that when people woke out of their sleep, they did not . . .

However, my dear, there shall be a liberal distribution of spotted muslin! only, will you tell me where it is to be applied? It is no use 'leaving it to our own consciences.' Our sympathies are imperfect on that point. I was told the other day, by a man who really was present in a Methodist chapel in Birmingham that the preacher, who was settling our parents before the Fall, said: 'It has been supposed by many learned divines that when Adam and Eve left the hands of their Maker they were guarded against the inclemency of the seasons by a sort of natural soft white down, in which their lower limbs were clothed, very similar to the plush of the present day!' Now, my dear, is our tale really true, or are we destitute of such a beneficent provision? Are there no traces of it to be discerned by spiritual eyes? For mercy's sake do send us some pattern or fashion by which to shape our garments, and they shall be dutifully worn! I think we have a natural hankering after the privileges of the state of innocence, for I once knew a man, rather a clever one, who set up to be an *esprit fort à la Voltaire*, and his grand complaint was, 'you see, Miss Jewsbury, that as society is at present constituted, man cannot be free; he could not even take off his pantaloons without being thought to commit himself!' As the grievance about 'the pantaloons' seemed a fixed idea, I at length suggested that he might enlist in a Highland regiment! One thing I have observed in my experience—viz., that if we are thrown among people totally dissimilar in their ways of thought and feeling to ourselves, we are tolerated, and we do not raise up any angry feeling; but the instant we begin to try to conform, everybody gets indignant that it should all be natural to us, and each one sets about examining and criticising whether the acquired thoughts and feelings are of the lawful fashion, and they are much more inveterate against a false copy of their dearly beloved gods than if we paid them no attention at all. It is impossible to catch any 'shibboleth.' You know it was a herb-woman who discovered that Themistocles was not an Athenian— 'thy speech bewrayeth thee!' And this is true all the world over. I think there is something truly touching in our destitution of what is called decency —an irresistible appeal to the merciful consideration of those who are gifted with it—a throwing ourselves on the charity of those more richly endowed. We make no profession: we clearly 'know no better.' Do you not think this will be taken in extenuation? Still, we will do our best to mend it! Now about the conclusion. I am at this present busy on the chapter where he comes to the conclusion of giving up his college. When a man has been born and educated in one idea, it is wonderful how impossible it seems to him to get out of it. 'Everard' found infinitely less of difficulty in getting out of his faith than in throwing himself out of his Church. I have been told that if you draw a circle of chalk round a goose it will starve to death before it will cross the line, and we have all of us more or less affinity with the goose; besides, the grand fault in Everard's character is indolence—a slowness to act. He is conscientious, but it takes time to rouse it up to the pitch of moving him. He has had feelings, but from time to time he quiets himself, as the greater number of all the priests and clergymen I ever knew quiet themselves. Indeed, how could they do more good if they were less human? And then, E.'s atheism is not a vulgar 'Tom Paine' hatred to religion? It is only the seeing a little further into it.

He sees that doctrines inculcated by religion stand on their own account, and that the religious mythology is only the coarse form in which they are made tangible, so that at first and for a time he might easily reconcile it to his feelings to stay where he was, especially till he saw his own way a little bit clearer. And then, the Catholic Church is not like one of the little, pert, prosing, Protestant sects! No man could remain in one of them a day after he ceased to believe; but there is room in the Catholic Church, when you are once fairly in it, for almost anything! It may be said of it, that 'in my Father's house are many mansions'; and he is a Jesuit, too, and a man cannot readily make up his mind to leave such an Order as that. I do not want to make it out a virtue in Everard that he remained for a while after he ceased to believe. I only want to make it out that it was highly natural. His real, true passion for Zoe opens his eyes to the littleness of all the motives which have held him, and you will see all the misery and shame and self-contempt he reaps, and the *bouleversement* he has sustained works him up to the point of decision. He writes to Rome and turns his back on all the honours and consideration he is enjoying, and you can hardly enter into what it costs even a common priest to leave the Church, so that to E., in spite of his atheism, it would be a heart-breaking affair. And it is just at that point, after the preparations for his departure are made, his successor appointed (only not generally known), that we thought of bringing home Schultz ill, and then all the dying! We once thought of making E. live on as he could in the world for some years after, but Betsy said—and I came into her opinion—'no, let it be as you at first schemed it; let it be a lost life! What are we to do with him in the world? Nobody can feel the least interest in him after he ceases to be a priest, and there is something more touching in his dying just when his eyes are open to the full worthlessness of all he has been living for. Let him die, and let them say Mass for his soul! for the Church would never go publishing that he had turned atheist!' And I must say this accords with my own feelings the most. The other day, reading 'Jeremy Taylor,' I found this quotation from some old Greek: 'Our wisdom never comes till we are past the using of it—that is, till we are going to die.' What are we sent into this world at all for? What ought we to do with our life? The whole book is to ask that question, or rather suggest it. I am sure I know of nothing that is worth doing. What can we set Everard to work upon? I have taken him as far as I can. I can tell him nothing more. I can give him no new faith. I can set him up with no new doctrines to begin to lead the remainder of his life-time. My dear love, what can any of us do? What do any of us know? 'For man walketh in darkness, and knoweth not whither he goeth. He walketh in a vain show, and disquieteth himself in vain.'

No, no! let him die, die in the consciousness

that he has failed in his task ; that his task is over, that his chance is over, that the significance of his life is sealed from him, and, passing along with the rest of nature into darkness where 'the light is as darkness,' let him sleep ! I cannot make Everard up into any theory of utility or usefulness to mankind. I cannot even make out his scheme of morality for him. He must grow shapeless and vague, and pass away, leaving all sorts of inconsistencies to be reconciled. What can we know till we are dead, and ' the end is not by-and-bye.'

My God ! I would give the rest of the years of my life to be able to know why it is that Life is given us, and I would say it and leave it behind me.

Now, my darling, I have explained at very full length my ideas on the matter, to give you grounds for judging from. It would require working out still more clearly, of course, if I took this tack, but what I want to know is, do you agree to it ? Do you think I am right ? Do not fancy I have said all this to justify myself ! I have only wished to make my views clear to you, and now I want your notions before I go on any further. I don't care what trouble I take, or what work is to be done or undone ; I only want to be, as St. Paul says, ' thoroughly persuaded in my own mind.' I shall send your letter off to Betsy to-night, for she will be anxious to see it. If there is anything entertaining in the tale it is thanks to her! If it had been left to me to manage it would have been very 'dree,' the tale parts that I attempted to tell were dreadfully long-winded. I always stuck fast among the ancestors. You may thank heaven that you do not know the biographical details you have been spared. However, it wants, as you say, rewriting altogether, and it shall be done, whether or no. But do you really, in sober earnest, think it will ever do to be printed and published ? Now if I had been with you for half an hour it would have saved all this writing, and I could have had your counsel warm and at once, without having it cut short by the plague of refractory pens. I cannot write well by candle-light : my eyes are burning now, so good night, love ! You have long since left the region of thanks behind! Still I can say ' thank you ' for the ' feather '—thanks are adequate to express female feelings about that. You don't know how I was tempted to buy one some time since, and I was actually prudent enough to buy my velvet bonnet without one because I could not afford it. So let no one say that virtue does not get rewarded.

LETTER 41.

[Fragment, undated, probably under date of 1844.]

. . . A time may come when my 'elective affinities' will break their bonds, and I shall find myself resolved into the elements some fine morning. I feel as if I wanted a leaden weight of some twenty pounds melted into my body to give it a due proportion of gravity. Miss —— came to me last Saturday. I admire her very much. She has escaped all the defects which I feared she must have had from her peculiar qualities. Escaped is not the word— they are neutralised rather. She is very agreeable, pleasant to look at, dresses very nicely, is rather stylish in appearance, and has a 'repose,' as one of my friends says, which is very soothing to me. I feel very comfortable with her, and there is a reality in her speech which is very good. —— almost worships her. You cannot think how charming he is with her! It is a position to test a man, and show whether he is a gentleman 'ingrain,' and I never liked him so much, or thought so highly of him, as since Miss —— came here. A man must be thoroughly good to keep up such a frank and intimate relationship with two women, not only at the same time, but in each other's presence. Miss —— deserves the influence she has over him; and if I feel this you may believe this. The other day I received a letter from Egypt, and I think that possibly may be the reason of the questionable state of my nerves, for it startled me horribly. I had been writing all day and had gone out for a while, and when I came back I had my tea and read Mazzini's article on 'George Sand,' and was in the most comfortable, innocent sort of spirit, and when I sat down to my desk again this cursed letter lay there! If I had seen a ghost I could not have been more upset. However, the letter itself is transcendental enough, and I could make neither head nor tail of it; it quite passes my understanding! At the same time I feel very glad he has written again, as it is some consolation to my outraged dignity. For however little one may hold to one's vanity, still I suppose there must be some leaven of it in one's human heart. All this time I am forgetting a most important event that has befallen me, which is a grand epoch in a woman's life. I have had—what? Guess. An offer of marriage? Never a bit of it. No man of my acquaintance has been so far abandoned by Providence. A lover, then? Still less. I am in no humour for human valentines; but what I have had is actually a real Cashmere shawl given me last week!! And upon my honour, a great many disagreeable things might come upon me which I should not feel now that I can wrap myself round with this mysterious and almost unknown production. It was reading the

memoirs of 'Madame Lafarge' which first inspired
me with an ardent passion for the unknown article.
Ever since I have had a secret aspiration after one,
and, lo, last Wednesday one gently and most unexpectedly descended to my arms. It is an immense
size, and not at all to be called pretty, but it has
occult properties far beyond beauty. It seemed to
me to want cleaning, and I went to a large shawl
shop to inquire about it. The man in the shop, a
sober Scotchman, grew quite enthusiastic. He would
not let me have it touched, and said his only desire
was to go into that branch of business (it is evidently
the poetical side of the shawl trade), and then he
sighed and said, 'So few ladies here know how to
appreciate them.' Like the lamentations after high
art! You never told me how the plaid dress looked
when it was made up. I have nothing more to tell
you, except that I want to hear how you are going on.
—— is, you will be sorry to hear, very unwell. His
cough and cold keep hanging on him. Miss ——
has made him promise to go to the doctor. If ——
were as ill I should be miserable. I am not happy as
it is? Finally, good-bye. God only knows when the
Devil will let me get to London. Miss —— now
cannot do with me till the end of April because her
blessed nephew is with her, out of real vicious perverseness, because we want him elsewhere. Miss
—— has asked me to return with her; indeed I

proposed it before I knew of this change, so now, whether I shall come or how it will fall out I don't know. When do you want me? How does your convenience lie? I shall not be able to remain more than a week or ten days. So, my dear, fix your own times and seasons, tell me when you wish me to come. About Miss ———. I was so sorry I had bothered you! Somebody said to me afterwards, 'it is like meddling with a porcupine to introduce any one to her,' and then I felt vexed I had asked you, and all my interest in her is gone. Write soon.

Ever yours,
G. E. J.

The visit came off, but mistakes and misunderstandings on both sides clouded it over. The Cashmere I gave finally to a young friend who lived at the Court of Hanover, and it did her more service than it could do me, and her mother had been, and still is, very good to me.—G. E. J. 1872.

1845.

LETTER 42.

Tuesday, March 20, 1845.

Dearest Jane,—Really you contrive that your sins of omission should look so much more like the best 'Sunday virtues' of other people, that when the time comes for your modesty to own to having done something excellent you will have to dress your head in a veil and turban *à la Moses*, or we, your contemporaries, shall not be able to 'view the mild rays and bless the useful light.' You have been better than good about that MS. Only to think of your streaming off to 'Chapman & Hall,' ill as you were! Really, my dear, I feel sensibly touched by it, and cannot resist scrawling this to tell you so. I had so carefully pruned any exuberance of imagination and all sorts of sanguine expectations—indeed, I had not ventured even on the smallest shade of rose-pink in my hopes—that the bare fact of getting the book printed without cost has, ever since the possibility of getting it published at all, been tangibly before me as the utmost stretch of my hopes. I mean, I would have been quite satisfied with that, and waited for money to another time. So you may judge that I will very thankfully conclude the present bargain. You mention the plague John Mill's 'Logic' and Carlyle's 'Sartor' had, to become successful! My dear, if I had deserved to succeed the least bit more than I do, I should have had to wait like other people of merit; as Mr. —— said to me, in our memorable conversation across his counter, 'The more nonsense there is in a book the better it sells; people can't stand sense, they want something racy.' But you don't need me to make more expounding to prove that I think myself very fortunate, and that I am profoundly satisfied, though I am too sick, and 'dished,' and miserable, and cross, and in such a concatenation of abominations to-day that I can hardly put my words together. God help the spelling! But I cannot wait till to-morrow to say the thanks for all your goodness. I will try what I can do with those horrid seven chapters, but I have not an idea at present to bless either myself or my book. I feel more inclined to die than do anything else just now. By the way, there is one thing that one may speak about now, and that is, I had rather not have my name stuck to the thing. First, because there are many things said in it that I don't want to walk about amongst some of my reputable friends as being guilty of holding. There are several I am very fond of, and I should be sorry to hurt their feelings;

and another reason is, that I myself have a general
sort of prejudice against women's novels, with very
few exceptions. I mean, I would not on any account
take up a woman's novel at a venture, unless I knew
something about the writer. Now, I don't suppose
'Chapman & Hall' care one scrap about a name being
tacked to it, or, if they do, may I not put some other
name than the one under which I appear in society?
There is my second name, for instance, 'Endsor';
that would do just as well, and if I might cut off the
feminine termination to 'Geraldine' I should feel
much more comfortable. You will perhaps laugh at
me, and call it affectation. I only say that I should
like it infinitely better. But I am not going to make
a fuss about the matter, and will be settled by your
opinion; only I hope you will feel as I do. As to the
spelling and grammar, I will have it all copied in a
clerkly hand. I know my cousin, whose matrimonial
affair I have advised and sympathised upon, would
copy it every word. Only within the last three
weeks he has entered into a business which does not
let him be idle, as he has been hitherto; however,
I shall make him help. Mrs. —— brought me a
beautiful print of 'Ary Scheffer's' the other day,
'Christus Consolator,' the picture that Miss Martineau
speaks of, and it moved me to tears. I wish I could
transfuse it to you. Her speech about it gives no
idea of its overpowering influence. There is the

figure of a mother over her dead child—that is wonderful. The face is swollen with grief, and yet there is an ineffable beauty and rest about it which almost consoles one. I shall buy it on the speculation of my 'profits.' I can write no more! God bless you, and take care of yourself.

G. E. J.

LETTER 43.

Brussels, Thursday, June 4, 1845.

Dearest Jane,—I did once in our wanderings get up energy enough to write you a letter, which I hope you received, otherwise you will think me lost. But you know I cannot do two things at once, and all my energy has been taken up in travelling every day almost without intermission. If we ever rested for a full day in a place without sight-seeing it was too great a luxury to be spent in writing letters, even to you, and besides, I had turned my mind out to grass, and all my wits were wool-gathering, and I don't think I could have written you a letter worth postage if I had tried, so I trusted to your faith in me to believe it was sheer laziness, and nothing worse. I sent Mrs. —— a letter last week (if she got it); it was begun a month ago, and has been travelling ever since in the pocket of my gown, waiting for a convenient season, till the poor thing

was almost in tatters; so if she sends it to you you
will know something, of course, of my proceedings,
and if she does not, you must wait till I see you, and
then you shall have it all, or as much as can be put
in the mortal space of a few hours. This note is
only to say that I hope to be in London on Saturday
night next, and that if I am able to move after the
sea-sickness and other 'devilments,' I will be with
you on Sunday morning. But if that would interrupt
any church-going, let me know. Let me have the
glad sight of your handwriting when I get in. Tell
me whether you will be at home on Sunday; address
to the care of ——, Messrs. Guest & Co., Loth-
bury, and I shall have it as soon as I get in. I
cannot tell you how much I want to see you. Tell
me what sort of health I shall find you in, and how
things are with you, for I have thought of you a
great deal, and in a 'diligence' have often said to
myself such nice letters for you; which, not having
ever got tangibly expressed, must remain in their
unknown fate, and you know Carlyle declares that
unuttered thoughts are infinitely more valuable than
those which are reduced to the parts of speech. I
have been in splendid health, and was getting quite
fat till within the last few days, when I caught cold
on the stupid Rhine, and I am looking as ugly as is
within the limits of my capacity that way, which is
saying a good deal, and just now I am very 'dished'

indeed. However, I am enjoying my journey more than I can express; it is something to be thankful for all my days. I have a great deal to tell you, and it is no good trying to write it; and adventures enough to fill a ream of paper. But they must all remain till I see you. I have had not a single line from anybody since I left, so you may fancy whether I am hungry to get some tidings of you; I cannot make this letter long now, as I am pressed for time. There are a set of beauty-sights to be seen, so, God bless you, my dear Jane! Let me find a letter when I get in on Saturday, and believe me,

Ever your most affectionate
G. E. JEWSBURY.

LETTER 44.

Monday (Postmark, June 25, 1845).

Dearest Jane,—I want very much to know how you are, and how you are going on, though if you are in anything like my own state of body and soul letter-writing is precisely the most unpleasant thing in life. I think of you much. Those two weeks I spent with you are a great comfort to me. They seemed to give you back to me with all the freshness of the time when you wrote the first letter you ever wrote me. For the moment one says, 'I will be your friend,' and you accept it, it is an era quite as notable, and as much to be accounted of, as if it were the lover to whom one gave oneself, body and soul, for ever! I was going to say perhaps it should be as long as he can retain one. However, I cannot tell you how thankful I feel to have you safe once more, because at one time I feared that perhaps the best period of our intercourse might be past; but you have shown both faith and patience towards me, and the time I was last with you seemed not the beginning of a new friendship, but rather what one might imagine to be the way we might meet in another life, after one had had the experience of a lifetime here to enlighten us on the follies and shortcomings of our friends. I care for you now more than ever I did, though I don't know why I am writing to tell you so; but I was lying on the sofa, where I have been all day, when an impulse stronger than my laziness made me get up. I could not help writing this to you. I know your birthday is either to-day or next Monday, but I have forgotten the exact day of the month, and I have been puzzling myself for the last three days; I think it will be next Monday, because —— says it will be, next Saturday, twelve months and a day since he sailed for Spain, and I know your birthday was the day but one following. So if I have mistaken, I have not forgotten.

It is an old proverb, 'As the year begins with

you, so it will end.' So, my love, for the sake of superstition, try to keep that one day as free from sorrow and annoyance as you can. It is a sort of moral 'St. Swithin,' and no rain should fall upon it. I have not been well yesterday or to-day; indeed, to-day I am in one of my old nervous stupors, broken by the necessity of going into the kitchen to see to the dinner, for I let Mary go out for the day, and the charwoman cannot cook. So I first woke up with a sense of guilt, and rushed into the kitchen and made a gooseberry-pudding, set a 'poulet au riz, en train,' then I fell off in a strange sort of half-dream for another while, and then my conscience roused me to go and see into their progress, and then I relapsed into my doze, and that was broken by the desire to have a talk with you. Otherwise I could have lain very comfortably from after breakfast till teatime, as this is the present state of my soul, or as my virtues are in a dormant state, whichever you please to fancy. I am rather uneasy at the continued silence of my Eastern friend, and begin to fear he is ill, especially as his last letter was written in a state of great bodily, as well as mental, suffering. By the way, that reminds me, did I ever tell you a horrible piece of consolation that I heard the conductor of a 'diligence' apply to one of his horses which seemed rather unhappy about something? 'Ah, viens,' said he, lashing it with his whip, 'tant que tu souffres, tu n'es pas mort,' and that is comfort for Christians as well as for horses! How is Mazzini? If he has any sort of translation he wants to get done, I shall be glad if he will command my services, and he may depend on me not bolting off again. Now, my dear love, good-bye, and God bless you, and send you well through this next year and all future years that are appointed you.

Ever your own
G. E. J.

LETTER 45.

Saturday (dated on postmark, July 14, 1845).

My dear Love,—Come to me directly, directly, do you hear? You must come to see me before you go to Liverpool! You may stay as short a time as you like, and come and finish your visit after your cousins are safe in Scotland, but you will never be able to go through all their small life details if you go there straight. They cannot (even if they get to know it) make case to any great grievance, as I earned the right last year to have you the next time you came, without opposition on their part. I tell you that you shall be free to do just as you like; you shall not be plagued to stay if you come, but if you want to get any good from your journey do not go there direct! My dear! I know from horrible experience all you are suffering. That depression which falls upon one in a moment, enveloping one, body and soul, for hours or days, as it may be, and the horrid lucid interval which we spend in dread of its return, knowing full well that it will come. It is not sorrow; one could endure that. Oh! it is too frightful to talk about! For two years I lived only in short respites from this blackness of darkness. Struggling is of no use; you are doing the only thing for it in changing the scene. If the most intense fellow-feeling can be any comfort, you may have plenty from me. For the last three or four years I have been comparatively free from this visitation, but God only knows whether I am fairly through this 'valley of the shadow of death.' Oh! my dear Jane! do come to me directly! I shall leave here to-morrow. Write me a line to say what day I may look for you, or if I do not hear before I will expect you on Thursday, if you can get off; if on Wednesday, so much the better. I have faith that I can do you good, Now, do not let anything hinder your coming. It is no good to waste your strength in struggling, you must try to cheat it. I am thankful there is Seaforth for you. It is a capital place, but not just at first. Poor Jane! you have been tried beyond even the ordinary extent of the torture of this life, but the hour-glass will be reversed. You will be taken off the rack. But I cannot tell you how much I suffer for you and with you! Oh! come to me! You may go, do, be, whatever you like ; only come, and that directly! You know I love you, and if I were to write for ever I could say no more than is contained in that one word. You will have no sort of *gêne* with me, for there is a sitting-room for yourself, as well as a bedroom, and it will be such a comfort to me to have you, for I have many things to tell you on my own account. To have you just now is the greatest blessing that could befall me, and I will meet you at the railway if you can say the train ; and you may set off as soon as you receive this, if you will, for I am not good housekeeper enough to be put out of my way. Only come, and God bless you! I have so much to tell you that will not come out in a letter.

Ever your own
G. E. J.

Your letter was sent here to me last night. I shall hope for you Wednesday, and expect you Thursday.

LETTER 46.
[Undated, but assigned to the year 1845.]
Warrington.

. . . You perhaps do not know where that is, and yet it is a town of no little importance in its own eyes, and some antiquity ; many generations of comfortable people have lived and flourished here. I came here last Saturday, and have an idea I must have died and transmigrated into a mite and am living in the heart of a large fat Cheshire cheese! My environments are altogether so different to what I ever knew them! Everybody is sleek and comfortable, and seems as if life for them were paved with feather-beds; only imagine a man saying quite seriously to me, 'Miss Jewsbury, you see us just as we are; I and all my friends are people of ample means, and we make up our minds to enjoy life! We none of us want to be grand, but we lay ourselves out to be comfortable, for, to my thinking, comfort is the best thing to be got for money. Some people have all they can wish for, and yet they cannot enjoy it; but I do enjoy myself, Miss Jewsbury, we all enjoy ourselves.' Oh, dear me! my dear! I have always made it a rule never to mention, under any temptation, what passes in a house where I visit, so I am obliged to refrain from making you laugh, and I am sure that is an effort of morality. But I have strengthened mine by reading Mrs. Chapone, and looking at the outside of Dr. Gregory, since I came here. But if I were only to describe all I have seen and heard said since I came, it would be a phase of social life you have not met with. I have thought of Carlyle's counsel to write a book about things I see, but I have shut mine eyes that I may not be tempted.

I had a long letter from —— the other day! He arrived safely at home, and found all well. Everything was right. All that had been written to him had been founded on mistakes! I feel so thankful. I cannot express the release to me, for I should have been deeply pained had it been otherwise! . . .

[Fragment.]

LETTER 47.

[Undated, but assigned to the year 1845.]

Sunday night.

Dearest Jane,—Thanks for your letter yesterday, but what have you been doing with yourself that you are not well yet? But I will not bore you with asking questions; only it will be a real consolation to me when I hear you are in a more Christian-like fashion. This letter must, of necessity, be very dry, so do not begin to read it under any hallucination. I am just beginning with the influenza, and am as stupid as an owl; besides, my ears having begun on the 'singing for the million' system, I am quite bothered. I am more obliged than I can tell you for your promise to take the MS. to Chapman & Hall, which is exactly the thing of all others I was wishing for; but do not go till you are quite up to the nuisance of it, for I assure you my 'constitutional patience' never feels delay when there is any prospect of eventual success. I am not impatient, except about little things; so, my dear, do not work yourself up into any fever of friendship, and go out before you are fit for it under the impression I am worrying myself. Really, there is very little temptation to be moral in this world. Only to think of my 'questionable' chapter being a bait for the whole book! Surely nobody indulges in enthusiasm except candidates for a strait-waistcoat. Anyway, it is well there are some readers as conscientious as a lady I heard of the other day, who, if she has proceeded to the third page in a book, fancies she has gone too far to retract, and whether amused or not reads resolutely on to the close. So you see the cardinal virtues are not altogether extinct, but *en revanche*. One day last summer I called on the man I get my books from, and we had a long chat over the counter. 'Ah,' said he, 'if only half the number of books that are sold in Manchester were read, it would be a different place.' 'Why,' said I, 'how do you know they are not read?' 'Oh, only last week, for instance, a gentleman came to me and brought me the measure of a new bookcase he had bought, and told me to fill it properly with books and to see that the bindings matched, so I just sent him safe works such as all libraries must have.' 'What are those?' 'Oh, Johnson's Dictionary, Scott's novels, Shakespeare, a Cyclopedia, and Hume's "History of England," and such like. The man will never open them, but he would be very angry if any of his friends should ever say, " Why did you buy this rubbish ? " So you see, Ma'am, I am put on my honour what to send.' He told me many vastly curious things which would have made me laugh, if they had not really made me cry. I have just finished the life of ' Gerald Griffin,' the most tragical thing I have read for many a day. Such a fine character and a powerful genius ground to powder, writing little tales and ' beating his poor brains,' as he says, for articles to gain daily bread, and ' you cannot conceive the intense drudgery,' he says in one of his letters; and his end is even more crushingly mournful. He was haunted ' by the terrible idea that it might possibly be he was misspending his time,' and all the rich amount of perseverance and endurance of hardship all wasted, and the ' half-name,' as he calls it, that he won in the struggle only came to make him feel its worthlessness, and when all desire for it had fled. In the life you only read his character through a veil, for he evidently let no one into his inmost heart, but that only makes the whole book inexpressibly mournful. I don't know when I have shed so many tears over any sort of biography. . . .

[Fragment.]

LETTER 48.

My dear Jane,—I wrote you a letter yesterday, but it was so dead stupid I could not find in my heart to send it. And yet to send you none at all I don't like to, though, *selon moi*, simple starvation is better than indigestion from bad diet. This morning my time is limited. I have a sewing-woman to provide for, and the clothes to send to the wash, and a variety of 'Monday' things to do, and I go out to dine with Mrs. —— at one o'clock, and to a lecture after, on what earthly subject I am in vast ignorance, and don't feel any great excitement to be enlightened. I was sorry to miss Mr. Scott's lecture, and to miss himself too, for I feel a great desire to know him; but lectures in general are a sort of purgatory, and I look at the clock very often. But I go to Mrs. —— as often as I can, for she is very lonely without her daughter, and I am sure she has well earned all the comfort or good I can be of her. She threw that 'bread on the water' many days ago, long before there was any prospect of my turning out either useful or ornamental, and I feel a special and peculiar affection to her that no testimony to my merits could elicit in these latter days. I wish, after keeping me waiting for news of you so long, you could have told me a little more of what concerns yourself. I can get little good out of that letter, and I fear, from a certain tone in it, that all is not well with you. I mean the average wellness. So write again soon. Poor —— has had another relapse; they sent for another physician, whose remedies were of the strongest, and I am not at all easy as to the result. I have had no letter now for some days, for which I am a little uneasy; as to the Chevalier,[1] he goes on charmingly, and is to take a drive to-day for the first time. I was there on Saturday. He looked at me with the new eye, and it is actually the first sight he has had of what I am like. But he is to have his glasses soon, and then he will be able to discover whether I am what you say he is; though, by the way, I never discovered it myself. For one thing, he has always been like Milton's 'Parent of good, to us invisible or dimly seen.' The room has always been so shady with a quantity of green blinds and curtains; and, besides, when we like people, they are always beautiful to us. At least, I never liked anyone, man or woman, without finding them very handsome indeed. Have you seen ——'s last lecture? It is very clever, I think, and there is at least a clutch at the practical in it; but one thing I protest against, and that is the audacity of his profession of inability to find any son of Adam who is a French tailor capable of making trousers worthy of

[1] The Chevalier Neukomm.

his wearing. He who never had on a Christian pair since he came into the world! It is the coolest piece of impudence ever perpetrated. However, the lecture is very good for all that. I have set up a superb velvet mantle that Mrs. ⸺ bought the materials for, and made up with her own hands, and put on the Emperor to make him hold up his head under his cloth-of-gold canopy; coaxing, persuading, and making me begin again. It seemed all part of the Drama, and you could not tell which were the real people or the actors. Then there was a meeting amongst the ballet-girls, very promptly and summarily disposed of, and finally the Jewess herself had to rehearse her execution twice, and that was by far the most exciting scene in the play. Altogether I have never been so far below where Don Giovanni goes to. Then we had to go up another pair of stairs as steep as if they were taking us to Heaven, and then through dark passages which finally led us into the lower boxes, and there we found about half a dozen people come by invitation like ourselves. The theatre very dark, only the stage all light; upon my word, I felt a respect for all the pains and trouble I saw taken, and the ridiculous little dramas that were going on along with the play. The stage manager, who never either swore or lost his temper, worked away in an energetic, spirit-pushing, really historical looking, and not theatrical manner. I wanted to see it, but had no mind or strength for the worry and heat of the theatre. Well, there was to be a dress-rehearsal, and somehow, I hardly know how, I received a most civil invitation for —— and me to go and see it. We went, but on arrival in the hall, the stage was so full of men in armour that all getting in was impossible, and the regular entrance was not open. So one of the satellites took a lantern and opened a door in a wall, and told us to go down some steps there were, and this led us to the strangest subterranean world . . . Here is something to make one shut one's ears. Poor —— said so naïvely the other day, 'What reason has she to speak ill of me? I am sure if I bore with her four years and a half, it ought to be a certificate of my amiability, so that no other woman need be afraid of her.' I am very poorly indeed; to-day I have been rather brisker, but in general I am only half alive. I had such a curious escapade the other night. There is a very grand spectacle got up here at the theatre; a procession that looks as if it had come out of Froissart. I could not realise that they were substantial people; and little —— looked very pretty. She is a sweet little darling, and —— looks like a man of genius *incompris*. We were all to have dined at Mrs. ——'s to-day, but this morning a cold, miserable, raw frost. —— must needs take a shower-bath, and the pipe, being frozen, burst, and all the water of the cistern broke over poor ——'s devoted head and deluged the whole house. So, instead of our going there everybody had to come to us, and I had to turn out to order in dinner, much to my disgust, for we had had a large family party only a few days previously. This letter was only begun on the First, and now this is the Sixth, so I may tell you that when we went to ——'s the ensuing day the house was dry, but the whole party was stupid and disorganised to a degree. —— and —— had a grand quarrel—he does not know what he wants or who he wants. He is ill and miserable, and very much changed, and I am very unhappy about him. As to ——, she has no feeling except through her vanity. No one tells me anything, and so how it will all end I cannot guess. I wish he could find some nice, good girl to have him. —— was in my mind as I wrote what was to have been the 'leading article,' and I got a most depressing letter from ——, making a shuffling excuse, that the 'Westminster' was bound to aid and comfort sufferers for conscience' sake, so that, therefore, my article was rendered 'incomplete.' However, it is, I hope, the last time I shall have dealings with him. If you do not see the ——'s in the course of nature, I will tell him to send you a copy, which is little enough for him to do, and I want you very much to read the article, because I took a great deal of trouble over it. It is the one on 'Faith and Scepticism.' I have just had a note inviting me to go with —— to see some Ragged School to-morrow morning, so we shall have a *tête-à-tête* after all, for Mrs. ——, having a ball in the evening, cannot go very well. I will send you word all that happens. The more I think of you the more anxious I feel about you. Dear child, do take care of yourself. If anything happens to you, what am I to do? I cannot lose you again. Do not worry yourself to write to me. I know the difficulty of it, and you must spare yourself. How does —— go on? —— was inquiring after you very tenderly yesterday. How is Nero[1]? I had a deal more to say, but somehow it is gone from me.

Ever your affectionate
G. E. J.

LETTER 49.
[Undated, but assigned to the year 1845.]

My dear Jane,—This is not intended for a letter, but only to say, how are you? though I don't expect to receive an answer. But whatever you do, keep chewing the cud of the idea of going from home, and it will take a practicable shape before long. I have many things to say, but this morning I cannot say anything except that I am stupid, for the fatigue of

[1] The little dog.—A. E. I.

the last two months seems all making itself felt at once. I can hardly move from my chair, or keep my eyes open; but I can love you with them shut, though I cannot write to you. I send you ——'s letter—is it not touching? And the idea of that man presuming to judge and punish her, forsooth! Bah! if he lives to the end of his tether without becoming a 'hissing and a bye-word,' justice is not executed, in this world at any rate! However, she is a deal too good for him, and he would only break her heart. He will never have anything a millionth part as good thrown in his way again, and, on the whole, it is rather a satisfaction to think his infatuation has made him throw it away! One might get into a magnanimous rage when one thinks of certain things—what he told me about his conduct to her, for example. But can one say, even, 'let alone' doing, anything? The weakest must go to the wall! I suppose by way of calming down my troubled philosophy, according to the most approved 'Goethe' recipe, I am this very day going (with my own hands) to do a wardrobe like your cabinet.[1] It has long perplexed me—for there it has stood, at the bottom of my bed, painted a clean sickly looking cream-colour, a beautiful emblem of innocence and negation! I grew sicker and sicker when I looked at it, but could think of no remedy till your example suggested one; so you see

[1] Mrs. Carlyle had been painting a wardrobe at this time.—A. E. I.

no deed can be transacted without bringing a family of consequences, and I am going now in search of some Manchester print, an humble imitation of Indian taffety. I have literally no news—neither spiritual nor worldly. I will write again soon as I can. God bless you, my darling! You are ever much on my mind.

Ever your own

G. E. J.

'All things are possible'—a text that came this minute jingling into my head. I send it you by way of a 'sortes,' and the Bible has as much virtue—that way—as Virgil!

LETTER 50.

[Without date, but assigned to the year 1845.]

Tuesday Night, Wednesday Morning.

Ma très chère Jeanne,—Heaven knows what sort of a letter this will turn out to be, for I have been walking nearly all day, and am cross and tired—if you know what that is—and not inclined to do any sort of useful or virtuous work. So whether any good thing can come out of what is good-for-nothing remains to be seen! I am really vexed: and reflect how my carelessness must have annoyed you, for it is just the sort of thing that would have set me swearing! However, in the nightmare of annoyances under which you are suffering, it is the most wholesome

thing you can do to give 'shrewings' right and left.
It is far better to work off your irritation in the due
course of nature, and let it evaporate, than to
suppress it, and allow it to work in the system, from
no matter what 'Unitarian' motive, universal benevolence, and 'welfare of others' principle! Depend
upon it, that suppressed irritation and suppressed
perspiration are both equally injurious! Better to
scold, scold, scold! My dear! is there no prospect of
deliverance from your ill-advised good deed? Because
you have had patience for three weeks, must you go
on having patience for an unlimited time? When
one goes to Heaven one must go on being good to all
eternity, but surely we have troubles enough in this
world without taking up that one. My child, do, for
God's sake, pitch your virtue in a lower key! An
archangel could not go on performing such feats of
self-abnegation as you lay upon yourself. If you
worry yourself to death it will be a much greater
loss than if you had left a few weariful things undone.
Do reflect upon this! 'Au reste,' I can picture your
present condition quite as well as if I felt it in my
own person. I know full well the weariful feeling of
being dragged along the ground that one always has
at the end of a series of worries. Would to Heaven
you could get away from home! It is the only cure for
you, but, like all cures, it is just now precisely the
one thing unattainable to you, something like the

prescription I once had: 'tachez de bien digérer, and portez vous bien'! Poor ——! I am really sorry for the vexation he has had. I can fancy nothing more mortifying to the person concerned, for he cannot be expected to realise how very much alike the successful and unsuccessful candidate looks in the eyes of the world; but I feel real sympathy for the waste of so much good trouble and money. I know nothing likely to make a man a misanthrope more surely than to hear himself constantly sneered at. It is enough to provoke a man to turn rascal, in order to force people to be serious about him. I have been so much used to people speaking of me with a sort of half-contemptuous smile, that I can have real sympathy for anybody else in a like case. It is no good to feel one does not deserve it. One's 'milk of human kindness' is sadly curdled by it, and I do believe that is the secret of my spite against 'too respectable people,' 'if they had been good, I would have been good too'—as the little girl said when she was whipped. After all, there is something in 're-pectability' that nobody can heartily sympathise with. It is like a 'set of best china,' never used but in fear and trembling—because if there is a breakage 'it cannot be matched again.' Respectability does not appeal to any common feeling of human nature; it is not a bond of brotherhood, but a 'sunk fence' of separation. No noble or generous thought ever had its sole root in respectability. It is a sort of antiseptic principle, which makes the world a safer place to live in, clears away a few obtruding nuisances, and puts down a few annoyances—in short, it acts like Rowland's Kalydor. But, if the world were really good for anything, there would be no such thing as mere respectability in it! It is a morality invented for the good of overflowing wickedness. However, I intend by the blessing of. . . . (I am sure I don't know whether it is presided over by God or the other person), but I am fully purposed to master the mystery of respectability, for it is a craft of which no woman ought to be ignorant, and I will dedicate the first fruits of it to the confoundedly respectable Glasgow gentleman. In the meanwhile, do you console poor —— for his vexations. Your consideration ought to console him for all the ill-natured speeches he can either overhear or imagine to his own annoyance. There was a speech in that tale of 'L'homme de rien et l'homme du bien' which has graved itself on my heart 'il faut se defier les mauvaises langues.' I am not clear that those are the precise words, but they did me a world of good when I read them. They seemed to set me free from all sorts of vague obligations. I am very glad you think the last article an improvement! Do just what seems good in your eyes with it, but don't plague ——, for he has a store of worry to last for the next two years. Still less plague yourself, for your daily bread just now is unprofitable worry, and I would not add a feather's weight to it for all the articles that were ever written. . . .

[Fragment.]

1846.

LETTER 51.

Sunday (Postmark, February 23, 1846).

Dearest Jane,—When I wrote to you last I had not received any message from you, but got it a few days after from Betsy. But that did not hinder me from hoping for one every day last week, because I fancied the cause had ceased by the time I got the message. Your letter of this morning has given me a headache. I have heaps of things to say, but there would be little good in saying them even were it practicable, for the best words are but clumsy indications of what we really mean. All my life long I have been very unlucky in making my words and meanings bear a true resemblance : they have so often guided clever people contrary to what I intended. I do hope there will be a 'day of judgment,' when there will shine a light, clearer than what we get now, and when we shall know things as they really are. It is the only thing I desire as a future at all! It would be so charming to be able to have a settle with people one has loved here, and to say to each other, 'Ah, you were mistaken there, but I can see how you got wrong. I can quite see now how all seemed to you '; and that will have all the effect of being just of the same opinion. But it cannot be now, to any extent, because—because, I suppose, it is, as metaphysicians say, 'that two bodies can never be in the same place at the same time,' and, as things shift every moment, no two people can see any one thing under the same aspect. We cannot ourselves see the same object twice. We only recollect how it seemed. So you see what a clumsy process has to be gone through, even when there is least refraction from unkind motives or wrong feelings. Dr. ——— told me the other day that he had been trying experiments in microscopes with all his might and main in the hope of seeing that which is invisible, and he says he took a number of strong magnifying-glasses and placed them duly, and the consequence was that the object to be scrutinised was diminished to an infinitesimal amount, and turned upside down. So much for scrutiny and judgment! I almost laughed when he told me, for it applied so well to other things. As to my getting knowledge, and judging you, my dear, that is just one of the things we will clear up after the 'Day of Judgment,' and then you will see how much more my dark lantern was turned to throw light on myself than on you, and you will see that to judge me by rules made for things in general will get neither shape nor make sense out of me! So, finally, I am come back to my old doctrine that knowledge in this world is not intended for men, let alone woman, and that faith is all we can have to supply its place. My dear child, I don't feel in the least in the world as if I were going to fall in love with ——. The old 'Père' is more cute than you are. He says of a changed affection, 'qu'il ne revenait jamais, dans la même place,' and, though attracted ten years ago, he is the last who would speak to me now. I doubt even if he could amuse me more than once or twice! He always reminds me of a man I once heard a surgeon talking about. He had that morning been present at an operation, and the man was in such a horrible state that when they came to tie the arteries they were so softened that the ligatures went through them. And —— has nothing to hold by; he has nothing sound in him; *au reste*, I don't think Providence quite means to abandon me, for last week it was pleased to scour up my virtues till now they stand shining like a row of brass candlesticks! It came in the shape of an old lady whom I knew years ago, when she was in prosperity and I a small, miserable, neglected child whom she helped to torment out of her own heart, and 'Locke' and 'Miss Edgeworth.' If not imbecile, at least her intellect is choked up to a single spark, and she is very infirm, and has had paralytic strokes, and all sorts of horrible things. Well, this same old lady invited herself to come and stay all last week with me. At first I was excessively annoyed at such an inroad on my time and comfort (for I was in a most perverse humour to be industrious just then). I felt in a very bad humour, when the thought of my friend at Cairo came into my mind like the inspiration of a good angel, and all he had ever said to me, and the desire to do something that would have pleased him had he been here; and you cannot think the change that came over me from that instant. I am sure I was very good to the old lady, but that was nothing. I began to feel a sort of pleasure in it, and when she left me yesterday I felt I could have gone on another week; only every morning I swore in my heart when the postman came and brought me no letter from you! It is very miserable to have Grand Cairo so far off, and in a sort of fabulous region, too, quite out of the pale of one's sympathies; but I would not be without it for the world! You know better than anyone how strengthening it is to care for one who desires to help us onward, to see us stronger and better, one who is better than ourselves. My friend is a long way off, and he plagues me to death by writing so seldom; still, the certainty that every better sort of impulse that comes to me would be approved of and sympathised with by him gives me a sort of inner life, and leads me to him in a manner

I cannot express. The flesh is very weak, and I am quite capable of amusing myself in a moment of 'ennui' with somebody close at hand; but he is the first one to whom I would name it, and he would wait very patiently till the humour was over, and if I were to do anything unwise would be the first to forgive me and comfort. And if one believe all this, it makes one care a great deal for a man, and even put up with his being so far out of the way! So you never told me of Lady ——, for fear of boring me! How many more things are lying blue-moulding for want of being asked for? Do, for God's sake, tell me all that interests you or amuses you in any way. First, I will guarantee you that it will please me more than anything else you can do, and next, if it does bore me, depend on it you will soon find it out; so don't worry me by keeping me in the dark about yourself as you have done lately! But about Lady ——; as I am not on the spot to see —— I can be most magnanimously disinterested; and I do really feel pleased that you have someone near at hand to love, and who desires to be loved by you. What you tell me interests me very much about her. I can so well understand how she seems to you of that 'inner circle' you describe; in short, you have made me understand her as well, perhaps, and better, than if I had seen her, which still I should much like to do! Tell me a great deal how you go on with her, and don't fear making an explosion of jealousy. I tell you I am not on the spot to see, and can therefore stand a great deal more; it makes all the difference. Some fine day she will let you inside that moral mystery, and will hate you for it afterwards. She was not brought up by a mother, you once told me, and that's the secret of her! She was not treated kindly, and was driven within herself, and then she had no one to trust. She learned to look through everybody, and her own thoughts have ever been a secret. If she once brought herself to speak of them she would feel as if she had been a fool! There is something hard, not natural, in all women who have had no mother! You got bored about Miss —— because I had not skill to tell you of her, and I did bore you about her, in short; but I am not bored about Lady ——, nor likely to be, and I want to be told about her, which is just all the difference in life. I would give anything to see her. Hem! my well of love is not exactly 'perennial,' and I think I already love all I have the power to love. All our capacities are merely mortal, and I have already given all I possess. One cannot have one's cake and eat it—both! I am so glad you like that little essay—more glad than I can tell you, not because it is my own inditing, but because I was afraid you did not care for that sort of subject, and now I shall send you everything without misgiving. I am in a much better humour to write about those things than to hammer at a novel. I had something else to send you, but on reading it over next day I did not like it, so threw it away and began again, and should have finished days ago if my old lady had not descended upon me. She was anything but an inspiration. Don't, if you can help it, be so long without writing to me again. You don't know how it fidgets me. If I make up my mind and I get no letter, it spoils the whole day. I can't tell you how I have watched the postman for the last ten days, and if you could know how disappointed I have been you would feel some pity. I had a note from —— yesterday, a very short one. He seems to have been dismally tormented, poor fellow. I wish he would leave London, and take a journey for change of air; he would find the state of his soul much mended by it. My cold is not well yet, but I am better in myself. —— has bought me the most lovely little lamp; it gives a charming light, and I am 'set up' with it. Since I took to rehabilitation I have got a great many pretty things. I have not heard a word from —— for nearly a week. She is not in her natural element in London, or rather, not in the element in which you and I have known her, and I can easily fancy you get little good out of each other. She complains of the short and unsatisfactory interviews she gets with you. It will be better next summer, when you go to Seaforth. That place was intended as a refuge for the worried; and —— ought to stay and preside over it. I wish I could see you for an hour, it would be good for us both. I feel a need to see you, such as I have not done this long while, but write to me very soon. Do that at least, and do not, unless you wish to pain me, allude to what is past. Oblivion contrives to swallow up many excellent things one would willingly preserve; and it is hard and very perverse if it will allow such a poor little morsel to stick in its throat. It is a straining at a gnat with a vengeance. I cannot tell you the pain you give me when you make any allusion to the past. It is not civil to contradict people, but so far as I am concerned you are wrong, mistaken. Your compass is turned completely round, and points to nothing right. It is no good your getting up a theory about me. I was born to drive theories and rules to distraction, and I want to beat yours to powder and then stamp upon it. The only effect the past has on me is to make me more sure-footed in regard to you. If the gulf between us had been filled with Birmingham ' solder '—what you say would have been highly sensible; but I believe, from my heart, that it is drawn together and closed by the same process that first drew us together. I suppose that in all human connections there is at first a sort of exaltation. There has been no strain, no trial of the strength of the bond, and when that does come (as come it inevitably must if it is to be a real connection and not a holiday sentiment), it is a much more 'tickle' crisis than the 'grand projection' in alchemy to resolve the glow and colouring and fancy part of the attachment into a living fact of mixed, good, questionable, and a residue of what may not be owned, which makes up a real human being. If the friendship can stand this crisis (and thousands perish in it!), depend upon it the basis is more stable than before, and the nature is not changed. The knowledge is not of good and evil. It is of good only: it does not injure love. One has a surer light to walk by. It is not a question of thinking better or thinking worse; it is a fact of being placed closer together, of seeing each other close to. Much as I have suffered, I would not for any consideration have had the last four months undone; it is not a crisis peculiar to friendship alone, it happens in all things of any value. In religion, no man ever properly believes or gets any stable principles until all the unquestioning faith of his youth be broken up, and he has passed through a sharp period of doubt and darkness, and worked his way through that to trust and belief. He cannot have anything to depend on till then, nothing that, if leaned on, was not liable to bend beneath him; but if he gets through the crisis, he knows in what he has trusted, he knows what he believes. I feel too thankful to be safe on the other side—to have got it over—to be able to complain of the soreness and exhaustion one naturally feels after a severe operation; but I know that will pass away. I grasp your hand more surely than I did before. You will have no more of those explosions of temper which horrified you so much, and which arose from my not being able to reconcile certain things—from being perplexed between my own fancies and real things. No, my love, your theory, begging your pardon, is very commonplace, and not the least in the world true; so pray renounce it, or keep it to yourself, for you see what a preachment it brings about your ears! Your notion is true—when people who have quarrelled say they will be friends, and have ceased to care for each other, the friendship is dead, and there is no healing a wound in a dead body. But I feel quite lively, and hope you do too, in spite of all this long letter! Remember your theory is to submit to be buried quietly under the weight of it, and to lie quiet there, and not rise again—a ghost. You are to renounce it like the Devil and his works, and you are to write to me very soon, or else I shall take up the Devil and swear; and if you vex me my wrath will most likely be visited on that poor unoffending ——, so be merciful, and write soon to your very fun-cleaving

G. E. J.

LETTER 52.

(Postmark, February 26, 1846.)

Dearest Jane,—Do you know whether Miss —— intends to leave Mrs. —— on account of the devilish slight and malice they have shown her? Because Mrs. —— asked me to ascertain whether she was at liberty just now. So please let me know, as somebody down here wants a first-rate governess. How are you, at all, to-day? I am poorly and trembling enough, and off to get a warm bath, which is my panacea for all ills my flesh falls heir to. I have been to two very 'still-life' parties this week, and what between the elaborate dulness and the late hours I am distressed, and feel as I should fancy the men feel the morning after they have been drunk— there's a respectable imagination for you! I am in a very bad humour, too. I made sure (more fool me) of a letter this week, and none came, and the field of speculation thereby opened on me is one of the widest and full of the most luxuriant possibilities of evil—ranging from the 'Plague' down to smaller evils—and all sorts of intermediate casualties. Bah! some of these fine days I swear I'll throw away all my heavy luggage in the shape of hopes and expectations, and walk the rest of my way with free limbs. I have been reading, or rather am reading, a book that has excited more sympathy than I have felt for ages—it is the 'Life of Dr. Arnold.' It has made me earnestly wish I had been born a boy and been educated by him. I would thankfully have 'fagged up' from the bottom of the school. I can't tell how it is, for he believed heaps of things that I neither do nor can, but the spirit of a man giveth understanding, and it was that which in him was so noble. I am in no humour for letter-writing this morning, so adieu! State some case of yourself. I am writing of myself, for you are mine, and when you suffer I suffer too; so just have a little consideration for people's feelings. I had a letter from —— this morning; she made me almost laugh at the philosophical way she spoke of all things; she says she feels like King Solomon without the wishing. I shall be very glad to get her home again. Now, finally, good-bye, and God bless you! Write as soon as you can, but don't worry yourself to do anything.

Ever yours,
G. E. J.

LETTER 53.

Saturday Night (Postmark, March 8, 1846).

Dearest Jane,—Thanks and better thanks for your letter. I went to town this morning with ——, and what between the heat and the dirt I had come home 'dished' to a degree, so you may fancy the blessing it was to find your letter waiting for me. The moral fitness of things could not have fallen out better; anyway, it gladdened my heart, which has been very anxious about you for some time past. But now you can go to sleep and are grown stupid, I hope great things for you. I am never witty (save the mark!) except when I am ready to cut my throat; when I am at ease I am stupid and content. Whatever you have, my only light is a species of combustion. Finally, your letter has done me more good than I can tell you—there are things in it I am glad to read. I like specially what you say about the Lady ——, and I can understand it, which says a great deal for my intelligence. But though you have given me a real interest in her, and I like hearing of her as much as you will tell me, yet just at present I feel at times when I think about her much as the old-established member of Austen's happy family may be supposed to do when he increases their circle and introduces a new member. What you tell me of her now just squares with what I had figured to myself from your former letter, and I am very thankful you have got her. She is good for you; she has had long practice in standing on her own basis—and it's like learning to stand on ship-board, one's 'life-legs' are as apt to come to one as one's 'sea-legs,' and a monstrous deal of sickness has to be transacted before we succeed in either. I fancy if she ever lets you into her inner case, you would only find just what has been tormenting and dragging your own life out of you—the same sort of things—only 'her great dragon underground, in straiter fetters bound,' had not been let loose for a long time. I often think of that angel in the Revelation who came out of heaven having a great chain in his hand, wherewith he laid hold of the dragon, *i.e.* the Devil, and bound him for a thousand years. It would be such a blessed state of things to live under! 'Au reste!' I cannot help fancying that Lady —— cares a great deal more for you than you suspect, and a great deal more, too, than accords with her general theory of things. Go on telling me about her, because I feel as if anybody who belongs to you concerns me too, in a sort of way. 'A broad basis of veracity!' Ah, my dear love! is it not a deal harder to be true and to tell true than anybody believes till they try? You know that the manuscript of the 'Nouvelle Heloise,' preserved in the museum, has hardly a blot or an erasure in it, whilst the MS. of the 'Confessions,' which profess to be gospel, is interlined, altered, and cancelled from one end to the other, and so I don't believe in human nature! I think men are born 'artistes,' and we can't help embellishing everything we touch—I believe that is the true original sin, the iniquity in which we are conceived. King David was in search of a 'broad basis of veracity' for the sole of his royal foot when he said that! As to ——, I feel what you mean, but I can do nothing that way; I have tried, and better tried, if I can succeed (and God knows that, just now, I have the desire) in making something more rational, industrious, and good for something half my own life. The example may have influence on her. She, too, feels vague desires that way, but precepts or words, however eloquent, would do nothing; she has no faculty for generalising anything one says. One no sooner tries to point out any tendency, or practise it as an indication of one's meaning, than she bolts off into some special individual instance, and begins justifying herself instead of trying to see what one means; she always seems counsel for herself to disprove what one is trying to make her understand, instead of using her own conscience to throw light on the matter for her own guidance. God knows one does not want people to plead guilty—only to try to understand; to examine their own hearts for their own edification, to see how matters really are. But Betsy seems to think that if she can out-talk one, the fault itself is done away with, like a piece of false logic. That sort of thing has tried me very much, and then, to mend the matter, she retains a sort of vague idea that one wants to think a lot of her! That is the side of her that has vexed and worried me; but the people who educated her had no coherence or consistence of character, and, with all her strength, she wanted something able to bind her together; she must weave up her 'thrums' herself, and she might make them into cloth-of-gold! By the way, she has spoken most warmly of all the kindness and attention you have shown her. One thing she said touching me—namely, that you continued just as kind to her since we (viz. you and I) had got comfortable again as you were before—that it made no difference with you, and that, though she thought you had begun to care for Lady ——, she felt sure you could care for us all the same. I have not got the letter by me, or I would give you words which were very nicely said, and showed a real warm feeling of satisfaction at the fact. As to my poor Egyptian friend, those things always find their own level; whilst one has to lead one's actual life, it always rubs smooth, to some sort of surface at least. The gaps in things wanting always get filled with something, so that no chasms are to be seen on the surface; at any rate, one's life rounds itself off somehow, and so my Egyptian is a thing altogether apart. I cannot waste much faculty upon him, because he is too far off, but it has been good for me—it *is* good for me. If I could lead my life beside him I should be a world better in all ways than I am, and it is something to know that there is in the world a man who would suit us, and to feel sure that man cares for us; it is like having the receipt for the 'philosopher's stone' in one's pocket, though one may have no means of realising it. Still, it has come to be a possibility. He seems to realise things as they are much more than I do, but still the little he expresses is like a 'chink,' letting me see how much lies beneath. Anyway, when our friendship does die, it shall be a mutual death. I cannot find in my heart to poison it with reason, even if I had the strength, but it is next to an impossibility to summon resolution deliberately to hurt oneself. Now for matters of business. Thanks for your hint about 'Chapman & Hall'; once on a time I was wound up to the pitch of writing them an imperious letter, and it did wonders, and I'll try again, wearing my leek 'with a difference' this time. I am more pleased than I can tell you that you like that last essay, because it is the first attempt I ever made to say anything practically. I feel a real want just now to indite essays. God knows if anybody will read them, and it is a pretentious thing, too; but a volume of essays I could get done very soon, seeing I have already accomplished several. By the way, Douglas Jerrold has behaved like a Briton in printing the little paper I sent him, written without changing a word, as far as I can recollect, and he has taken the one I wanted printing—viz., 'To-day.' But articles run up in print are like flannels the first time they are washed—this only fills about two pages! Whether he will behave like a brick and pay me, I cannot speculate, but as I am like the ghost in 'Hamlet,' and 'want a hearing,' I am content either way. I shall send him the second part—the one you have—unless you counsel the contrary. I suppose I can reprint it again if I want to, and, as it is questionable matter, I had rather it had an introduction from somebody responsible. But this number is woefully inferior to all its predecessors. I don't wonder the least in the world that Carlyle saw no reason for my 'printing all that'; an individual attempt at a conclusion, however honestly meant, always does look impotent to one always dwelling in large, broad, general principles. All things in this world are done like Mosaic work, by pin-points of endeavour—each looks of no use by itself. What you say of translations settles the matter; only it is vexing to see that trashy thing, 'Priests and Women,' run after and nobody troubling themselves! That book of Quinet's is really worth reading, but I agree in all you say thereanent. Tell me what you think as to the Douglas Jerrold business, and if you are favourable, send me back the first essay I sent you. I am half-ashamed to make such a long talk about my schemes, but if 1 am to work at the practical I can't help making a grating noise just at first. I shall work smoother after a time. I am reading 'Niebuhr' very diligently, and now I have got rid of those dreadful Pelasgians I go on very well. Every now and then I come to a little golden passage which leads me hoping forwards. Likewise, I have got a servant, one who lived twenty years in one family and who snubbed me as a 'little girl.' If she be not too old I shall be well set up, for she is faithful and industrious; also, I have been beginning to help my next-door neighbour, though I had never seen her, but I heard such a pitiful account of the way she was left, with a little baby—the monthly nurse just gone—and no servant in the house. She called next day, and since then I have been very zealous in her service, for she has a look with her eyes like you—in fact, her eyes are like yours, and I 'cottoned' to her on the strength of it. Poor ——! I am thankful to say his cough is quite gone, but he is not well. He is dreadfully worried—by business, for one thing; he is going to have some shower-baths if I can persuade him. He has an almost constant headache, but now that he has lost his cough I don't seem to care for the rest. —— is in London, so you will hear his voice again, which is better than seeing his face. Oh! I could make you laugh at a conversation —— repeated to me the other night that he had had with —— (I fancy it had been said with that intent); it would make a cat laugh! but it is too long to tell you.

Oh, only fancy! that satin cloak I told you of last week has miscarried on that vile Eastern Counties Railway, which loses everything and seems born to be unlucky with packages, and the *père* is not here to see after it. Now good-bye, and God bless you, my darling! Sleep well, and send me word how you are. By the way, never fear that I shall discuss you with ——; it would be *lèse-majesté*, against my creed and inclination, too. There would be a want of reverence in it, if you understand what I mean. Good-bye, once more.

Ever your own
G. E. J.

LETTER 54.

Thursday (Postmark, March 19, 1846).

Dearest Jane,—Your letter came just as I was finishing breakfast, and I sat down first thing to thank you for it, and beg you to be pacified and not provoked at the present want of success. What you have done for me is far better, far more really valuable, than if it had been compliments and flying colours from ——! Thank you for sending me his note, whole and entire; you do not see that, living as I am obliged to do without any professional judgment and advice to guide me, a good, hard, professional, practical opinion is worth to me, personally,

a great deal more than the most flattering criticism!
—— is a practical man of some years' practical knowledge of business, and he knows what he is saying—as far as it goes. If my sister[1] had lived she would have said all these things, and given me the 'drilling' necessary and taken all the dilettantism out of me. It must be done for everybody if they are to do any good, and I have nobody at my elbow to do it; therefore, I am on the listen for practical, professional judgment, and thankful when I can get it. I have produced a certain effect of 'maundering,' instead of clear, definite conclusion, as I intended. —— may not be a genius, but he can speak to facts and impressions produced on himself; and I am glad to get a definite, practical opinion, not frittered away by civility, or the sort of gallantry (God save the mark!) that adulterates all the little bit of straightforward dealing women meet with from men, and is the reason they do so little that is really worth anything!

Another thing you may have found out about me—or not, I can't tell—but it is the truth, namely, I can do no sort of good on praise. I cannot work on it. I require pounding down with criticisms from people who know things better than myself. If —— had sent flourishing compliments and a promise of speedy insertion, I should have done no better next time.

---

[1] Mrs. Fletcher, Miss Jewsbury's elder sister.—A. E. I.

Now I see (though I had a sort of suspicion in my heart all the while) that there is a degree of truth in what he says, and truth must be attended to. At the same time I feel sure and know that the insight you brought to the matter has more of the spirit of truth in it. I know what is wrong with that essay in particular, and with my writing in general, and it shall be mended. I have shut my teeth together, which is my way of 'girding up my loins'; but, my dear, I would pay infinitely more respect to ——'s fault-finding than I would to his praise. If *you* tell me a thing is good or has truth in it, I feel confident that it is there, and that you have overlooked and seen through the artistic form and manner and practical shortcomings. But if the good it may contain is not to run into water, I must listen thankfully to all that —— and such people can or will tell me. So, my dear, if you will tell me plenty of those things that you hear, I will be glad of them. If, instead of running wild and trying to 'make a silk purse out of a sow's ear,' I had kept to a strictly professional friendship with ——, I should have got useful hints and good instruction in practical workmanship; but I made a horrid mistake! So now, my dear, are you better satisfied that you have done me a real kindness? You have often wondered— and I daresay have half taken a disgust to me for keeping up an intercourse with ——. The real hold he has had on me (for the fancy has been of ages and ages, if it ever were a real one) has been, that he has given me a practical insight into the working and practice necessary to make even talent visible and available. I can't put it in words, but if you had any work for a definite purpose to do you would feel what I mean, and see that, with all drawbacks, he has been useful to me, if it were only that he has enabled me to take quietly and in a business-like way the check I have met with and the general disappointment in ——'s note. So, finally, my dear, send me back my MS., and Carlyle shall hear what a bonfire I will make of it; but there is good in that article, and I will work it out. I am not going to throw it away. I will try if by judicious treatment the 'maundering' may not be made into something worth the hearing. If you, my dear, won't take a disgust, but try to read it when it is done, and not get tired of my steps up the battle of learning—it is all I ask. I must have the encouragement of knowing that you can feel an interest in my things, even in their neither flying nor walking state. Oh, about 'St. Simonism'— let me set your heart at rest (at Seaforth you forbade me, or you might have had it then). I should just as soon think of professing myself an adherent of any of the million dead-and-gone heresies by which people travestied Christianity, and disturbed the peace of the Church, and roused the 'Anathemas' of the Popes and the squabbles of the Councils, as I should dream of writing myself a 'St. Simonian.' My dear, I have not lost my instinct for the ridiculous; but in spite of all the theatrical nonsense and dressing up *à la Sainte Famille*, there is a great deal of beauty, truth, and excellence of purpose and sagacity too, in many of their views. I like their books, and the men, since *la Sainte Famille* was dispersed, have shown themselves men of practical ability. Guizot's 'Civilisation,' which made him famous, is to be found under an unpractical and impossible form, but the whole of it—that is good for anything—is to be found in the 'Exposition Seconde Année' that I got from Mazzini; but it is, as the 'Times' said of Mr. Villiers's motion, 'the little difference between his will and the plan proposed by Government: it makes all the difference between the practicable and the impracticable; between Sir R. Peel and Mr. Villiers; between the practical man and the philosopher.' Now, my dear, are you satisfied with this? I have, and can't help (being a woman) having, a sort of *tendresse* for the whole set of them. 'Are you a St. Simonian?' 'No. But I have a friend who is.' This is a long, rambling letter (I do believe it's the habit of writing long letters that has spoiled my hand for business), but I wanted a 'settle' with you after yours of this morning, and I want a letter about yourself; and you might just have told me how you were and when you go to Lady ——'s, just by way of a spoonful of currant jelly, which is always given to children who take their physic well. So give me a kiss and tell me some news of yourself. By the way, —— says she has bought (extravagant woman) Douglas Jerrold's Mag. for this month, and I want you to see my article, or *particle*, of two pages. Now, thanks for all your real, practical, work-a-day friendship.

Ever your own
G. E. J.

I open this to say that on reading your letter over again I found a sentence I had overlooked, viz., Carlyle's good nature about Fraser's Mag. I need not tell you that I am grateful to you—if one goes to the fountain-head, I will shew myself biddable; but do write me a note about yourself! God bless you, my dear love! It is worth while to get 'snubbed' for the sake of getting comforted by you after it. I am like a rhinoceros to snubbing in general—but if the 'snubs' came from you, they would find me very soft. I am away at old 'Niebuhr,' and it's like getting into a granite pestle and mortar. Doctrines fly like bats! Anyway, I have put my soul on a course of tonics! . . .

[Unfinished.]

LETTER 55.

Sunday (Postmark, June 22, 1846).

Dearest Jane,—Your letter came to me as I was dressing this morning, and very sorry indeed it made me, to find you in such an unsatisfactory state! I am really uneasy about you, and the only comfort in your case is, that you will so soon be at Seaforth. It is the only place for you just now. All those grand people may be very well—a great privilege to know, and all that—but just now you want to be out of the hearing of 'wits,' and with somebody that loves you, and to whom you can speak. I have an hypothesis that it's not good to live altogether with highly civilised people! After being some time in that sort of society one needs to go out to grass; it is an instinct of nature, as well as friendship, that moves you to go to Seaforth. It is such a plague to make new friends, or else I guess you would make something of 'Hahn Hahn.' She must have known sorrow! I feel very interested about her, although I have not read a line of her books. I had the 'Countess Faustin' ordered the other day, but it is not come yet! I fancy, after all, the world has sense to know realities when it actually sees them (though it puts up with make-believes with wonderful faith)—and that 'Hahn Hahn' and the Baron, being really respectable and neither feeling nor seeming ashamed

P

of themselves, it makes no fuss! I think it is a very good sign of the times, for people just as high in rank have been tabooed, and her being an authoress hardly explains the charitable solecism! Do tell me something about her; her experience and history would be worth all the novels—and she could write—if she would speak a word to women good for them to hear. But Carlyle putting up with her is the most wonderful thing possible; I thought he was of a real Scotch strictness in those matters, and could not stand 'George Sandism' in theory, let alone practice. The real George Sand seems to have got herself 'dished' (spiritually I mean) in her relations with the sterner sex! She has been the better of the two always; and has gone from one to another, finding nothing but disappointment, till now she is 'blasée' and hardened. 'Hahn Hahn' has been fortunate.

I have been working very hard all week. It is only expiating past idleness, or else I am sure the blessing of industry ought to fall on me. But all I have got yet is a headache and giddiness, anything but encouraging. However, I am working in faith; the heat is terrible, for our air is so thick and heavy that, when heated, it is like a casing of hot lead. London air is fine and clear compared with ours, which is oppressive to death! We have had Ibrahim Pasha, or as people here call him, 'Abraham Parker,' and nearly wore him out with taking him over cotton mills, up and down flights of stairs that would seem fabulous. It was reported, to the great scandal of all the women here, that he had brought five wives with him. One good lady was very vehement the other night. I stood up for the poor women's respectability, as they were all wives, and I said his religion allowed them. 'Religion!' was the reply, 'I suppose he expects to go to heaven in spite of such conduct.' 'Well,' I said, 'he will go to one of his own!' 'Indeed he had need!' But if your breakfast comes off on Wednesday you'll not thank me for hindering you! I know what it is to give parties myself, with a small establishment! Your breakfast tempts me terribly. I should like to be there, and no doubt there would be many of the same opinion. God bless you!

Your affectionate

G. E. J.

LETTER 56.

Tuesday (Postmark, September 2, 1846).

My Darling,—I am not sitting down comfortably to write to you at all—I am in the empty office, keeping it till somebody comes. —— came directly after breakfast, and we have been walking all over the town, and after coming home in a cab I have come here for rest, shelter, and a pot of porter. I am making use of the time to write you a word of welcome! I should be physically incapable of it if

I waited till I got home. I am thankful beyond measure that you will be home to-morrow, and out of the roast meats and proprieties! I shall feel more settled now you are at home, for I did not fancy your being in Liverpool at all. I miss you still more than I can tell you. I was much struck with —— this morning. I said: 'Mrs. Carlyle is going home to-morrow!' 'Ah!' she said 'it is well for her that she has a home to go to,' and then she sighed, poor old thing, till it was quite pitiful! —— was in an ecstasy of astonishment at your brilliant spirits and brilliant appearance on Saturday. She had been puzzled by your manner when she called, and I gave her your message—which I was glad to have, as it evidently comforted her—and then she seemed quite satisfied, only a little—what shall I say?—a little conscious of a bit of human nature that you have here in Manchester instead of Seaforth. But that nobody can help, only be very glad of! She was looking ill, and little —— worse with toothache! I came into town with them, and we went to ——'s, and I got a nervous headache with looking at 'casts' with exaggerated developments, till I felt my own brain all contracting and expanding spasmodically. —— had his head examined first—it is very like fortune-telling—and then little ——, and then ——. I refused doggedly. I should have had a brain fever with the painful consciousness of my organs. He—

the phrenologist—said some good things, very good guesses indeed, as to character, &c., to everybody, but it was like being in a German nightmare, with all the little deformities ranged on shelves and labelled! —— and I got very little talk; she did not seem natural somehow, and began to explain how it was she had hit on a wrong method of amusing you at Seaforth; but, as if she felt it required excuse, she spoke very kindly and affectionately of you, and seemed really relieved when I told her you never 'settled' with me, and had taken a horror of all that sort of thing. She feared you were vexed; still she was not natural, though perhaps the prospect of having to go to a dentist's with little —— might have somewhat to do with it. —— was making a bust of James Martineau, and said he had great self-esteem, as I suppose all Unitarians have. Your note threw poor —— into such an ecstasy that I have received a letter more incoherent than ever on the strength of it. He declares that if he had been a painter he should at that moment only have been able to paint flowers, that his emotion was so indescribable that it overflowed his eyes, and accumulated beyond all his power to express! For how could the man have power to say what he felt, when he resembled 'a dwarf mushroom to an oak'? There, that is all I can recollect! No doubt you will receive an exposition of his sensibilities. He has sent me a volume of

'George Sand,' which I am in a great humour for reading, instead of an unmanageable History of Sweden, which I have begun. I have finished the Utopian part of my essay, and despatched it, along with a most seductive note begging for money. If it does not bring me some sovereigns I will doubt my powers! I shall never persuade people to anything if I cannot persuade some money out of his purse into mine. —— declares the Utopian part was very good. I am just hungry to set to work on the book, but I shall be out again with —— all day to-morrow. Do, I beseech you, keep up your good intention about one book, *our* book! I don't feel up, at this instant, to anything but going home to dinner, for I am 'dished to death,' but as soon as I can get the steam up you shall have an official letter!—the revising and correcting must come after. Now, my darling love! good-bye! and God bless you! Whenever I say my prayers I put one in for you, and God will bless you and keep you, of that I am sure, and have faith! Be strong and faithful, and remember always that I love you! Come to me or send for me whenever you feel that I should be a comfort to you! I love you always. Ever your own
G. E. J.

Give my kind regards to ——, and tell her to make much of you.

LETTER 57.

[Beginning fragment.]

October 19, 1840.

. . . You must excuse this writing, for I can do no better! I like your account of your poor street-sweeper beyond everything. I do believe it is an acquaintance that will do you good. The man has got the divine idea of his condition, and he is worth a thousand other people who can speak eloquent speeches and construct theories! As to that Miss ——, I loathe her heartily from your description. I have no patience with theoretical profligacy. It does the heart and soul more harm than a course of blackguardism! She must be, and cannot help but be, a hypocrite, if she be tempted to death to live 'a free and easy life,' and yet keeps herself strait-laced up in practice to keep in with Emerson & Co.! I am extremely charitable towards people who honestly work out their own inclinations, but it makes me very poorly to see them putting on a grand fancy dress or transcendental philosophy to dignify their inclination! Anything else is far more respectable and honest to my thinking! And then those doctrines from an irredeemably ugly, uninteresting woman are really 'damnable.' Somebody was talking about that woman here the other night. If she comes to Manchester I shall see her. I had a visit yesterday from a man I have taken the greatest possible regard for—and I took his visit (busy as he is) as a real honour! You will not like him so much as I do, but to me he is a real God-send. He is Mr. J. J. Taylor, the editor of the 'Prospective Review.' He is a Unitarian minister, but not such an one as you ever saw. He is really well read, and so mild and candid and un-pedantic, and so—what shall I say?— Humble?—unpretending would be better. But anyhow, I can ask him questions and listen to his answers with great comfort and profit. He is worth a bushel of ――s! He is rather an elderly man, very shy and timid in his manner, but he must have something about him to impress me so much. I would not make a scandalising speech to him for the world, and yet I can settle any doctrine, and say anything I want to say, only I feel in earnest with him. I have had a book lent me which I am reading as fast as I can, a few pages at a time, but I am just wild with it; it is Fichte's 'Nature of the Scholar.' I have only just begun the lectures, but it is the life of Fichte at the beginning of the book that has fascinated me. I know not when I have been so moved; and yet your poor old blind sweeper has been moved and made on the self-same principle—the one learned his own secret and was a philosopher, and the other only had it in his heart as the 'gift of God,' and has lived on it. I don't think, perhaps, you feel tempted

at the philosophy, and yet I don't know. When you
found out how it was all lived out and worked out
by him on the most trying occasions, with unfaltering
faith, even you could hardly help reverencing it.
Anyway, read the life. It is in a number of Chapman's
'Catholic Series.' I am writing away at my book,
and have got two or three more chapters done, but
I cannot get on fast; I must go through a certain
process, and cannot make haste. I have a great deal
made out roughly, but it wants writing again. By
the way, little Dr. —— called on me last week, to
introduce that friend of his—the young lady who
wants to come to London to board in a literary
family. She has got her wish, for a while, it seems!
She is really a very pretty, nice-looking young woman,
and I guess Dr. —— likes her. There is something
very tender in his tone to her. I don't know whether
she is clever, but she seems to think the summit of
earthly happiness is—to know clever people. She
has not seen much society evidently, and yet she
seems so nice altogether that I think Dr. —— will
be lucky if he marries her, judging from a first
appearance. I don't know her name, and could not
catch it. I wrote a note to Miss —— yesterday.
Now guess about what! A friend told me of two
protégées of —— who aspire to be governesses,
and Miss —— had written to ——, and I thought
if one would suit —— it would be no harm to

inquire. —— said he had received your letter, and that he proposed writing very soon; he is most discreet about your letters, as all men should be when women do them the honour to write! He said he wished he had you for a clerk in his warehouse, you were so clever, and would make a first-rate man of business. I had not seen him for nearly two months! though he has sent me plenty of notes. I thought he would come to-day, but it is such dreadful weather.

—— is really better, if he will only take care of himself. If his shares would get up you would have a very tender letter, but he has no heart, poor lad, as it is! He is at church now or would send a message. Write to me soon, there's a darling! I can see no more now! God bless you!

Ever yours,
G. E. J.

LETTER 58.
[Undated fragment, belonging to the year 1846.]
Geraldine Jewsbury to Mrs. Carlyle.

Dearest 'Kadijah,'—If sympathy, and indignation, and being fit to set off to get a little news about that dreadful —— would do you any good you would find yourself solaced directly! for I am in a fit of excitement. What a shocking woman you tell me about! There must be some reason why governesses get so badly treated as a race, and people do get as much as they deserve, as Carlyle says.

Who could treat —— and such people well—viz., like ladies and 'one of the family'? My old —— is more likely to get well treated than a dozen such. Well, you will send her off forthwith, of course—and yet, poor thing, what has driven her to it? Perhaps something that would make us sorry for her if we knew; but anyhow, pity will not mend her, and she is disreputable—next door to a scamp for drinking, we know that! I was going to write to you this morning about a heap of things, and your letter has put them out of my head. Primo, I had a 'swarry' last night on the voluntary system, which went off very well, only like nothing else in this world! Dr. —— told me at Mrs. ——'s on Wednesday that he wanted to bring Mr. ——, Mr. ——, and M. —— on Saturday (they had all made various starts, and finally it was really to come off). So accordingly, about five o'clock, M. —— and another man arrived, whom I affectionately greeted for ——, but it proved to be —— (the other was ill of a fever, and in bed); then came little Dr. ——, and we began to talk about all sorts of things. They like settling books. But however, we got on Miss Cushman. They like her, but are not wild about her; people must have time before their reputation is settled, and Miss —— is only one year old, in these parts at least. Then —— came in and we had coffee, Ireland[1] talking away as

[1] Mr. Alexander Ireland.

fast as Carlyle, and speaking Scotch as broad as possible, He is ——'s great friend, they swear by each other; but he is a great improvement on ——, and he is a nice comfortable, sensible, fatherly sort of man, and I got at home with him directly. He has black eyes and great strong black bushy eyebrows, such as Carlyle's soul delights in, and is very pleasant and genial —not at all a Unitarian, but a strong, striding, healthy man. I want you to know him—make —— bring him! He has a splendid library, and knows all sorts of nice people, and it's fine making fun of —— & Co. They have all the people worth seeing who come to Liverpool; all their people do something, and though not high grand heroes like Carlyle loves, still wonderfully different to the insipid of every name! Make up to —— in spite of his 'm'ams.' I like Mr. Ireland amazingly. He is just the sort of man for me to know—quite sober and respectable, and therefore to be believed when he fights one's battles, and he is bringing me translations from Fichte and Schiller; in short you must know him! Tell Mrs. —— I like him extremely, and thank her for speaking of me to him, for she has done me a real good! In the middle of coffee everybody began to smoke!—(one can always get on with people who like smoking)—and then Dr. —— said 'I wish —— were here, I'll go and fetch him!' Now —— is staying at the ——s, and he had got Mrs. —— to bring him to call here in the morning. So it was 'un peu fort' to fetch him at night, but Mr. Ireland could serve him, so it was agreed, and Dr. —— set off and brought him back! Then the room was full, and we all smoked and talked, and settled just what came in our heads!

—— I like much better than I did at first; still, I don't much care about him. He professes to be a great friend of ——'s, but I guess —— would not care much for him. Still, he is evidently pretty intimate with him. He had to go away at ten, because they are early, but the rest were not tempted to go, and sat down again. Mr. Ireland settled Shelley, about whom he is wild, and all manner of queer old books, and mentioned several I ought to read, and has promised to bring me whatever I want! He is a kind, thorough man, and I am delighted to know him— even M. —— 'came out' in his presence. In spite of his somewhat conceited manner, the latter has read an immense deal, and is a good fellow! Then as they were nearly all teetotallers, they got hungry, and we had some supper, and finally, about eleven, they took themselves off! To complicate my affairs, who should come in about seven o'clock but old Mr. and Mrs. ——, to sleep all night. Only fancy!! She is quite silly.

[Unfinished.]

LETTER 59.

[Exact date doubtful, but of the year 1846.]

Friday.

Dearest Jane,—I don't know if smoking be bad for the health, but I am sure swearing is, and my digestion has not got right after the awful—what shall I call it?—ejaculation I bestowed on Miss ——. My dear, I quite think with you, and agree with all you say thereanent, and I believe you too, as firmly as a Mahomedan! I do the same myself, but the difference is—when I wrote on the subject, you were out of the right perspective to me. Still I am glad you say what you do (though I did not need it); it is a written testimony, and the Church, you know (that model of all knowledge), always enlarged her written creed to meet any heresy that might be just then rampant, clinched in a clerical black and white garb. So you have been preaching against my heresy, and articulated your own doctrine! Had I been always one of the faithful, it might have remained one of the silent celestial harmonies! Finally, our dispensations have an inverted sympathy, decidedly! You sat down to write to me, and Miss —— spoilt the purposes. I had invited a sort of Miss —— with others to come here this afternoon: she sends me back word—and as the others were contingent on her, I am free, and give you the benefit of it, being

in a great humour for a 'settle,' and all inclination
and ability to work were dissipated for the day in
search of a large fowl to be roasted 'turkey-fashion,'
which my cooking damsel insisted on having for
supper. I have plenty of things to say, and don't
know where to begin. I never told you properly
about —— and his visit. I want to know what you
think of him—sheep or wolf? Do you like him. He is
not what he used to be, and I feel very sorry for him
out there with his horrid wife, and all sorts of vulgar
wretches—vulgar in their body and estate, and just
left to die or drink as the case may be! I want to
get him back into civilised society. I have no
vocation for being a saviour, God knows—except
unlimited good nature, and that is all the feeling I
have for him, really and truly all. And he protested
he had subdued his love for me into friendship (I
don't believe it was ever anything but pure 'ennui'
and an effort at self-preservation); but this time he
behaved in a most touchingly discreet way. He sat
in the armchair, smoking; I sat on the other side of
the fireplace, doing the same—both in a very composed frame of mind apparently—but he suddenly
broke silence by saying: 'Geraldine, you ought to
have been my wife. I have done no good since,
and every step I have taken has been downward.
You would have been a happier woman, and
I should have been a better man!' Ten years

ago that speech would have raised me to the seventh heaven; now I only said, with a most heartfelt composure, 'God knows! We never can tell about those things. It is best as it is,' and took up a piece of hemming, and never even pricked my fingers! What fools we are to make ourselves miserable about anything, when we may be quite sure we shall get to care nothing about them in a very little while. I lose all faith in love when I see him! I did care for him once, long and well—better than I have it in me to care for any man now. He seemed in a capital good humour with me, which I am glad of, because he was very bitter a while since. On the whole, I guess he has not energy enough to come so far out of his way as to come to see me pretty often. His laziness is, was, and always will be, paramount to all other feelings! So the odds are greatly in favour of my guardian angel, and then I shall only be a memory! I think he has taken to you, for he spoke spitefully of ——, who, he said, 'threw his eyes on you without ceasing!' He wanted confidence, in a sort of way, to speak about you, only he said 'one expression of her face (*viz.* her eyes) is divine!' But he professed to me to think that Carlyle was the only man you really cared for, and I encouraged that, telling him with a most confidential air he was quite right in that surmise, and that as to all the men about you they just were obliged to live together like Austen's 'happy family,' and that you were the innocent little lamb in the midst, to tempt them to death, but which they were none of them to touch! He talked very little about you. The worst of —— is, that he is like spun sugar! you may draw him out in any shape you will, and then he melts out of it again! I myself cannot believe now in his dangerous powers, but, ma foi! it was different once! So finally, my dear, I fancy old friends are like old fashion-books, charmingly becoming and tempting at the time—and one wonders afterwards where the beauty lay. Still, it's of no use pretending! I have a great regard for ——, and when he is with me I forget all his sins! Now, I have told —— no details, so keep all this to yourself. She got me into a quarrel before; all with good intent, and not at all believing she had done mischief. I told her, in the general—'I think —— has got, or is inclined to get, into trouble again!' So give her neither chapter nor verse! Oh that Mrs. ——! I heard of that party through Mrs. ——, and wondered if she had cast out her net once more, though she had toiled so long and caught nothing! If people will hunt up lionesses they must make up their mind beforehand to get scratched! I think she wears an under-jerkin of brass, or leather, or something equally impenetrable. Poor Miss —— is terribly patronised by her, and there is a sympathy between them, if you only knew.

But Mrs. —— has been able to serve her, and her position is not one of absolute free-will. I can't help hoping you will meet with her yet, under better auspices than Mrs. ——'s. It is all very fine to tell me to walk a good spell! The rain has poured down every day for a fortnight. It took to clearing up for two days, and has begun again to-day. The rest of your prescription I will follow, and this, too, as soon as I can. I am seeing after a servant in real earnest, and have heard of a young woman who had expressed a great desire to 'live with Miss Jewsbury,' so whether it will come to pass I don't know. I am in very low spirits about another thing. —— has had a cough for a long time, and the other day he told me he had a pain in his side, and what he spit up had for the last day or two been marked with blood. I have put him a plaister on his chest, and he has given up smoking; but I hear him hacking at night sadly. For the whole day after he told me I went about like one stunned with a blow. I dare not think of it, if anything should happen to him! I don't know that I can tell you anything more. I will write again soon. Take care of yourself, and don't you get a cough! God bless you! Ever your own

G. E. J.

Have I not a right to feel affronted? I wrote Mazzini a letter on New Year's Day and sent him his bookseller's accounts, and also a post-office order for eleven shillings (all the poor pamphlet had realised). He has never answered me. I send you the thing to read. Douglas Jerrold has the first part, and has not yet printed it. I suppose editors' promises are like Bank of England notes—it is not expected there should be bullion enough to cash more than one-third. I must tell you something I met with in an Exeter newspaper this week. An old lady of that town died, and there is a row about her will. In proof of her eccentricity one witness said: 'She used often to say that if Jesus Christ came on earth again she would invite Him to dinner, and treat Him like a gentleman, for she had plenty of plate!' There is a beautifully respectful notice of 'Oliver Cromwell' in the 'Shilling Magazine' for this month.

1847.

LETTER 60.

(Postmark, April 6, 1847.)

Dearest Jane,—You will not get much good out of me to-day, for I am bilious, and lazy, and good-for-nothing—enough 'to point a moral tale' about the disadvantages of women who take to sewing and female employments. For it was only the other day that a very wise woman told me she was sure all my 'ill-regulated nerves' and illness came from not employing myself regularly, and said if I would do some knitting or sewing I should be quite another person. I made myself a habit-shirt on the strength of this lecture, but every day I am getting more and more like a lump of sugar that is melting away at the bottom of a cup of weak tea, and all the sewing in the world would not revive me. There now! I have groaned my groan, like 'Molly Brown' before she awoke at the ghost of 'Giles Scroggins'; so let us see what there is more profitable to tell you. I have learned the mystery of 'Mudieism.' Oh that it should never have struck any of us before! My dear, Mrs. —— has no less than three novels written and ready for the press; and Juliet[1] has written a novel, too, which has, moreover, been 'spoken of in the highest terms' by some unknown gentleman of the greatest judgment! Is not that enough to take the shine out of what I once overheard somebody call the 'purple light of literature'? For a minute I felt inclined to place my MS. on the kitchen fire, and let it lie there till utterly consumed. How did I get to know this? you will ask. Well, then, ——, though very reserved with me, is much more confidential with Mrs. ——, and she told her this, and Mrs. —— told me. Now it has made me think a great deal better of Juliet's sense and good conduct. Ever since we have had to deal with her, certainly nothing can have been more like a good girl and less like a heroine in disguise. Of course I shall not let her know that I have been told of her confidence to Mrs. ——. The place I secured for her turns out not to suit. There has been a deal of bother about it. Finally, it is settled that she is to remain at present where she is until Mrs. —— suits herself, and my business now is to find something for ——. Everybody does what is right in their own eyes, so I suppose does Mrs. ——; but I am out of patience with her. I cannot make her out. I think she intends to be kind, but it is in such a cold-blooded manner that an interview with her always

---

[1] Juliet Mudie, a maid-servant, in whom Miss Jewsbury took an interest.—A. E. I.

embarrasses me, and yet there is nothing to take exception at; but I can never do any good with people who have light flaxen hair and round light-blue eyes. Anyway, I shall not go from home till —— is 'fixed.' I am rather anxious to get her away from this neighbourhood for another reason. —— told me she had been followed whenever she came from church by a 'gentleman.' It seems to have annoyed her very much, for she was afraid there was something in her manner which might have misled him; but she never replied to him, and when I asked what he was like, she said she had never looked him in the face. She said he sometimes placed himself right opposite to her in church, and that she felt him staring at her. However, as she will come to this end of the town she will be out of his way, as she seems quite to have a notion how to take care of herself; but it roused a great deal of virtuous indignation in my bosom. Women seem sent into the world to be hunted down like hares, and if they are caught they are worried to death without hope. I don't know what else I have got to tell you, for the united demons of a century of Fridays seem let loose on me just now, and I don't know how to exorcise them. I am just at my wits' end with one thing or another. I ought to go to a conversazione to-night to hear a paper read on 'Eremacausis,' which, being interpreted, means slow combustion, and it is the secret of the process by which we live and at length die—*i.e.* when we are burnt out! But I have beguiled —— to go instead, as the paper is by an acquaintance. One of us must go, and so I have victimised him. Then, if I escape that, there is a 'Charybdis' on the other side in the shape of an Evangelical party, and I so seldom get invited to those that I am half-inclined to go if it were not for the bore—my 'eremacausis' is very low just now. I fear all the fuel is done. By the way, a lady—or rather, a female—has been lecturing here, and to a respectable audience too, on 'Phrenology as applied to Matrimony.' She is the wife of the principal tragedian at the theatre here ; like all theories, it did not answer in her own case, for she cannot live with her husband. Perhaps her theory is founded on experience. And a Mrs. —— has been lecturing at the Hall of Science on the 'Rights of Women.' I believe she is rather an interesting woman, and was described to me as very modest-looking, fat, and self-possessed, and wore a blue dress and a red handkerchief, and her hair braided, without cap or bonnet or any such thing. There was a woman some time ago who lectured here—I forget her name. The subject was 'Phrenology,' and she stated in her circulars that, as the female part of her audience might be revolted by the sight of real brains, she should fold her pocket-handkerchief so as to resemble the convolutions of the brain, and lecture on that. I know not what possessed me to let such a choice *morceau* get destroyed, for I read what I am telling you with my own two eyes! Well, my dear, I close my anecdotes of illustrious women by sending you a little book I bought for you—'Cookery Rhymes.' They are written by a lady I know. She has also written one or two polemical tracts. One, called 'A New Tract for the Times,' was commended by several high dignitaries of the Church, who, not knowing it to be a feminine work (God help them!), prophesied great promotion to the unknown Curate who, as they supposed, had uttered the oracle. She is, without controversy, the most triumphantly ugly woman I ever beheld, but excessively witty and agreeable. Another woman has been writing on the 'Millennium,' and settles quite coolly that in the space of a very few years the whole batch of unregenerate and worldly wicked inhabitants of this earth would be destroyed, by some supernatural means, in the twinkling of an eye, the dead saints and 'elect' all raised up, and a pleasant family party made to reign and have it all their own way on the earth for a thousand years. The Jews all to give up their old clothes to the lawful owners, and be transformed into soft-hearted Christian and respectable freeholders in their own country, which is to be miraculously extended for their reception! There, my dear, the

force of nonsense can no further go, unless you and
I begin to feel uneasy at our chance in this new
dynasty. Certainly it is a poor look-out for us. But
just console yourself, and try to get rid of all your
illness and biliousness, and write me a line when you
are in the humour and say how you are, and let the
'Millennium' go to the Devil, or the moon, which is
the receptacle of all plans and projects that don't
prosper here. God bless you and take care of you.
                               Ever you own
Monday.   G. E. J.

LETTER 61.

[Fragment. Date uncertain, probably 1847.]

. . . I did not believe you. You said he was an
'Egoist,' and now you have the comfort of having
been right, and I may save my soul by owning myself
wrong. I would send you the letter, but I cannot
find it, and fear I have dropped it out of the pocket
of my dress. Luckily the envelope was not upon it,
and no names were mentioned except Christian
names. So no one who picks it up will see anything
but a letter with most profound worldliness and *naïve*
self-complacent sentimentalism mixed up. I have
not yet got beyond astonishment; it is more like a
transformation in a pantomime than the act of a
rational being. However, one comfort is that I
have discerned this last and solitary act of sincerity

for myself—out of the mass of sentimental melancholy. The truth has nearly frozen me to death, but thank God it is the real truth I have got at last! The fact is, that the correspondence has grown to be a terrible bore to him, and he confesses that he has 'long lost the bright hope which he took out with him, that we might some time be something nearer to each other; but that he did not tell me, because he did not think it would have made me happier to know it beforehand, and before time had lessened my attachment to him!' And all the letter is full of explanations how and why it is impossible, formally setting me at liberty, and finally you never will guess what he falls back upon. My dear, he is a respectable man, 'and it would ruin his reputation with the really good Mussulmans' if he were to take a European wife, and also be a scandal to the respectable and numerous English with whom he is in contact!!

I wish I had the letter; in spite of the shock to my tender and lacerated sensibilities I shouted again with laughter over it. It would have made a cat laugh; it was like a man speaking in Madame de Genlis' 'Palace of Truth'—fancying he is saying the most tender and beautiful things, whilst all the while he is uttering the grossest insults and absurdities. The letter was ineffable. I recollect nearly every word of it, and swear I will put it in a book some day. I could not invent anything so rich. Don't think very ill of me, my dear, but I really cannot make myself unhappy. I am very much ashamed of my romantic faith. I did care for him (for what I fancied him, rather) more than I ever did for any man; but now it is as if he had vanished into air. It is a clean case of annihilation! I should tell you there was a P.S. full of compliments and messages to all his acquaintances here by name. I don't think I ever shall have luck with my lovers. God grant I may prosper better with my friends. Other people find the world full of villains and rascals; for me it is full of respectable people. I thought with a Mussulman I was safe, but respectability, like Monsieur Tonson, ' is come again.' How are you, and where are you going? And how is your servant? I have no time to write more. God bless you. Let me hear from you, and believe me, in haste,

  Your affectionate and very consolate
        G. E. J.

All right.—G. E. J.

LETTER 62.

[Fragment.]

Emerson has taken his departure. He called here on Sunday, but I was out. I don't fancy he took to me. I am too tumultuous for him, and he is not quite sure but that I am satirical. At least, such is the opinion of one likely to know! I had far rather the Quaker liked me. He wrote me a very nice note the other day. But, my dear, there is one difficulty in my going to ———. I am not invited yet. He sent me some books to read, and I hope he will come and have another 'profitable mutton chop.' As to Hastings, upon my honour I feel it is a relief that it has not to come off! But still I am vexed you should have had any annoyance. I don't think Mrs. ——— has been respectful to you, or very polite either, for the matter of that. I have ——— very poorly again. ——— is ill, too, and in a queer, morbid sort of way. He was up here the other night, looking even worse than ———. Now do write to me and say how you are. Recollect I want some sort of 'cordial' over my work. Do tell me how you are yourself. Please give Carlyle the enclosed note. I have been setting up a thick quilted satin petticoat for this cold weather, and my eyes are not well. This is all the news from

Ever your affectionate
G. E. J.

LETTER 63.
[Fragment, assigned to 1847–8.]

... The tears stood in her eyes, and she looked quite handsome. I felt to love her! She is so thoroughly honest—I should say, only too apt to take everything everybody says 'au pied de la lettre'! . . .

It seems like a dream that you have been here. What a short visit it was! and I can have people I don't care for, and would thankfully dispense with, for weeks at a time. Recollect, there is that room always ready for you. We went (——— and I) to dine with Mr. ——— according to programme. I think he had been rather frightened at you, for he would not make up his party until he knew whether you were coming. I don't know who he would have assembled in your honour; but, though I was sufficiently amused, I am glad you were away. It is very odd how one can not only endure but really find amusement on one's own score, whereas the bearing of it for another would turn it into Purgatory. There were two other Aldermen, a Mr. and Mrs. ———, very nice Germans, whom I have known a long time, and a young German lady, ——— and myself. The dinner was 'aldermanic,' but there was no fire, and the room got very cold. All the talk was about the robes which the 'Mayor and Corporation' are to wear before the Queen, which had that morning been ordered after a stormy debate. The Queen little knows all the perturbation she causes by her visit. The whole town has gone perfectly frantic, and what with flags, and banners, platforms, and laying down extra gas-pipes for the illumination, the streets look as if they were 'on the spree'—quite dissipated, in fact. There were several places we ought to have gone to whilst you were here and we didn't; and I am quite provoked. The other day I went on an expedition 'to Peel Park,' one of the 'people's parks,' as they are called, and really it was worth seeing. Originally it used to be the family residence of one of our rich men, and when it was bought for the present purpose several fields were added to the grounds and laid out with great taste, and you cannot think what a pretty place it is now. The house is turned into a museum and library, reading-rooms, &c., and dirty-faced, painful-looking mechanics were to be seen through the windows, with a grave attention which showed that to them, at least, books were very reverend realities. I could not go into the room, for ladies, though not absolutely excluded, would be startling novelties, so I contented myself with going into the library, which had a large collection of books of all sorts, from the 'Cyclopædia' down to 'Pendennis.' The museum is a capital beginning, and all the people, especially the women and children, seem much attracted by it. The grounds are in beautiful order, and the people behaved just the same as the genteel people in Hyde Park, only that one saw pipes instead of cigars, and fustian jackets, and not at all white hands. On a garden-seat two little dirty, ragged, barefooted urchins lay stretched at full length, most luxuriously. Had they been dandies born they could not have done it better; and then the men with their wives, or the women with their children alone, were scattered up and down, looking quite at home. It made me see that the 'people's parks' are no 'make-believes,' since they use them and enjoy them. I suppose that I and Mrs. ——, who was with me, were the only two people there not belonging to the working-classes. In the omnibus, as we were going, there was a fine, intelligent man, dressed in black, with a Peninsular medal, and with at least six or eight silver bands above it, each inscribed with the battle in which he had served. He was a retired soldier, and he was going to the Park along with his wife, a nice little old woman in a black satin bonnet and close cap-border. They were quite a picture. It had been a sudden thought to go when we saw the omnibus standing, and I felt so provoked I had not thought of it whilst you were here. But you must see it some time. I think I have now told you all I have done since you have left, except the tea-drinking at ——, and one that should have come off with Mrs. ——, only I had a headache and could not go. I have been mending ——'s shirts occasionally by way of recreation when tired of writing, and all my letters have gone to the dogs. I have not written to

Mrs. —— all this month, and naturally she is hurt at me.' I had a letter from ——, who is better. He went to call upon her, and really it has been almost like seeing him myself again. I could not have believed that second-hand sight could be such a comfort. Mrs. —— wrote to offer me anything to finish the 'Sorrows' for her magazine, but I refused. It is now combined with the 'Belle Assemblée,' and if I do finish it, it must be for a better place. I hope you are thinking of our tale. Do make an effort! It will take your thoughts off disagreeable things. I can tell you, from experience, that whilst one is in for writing a tale, it becomes the reality for the time being, and all other things grow shadowy, and I don't think it is one bit more wearing than it is to worry one's self about the things of one's own life. Have you written to ——? I wish you would, for he felt very hurt that we did not call that day. —— intends to write and thank you for the paper-knife after the fifteen days are expired. At present he has to send 150 letters a day to the post.

1848.

LETTER 64.

Wednesday, March (no more exact date) 1848.

My dear Jane,—I was going to write to you —indeed, I should have written days ago, only just now I have to snatch at my moments as well as I can, and it is like trying to pick up peas with a two-pronged fork, or, to use a more elegant illustration, like the lady in the 'Arabian Nights' who picked up her rice with a bodkin. The result has been equally meagre. Your letter came this morning, and I had to look at the handwriting twice before I could believe my eyes. Do you know I feel to have been not well treated. You have been ill for seven weeks, and until —— told me I had not the least idea of the fact. Your last letter, which came somewhere about seven weeks ago, stated that you were starting for Alverstoke [1] next day, and in the one previous, which I got on January 3, you entreated me, after finding fault with me for wasting my time (which I was not doing), that I would not write letters, even to you, until I had got out of difficulty.

A country seat of the Ashburton family.

There was a tone in both letters that very much annoyed me, for, after the very solid obligations you had laid me under with regard to the book, I was doubly athirst for a word of affection to take them out of the material region of 'so much value received,' and I never received two such utterly, utterly, unsatisfactory letters from you since I knew you. At that time I was very worried, and I felt as if the least thing would throw me off the rails. I had no idea but what you were very nearly, if not altogether, restored to your usual average of health, or I should at once have set down what had pained me to the fact of their being written under difficulties which would have been fatal to any mortal attempt at utterance. I only want you to know how it fell out that you got no letter at all for so long, and then only got one which was good for very little. Your letter of this morning is, I suppose, quite as good as, from your point of view, I seem to deserve, but to me, knowing myself, I feel it is not any such thing. I do not deserve to be kept in any such ignorance, and if you are not up to writing, you might set some of your people to write me a line. For, to tell the truth, the letter I have just got has a wonderful funny likeness to one or two I wrote to —— when, without a blow-up, I wanted to put her at arm's length, or rather, out of reach. I do not suspect you the least in the world of doing it with

such deadly intent, but it will account for my dislike
to it. Besides, even if you did, it would not take
effect; there are two sides to every bargain, and I
am not a subject for 'painless extinction.' I should
first squeak for my life very sonorously, and try
what moving speeches would do, and if they did not
answer, I would wait patiently till the tide of things
should bring us into our right relation again. You
may give me pain—you have often done so—to a
degree you would hardly believe that one woman
could inflict on another—(no one has ever made me
suffer so much). I see now how very much was my
fault, and not yours; but I only say this to make you
feel how utterly it is beyond your power to vex or
estrange me permanently; as long as you are in this
world the tie exists, with a strength that has been
proved, and which is far beyond any control of your
own. If David, with all his sin, was called 'a man
after God's own heart' because love lay at the
bottom of his 'Pandora's box,' I am sure I ought to
be called a woman after yours. You know I don't
hold to your theory of 'wounds and bruises' at all.
Nature heals soundly over all mortal casualties.
There is no such thing, either morally or physically,
as living with incurable wounds. And besides, the
Bible tells us we are all 'soldiers,' so if we have
scars it is all as it must be, under the circumstances.
If, however, there has been any reason for the cold-

ness I may have fancied, but which I have suffered from all the same, either kill it yourself, or tell me, that I may destroy it myself. I sin against your notions of good taste very often, and that is quite enough to give you a distaste to me for the time being, but I don't see how it can be anything of a graver nature—anyway, I feel very innocent. All through the spirit has moved me to write, because I do not feel satisfied with your late letters, and it is much more likely that there should have been some fault on my side, or disagreeableness, and so I want to get right with you. Don't bother yourself to write a formal explanation; I shall feel in a moment the next time you write whether I am as I would wish to be with you. As to poor ——, —— looks very grave about him; he is here now. Before he went to ——, I asked him if he were out of danger; his reply was distinct enough: 'No, he is not, and he will require very great care.' There is no prospect of his getting out of the house for a long time; —— says he is too thin, which is an unpleasant sign, but as we have got him safe in the house I begin to feel more at ease. His cough is less troublesome, but his breathing is still difficult and oppressed; he is very pleased with your kind message. —— was here yesterday; how very kind he is! He came to carry off —— and me to ——; he declared change of air was the one thing needful.

I cannot tell you how good he was, but when I mentioned it to —— he laughed at the idea of sending a patient threatened with inflamed lungs from home in March, and was imperative in his negative. But when warm weather comes I hope we shall get there, and perhaps you will come too? Oh, have I not from the very beginning lamented after ——? It is very mournful that after a life of expectations which looked Utopian, he should have been taken away before the dawning of the day; but I have great faith that all that is best and noblest of a man lives after him, with wisdom not his own. He has not lived in vain, and, though dead, yet he has not passed away; his spirit is still working at the events of the day. I have a just faith in the future, and more hope than ever I felt in my life. Are not the people behaving nobly? I had such a beautiful letter from my old friend the other day, making me feel, for the time at least, so strong and full of noble instincts. I don't know when I have had anything which so has spirited me up. I never told you the escapade I had yesterday after tea. He said he wanted to go and see Emerson, and declared I should go with him. —— said, 'Go'; and so, though it had come on to pour down straight with rain, I got ready.

* * *

[Fragment.]

LETTER 65.

Greenheys, July 13, 1848.

It was time you should write to me, and now don't let it be so long again! Recollect, that in the course of nature (human nature, at any rate) it is just possible that I as well as yourself may require some patience to make good movements permanent, and to enable those returns to old faith and old affection to go on, as a renewal of early times, with all the advantages of experience added to them. What has pained me most in you has been your insensibility to all the pain you inflict yourself, and the absence of all consideration for the natural effects of things on others. No matter how hermetically one's ears may be sealed with a real affection and a faith which, in the main, is proof against even unkindness —still, one may get warped, and it may require some gentleness and management to restore the new distortion to the old 'squareness.' I am conscious that you must find me unsatisfactory in a thousand ways, from habit, disposition, and natural shortcomings of many kinds. It is an original defect in structure, with which you must have patience; but still, whenever you have any specific point to complain of, you may be quite sure that it is the effect of something on me, and not a cause in me. However, you may be quite satisfied this time that you have made me suffer quite enough,

not only from your silence and in not knowing what
was becoming of you, but in the consciousness that
I had given you pain; for when that happens to me,
no process of self-justification or amount of provocation can prevent my suffering more than you do. And
so, as it is your birthday, turn over a gracious 'new
leaf,' and start fair, for we may have only a very few
birthdays left for either of us. 'If crushing your
great toe' may sound an unromantic accident, it is
nevertheless a serious one. Do not neglect it, and
don't forget to tell me how it goes on.

—— is better; *i.e.* his cough has disappeared
this fine weather. But he gets very little strength,
and he is working too hard at the office. I think,
however, he is to go to Blackpool for a few days
on Saturday, and I hope good things from that.
Miss —— is to come to me to-morrow, and I am
very anxious to make her visit pleasant, and I feel an
awful responsibility, when people come 200 miles to
visit me, how on earth to make it worth their while.
But I am quite looking forward to seeing her. All
the good I have in me I owe to her, and she has
grown to be more like a relation than a friend. I
do not remember a mother, but I feel the need of
one, and I cling to Miss —— with what I suppose
is the instinct I should have had for a mother. How
can that woman's nature be anything but unequal

¹ The lady who educated Miss Jewsbury.

and unwise who has never known a mother and never had a child (so that she might, as it were, learn backwards)? There must be moral deserts in the nature amounting to the absence of all balance. I had a very nice letter from —— the other day. I fancy there will be what —— calls a 'metaphysical prayer-meeting' to-morrow. Emerson is to spend the day at Seaforth, according to a long-standing promise that he would not leave England without going there again. I have a great affection for Emerson, in spite of the provokingly serene ether he always seems to breathe. He has such a fine spirit in him, and so much humanity, too. I am melting away whilst writing this, and my head aches most stupidly, and I am going 'to do music' this evening. There is a grand concert, and Mrs. —— is taking me. I had something else to tell you, but I forget what, so

Believe me ever,
Your affectionate
G. E. J.

P.S.—That letter was not an offer of marriage, only a note from a nice little girl—she who translated the 'Campaner-Thal.'[1]

[Written after a long misunderstanding.]

[1] Of Jean Paul Richter.—A. E. I.

LETTER 66.

Monday night, August 10, 1848.

Dear Jane,—I was out in the country all yesterday, at Mr. ———'s new place, and only got home a little while since, so was hindered of my letter to you, and I don't want it to go on till next Sunday, when something else may hinder. I never was so glad, for a long time, over a piece of news as I was to hear of ———'s marriage! I cannot help looking on her with a certain respect—to have gathered herself together out of the horrible mess she was in, to say nothing of the suffering she had from all the 'finer feelings.' M ——— is a great brute, but surely even his infernal vanity will not lead him to be so cowardly as to torment that poor thing any more, unless indeed the Devil inspire him with something that strikes him as a piece of powerful writing—then indeed it will be a bad look-out, for he has not shown himself very strong in the gentlemanly line. . . .

Wednesday.

My dear Jane,—The Devil has been in it, as he always is when one wants to do a thing! He hinders us just out of his own perverseness and nothing else, and this morning, as there is something else I ought to do, he has inspired me to write out this letter. I don't think he will so much hinder me

from going to the Kingdom of Heaven as he will make me too late for it! Last week was smashed into little bits, and this week will be broken into bleeding fragments, for I am going with —— at three o'clock to see the Brights, at Rochdale, and stay all night! I was out at Mrs. ——'s again last week, and only came home yesterday. I was fetched, which is the surest way of getting hold of me. Miss —— and Miss —— are staying there. On Monday, who should come out in a cab all the way but ——, who has never given me a sign of his existence for near a twelvemonth? I fancy, in spite of all the flattering looks, that Miss —— was the attraction: he wants her to come and stay with them. When she was acting there last week he went to fetch her to supper, and introduced her to his wife. All the news of myself I had to tell you has grown out of date. I had Miss —— on the 14th of last month, and she stayed some time, to my great comfort. I wish she could live with me, though the amount of church-going she made me do was enormous. Still, I felt better for her visit; she did a world of practical good things for me! One was fitting me up a study—
—— had established a 'right of common' in the back-parlour, and it was beyond my force to eject her, but Miss —— set to work in earnest, and now I have most comfortable and complete quarters. I wish you could see them, and I want you to send

me either a picture or something to put up as a
memorial of you. You have many old-fashioned little
things, and I want you very much either to give me
something that has long belonged to you, or else
something you have done yourself, for I am like a cat,
and must have my feet rubbed with butter to keep
me in a strange place and make me settle to it
cordially! I hate back-parlours, except when they
have some special attraction in them, so please send
me some scrap for a remembrance. A note from
—— yesterday told me you were going on September 1
'to the Grange for an indefinite time.' Well, God
send you well through with it, and with everything
else you have either to do or to suffer, as it may be!
Whether I express it or not, you have my sympathy
—very true, and not to be changed either by squalls
or foul weather of any sort. I am in the depths of
the 'Life of Defoe'—very stupidly done, but of a most
painful interest! By the way, did you ever read
his 'Religious Courtship'? You could not help liking
it. The thing that has struck me lately in the course
of my reading is, though we are terrible unbelievers
in this age, without a rag of a creed to cover us, yet
we have a much deeper reverence for religion, a
more religious sentiment is spread abroad, than was
general in Defoe's days. I am in hopes of going to
see Macready on Saturday—in Cardinal Wolsey! I
got a present of two little books on Geology and

Philosophy, to supersede all received authorities, bound in deep rose-coloured cloth with double-gilt leaves. I have not had courage to read a line in them, nor grace to thank the author! By the way, I met the author of the 'Life of Mirabeau' the other day, and I quite repent all my hard speeches. He is quite a boy, not twenty-one, and where all his 'Carlylism' comes from I cannot think. He is the most natural, simple, good-hearted, almost rustic little fellow one can see—as good-hearted as possible, with a little round, fresh-coloured, beardless face, and sparkling black eyes—as unlike his subject as possible. I was pleased with him, and intend to invite him; he is full of fun, and made me nearly die with laughing at his account of a violent friendship he swore to a German doctor in the belief he was a man of genius, and how he got undeceived by finding him a swindler. He is a very nice lad, and will do something one of these days. I had a very becoming, nice letter from —— the other day. How does —— go on? I must go and pack my carpet-bag, so good-bye. Don't go to that grand place without sending me a line first. The blessing of God and the Virgin go with you. Ever yours,

G. E. J.

P.S.—I must tell you one thing, George Sand corresponds with Miss ——, and calls her the 'sister of her soul.' Ahem!

LETTER 67.

Monday (Postmark, October 10), 1848.

My dear Jane,—I don't know where this will find you. Indeed, I have a notion that it will not be intrinsically worth the carriage; only I don't like to miss writing, and feel more inclined to write than to let it alone. I have had a very uneasy, anxious week, and I am not easy yet for the matter of that. My dear old friend the Chevalier [1] has actually gone through the operation for cataract, and God knows how it will end! Nobody knew of it. I was there all last Monday, and never suspected what he had in his mind. He kept it from everyone, and so wisely saved himself much bother, for no doubt everyone would have had some sort of counsel or entreaty to impart, which he happily escaped. But I must candidly say I would far rather undergo a dozen operations, from tooth-drawing upwards, than suffer all the anxiety I have had lest his should not turn out well. Your friend Mr. —— is here lecturing on the 'Exciting Elements of English Society, Historically Considered.' Mrs. —— is taking me, for, as it is in our beautiful 'Royal Institution,' none but members can go; and oh! if you saw those members! Lady-like old gentlemen, and evangelical elderly ladies, and depressed-looking young ones, who do not frequent

[1] Neukomm.

public amusements, being seriously disposed, make up
the audience, and a few occasional visitors, exceptions
to the rule—Mrs. —— and myself, for example—to
redeem its character! I was there at Mr. ——'s first
lecture, but just before entering I had heard of the
operation, and I got so stifled that everybody seemed
to look like a bad dream, and as to hearing a syllable
of what was passing I could not—Heaven above only
knows what it was all about! I made a retreat in
less than ten minutes—from real failure of my powers
of patience. I hope he did not recognise me, or he
would think I was paying him a sorry compliment.

—— came here one day last week; his father and
mother are still with him, and he is deep in his
lectures. His poor mother pitched upon a volume of
Robert Owen one day; only fancy her horror and
dismay! I am glad he is amusing himself, and doing
some good beside, with these lectures, which I daresay will be as good as lectures can be as a rule!

—— is laid up with gout, and I am going to see him
as soon as I can: they talk of going to some of the
German baths as soon as he is better. —— is still
better, but I am anxious for the winter. For me, I
should be well enough, if only my head would keep
from thinking. But that is a great deal to expect
from a mortal head—mine, too, of all others. By the
way, I must tell you a ridiculous thing I heard the
other day at my baker's. A lady was complaining

that the yeast he had sent her last was bitter, and wanted to know why it was so, and how it had happened? 'Indeed, ma'am,' he replied quite gravely, 'I am sure I cannot tell, but it is one of the laws of nature that it should be so sometimes '—and it is one of the laws of nature that my letters should be stupid sometimes. I am writing this in the hope to have a speedy answer from you, to tell me how you are, how you are prospering. God bless you!

Ever your affectionate

G. E. JEWSBURY.

LETTER 68.

Wednesday morning, October 4, 1848.

My dear Jane,—I was very glad to get your letter, though I wish you had told me more definitely about your state of body, if nothing else. I feel in a humour to answer your letter directly. It is more like talking or dropping in promiscuously, instead of coming to a solemn dinner. I wish you knew how much more pleasure it gives me to have done anything you like, than to have the sunniest side in the 'career' you prophesy for me.

Sunday morning.

I got up to write to you before breakfast on Wednesday morning, intending this to reach you before you start for the Isle of Wight (if it be decreed you go there); but I only got so far on the other side, so my good intent is all you have. My life does not get along half so smoothly as it used to do. I get so many more hindrances than I used to have, in all things. I suppose it is more prolific in incidents, and they jostle each other; but understand that when I do not write to you it is really a hindrance, and not a want of inclination, that has intervened. I wish you had told me a little more, especially the state of your health, for your letter is as vague as need be about all I want to hear. Do find time to send me half a line, at least, to say how you are. In spite of all the faith I have in your judgment of people, I cannot get interested in Sir ———. He is too like one of the heroes in 'May You Like It'—if you ever read that remarkably good book, written by a young 'cleric,' many years ago now, to circulate in families, and as mild as milk-and-water. Perhaps if I saw him now I should take to him better, but I should think better of his theology if he were a Catholic out and out, instead of giving in to dandified 'Church-of-Englandism,' which bears the same relation to 'the Church' that a polite assemblage of ladies and gentlemen at a 'bal costumé' bears to the countries after which they have dressed themselves, and are at such pains to look in character. It requires the eyes of a milliner to see the resemblance. I do hate all fancy religions, and that sect of the Church of England playing at Romish rites makes me feel very poorly indeed. It is like a parcel of children making gardens, and sticking flowers in the ground to make-believe for plants. Let people be Catholic, and welcome, or let them be of no religion at all, if it suits them; but these half-and-half sects, where there is no more reason for stopping short than there is for going on, are my detestation. They certainly resemble eternity in one respect, for they have neither an authentic beginning nor a legitimate end! However, when either a man or a woman has a real genuine love of religion in him or her, one can get on with them, whatever crotchets go along with it. I had such a pleasant day last week. I went to see my old friend. He took a fancy for me to read to him, and he fetched a book that, on seeing the title-page, struck me as dreadfully dry. It was called Nichol's 'Architecture of the Heavens.' But of course I began it peaceably, and it is long since I have been more entranced. There are no bothering algebraical calculations as far as I went, but glimpses, as it were, into the 'everlasting universe of things,' till one is taken out of oneself completely—indeed, it takes away one's breath for a time. The style is majestic and noble, and the man seems to feel what one does oneself. He says what one wants to hear of a subject, and does not show himself at all. I am sure you would not regret reading it, and you will be glad to get out of the reach of all men and women so com-

s

pletely. Indeed, how they, the men and women, ever came to pass seems an obscure accident, too small to detail. I thought of you whilst I read it, and determined to tell you about it. And there are the strangest and most mysterious plates in it, at which I sat looking for half an hour, till I felt 'eerie'—that vague, half-frightened feeling as if something supernatural were about one. After we had closed the book, the old man sat down to the organ, and the music sounded as grand, and infinite, and mysterious as what we had been reading. I would give anything if you could hear him. He is deep in Carlyle just now, and after tea I read to him and Madame Schwabe half the evening. He was highly delighted. By the way—to come down from grand things to very ordinary details, which, however, must still get done or the world would fall to pieces—Mrs. Salis-Schwabe said to me that she had heard you were very good, and would I do her a favour with you? I said I would do anything I could for her. Well, it was that I would send you the card of one of her 'protégées,' whom she had known many years, and who is now married and settled in London as a nurse. She understands both French and Italian, and I think German, but of that I am not sure. She is excellent in all ways, and if you have any opportunity I beg you to mention her. She has attended Mrs. ——, and has very high testimonials from medical men. I know it is not a thing much in your way, but still in the calculation of chances it is possible some occasion may arise when the question, 'Do you know of a good nurse?' may be put to you. So I send you the card as requested. Indeed, Mrs. Salis-Schwabe is too good to me for me to decline doing anything she asks; and if you knew her, and saw what a good, kind-natured, hearty, handsome creature she is, you would feel, as I do and as her husband does, that you could refuse her nothing. By the way, I must tell you something about her husband you will feel sympathy with. He has all his life felt an intense interest in the condition of the insane; he has travelled abroad and through England to learn the different modes of treatment. He is one of the trustees to our infirmary, and the insane patients have cause to bless him, for until he came the custom of chaining and beating them was kept up. He has collected, almost alone, 25,000*l.* to build an asylum. He has given immensely to it himself, and taken all the trouble, and now it is finished. You would have almost loved him if you could have heard the wise and kind manner in which he spoke of the sort of superintendent he and the trustees had chosen; he is such a quiet, modest, almost shy man, without one bit of dryness or systematic philanthropy about him. Both he and his wife are such natural, quiet, unpretending people as I have not seen for many a day! We were talking of the asylum and insane patients, and I told him about you, and the influence you had over insane persons. It seemed to make an impression both on him and on the Chevalier. Well now, my dear child, I have bored you, for I have not, like you, the gift of making people take an interest in those they never saw. I can only tell you of the things and people that interest me, and make up the details of 'my life and errors,' as an old Presbyterian wrote. I suffer from a very nasty feeling in my head, as if a mill-wheel were in it, and all the blood at the top of my head. It makes me very stupid. By the way, on due reflection I cannot see my shortcomings in the way of letter-writing. This is the fourth since you were at 'The Grange.' I think so, at least, for I have written every Sunday but one since you went, and then I did not miss willingly, but I was doing hospitality, and not entertaining angels, nor anything related to them. God bless you!

Ever your affectionate

G. E. J.

LETTER 69.

Seaforth, Monday, October 17, 1848.

My dear Jane,—Figure to yourself the state of things here! —— has the gout. He has been very dangerously ill; in fact, when I got here on Thursday he was not out of danger. Two doctors come to him every day, and he cannot be left alone a single moment, night or day. They have got a regular nurse for him. I had no idea I should find him so bad. He is, however, getting round again now, but we are obliged to be very careful, as a relapse would be apt to be fatal. They have been so terrified lest the gout should reach the heart. In addition to all the natural miseries of his condition, he has been severely salivated, and his mouth is quite sore yet from it. He is so weak he cannot bear to hear anyone moving about. I am come at his especial desire, as he had a fancy I could nurse well, which is rather true, it being one of the few useful things I am up to. In addition to all this the coachman (who had been very delicate for a long time) ruptured a large blood-vessel in the lungs one night last week, and is under severe medical treatment. In consequence, I found poor —— nearly worn out, for at the beginning of ——'s illness (before the nurses came) she was in his room all day long, and just on the heels of illness of her own. She has been hardly worked, and is not looking at all well. —— has just dropped asleep, which enables me to write this, and —— has gone to take a shower-bath. I received your letter just before I started to come here. I would have written you a line on the moment, but I had been ill all night—more dead than alive—and writing even a word was quite beyond me. So you will have no letter good for anything till I get home again. This is only to tell you how matters are. I am in the depths of an infernal cold, which makes me ill, and ugly to boot. Carlyle's letter to Mirabeau came here this morning. I, too, have forgotten his address, but have sent it on to the lady at whose house I met him; so he will get it in time. I am very glad to know you are safe at home again, and I should much like to see your room under its rehabilitation. I was wondering why I never got those prints you told me you had sent for my room, but I shall see and fetch them before I leave this! Thanks for them. —— is lecturing in fine style, and I fancy finds it 'very amusing,' like your man with the marmalade! The Socialists have not felt flattered by his portrait of them, and have sent for one of their own men to do it more like 'the angelic original.' I am still in great anxieties about my dear old friend. I fear he is suffering from the confinement to one room, though his sight is now safe. He can see, and the eye is healed, but the notes I receive are so vague that I get little comfort from them. He is not allowed to see anyone yet, and the medical man is such a strong-minded fellow that I know he will hinder anybody from going near him as long as he can. I am glad I am here doing something useful, at any rate.

It is a great nuisance people cannot answer plain questions when one asks them. All my notes are written by the English governess, whose specialty is certainly not letter-writing. I suppose I ought to be grateful to her, for she writes a note, such as it is, every day. It is no good trying to send you an amusing letter. I am as little up to one as my governess, but when my friend is well and I am 'at ease in Zion' once more I will write to better purpose. Don't send that letter till I get home again. I hope you will have comfort of the renewal of your lease on ——, but I fear. How does your new maid-servant go on?

Ever your affectionate

G. E. J.

Has —— sent you a report of his lectures? If not, I will send you the one he sent me.

LETTER 70.

Sunday, November 5, 1848.

My dear Jane,—I wrote you a short note out of a dried-up inkstand, and with a pen that would hardly write, a few days before I left Seaforth. But it was written in ——'s room, and at a moment when I could not make a bustle by going out to seek better things; and even this, written under difficulties, I fear never reached you. I gave it to —— to stamp and send, and she 'put it down a moment'; so, unless some special Providence watched over it, I fear my little venture got swamped amid the chaos of French newspapers, 'Family Heralds,' and business letters which were piled about. If so, it will never be found till there comes a great day of investigation and sweeping after ——'s recovery. Not having heard a word from you so long makes me think that this must have happened. I wish you would write just to say how you are, for it was an entire month last Thursday since I saw the scrape of your pen. So it is my turn this time to complain— if complaining were of any use in this world, except to a very scanty number of primitive souls, who think they must mend when there is any shortcoming proved against them; and these elect are dying off daily, leaving no descendants. Before I left ——. had begun to take a turn towards recovery, though, by what —— writes, it still goes on very slowly. —— is there now; she came to take my place a day or two after I left. I did not write to you last Sunday because I was sent for to Cheetham Hill, the Chevalier[1] being able to see me for the first time since the operation. He progresses very slowly; it has shaken him sadly, but I hope all will be well at last. Except his nerves, which have been a good deal weakened, I don't think his bodily health has suffered

[1] Neukomm.

much; but, as those who have suffered can testify, nerves are everything in the way of comfort and suffering. I hope he will regain a good average sight. The doctor speaks very hopefully. I went to see him again yesterday, and he was decidedly less of an invalid. Really, I begin to think I would rather be without friends altogether—one feels so horribly anxious when anything ails them. It is like getting a large fortune: one begins straightway to fear robbers, casualties, distress, and destitution, which one never thought of whilst one was poor; and, in spite of all the philanthropy one can cultivate, the whole generation might die in peace without disturbing one's sleep in moving anything but one's abstract sympathy. But the instant there is a friend one cares for, the dice are loaded, and one is afraid to trust Providence itself. Have you seen the 'Mémoires d'Outre Tombe,' by Chateaubriand? It is a pity they were finally destined to an after-life—such a poor, rickety, vain, stupid attempt at a biography, and such a theatrical *mise en scène*! I was asking the Chevalier about him; he knew him well, and does not seem to have thought much of him. But just as he was beginning to talk I was fetched away, for he is not allowed to see anyone long at a time. Only fancy! he has heard many chapters of Talleyrand's 'Mémoires.' These he left not to be published for thirty-one years, and you and I

will be dead and buried before we can have a chance
of seeing them; he spoke highly of them; and would
they not be worth reading? I wish the Chevalier
would take a fancy to write his own, for they would
be almost as good—rather better, I should think, for
he is so simple and direct in all he says. By the
way, he has taken a great notion of hearing 'Zoe'
read to him, having heard that it is a most disreputable work, and I am to read it to him as soon
as he is well enough to stand it. Whilst in Liverpool I sent for the two prints—for which many
thanks. I told you this in my last, but repeat it
now, as I want to know whose the portrait is. I
admire the look of it. Amongst 'all the chances
and changes of this mortal life' did I ever tell you
that —— has been sent by —— as his representative to Frankfort, and has been made a Knight of the
Order of St. Lazarus and St. Michael? What a different
world it would be if we did the things we leave undone! Do you (who hear of everybody) know anything of 'Jellachick?' who somehow interests me.
—— (of Bowdon) was here on Thursday. He came
in late, and my brother made him stay all night.
It chanced to be a party, so I saw little of him. He
seems very full of his lectures, which have been well
attended, and there is to be a discussion about them
next Tuesday; he has been expecting Louis Blanc.
I wish you would write to me. I seem to have got

out of your reach altogether, and I want to know
how all things fare with you, from the renewed
face of your room down to the doings of your maid-
servant's 'second advent.' Do write and tell me as
much as you feel you can; at least, let me know
how you are.

Ever yours affectionately,
G. E. JEWSBURY.

LETTER 71.
Sunday, November 13, 1848.

'Cara Mia,'—How do you get on this horrible
weather? It seems there is a perfection in the very
detestable, for when I complain I am met with the
cry of 'fine seasonable weather.' Perhaps it may be
better with you than with us. But I am just getting
desperate—my spirits are seasonable too, down, down,
far below 'change'—floundering in the Slough of
Despond was a joke to it. There is nothing for it
but to go on peaceably sinking, and I will perhaps
find 'ground at the bottom,' as Brian O'Lynn says.
I have thought a great deal of you, for you always
suffer more, every way, than I do. This comes, then,
sympathising, for I have no comfort for you, and no
news either. I have a vision of you lying curled up
on the sofa—pale and miserable-looking, as if the
damp had struck into your very soul, and I can only
hope that —— recollects to bring you a tin of hot

water for your little, cold feet. I wish I were near you, to make you a little comfortable. I sit rolled up in a shawl with my feet one on each hob. —— has bought a new carpet for the other sitting-room where the sofa stands, and I cannot fancy sitting in it, for I am like a cat, and don't take to new furniture —so I sit in an ordinary chair and pity myself exceedingly. Neither can I get any new novels, for which I have a strong appetite now. It is great nonsense when people talk about occupation being a certain method to obtain an always happy result! It is very much like a receipt that I once saw in some cookery-book for preparing a dinner when friends come in unexpectedly and you have nothing in the house. It begins, 'take a good-sized turkey!' Sure enough, a very satisfactory meal is produced. But then, cavilling is contemptible, as all controversialists declare! By the way, I had a letter from —— the other day. She says that she had sent you the caricatures, and as soon as they were gone she was seized with qualms—or, as she says, 'got nervous'—lest you should in the first place think it strange to send you caricatures of people you don't know, and in the next place you should feel annoyed at seeing me caricatured, and by her. She entreated me to tell you that 'I asked you to do them;' and as by another letter to-day she seems really distressed about what you may chance to think, I beg you will hereby understand that I not only 'aided, complied, and abetted'—as indictments say—but actually suggested the same, and gave her free leave to caricature my illustrious self! Of course you are not to translate caricatures 'au pied de la lettre.' As I have not seen them I don't know what they are like, but if they have made you laugh, it was all they were intended for. When this letter will get itself finished Heaven knows! It was begun on Sunday, and this is Tuesday, if day it can be called which light has none. I am nearly asleep, and, for my sins, have the prospect of being obliged to turn out to a 'friendly tea,' there to be stupefied and ennuyée to a pitch that human fortitude shudders to contemplate; and I am going out to dinner to-morrow, and to a party the night after—and all with the pleasant reflection that, however insipid these 'réunions' may prove, the people must, one and all, be angels not to have been affronted and cut my acquaintance long since. Before I close this I must not omit to chronicle a great act of heroism that I perpetrated by my own spontaneous impulse the other night. My brother had gone out of town, and only my damsel and myself were left in the house. I don't know what time it was, but I woke with a noise of a saw working steadily, and, as it seemed, stealthily. I lay and listened for a while, 'reasoning with myself' as —— would say, and then it struck me that it was very ridiculous to let people get into the house just because they felt disposed. So I got up, and, throwing on a shawl, I descended, a grimly ghost, to see for myself what was the matter. The parlours were all safe, and so were the doors. Then I went down into the regions of the kitchen and coal-hole, but all was quite still, and I could not help thinking that if there had been thieves they would have been quite fools to have been frightened away by me. So I went quietly upstairs again, feeling a little bit nervous. The only neighbour I could have hoped to make hear in an emergency is a neighbour who is lying ill of a nervous fever. I looked out of the window, but neither man nor mortal was to be seen. There were stars shining helplessly, and the gaslights gleaming, but nothing at all ' to the purpose.' So, after a little while, as neither the noise nor the thieves came, I got tired of expecting and went to sleep again. I did not come to the consciousness of my own courage till the next night, when, seeing the active inspection of bolts that my brother instituted on hearing my tale, the soothing sensation of my own virtue arose within me, and I have recorded the fact for your admiration. By the way, as I am in a narrating humour I must tell you a little trait that came before me lately. A young lady of my acquaintance, rather addicted to the tender passion, and whose last lover had set sail for New Zealand, leaving her much afflicted at his departure, is on my mind. The vessel in which he sailed has not been heard of since, and she begged me to make some inquiries, for, said she, 'you know, Geraldine, it is no use wasting my feelings, and I should not like to go thinking about him when it is of no use; you see, the uncertainty makes me feel so unsettled! I should like to know one way or other; but I will give him twelve months from the time he sailed, and if he does not write by that time I shall consider myself free, for I should have a very poor opinion of any girl who could go and think of anybody else directly, as it were! I will be faithful as long as it is of any use.' However, it seems more than probable that the vessel is lost, and she has promptly consoled herself with a 'Whiskerando Pole.' I was put into a pair of scales the other day, and weighed—how much do you think?—(surely it was Troy measure, not Avoirdupois)—98 lbs., including a heavy bonnet and shawl, and a dress that I am sure was exactly as much as I could carry. What a little grain one is in the world—if one could only think so! Now really I have no news, and I want this letter to get sealed before I get more hindered. Now good-bye, and God bless you and take care of you. If I hear anything worth telling you, you shall hear it straight away. Now good-bye once more!

Tuesday afternoon.

LETTER 72.

Thursday night (Postmark, December 1, 1848).

Dearest Jane,—I have only time to write a line; but if I don't do it now I know I shall be hindered to-morrow. I turned quite sick to read of Charles Buller's[1] death; his poor mother will die of it too. I feel very glad you have all this nursing and comforting laid upon you. It is a comfort of the best sort to find that anything, even a 'cut,' is the better for us! Don't go letting your poor heart sink, and fancy you would be better dead and out of the way. A great many people are the better for you, and will be the better for you yet. We are no judges of what we are, and just when one is the most broken-up and flung down in one's own eyes, it is just then that something turns up that we are wanted to do; and I fancy no one who is in readiness to embrace the occasion can say with truth and soberness that they are useless. It is only when no inclination or capacity for good exists that people can be spared, and it is just those who think themselves indispensable that the world would soonest be tired of. One-half of those *soi-disant* useful people ought to be turned over to a moral nuisance committee! I could almost be glad of all this trouble which has come to pass; the comfort you give will be returned an hundredfold.

[1] The pupil of Carlyle, who died, full of brilliant promise, in his early manhood.—A. E. I.

Do write me a line when you can to say how poor Mrs. —— is; poor Lady —— too. I had got very weary at the delay in your letter, and fancied you were laid up again. I was just going to write again. I have been very uneasy about ——; he has had a return of his last winter's illness, but I hope it is going off. I am going to Cheetham Hill next week for a few days, if he keeps better, to stay with Mrs. ——. The accounts of poor —— are very unsatisfactory; he has had relapses again, and is about what he was when I left him a month ago, but is fearfully low-spirited. He cannot bear even to have the paper read to him; as to ——, I don't think words will ever touch her. I have tried them. She takes all I have said in excellent part; but in this world we must have feeling brought home to us, or we do not understand it. Sorrow finds us all out, and I fear great sorrows are in store for her to break that audacious hardness and mellow it into a virtue. I know that her presumptuous, hard judgment gives both her father and mother great pain. —— has lamented over it to me, but no exhortations, if even they came from St. Chrysostom himself, would touch her. It must be experience. I have great hope that she will turn out well; she has strength, and that is the main thing. She will have the grace to be ashamed of her childish presumption when she finds how small a basis of knowledge she has to go on,

T

and the mistakes she makes. My candle is going out. This letter is hardly worth sending, but Heaven knows when I could send a better! Take care of yourself. God bless you, and Good night. Though I am far from wishing to put any sort of pressure on you, yet I would be glad if you were brought here. It would do you good, and I would rejoice to receive you.

Yours ever,
G. E. J.

1849.

LETTER 73.

(Postmark, January 10, 1849.)

My dear Jane,—I have just been writing to Carlyle to thank him for his New Year's gift, which it was very good of him to send. If you could have foreseen all the fine new editions it would go through at the time you came up first to London, and nobody would take it; and yet all the desire of one's heart seems to come in a shape one cannot make use of. Is it our own want of skill, or is it the want of intrinsic value in the things themselves? I don't know; but I have got up this morning before anybody else, and my fire was not laid last night, so I am writing this under very shivering auspices. But the fact is, I have given in to a shameful, lazy, good-for-nothingness lately, and this morning I woke up in a better fashion, and, being minded to get up, I would not let the brisk inspiration be lost for the small want of a fire. But it is cold, so that will explain all the jerking shape of my letters. I did not go to my grand ball after all, and thankful now I am, for my brother has caught another cold, and has been in the house some days. It came to him whilst he was after his lawful business; but if it had followed his going out with me, I should have reproached myself. Jenny Lind, who was the great attraction, sang three songs; but I went to see the Chevalier the day after, and he gave me some music on the organ, which made up for all the songs she could sing. When I hear his music I feel so ashamed of all the little sordid feelings in which I have lived; both the pleasures and annoyances that have moved me seem so little and foolish, that I wonder how I can ever give in to vain or bitter feelings again. I can quite believe in Saul and David. I am afraid he[1] is going away soon, and then God knows when I shall hear him again! Do you remember those lines in Milton's 'Hymn on the Nativity'?

> For if such heavenly song
> Enwrap our senses long,
> Time would run back and fetch the age of Gold;
> And speckled vanity
> Would sicken soon and die,
> And lep'rous sin would melt from earthly mould.

I never felt what they meant before. I wish you could hear him; but as you cannot, it is no use talking about it. I want to know how you are—body and soul; is that dreadful sickness gone? How are you, in short? and how is ——? and how does your servant go on? I have got a cold and sore-

[1] The Chevalier Neukomm.

throat, and if it is not well to-night I shall try what a wet bandage will do towards bringing it to its senses. I tried one on —— last night. —— told me vaguely that —— had left his charge suddenly. Is it so? Have you heard where he is gone? You will feel very anxious if it is so, as I fear from ——'s manner of speaking that it is a return of his old wildness. I have often thought of him when hearing of those political commotions, and feared for his sanity. He is a noble creature, and it is heart-breaking that all his fine qualities should have gone into chaos; it seems as if there were only the smallest touch needed to make the highest wisdom mad, and the wildest madness wise. This, the only thing of consequence in this letter, comes, as you see, at the tail of all. God bless you, and help you in all your need!

G. E. J.

LETTER 74.

Friday (Postmark, January 12, 1849).

My dear Jane,—Your letter has come, and, of course, was burnt directly. I only wish —— and that other person could be served the same. It is something enormous to see how men may lie, and yet keep their fame and go current as 'honourable men.' They cannot know what they do, or surely they would set some limits to their recklessness of speech.

The world allows them great latitude; but even so, these men have proved themselves scoundrels, and utterly unfit to be received into the pale of society. I say nothing as to what gentlemen ought to be, but as men they are infamous. The name of one, at least, will suffer, because, as in the chance and change of things, I may come in contact with him; I shall speak the truth to him if I can only get the chance. Why, he is worse than ——, who had the excuse of being more mad than sane. Is there no way of making people amenable to common decency, if no other feeling can touch them? I do not call it, with you, 'a tempest in a teapot'; I am bitterly indignant; I cannot tell you the shock it has given me. It opens up such an abyss of wickedness and cruelty and heartlessness as turns me sick! How is one to live in such a world? It seems like a very 'babe in the wood' to wring one's hands over the world's wickedness, but this is something beyond the bounds; it is at these times that one's own self-respect outweighs all that man, or woman either, can say. It is not in the power of such coarse, lying natures to do you any outward harm, but I feel bitterly the sting it will have for you, of which they do not dream. I have no words to express all the indignation that is boiling within me. Bah! that such creatures have a right to decide on a woman's good name; it is enough to make one trample it under one's feet as a thing utterly worthless when held by their permission. I am quite sure I feel more about it than you do, not for the slur on female purity, but for the loathsome insight into the position women stand in. Why, the very form of the thing is enough to make a woman fold her arms and assert her perfect right to dispose of herself in any way she chooses. I have no temper to write; I feel an intense indignation that you have been the subject of such a lying legend, but I feel as if the whole sex had been injured at the same time. I'll be hanged if I don't ease my mind in the next book I write! I have not felt so indignant in my life, and I wish I were a man for five minutes to kick them—*ma foi, ma foi!* I will have a little bit of 'settling' yet; if I cannot do that I can preach a gospel—a set of lying, hypocritical beggars! Well, it's no good swearing—only, I am angry, and it eases my mind. Do not let it make you regret anything you have done which your heart tells you was well and honestly done. The result does not lie in our province: we can only set ourselves in what seems the right path; the event lies with God, and He accepts the intention, and burns up all that may be defective in the execution. Therefore do not let your heart turn to bitterness against yourself, even though you may see how and where you might have done wiser. Yet true wisdom is not to depreciate what you did believing it to be for good, and how can you know that it has not been for such? Be firm and of good courage to abide by your own act. Is there a step we would any of us take over again in precisely the same manner? I remember once hearing a very good and a very wise woman say, 'I believe God always allows us to suffer by the particular virtue on which we pride ourselves. I used to pride myself on my good-sense, and He has allowed me to fail most signally, so that all my acquaintance can point to me as a warning. But I accepted it as a chastisement for my complacency!' She was a woman of very strong mind and singular good-sense, but she made an ill-advised marriage, led by some high, transcendental motive, which she conceived to supersede ordinary rules. My dear child, do not put a sword in your own heart to aggravate anything you have done. Insomuch as you thought it right, *it was right*. Let me hear from you what were the other things you had to say. I have no news, except that I have got a cold and have deserved it, and I have fairly begun a new book—settled the principle of it, and got it nearly worked clear as a programme, and I shall now work like the Devil. I feel relieved as from a nightmare now my work lies straight ahead. I woke up the other morning with an idea. When I have done a chapter or two I will send them to you. I hope to keep clear of scandal in it, but, in fact, at

this moment I feel tempted to go and preach at
Paul's Cross many things which would rather startle
Messrs. —— & Co. Thanks for the good intentions
to the ——. Did I ever tell you that man[1] has
travelled all over Europe to learn details about the
treatment of insane people, and has built an hospital
here, where the treatment is to be quite on new
principles? He collected of his own exertions and
contributions 25,000*l*. . . .

[Unfinished.]

LETTER 75.

Tuesday (Postmark, February 19, 1849).

My dear Jane,—It is precious little good you will
get out of a letter from me to-day! I am mesmerised
by my 'entourage,' and feel as if I could not even sit
on a chair in peace. I have two visitors, both relations: one a very comfortable, good woman, whom I
like; the other a large, bony, uncomfortable person,
who never can get into the right place, and is always
in the way, and makes a room look untenantable by
the mere fact of her being in it. She pulls the chairs
and tables out of their places, and is as restless as a
great bird fluttering about, so you may fancy if I am
possessing my soul either in peace or patience. Lewes
is still lecturing here; I have not been to hear him
yet, from having no one to go with me. He went to

[1] Mr. Salis-Schwabe.

see Mr. ———'s works the other day, and stayed there. He takes extremely well to the people here, and they all seem to like him. He and ——— are become very good friends. I like him so much better than I thought I should in London when I saw him; he really is a good fellow. ——— came over for a day to see me this last week; she is not yet allowed to read or write, but her eye is quite recovered now, as far as appearance goes; it might have been a most serious thing. As for poor ———, he is just at the end of another attack. Figure to yourself that he had not been dressed for five months. I do wish ——— had more feeling. What trouble lies before her; for those hard natures are always broken sooner or later. She wrote me a letter instead of her mother one day, who could not write, and I was quite pained by the callous tone throughout. ——— is very poorly, and business worries him. I am trying to persuade him to go from home for a little while. I want very much to know how you are, in all ways. Do write to me; you would do so if you knew how much I desire to hear. We are going to a grand concert at Mrs. Salis-Schwabe's[1] to-morrow, given by her in honour of

---

[1] This honoured lady frequently entertained Jenny Lind (the late Madame Lind-Goldschmidt), with other eminent representatives of music, art, and literature. Her hospitable home at Crumpsall, near Manchester, attracted all the cream of talent which came near enough to enter those princely and cordial gates. Her husband, the late Mr. Salis-Schwabe, sympathised with all his wife's fine tastes, and was much beloved.—A. E. I.

her husband's birthday, and it is to be a surprise to him. Fancy the poor man going innocently into his drawing-room, and finding it full of people, all come to do him honour, and themselves pleasure! And he will take it as it is meant, and be as pleased as she can wish. This letter is not worth the postage, so I send you a note —— wrote me, which made me laugh, and will perhaps do as much for you. Now good-bye, and believe me, whether bright or stupid, to remain

Your affectionate

G. E. J.

LETTER 76.

Sunday (Postmark, March 5, 1849).

My dear Jane,—If you want to know the reason why I have not written, it is that I have been dead-stupid, and as to writing a letter worth reading, I could as soon have 'jumped over the moon,' but not a dog would have laughed at it. It is very odd, but I was thinking of —— only the day, before your letter came, and thinking that the Devil had been singularly forbearing if he had not 'marked her for his own' during her absence. However, you have kept in a state of salvation many years longer than the time originally fixed by destiny. The dial of ——, like that of King Ahaz, went ten degrees backward, but, you see, she has fetched it up. However, as

you have picked up a jewel by the way, I can send
you nothing but congratulations, double-edged, at
being off with the old and on with the new. Lewes
is making a prodigious sensation down here, only his
moustachios have hurt people's sense of propriety, and
nothing but the report of his wife, and an unascer-
tained amount of family, could have stood against
them. People here are morbid about moustachios.
He might have brought a 'harem' with less scandal.
Still, he is a great favourite in spite of them. Dear
Mrs. —— has taken him in great favour, and I like
him extremely. I think there is a great deal of
genuine kindness at the bottom, and there is a
geniality I enjoy amazingly. He and —— are great
friends. He has taken to —— extremely, and will not
hear one word in qualification, even from me. He
declares she is 'a rich organisation.' Poor ——
is still very ill; he was on the point of another relapse
when Lewes was last there. If you wanted to do a
real good deed—from which you might triumphantly
appeal to Providence when it ill-treated you—you
would write him a letter 'all to himself.' They are
the only things he cares for; he is past reading or
hearing read the newspapers. I read your last letter
to the 'Chevalier,' who, delighted in it, would have
it over twice, and declared that it was the best piece
of description he had ever read. Mrs. —— gave me
a long message to you, which she insisted on my repeat-

ing 'verbatim'; but as I can't, you must take the substance, which is that she and Mr. —— are very anxious that you and Mr. Carlyle should come and stay with them—that it would do you good; and I am sure that it would do me good for you to come. So send us some sort of hope, please! —— was here calling on Friday, but I was out at Cheetham Hill, and so did not see him. As to more chapters, the 'Chevalier' is going away in a few weeks, and then you will get more, but I am with him a good deal at present. I can write books when I cannot have him, and I am getting more than I am losing; in other words, it is very good for me to go there. I will, however, send you something very soon. The other day I received wedding-cards from Madame —— somebody ——! She is married, and gone to live in Paris, on a basis of 'George Sand.' Ireland[1] gave me a picture of Carlyle the other day. What a disagreeable likeness it is! I should fancy it is how he looked when he came home and —— would not open the door. I flatter myself this would have been a better letter than it is, only Mrs. —— came in—the wife of the child born in the Reign of Terror who never came to his full senses! He is now travelling in the East, and she came to read a long letter from him, and I think that has absorbed the little sense I had. —— sends his love to you; —— is very poorly.

[1] Mr. Alexander Ireland.

—— dined here the other day to meet Lewes. He seemed misanthropical and flat, as I am now.

There is a secret I want dreadfully to tell you, and I must not, and I am like one of those bottles of wine with a cork in the throat of them. It stops the way of everything else; it is burning my paper, my pen, and my tongue, and it would make this letter explode like detonating powder if I might only put it in the postscript! I can hear the claps with which your two little hands would go together, and the exclamations that would follow. —— sends you his best love without qualification.

Affectionately yours,

G. E. J.

LETTER 77.

[Presumably from Mrs. Salis-Schwabe's house.]

Crumpsall House, March 29, 1849.

My dear Jane,—Here is an hour in which I am left to myself entirely, so I give you the benefit of it—to comfort my soul by abusing you; for if I don't get a better letter from you, or at least a letter with something in it, you may pass 'a month of Sundays' at breakfast without any letter from me. I want to know how you are in bodily health. You are going on pretty well in your worldly matters, I can see; you always have a certain tone when you are 'well-to-do in Zion' which is

good for telling that, if it is for nothing else; but
still I would have been as glad to have some news
of you after such a long silence as to be scolded
about a matter which was a harmless caricature.
Never abuse 'surfaces'; cream lies at the top, and
there is nothing but skimmed milk underneath;
and, besides, the surface is the result of all that
is gone before, and is generally the best worth
seeing. As far as I am concerned, my surface is
like those strata which go down all the same as
deep as people can dig below, so it is not much
worth exploring. I could not help laughing at
your assertion that I keep all sealed up with Solomon's seal. I have actually and literally told you
all there has been to tell, what has filled up my
days and my hours, and because it has been simply
barren, you think I have secreted the crops, when
in fact none have been grown. I come here much
of my time, and shall do so as long as the Chevalier[1]
stays, and when he goes I shall be very sorry. He
has begun the almost impracticable task of making
me speak French correctly, a feat I have never
achieved in English, and when I am at home I have
often been in a dead-fix about my writing. I think
the simple mystery of my existence just now—
(your letter forced me to a self-examination)—is
that I am 'bone lazy,' as my nurse used to phrase

[1] Neukomm.

it. But I have great faith in 'lying fallow,' and when I have a spell of laziness on me I follow it religiously, looking on it as the Orientals do on idiots—as an inscrutable manifestation of the Deity. I am sure I am glad to hear that a good novel is coming out. I want to read one sadly. I was not grateful for 'Jane Eyre.' I did not take to it somehow. I wish Lewes would write another. I like his very much. He is coming back again for his play, which is to come out after Easter, and I shall be quite glad to see him again. I took to him like a relation. He and —— have sworn everlasting friendship. You really ought to come down amongst us again; you would see how the warmth of your presence would dry up all the marshy exhalations. And how you would enjoy it! As for me, be quite sure we should prosper; we are always glad in each other when we see one another. It is in absence that all the mischief arises—in the night the enemy sows tares; so just come, and send obstacles to the Devil; but you will be seeing Mrs. ——. I had an event the other night. I went to hear the 'Creation,' the very grandest thing in the shape of music I can conceive. It seemed to take one into a new world of sounds; it broke one up altogether, and called one out of oneself, possessed one like a new spirit. It was music that had nothing to do with passion or emotion, but when it was over one felt as if one had been

banished to a realm of common things, without
sunshine, and nothing but an east wind. I have been
miserable ever since, as I used to be, when a child,
after a great pleasure. Jenny Lind sang very wonderfully, but the music itself swallowed up all she
did. One never thought of her, at least I did not. She
seemed to do what she was wanted to do, nothing
more. The music was too grand to let anything else be
thought of. There was a prayer, an old Catholic one,
which I wish you could have heard. It was Per-
golesi's 'Lord, have mercy upon me, for I am in
trouble.' It went down to one's inmost soul. Jenny
sang a very wonderful song, a sort of 'Cheval de
Bataille,' about the 'Bright Seraphin,' but it did
not touch anything but my organ of wonder. Here
I am interrupted, so good-bye, and write me a good
letter, and not a perverse one!

Yours,

G. E. J.

LETTER 78.

August 20, 1849.

My dear Jane,—When are you coming to me? I
am looking for you, and hoping for you, so do not
delay much longer, or I shall be out of all patience;
and why the Devil don't you write to me! Your
letters are always scarce enough, and now you are

making quite a famine of them. Do write, and, above all, say when you can come. I intended to have written yesterday, but was hindered by people to dinner. How are you? I am not at all well; I have a constant, dull, heavy pressure on the top and back of my head. I have not felt well this long while, and yet I don't know what can or ought to ail me. My tale is progressing, and —— says it is interestingly innocent. I am sure it is, and I want you to read it, to see if, as the homœopathic cookery-books assert, 'the most savoury ragouts can be made without pepper.' (A small kitten is running up and down my dress, playing with my pen, and amusing itself in various ways at my expense, and yours too, for you will never read this.) I want very much to know how you are, and how you continue to go on. I wish you would write me a real good proper letter, with some information about yourself in it. Only fancy, in two days it will be my birthday! Do you remember that one you spent here—when we went to Dunham Park, and in the evening to hear that Delilah-like woman sing? What was her name? She shocked all our notions of womanly decency. I wish you would be here for this birthday, but that cannot be according to the laws of time and space. I am not half so happy as I was this time last year. But bad spirits, like bad weather, do not last for ever, it is a comfort, and I am looking out for a brighter season. Birthdays are nasty high-water marks. One just sees how far the tide has receded, and all the sand-banks on which one has a chance of getting stranded. I am deep in Hungarian reading—such a fine, noble set of people as they are.

Did I tell you that our meeting of sympathy came off with *éclat*? but they were all men. I tried to go, but there was not a woman in the place, so it was too strong for me to go as *femme sole*, representative of the women of England. But, really, a meeting all of men looks a deal more imposing than when interspersed with white pocket-handkerchiefs. I had just a glimpse (for tickets were sent me), and such a surface of upturned, rough faces was very stirring. They had all left their business to come, and every presence there meant something, for each had come at a personal sacrifice of time and convenience. The people were very civil, and as I declined going in when I found how it was, a gentleman most gallantly took me and Mrs. ——, who was with me, into the Council Room behind the platform, and opened the door; but as we could only hear one word in five, we soon retired. I would do anything to help them. Have you heard anything of Mazzini? Mrs. —— has come home again. I am trying to tempt her over for a sort of 'swarry' in honour of Goethe, which some people are getting up. If she does not come, I have an idea that my headache will be supernaturally bad for that evening, and that I shall go to bed instead. I wish you would be here for it. I daresay there would be some fun, and, besides, the 'Lieder-tafel' have promised to sing, and that is worth something. I am going out to-night to meet the author of 'Nemesis of Faith,' a very nice, natural young man, though rather like 'a lost sheep' at present. He has only been used to the Oxford part of the world, so that sectarians and unbelievers are strange to him. He is engaged to be married to a very handsome woman of good family and good fortune, a sister of ——'s. —— is not at all well. —— is gone to see Mr. ——. Only think, a sober, reputable Scotchman—Mr. ——, no less—wrote to me the other day his gratitude for the loan of 'Lucrezia Floriani,' declaring that he had known many Lucrezias, and that Madame Sand had shown her profound knowledge of the human heart. Pretty well, upon my honour! Codes of morality require revising as well as codes of religion, it seems. My head is so heavy and surging that I must lie down. This letter is only written on the Christian principle of 'heaping coals of fire upon your head,' which I hope will burn bright and make you miserable till you write to say when you are coming to your affectionate

G. E. J.

LETTER 79.

Queen's Hotel, Saturday (Postmark, September 6, 1849).

My dear Jane,—I have seen old ——; his servant was out, but the nurse let me in. He is not much changed in appearance, but he is very feeble. He spoke quite rationally, and desired me to tell you that he is most grateful to you for sending to inquire after him; that, of all people, you are the one he most desires to see, but that he is not up to speaking to you, and that he will communicate with you as soon as he can. The servant, ——, says he is much better, but that at times he does not recognise him, and though he knows, he cannot express what he means. He is not able to be removed, and will not be for a fortnight at least. Those are his servant's own words. The doctors are very kind to him, and they say a fortnight will decide everything. Captain —— has been down for a day, but was obliged to leave again. The old man wants for nothing, and is well attended to. I offered to go and see him from time to time, and —— said that a little company did him good occasionally, and that if I would come, I might sit with him when he was 'up to it.' So I am to come on Monday, at eleven o'clock, on speculation. Poor old man! I am really sorry for him, and will do anything I can. One thing I can set at rest for you—viz., do not come over on purpose to see him. I don't think he would like to be seen by you in his 'humiliated condition,' as he calls it, and he is made very comfortable as things go, so there is no sort of necessity. Mr. and Mrs. —— have been very kind, but are now out of town. On the whole, Mr. ——'s letter was not so foolish as it seemed. He could say nothing more than he did say—viz., that you are not needed. I can speak from my own eyes and positive knowledge to the same effect. . . .

[Disconnected.]

. . . If you were always here, of course you might see him as much as you liked, but there would be no good in coming over; and even when he is able to be removed, 'no stranger can go with him,' he is so ill; so the servant told me. What it is I don't know. I did not remain two minutes in his room; he was in bed, but —— says that he sits up a little every day, at eleven o'clock, when his grandson sees him. I will write to you again on Monday, and tell you whether I have seen him. Poor old fellow! he looked so like my father when he was lying in bed that I was quite startled. He had, it seems, been over-fatigued with travelling for several days previously, and the doctors say his attack arose from that. He had been told of your first message, and expressed himself very grateful, but said just what —— told you. This is a confused letter, but two hours on the railway and no dinner have made me very faint, and I can write no better. I will write again on Monday. God bless you!

Ever yours,

G. E. J.

LETTER 80.

Friday (Postmark, September 21, 1849).

Dearest Jane,—I was looking out for the postman very anxiously, and in due time he brought me my own envelope, as a sign of your safe arrival, somehow, in London. I thought that would pacify me, but it has only made me more impatient and restless to know in what state you arrived. It seems only a moment ago that the train started with you—as if I could put back my hand and snatch your's to me again, and seeing my own writing again was just as if the ghost of yesterday morning had really appeared. I wish you would get someone who knows how to write to me to say how you are, for I don't want you to be bothered with letter-writing, and yet I don't want to wait for tidings. I feel as if I must have seemed very cold and indifferent whilst you were suffering, but you know it was not so. There are many things I wanted to tell you, and I cannot write them this morning. I am too 'dished,' partly because those people stopped till after twelve last night, and partly that I 'dished' myself this morning with strong tea, which has shaken

out of me all I have thought since you went. ——
and —— were both very anxious about you, and I
shall call and tell —— my news as I go into the
town. I had ——'s letter after you left, and I sent it
you, and its enclosure. If you have read Newman's
'Soul,' you will laugh at the notion of Lewes's finding
it so sublime. For all the world, that book is like that
story of the lady in captivity who picked to pieces
some old tapestry, and with the faded and moulder-
ing threads worked an emblem of her own sorrows.[1]
It is the ghost of a book. As to ——, I hope you
will get more good out of his philosophy than I do.
The fact is, that when Lewes got that cursed article,
he said it would scandalise every review but ——'s
(who, however, pays nothing, or at best next to nothing,
for I suppose contraband notions are sold in the same
market as stolen goods). So, finally, to —— it was
sent, and ten pounds asked. He declined it on the
score of being full, and that by Christmas the subject
would be 'passé,' which it cannot be, for the subject,
unhappily, is going on, and the problem won't be
solved, this long while, at least, of 'Modern Scepticism
and Modern Belief.' So I wrote back to say that as
Lewes thought it was the ten pounds which made the
obstacle, in the Devil's name to let him have it gratis,
on condition it was printed this next number. So

[1] Possibly the daughter of Louis XVI., afterwards 'Duchesse
d'Angoulême,' during her cruel imprisonment in the ' Temple.'—A. E. I.

now you may appreciate his 'Dissolving Views.' The article, I know, has some good things in it. I did it as well as I could, although, like young actors and young singers (I mean beginners), I can truly say I wore out a deal more force than the result indicates, and I want an article in print as 'a specimen of my handwriting.' I have not let —— see it, because, though I am sure it is all as natural as the day, yet, as the 'Correspondence philosophe et réligieuse,' the ' Père's ' last book, printed for private circulation, is taken as the type of the modern tendency of 'belief,' and the ' Nemesis of Faith,' and all that sort of thing, as the type of the *other*, I think he would rather I had not meddled with either; though it was a comfort to my soul to 'say my say,' and I am sure it was all true, and, to my thinking, more like a sermon than a scandal. So, if it had not been for the vexation of not getting more money, I should have laughed at ——'s note, and felt obliged to him for 'doing' such a correspondence. When I write to him I shall send you the note for counsel. It is a shame to talk on at this rate, and I am haunted by the idea that you are in for another day of suffering. For Heaven's sake, don't waste your strength in struggling against obstacles which seem stronger than you are! You have enough of all kinds of suffering to endure without cutting yourself to pieces for people who are too idle to amuse themselves, and only want some teetotal substitute for the excitement of dram-drinking. Let them go to the Devil! You have enough to bear of your own. Do not, for God's sake, spend all your remaining strength, but retire whilst you have an existence left! Those who love you don't care a pin for your social excellences. You are *you*, and that is all they want. As to the others, who only want you to lighten their fog, let them go elsewhere, but do not spend your strength for naught! I am so thankful for the few days we have had together that I cannot be very troubled by anything that may now happen to me. It is like receiving back a loss with compound interest. God bless you, and send you better!

Ever your own, as ever,
G. E. J.

[September, 1849, after one of Mrs. Carlyle's visits to Manchester.]

LETTER 81.

Sunday (Postmark, September 27, 1849).

Dearest Jane,—I was very glad to get your tiny note. Don't write till you are quite better. I will not have you waste your little strength in letter-writing. I have thought a great deal about your headache since you were here, and I do most earnestly entreat you to consult either Dr. Elliotson or Locock;[1] but Elliotson has an inspiration for knowing what ails people. I don't recommend you to let him try

[1] Sir Charles.

to cure you—his treatment is too strong; but do not
go on in ignorance. 'If you must perish, perish in
the light.' Do try to get well. I am of Carlyle's
persuasion, that the darkest hour is past, and that
there is light coming if our mistakes have been
cleared up and cleared away, along with their train
of aggravations and collateral sufferings. I am sure
there is no need to despair of anything, of yourself
least of all; the one thing needful is, that you take
care of yourself. I had a great deal I wanted to say,
but this morning my head is very painful, as well as
stupid; but that is not supernatural, for we went to
Franconi's last night, and this morning, instead of
getting up I lay in bed giving wise counsel to ——,
who came yesterday. She is a very nice, natural
girl, and has a world of good-sense. I do not believe
she has any more love for —— than we have; she
speaks of him quietly and sensibly, and with no
blushes of confusion, that I can see; in short, she has
been looked at through a Seaforth mist, which is re-
fracting, as you know. Oh! I had such a ridiculous
evening on Friday. I dined at the ——s, to
meet Mrs. Follen—Gambardella's heroine. She is a
nice, mild-looking woman, whom Nature once intended to be agreeable and good, but her 'circle'
have surrounded her with so much adulation that she
can neither move nor speak without an emphasis of
'superiority,' which makes the least action look as

if it were a specimen of some 'tesselated pavement' fit for a museum, and not a pebble is to be found in its natural state. Everything has been weighed, polished, arranged, and labelled. And then her conversation was elocution, and flowed on like a river of oil, which fairly carried me 'povera' away in the flood. And yet Nature did her best to make Mrs. —— a very charming woman, only poor Nature was sadly thwarted. Only figure to yourself my perplexity when Mrs. —— began to come out strong about 'hanging.' Some 'Nemesis' had driven her to travel in the same train with the man who hanged Gleeson Wilson. He was in the next carriage to her, and, of course, people looked very hard at him. And did she not talk me down because I said I hoped Mrs. Manning[1] would be safely hanged before the 'drop' was abolished. I am sure I felt very sorry for the Jews and heathens who have missionaries sent to preach at them and touch their feelings. I never felt so aggravated in all my life as I did at her pathetic appeals to my 'sense of humanity,' and her proposal that some humane person should 'take charge' of Mrs. Manning, and bring her to a sense of her conscience. —— hereupon laughed, and said that Mrs. Manning had a far better prospect of doing well in the next world than of doing any good in this. Don't say that man has no fun in him. Well, finally, though

[1] The murderess.

this letter was begun on Saturday, it is Wednesday
to-day. This time last week you were lying ill with
your head. I hope to Heaven that you are better off
to-day! Carlyle wrote me a very kind note. You
see, you might have stopped quite well to the end of
the week, and it would have been such a comfort to
me. It is so long since we were really together. By
the way, I have not written to —— since you left.
She must get miserable again before I can write;
when she is 'at ease in Zion' I feel out of all patience
somehow. I have written to invite little —— to come
over for a couple of days, and I am racketing about
with —— in grand style. I suppose the exercise
and air are good for me, and I am so disgusted about
my 'tale,' that if I can break the engagement I will.
Only fancy, after all the bother they made, and hurrying me as they did, they won't now print it till
January. I am just disgusted! I was 'left to
myself' when I undertook to have any dealings with
them. —— is not well, but I suppose he is amused
at having a visitor, and so is in a better fashion. He
regretted your absence, especially when he found you
might have stayed. By the way, I must not forget
one thing I want to tell you. Mrs. —— said that
some tribes of Indians want to be civilised, and to
have 'constitutions,' and when I said, 'Oh! I hope
they will keep to their costume,' she said, with mild
wisdom, 'You surely would not wish them to keep

their blankets! Nor will they ever become civilised till they adopt a dress which is not open to such serious objections; few families would like to admit them to their society in their present costume.' So you see 'breeches' are the first principle of civilised life; and at Franconi's I could not help being struck with a slight indication of that 'indispensable' which satisfied the 'feelings of society.' This is a stupid letter, but I am not up to writing more, and am vexed and worried; so good-bye, and God bless you, and send you well.

Ever your affectionate
G. E. J.

LETTER 82.
Friday morning, night, and Saturday.

My dear Child,—What a wonderful being a clever woman is! To think that I should just now, 'at this period of the debate,' have discovered for the first time that it was better to wait for the season when time and strength set in for a regular letter. Good Heaven! if you only knew how anxious I am to know every minute how you go on, and how you feel, and how very little I care for 'good letters,' you would never waste another upon me. Just scratch me a line as often as you can, even if it be only a sentence you want to say, and send it without feeling any moral obligation to fill the paper. I will send you a quantity of stamped adhesive envelopes, and then all the material bother of sealing, &c., will be done away with. At first I was in a great rage with that remarkable woman for interrupting you in the middle of your letter to me. Then I got into a worse rage at finding it had been burned. Why could you not have begun another, and sent the fragment on its own basis ? Just as if I did not know well enough how gold and purple clouds of sunset change into leaden-coloured mists, and no fault to the sun. And then I thought that perhaps she might have come to you for some comfort in her perplexity, and then I got very placable towards her. I am more shocked at the mode in which she lives with her ' lawful love ' than with anything else. It is the common instinct of human nature to say so. No system of philosophy, either Satanic or transcendental, can make it otherwise. As to the man himself, there is a point at which virtue becomes vice, and *vice versâ*, and his pusillanimity in shrinking from the inconvenience and terrible disagreeableness of ' making a row ' coincides with his good-nature. People like him always slide into what comes handiest. And then he has filed down the edge of his feelings by the dreadful promiscuousness of his way of talking of everything to everybody. It is an experience he will put in a novel some day—or might do ! . . . .

[Disconnected.]

The thing you intended for the best and noblest dedication of yourself has not borne the fruit you have reason to expect. Dear friend, do not let yourself be made bitter by this trial. Yield yourself up, and bow your head to Him who is the Father and Director of all. Don't worry yourself by thinking over all you might have been, if you only can resign yourself into His hands (to no earthly or second cause), but accept as from His hands this humiliation of not having any visible, successful result of the great step of your life. Yield yourself and your sword to Him, and do not fight any more, and all the bitterness and the poisoned suffering will pass away, and strength and healing will descend upon you. It is not with men you have to deal. Look away from human beings. You are in the hands of God, the Master of all, and it is to Him you submit. He is your Judge. It is a small thing to you to be judged of man's judgment, to be understood or misunderstood. Leave husband, friends, all alone, and resign your destiny to Him, to do with you what seems good unto Him, and you will find your sorrows cease and your way made plain. Do not degrade yourself by any second motive. I cannot describe the state of mind I mean, but I only know that more than once in my life I have thus flung myself, broken, helpless, and prostrate. Destiny only meant that I might be in His hands. I cannot describe; it has been like being taken into the invisible world, and all the littlenesses and the pitiful things are broken down which separated me from Him. It has been rest and healing, and everything one's shattered being needed. One gets hard again, and sets up for oneself. One has to come out of this mysterious sanctuary; but one comes out able to go on, and then it is there, and a time of need opens it to one again. I have tried to say this to you more than once, and I cannot express myself, and you will be weary of hearing it; but I don't want you to think I am using mere words in a vague sense. If I could only say something which should move your heart to feel as I do! One hears things very often without attaching any meaning to them, and then, some fine day, after listening for the fifteenth time, a meaning flashes upon one; and so that is my excuse, but I tell you nothing but the most statistical matter of fact. Do not be out of patience with me, or think I want to preach. . . .

Saturday night.

This is the third time I have been interrupted in this letter. If I were to read it over, no doubt I should put it into the fire; but I shall not do so, and you must take what you get. I have been out all day. —— has a whist-party, and I am writing in the midst of the aces of diamonds and clubs, and what not! There is a heap of things I want to say, if I only

x

could think of them. I like that poem; indeed, I like all those you ever showed me by ———. My dear child, my conclusion of the whole matter is, that you may be trusted to manage all your own affairs, and good advice, the very superfinest and best, would only mislead you, if you were to take it. Now, is not that generous, considering my turn for giving advice? I feel quite easy about what you say, and you will and must get good of some sort out of such really generous devotion, which it is, in spite of drawbacks.

The only thing I don't like in your letters is, that you do not seem disposed to come here to us, and I had made up my mind that you would. It is all nonsense what you say about 'generosity,' and so forth. Don't get that into your head. I want you to come here, so, for God's sake, don't take into account any other consideration than how to get here! Will you promise me not to do anything till you have been here? What do you think I am doing in the way of handiwork? You will never guess. I am making blue petticoats to frighten away the cholera. It's not often I do anything for poor people, but my feelings were roused to think that the 'house-to-house' visitation was to give the poor wretches physic, and I thought if one only could go from house to house with clothing it would be more practical. . . . .

October 19, 1849.

[Fragment.]

LETTER 83.

Thursday night (Postmark, October 26, 1849).

How nice it is to get your tiny scrap! The reason of my Sunday failure? The Devil kept me in bed very late, and then he came in the shape of Dr. —— to take us a long walk, and then the people came without end till bedtime. Among the rest came ——, who was extremely—what shall I say ?— companionable and communicative; and then I went to bed, and 'slept the sleep of the just.' I am obliged to get things done and written as I can, and I think letters to you, and then forget that I have not written them. I want to know how you are. How much I wish we had an electric telegraph apiece. Well, finally, Mrs. Tom [1] is come home looking really very handsome, and a deal more amiable than when she went away, and Tom told me that Miss —— had made up her mind, and accepted ——, who does not know this exactly, and is still balancing in his own mind what he shall do, while the thing is done for him. I feel to like the girl a great deal better now I know this; indeed, I feel quite amiable towards her. And as to the young man, he is a very good fellow, and I don't know that I would have refused him myself. You are a real darling to like my old friend, though I fancy the love

[1] Her sister-in-law, Mrs. Thomas Jewsbury.

was most on my side. I have actually not written to him this age, but he will stand a little starving. It used to be such a white day for him when I had one of your letters to read to him—he used to appreciate them. He did me a world of good; but what touched my heart most of all was a little sentence about me in a letter to Mrs. ——, and not intended for me to see. Would it amuse you to see the 'memoirs' we wrote together? But had he not used to tell me nice tales, and then wind up with 'Mais, ma chère, ces choses ne s'écrivent point'? He was a darling when he was in a bad temper, because then he used to abuse people so wittily.

Mr. —— has begun his paper. Have you seen it? He sent to ask me to write him an article on 'The Influence of Cheap Literature on the Female Mind.' What the Devil is its influence? I'll send it to you if it turns out anything, but my head is so crazy that I doubt if I can ever write more. It is coming off now: my head, not the article. God bless you, dear love.

G.

Yesterday was a public fast-day, and felt to me like Sunday.

LETTER 84.

Tuesday (Postmark, November 6, 1840).

My dear Child,—I am very glad that you have got —— back out of the region of lies; but your letter has made me very sad. How is one to do in this world when things are told one, sworn to one— and one is tied hand and foot to secrecy and honour? I thought I was condemned, of necessity, by hard labour and silence, to get over that tragedy; and when I had, and when all the pain and suffering had done their work, now to find that it was all lying, is dreadful! What a waste of our life! For —— did tell the truth as regards all I suffered; and, anyway, she has put us right together, which we could not have got without her, and I am too thankful for that, to be able to get up the steam to be indignant. I am very sorry for Miss ——, because, though I have forgotten the details of all the horrible allegations, yet I recollect well how —— said they came about, which no doubt she told you as she told me; but I have suffered a deal too much in the business to be able to be very sorry for anyone else, for the communications were humiliating for me, independent of all the shock with which they came. I am very glad that Miss —— has not done this thing, and that you have lost nobody you cared for. In short, I am too thankful altogether, that it is not true—to have room for any other feeling. You see, straightforwardness does bring people out of all difficulties at last, and when the main grievance is set right, all the collateral grievances which arose out of the supposed fact, fall to the ground. One thing I am very thankful for, on my own private account, and that is, that I have not been able to help myself in all this tangled affair. The cloud settled over us, and the cloud has cleared off, and I have had no part in the matter, except to sit as quiet as I could, as, of course, anything said or thought under such an impression is as though it had not been; and, indeed, it is all a dream together. I am very content now, and the memory of former things has passed away; only as to Miss ——, I am very glad she has cleared herself so soon—she might have been years over it, as we have been. As to ——, we had better make no theories about her, except that she is like someone's lawyer, who 'hatched great hens out of little eggs.' She has not answered my last letter. She wrote one, but burnt it. —— told me, and so I shall let her run a little more of her present course. I have known her longer than you have, and have suffered more by her; but, in the face of all the shame and suffering that lie before her, I cannot feel resentment for what is a touch of insanity, unstrengthened and unpurified by any sort of education, as the wise understand that word. Her intimacy with her brother during the first part of her married life was disastrous; but she has fire in her, and the fire she has to pass through must and will purify her, burn up the dross, and leave her less of 'alloy.' But I must give over all this, and go to work. I send you our friend's modest note. All last week I could not write a stroke, and I wanted you to see the article before it went back. The Devil fly away with—not it, but other people! Another mail, and no le.ter from Cairo. If I had one I should be too comfortable to be disturbed by anything. As it is, I am too uneasy to be vexed by anything else. God bless you, and keep us safe together now, henceforth and for ever.[1] I promise to make a real 'row,' and no mistake, if ever you give rise to unpleasant reports again. I will not chew the cud of a grievance any more.

LETTER 85.

[With fragment.]

Saturday (Postmark, November 12, 1849).

Dearest Jane,—In the hope that the 'Desecration of the Sabbath in the Post Office' may enable you to get this note to-morrow morning, I scrawl this on the spur of the moment (though I hope to write you a

---

[1] It was so.—A. E. I.

better to-morrow). I have two of yours to answer.
When I came to reflect upon what I had written along
with ———'s note, I thought I had spoken foolishly.
No amount of explanation would ever make her
confess herself in the wrong, or would ever make
her see the question as a whole: she would go dis-
tractedly into details, and I thought with a shudder
of all the isolated facts she would dig up; and all the
dreadful things that always get said, are recollected
by her as if she were a demon, and no human being
at all, let alone a woman—my experience of all that
is deeper than yours, alas! It was an abstract sense
of justice that made me desire she should know, but
the very writing of that note cleared my judgment.
No good, but much harm, would come of it. You and
she can never be friends again, so that reason for an
explanation does not exist. As to me, I know her,
and she would only say things that would make me
like her less than ever. I feel, besides, quite strong
enough to do her justice, and make allowance and
all that, which I should have to do, after all the
affirmations and explanations she could make; and
this is a case for an arbitrary and summary process,
rather than the application of any constitutional form,
and, besides, it is in reality no concern of mine. She
has set me right with you, and in your esteem, for I
must have seemed untrustworthy. That is all I care
for, and that one act may save her life: as they pardon

criminals who turn 'approvers' and help to make restitution. I never intended to let her enter on the subject with me—God and the Devil forfend!—and I am glad your practical sense has hindered your doing it. She is not a subject for ordinary treatment; it would be like treating savages to a legal constitution. No, let her be; I don't want even to speak on the matter. I have got all I want; indeed, *that* I got, the moment you said 'it is a lie,' and I could feel no interest whatever in any other verdict—'guilty' or 'not guilty'! I am glad to find a 'rock' somewhere, and I am glad she won't tell what —— said. As to ——, she is like the Goodwin Sands, which at high tide are water, and at low tide, shoals and the wrecking-place of thousands of ships. —— never hinted to me that she had told —— anything; but no one who knows her would need to be told that she did. Many years ago, —— and I had a grave misunderstanding, which broke the neck of my romance for her; I ought to have withdrawn then; I foresaw, I felt, I *knew*—all that has happened since. I shut my eyes weakly and falsely, for I did not deceive myself. But she behaved as one woman should not behave to another; and other things were mixed up in it which disgusted me, but she pacified me (when she found I was displeased), and one or two instances of singular affection and kindness which she showed afterwards, kept me bound to her; though I knew where the danger of her lay. And though I have trusted her since I had 'settlings' and all that, it has always been with a certain reserve. I had felt bitterly that she was not to be trusted with impunity: everything I had ever said in a moment of 'abandon' she had always brought up afterwards, like half-digested food, and flung it at me. —— has trusted me implicitly, but I have, to a certain extent, been always on my guard against her. Now, as I did not withdraw when I might have done, when the unsoundness of her character was revealed to an extent that injured all my intercourse with her—it is not justice to fly off from her *now*; so matters must go on in their natural course, and fall, like the leaves in autumn, of their own accord. Can you, and will you, trust me, and not fancy I am double, or inconsistent, or false in any way? God knows that being 'true' is not a virtue that 'grows wild' in anybody, and is not so easy as truth professed in letters would have us believe; but I wish to do right, which is all I can say for myself, so will you let me go on in my own way, according to my own instinct, and not fancy that I am acting a double part in any way? as 'telling the truth' and 'a sense of sin' form no part of my profession. I can only lay hold of the chief thing, and strike the best balance I can, without bothering about minor details, therefore, as the main thing is to put a stop to this bottomless grievance, —— is as an 'Irish

Bog,' only to be reclaimed into solid land by some yet unknown process (though in this case the Bog contains materials of much value). Yet I cannot be ever resolving her problem, so therefore I shall not only say nothing of the late 'éclaircissement,' but if it should come to her ears by any other channel, I shall emphatically deny all knowledge of the same; and if she further inquires of me concerning your silence, I shall reply that you have never mentioned the subject, and that I am altogether ignorant of the reason why you have dropped intercourse with her.

Sunday morning.

Here I was interrupted, and have been hindered ever since. I must write my Sunday letter to-morrow, for this is only a word spoken in haste. I feel like a child in the dark, afraid to be left alone. I want to keep hold of your hand, for fear you should again leave me. One thing is very true, you see, namely, that in the long run it is oneself that one blames the most. It may be that in this business the people might have behaved better than they did, but their doings have all faded away for me; the only point that stands out is, that I behaved very wrongly in condemning you unquestioned—the more I think of it the worse it seems. I cannot get over it, and the only thing for it is to bury it along with the rest of the wretched business, and to put up a stone over it to show it is an accursed place! One comfort is, that I think I am better worth your having now than I was then. I have seen an example of a friendship between two men which has revised my notion as to what a grand thing real friendship is—and long ago my conscience made me feel the irreverence and shortcomings of my own attempts that way—my darling! I will be better for you than ever I was before. Is it not the use of love that it shall fill up gaps, not of centuries alone, but the mistakes of the whole life? Oh! do you forgive me, and love me, and be very sure that even this wretched interval shall have been a golden seedtime. I will write again the first hour I have, but my time is a good deal cut up just now. I am only snatching a moment to finish this. How are you? God bless you dear, dear love!

G. E. J.

LETTER 86.

[Written next day.]

Dearest Jane,—I have received the enclosed this morning, which I have read over four times, and can make neither head nor tail of. You see, there are things I am to tell you, and things I am not to tell you, so I send all just as it stands, for, hang me if I can understand one more than the other! You must pick them out for your own self. What do you wish me to do about that affair? I think when so much useless suffering has come to pass from my keeping all that in, instead of sending the letter straight on to you, that —— had better be told all that has passed. What sort of a memory has Miss ——? I think —— could not have invented everything, because I most particularly recollect that —— told me Miss —— said, 'I consider what we have said to each other to be a very solemn thing'; and then they bound each other under the seven seals to secrecy. I know —— proposed not to tell me one-half, so what the suppressed passages must have been the Devil only knows. I ought to have been able to discern the greater from the lesser-duty. I ought to have sent you on the letter, and defied the Devil and all his works. But you cannot know how circumstantial all the evidence was; and then I had as great an idea of ——'s 'sense of truth' (how I hate that word truth!) as you had, and even now I think she must forget some of the conversation, for by the solemn way in which —— reported it to me, in the heat of the moment, I do not think Miss —— could go away and 'never think of it again.' All my magnanimous holding of my tongue has proved to be like all those virtues which lie out of the way. It has simply been a mistaken view of the matter. I confess that I believed it, but thought it best to say nothing, for fear of making yet more mischief; so I behaved very ill to you in not giving you the chance of contradicting it, for one word from you would have satisfied me. So I have been punished enough by all these years' estrangement—puzzled to death various times at your want of conscience, for, naturally enough, you did not know what you, so far as you believed, had never done. And I had been made so miserable; all from not trusting to my natural instinct. I think you should tell —— frankly what has happened, and let her see ——'s note. I know ——'s power of reflection well from experience. I know her exaggeration, the looseness of texture in what she asserts, her want of reticence, her want of common delicacy (all which I have suffered from), but I never yet found her malicious, or capable of deliberate mischief-making from bad motives, and she must have been a very devil to have invented all this. *She* is very real, though she so seldom says things to be depended upon when looked into. She must have deceived herself, or she never would have said all that; and besides, she said it so guardedly and yet so circumstantially, so afraid to exaggerate, that I am sure she did not mean to lie. How the phantom was raised, the Devil only knows. I need not tell you, my darling, that there does not remain a shadow on my mind. You have been maligned, and I have been imposed on, but, knowing Seaforth, and knowing also how very harm-

less speeches have been repeated with a meaning I
never dreamed of, and motives lent me I never had—
and that I could not act from—I can see how a good
deal arose; still, ——— did not know she was wrong.
She is so fond of acting, that she would set the
angels in heaven by the ears; but to me she has
always been good and true, in spite of all the mischief
she has done. Still, tell her what has happened, and
give her a chance. This connection with ——— will
loosen the intimacy gradually, and bring it to a
natural end, for of course I don't choose to be mixed
up in such an affair, and, besides, I have all but cut
———. We barely spoke the other night at ———'s,
and I know he will do all he can to separate us, and
I shall not struggle against the stream; only, if she
gets into trouble, I cannot be cold to her. It is not
now that I ought to leave her. This is a rambling
letter, but I am very anxious ——— should know the
mischief she has done. I am sick to death when I
think of all this ' coil.' I wish you would send me a
nice, comfortable note, with nothing of all this in it.
My only comfort is that now you know how strange
it has all been: and you know that it cannot come
again; and if I could forgive when I believed, you
may be sure I love you more now that I know I did
you such injustice. . . .

LETTER 87.

Thursday (Postmark, November 22, 1849).

Dearest Jane,—This is only a line written in haste to ask you how you are. There was a chance I might have come up to take a peep at you, but it is past. Mrs. —— was most anxious that we should have come up to London with her, but —— cannot arrange it, and I must stop at home with him. Do you know I am very uneasy about him? He is not only ill in body but he has also a desperately sprained wrist, and he has grown so miserable and unsettled since —— came home, that I am very unhappy. If I needed any finishing touch to bring me back to ancient notions of decorum, here it is, with a vengeance. I think his entanglement is now more habit than anything else ; but he is unsettled, and I would give the world to see him married comfortably. As to ——, there is a mystery there I cannot understand. I only know that amongst them all poor —— is in a bad way for his domestic happiness. If he would have gone up to town with Mrs. —— it would have been a break for him, and he would have been well taken care of, for she is a real darling, and I am very put out at having lost her. So it is no good expecting an amusing letter, for I have not been in such bad spirits this long time. I am very anxious about you. Do make some of your people write me a line, if you are not up to it yourself. I am not well either; but just now, being worried, I don't know how far that will go towards accounting for it. To make this letter worth the stamp, I send you the proof of a slight thing I wrote for Mr. ——. It is too short for such a long subject; but some day I hope to be able to have a 'say' at Mrs. Ellis and all her school, and develop my own theory more at length. We only want to be let alone, and then we shall neither be 'strong-minded' women nor yet dolls. I have not written to ——, nor have I heard from her either. She seems quite willing to let us go. By the way, when —— was here she one night launched out against —— in the most ridiculous style, making fun of him like a girl, with a genuine fun and heartiness which kept us all laughing. Nothing was said but what was quite true, and nothing that would break bones; but certainly she was very sarcastic. Well, —— was here amongst the rest, and he went and repeated everything to a friend of his who was going to see ——, and this ill-advised friend went and repeated all to ——, with the addition that I said it all (certainly, in these cases, the receiver is as bad as the thief), and —— went and complained to ——; so there is a 'kettle of fish' which will tend to separate us all. I am not sorry for the result, but I am very displeased with —— (he has owned to his fault). People must learn a certain tact *en attendant*

Y

that 'reign of peace' upon the world, when people will no more make fun of their neighbours. Till the armour is strong enough to stand heavy blows—we must be careful to hit it gently, as Don Quixote treated his patched helmet. I cannot write any more; my eyes are heavy, and I am not well, and too desperately out of spirits to say anything worth reading. Send me word how you are, and God bless you, dearest.

Yours ever,
G. E. J.

LETTER 88.

Christmas Eve, 1849.

Dearest Jane,—It is so great a comfort to sit down and write to you after all the bothering things I have had to do to-day! But I shall have to hurry to be in time for the post, as I would not have Christmas day shine or snow without bringing you a word from me. It is the best Christmas I have had for a long while, and being right with you makes up for a great many things that are plagueing me. I enclose you a note from —— in reply to my refusal to go to their party, and inviting her to come here. I can see traces of —— in it. The tone is very different to the two last. The more I reflect, the more content I feel to have done with Seaforth; and yet I used to wonder how I should live without it. I want to know how you are going on. It seems a long time since I heard from you. Lewes turned up again last week. . . .

[Disconnected.]

Be very sure you will have me to the uttermost moment. I want sadly to see you. Where on earth do you think I am going to-night? I will give you as many guesses as you like, and you never will hit upon it.

Well, then, I am going to the gate of Heaven. I am actually going to turn out to hear the 'Midnight Mass.'

Really, it sounds anything but decent, and yet one goes to balls at equally untimely hours. However, I am going with —— and his wife and a servant, so we shall keep each other in countenance. I will send you word what it is like. I was very bothered not to get a letter from Cairo either last mail or the one before. You don't know how much those letters are to me. Well, I shed plenty of tears—enough to have turned the tide, and last night I had a nice dream. I thought I was at Cairo, and that I was in his house, and that we were all at supper. I sat beside Madame ——, who was a handsome woman like ——, only with a snub nose. It was very light, and I saw my dear friend looking so radiant and so

happy—his face seemed to have a light within it—
and I just got one look of such intense content and
pleasure that I awoke quite happy. I so seldom see
anything in my dreams (they are, in general, only
half-consciousness), that this real glimpse has had all
the effect of a real occurrence. You will only laugh
at me for this. Have you read —— ? I got it
yesterday, and began it. It is a strange, tragical sort
of thing, and has taken my fancy very much. I have
always had queer, dreamy fancies about those huge
monsters who had the world all to themselves, and
there are the most vivid descriptions of the earth as
it was, according to geology, in those days. I wish
you would get it. It is so different to any other
book I know. I had other things to tell you, but
I shall be late for the post. God bless you, dear
love.

Ever your affectionate
G. E. J.

I have for you Mr. Neuberg's[1] address, and this
letter ought to have been written a fortnight since.
It is about a young German he wrote to me to speak
to —— about. . . .

[Disconnected.]

[1] Carlyle's friend.—A. E. I.

LETTER 89.

(Postmark, December 28, 1849.)

Dearest Jane,—I send you a 'golden letter' to begin the New Year. It is not such a horrid anniversary as Christmas Day, for one always feels glad to see the milestones getting behind one. A thousand thanks for the little cross. It is indeed an inscrutable imagination; one wonders how the Devil it came there. Still more for your long letter and little note I thank you. It does me more good to be praised by you than anything else in life, or perhaps I should say it is just the pleasantest thing for me in life. I could hardly help laughing at your definition of me. It is possibly a *couleur de rose* version of the fact; for one night lately I was at a dance, and there was a great philosopher, phrenologist, and mechanics-institute man present, when a friend of mine, who has great faith in his infallibility, said, pointing to me, who was dancing in the innocence of my heart, 'Look at that young lady, and tell me what you would judge of her by her head?' 'Full of inconsistencies' was the laconic reply, which my friend thought fit to report to me. I cannot express the comfort it was to come to the end of your story about Mazzini, for the shock your beginning gave, is indescribable; that would indeed have been a climax in sad keeping with the rest of his life. I was talking about the dreadful disease that is worse than 'a possession of a devil' to a surgeon, and he said that it was wonderful to him that, under such hopeless torment, people lived on to the last; and yet, strangely enough, there is no record of anyone committing suicide under those circumstances. At which I marvelled greatly, for certainly it would be the first thing I should do if I were once assured that one had declared itself in me. He little knew how nearly I was interested in the subject. Pray send me frequent news of him. Juliet Mudie [1] duly received your packet on Tuesday. I was driving with Mrs. ———'s mother the next day, who expressed much interest in her. It seems that on that Christmas day ——— had been invited to spend the day with Mrs. ———, but was obliged instead to go with her mistress and the children elsewhere. There was a large party and numerous assembly of servants. Mrs. ———'s servant-of-all-work, seeing poor Juliet looking very shy and uncomfortable, came up and shook hands with her, saying, 'I am very glad to see you.' 'Everybody else was in their best,' said she to Mrs. ———, 'and I was not over clean, having had to help the cook, but I did not mind that. I went and sat by ——— at dinner, and talked to her, and she soon got as friendly as possible, and we had a great deal of

---

[1] A servant-maid.—A. E. I.

talk before dinner was over; she was quite at her ease. She is a nice, good girl, and I like her.' Now, if that was not true good breeding, I should like to know what is. By the way, that horrid Mrs. Mudie has contrived to drain her of all she has earned, and is constantly writing for money; however, I am thankful to hear that Mrs. —— now refuses to give her any, but has undertaken to spend it for her, and that —— is living in idleness. If you want to communicate with the creature, you had better address her through a certain brother-in-law, who seems a decent sort of man. His address is 22 Lower Kennington Lane, Kennington Cross. . . . Juliet told me herself that I had better write to him, as her mother's address was not certain for long together. Pray, if you write to Juliet again, warn her, under your displeasure, to send no more money to that wretch of a mother. I am very glad that Mrs. —— is in harbour for the present, even though it be only a 'lodge in a garden of cucumbers'; it will give us breathing-time, but I will not rest till something really eligible turns up. I have got into a horrible strait—in fact, I have committed a sort of *lèse-majesté* against good breeding. A lady wrote to me months ago to beg some autographs, and I have never either answered her letter or complied with her request, and she has written to Mrs. ——, saying that she has no words to express what she thinks of such manners; so, my dear, if, without worrying yourself, you can send me a signature of Harriet Martineau and a specimen of Carlyle's caligraphy, you may save me from a torrent of abuse, and it is as well to stop crevices when they fall under one's hands. By the way, please send me a good large piece of Carlyle, because I promised a very nice little damsel, who just worships the sound of his name, that I would try to get her a piece, and I don't want to disappoint her, partly because I like her, and also because she is my sheet-anchor about Mrs. ——. By the way, Mrs. —— is intending to return the visit you paid her months ago, about the Mudies (she has been from home nearly ever since). I wish you would mention the matter to her, because she is a very likely person to be useful, and has, I know, all sorts of good intentions. I was upset in a cab the other night, in the middle of a dark lane with a ditch on each side and mudholes everywhere, and I actually perpetrated the heroism of walking home by myself, all in pitchy darkness, and sending assistance to man and horse. I had no idea how utterly helpless a woman feels on such occasions. Well, my eyes are stiff with candlelight, and this letter is too stupid to be redeemed by any addition, so the only thing is not to make it any heavier. So God bless you, my darling, and may the New Year bring you good—the sort of good you need! If wishes were helpful at all, you would prosper indeed. I can only say God bless you and keep you.

Ever your own
G. E. J.

Saturday night.

LETTER 90.
[Fragment, apparently dated 1840.]

... I had a genteel 'swarry' the other night of respectable married people, clearing the old scores of civility due for all manner of respectable tea-drinkings. I was disappointed of half my men, who all had such valid excuses that they might have passed muster at the 'Wedding Feast' in the parable, but that did not make things pleasanter. We were 13 at supper, an accident I did not like. However, we had a pleasant evening enough, and my supper was highly successful, and might defy the criticism of the good housekeepers present. I hope you will come to us. We should have such a pleasant time of it; and —— bids me say how delighted he would be to see you. If you come it would put him out of conceit with the idea of marrying any of the young ladies in white muslin going. Do write to me. I was told the other day that the Schwabes had met Mazzini in Switzerland, and that he was quite old and grey, with a long grey beard down his breast. Those poor

Hungarians! I am more depressed about the news from Hungary than I can tell you. It even drives my own concerns out of my head. I can only pray to God for them—the last refuge of desperate humanity. If I did not also trust in Him (despite my heathenism) I should cut my throat; but I do trust that all things will 'work together for good' in the end. He has never abandoned the world, and though belief is difficult when one is deeply interested and things seem to be going wrong, yet still I believe that what is right and true is stronger than all the laws and swords and spears made to crush it down. All they can do is to burn out and destroy the dross and error which have got mixed up with better things. The wood and stubble must be consumed—and that is not a process to be regretted, even though we may have to wait for the blessed result. I cannot tell you how deeply, how gravely I feel, in all that concerns the struggle of opinions—that many of them are wild and cloudy, and that their discussion seems to lead to no good, only tends to make one's interest the more pitiful. Write to me, please, and tell me how things fare with you. God bless you.

Ever your affectionate

G. E. J.

LETTER 91.

[Fragment, 1849 or 1850.]

Sunday.

My dear Child,—You have no need to tell me that you are not well: I should have found it out fast enough from your letter. What the Devil do you let all those stray women take all the goodness out of you for? Eh? It is only a new version of 'the birds of the air picking up all the seed that fell by the wayside.' I am in a bad humour with them, partly in that they tire you to death, and do you no good, and next, they hinder you writing to me. And even then I don't get a comfortable letter, for the one that came this morning bore the exact impress of this life laid waste that you are leading. Benevolence does not agree with you, and I wish in Heaven's name you would give it up. As to the money, I hope the dividends will become satisfactory by the time private friendship has paid up its calls— and if not, I will always be ready to do what I can down here. Only, my dear child, do let me correct an error you have fallen into which touches my conscience. Don't think it is my maxim to make use of my friends. I never ask anybody to do more for me than I would do for them either in kind or in degree, but some can do one thing and some can do another —and I always ask my people to do what they can with least plague to themselves, and the only

'Manichaeism' I am ever guilty of, is in judging who is the right person to go to when I want a thing done. If it is a thing very near my heart, I use all my discretion as to the best means of setting them in motion and getting at them; but making use of my friends in the sense you understood it—is an odious thing, that I hope I shall never feel even the temptation to do. Merciful Heaven! I only do to others what I am very willing they should do to me, and what they do, too. At this very moment I have been working, at the suggestion of Messrs. —— and ——, for a man I don't know and don't care for; but he was in trouble, and as I know people who did know him, and do care for him, I only set them in motion; and two of my friends who are well-to-do gave me ten pounds, almost without asking, and the whole set have bestirred themselves in a way that is wonderful. But I don't consider that I 'used' them or laid myself under the slightest obligation. I went to them thinking they could do what I wanted--'voilà tout,' and they will come to me when I stand in the same relative position to anything they may want; and besides, I have such a real, cordial response from everyone of my people—that I could carry the weight of any amount of service I am likely to want. All this is that you may not misunderstand my simile of 'pawns in chess,' made for the gratification of self-mystification, which is a woman's foible. But as to the particular instance of Mrs. ——, I was only proposing that you should give her 'value received' (or rather requested) by writing to her yourself, which would be a good deed. . . .

[Disconnected.]

I am not well yet, but a great deal better, though I am forbidden to go to parties, and ordered to be 'very quiet,' and the Devil throws all manner of difficulties in my way. ——'s affairs are not flourishing, and what the catastrophe will be I don't know. But I am very anxious, because it is a crisis in his life, and I wish he were well through it. I would very much like to see him happily married. When brothers and friends are in question, how differently one sees things to what one does in abstract cases of 'George Sandism.' I begin to think I am a most cold, matter-of-fact woman, spoiled—or at least 'incomprise.' My brother has always been so good to me that I shall be miserable till he is happy; and then I am bothered with my 'tale,' because I know I ought neither to write nor to read at this present, and I must write, for I have let myself run sadly too near the shore—alas! You suggest my living in London? No, I would like a cottage in the country with you! You should keep the house absolutely—keep the accounts, keep the money—and I would write; and you should make me work, and we would see each other alone, as wisdom inspired, and that is what would tempt me. But the bare thought of a 'London Season' gives me a nervous fear in my present state which exceeds the usual license, even of the 'irritability of genius'! Figure to yourself that the first question my doctor asks is, always, 'How is your temper?' . . So it would not be good for me, even to try me in that way. It has been the one fortunate chance in my lot to be knocked about—and nobody to think me even an addition to a tea-party! I have not sense enough. And I would be sorry to be thrown on such a precarious resource—it would be worse than a railway dividend! No, we will have a cottage together, sometime, up in the wilds of Scotland, or else I will go to—where? I won't tell you. I send you a tale to make this letter worth postage. It is Gospel! . . . . Believe me!

[Fragment.]

LETTER 92.

[Fragment, ascribed to 1849.]

Truly it is a time when one can neither breathe nor hope! I am very miserable about you. I can say nothing and do nothing; only it will not be for long. I expect firmly that such great things are close at hand as will take away all thought or feeling of one's own affairs. No matter how close it is. A woman, a plain, natural person, the wife of a provision-dealer, so not at all likely to have any philosophy, said to me lately, 'I do not expect to have as much pleasure and comfort in my life as I have had. I expect the events that are coming upon the world—war, and cholera, and such-like—will change all our prospects, and leave us no time to think of comfort. I shall not dream of saving money for our child—he will never want it!' This was said quite calmly, and as an ordinary observation, and it is a great comfort that one need not feel smothered up by one's own personalities—that they will be broken up by things of greater importance. Cobden was at Mrs. ——'s yesterday, looking very sleek and comfortable. There was a certain self-complacent common-sense about him, repudiating everything that could not be seen, measured, and the probabilities thereof calculated like a trade speculation; and the entire absence of all religious ideality gave the idea of a want of sagacity. He was speaking of the excitement caused in Scotland by the affair of Miss ——, and he gave an amusing account of a demonstration in her behalf, in which Government was memorialised to go to war to deliver her, if need were, and which was held just underneath the committee-room of the Peace Conference. It was breaking up as he was leaving his committee, and he said he could not help laughing at the fierce looks of the ladies, with their lips compressed, and looking 'daggers' and 'needles'; and, as he said, 'Only fancy how the Grand Duke would fare if he fell into the hands of those gentle Christians!' I am reading the life of Margaret Fuller d'Ossoli.[1] It has deeply interested me, and yet it is one of the most oppressive and painful books I have read for this long while. All that intense self-culture and self-production does not seem healthy, somehow; and all that deference and admiration must have been very bad for anybody. But it also makes me feel very much ashamed of myself when I compare my own self and my own attainments with her's. I remember you did not like her when you first saw her, but thought better of her after. Do tell me something of her, and will you let me see the letter she wrote you from Paris? I don't know how it is, I never either talk or think of the great things she seems to have had her thoughts filled with. But she must have been a noble creature, and I wish I had known her. By the way, I heard tidings of poor —— the other day. He had risen high in the Egyptian service—received the rank of Bey, was Governor of Suez, and director of the railway begun at Alexandria, and—for a word misunderstood in one of his written despatches—he has been brutally degraded, and deprived of all he had, and he is now on his way to France, there to find some employment and begin the world over again.

[1] The Countess d'Ossoli (born Margaret Fuller), Emerson's friend.—A. E. I.

His daughter, by his first wife, will, of course, remain with her mother! His present wife comes to Europe with him. I have heard no particulars of his life, nor how that marriage has turned out. It was in a short note from —— I heard all this. Oh, my dear, if you and I are drowned, or die, what would become of us if any superior person were to go and write our 'life and errors'? What a precious mess a 'truthful person' would go and make of us, and how very different to what we really are or were!

But for pity's sake take care of your letters. I have burned all those of yours which could be misunderstood, and I don't think a rummage amongst my papers would return any significant result—except one series, that I must burn when I can summon resolution. If anything should happen to me suddenly, will you write and ask —— for a box done up in brown paper? If anything happens to you first, —— will deal with its contents! They are all the reserves' I have in the world, but I hope I am not going to die, but to live to see the end of all the great things that are coming to pass in the world, and you must try to live too. The next few years will be worth seeing! . . . .

[Disconnected.]

. . . I did not desire to do it, or anything like it, but when once done I think it may stand. There is a sense of relief and comfort inexpressible, like nothing else I could think of; and if I am long without writing, I get morbid and miserable. So you see, it is rather a good look-out if only I can find work. I shall get you to help me read the novels. Oh, my good gracious, such unutterable trash as some of them are! I began to get quite ashamed of spending so much life and strength in nothing better than slowly writing one, but one day last week there came 'Hide and Seek,' by Wilkie Collins. Get it and read it; it is the most lovely story I ever remember to have read! It left me feeling inclined to pitch every sheet I had written of my own into the fire! Really and truly, I felt that is what my own tale deserved, though I could not afford to do it. Please get 'Hide and Seek'! I don't know whether I did most laughing or crying over it. It is so pretty, and so healthy in its nature! I am sure Wilkie Collins must be a good man, though he did once write that atrocious 'Basil.' Please remember that my chapters, sent to-day, are to come after the last. It is supposed —— has been in London, and —— is beginning to fall in love with her. I have sent the rest by Miss ——, who is going to-night; so I finish this letter for the postman, who has just come. You will understand, I hope, how it is I had not finished when my friend Miss —— had to start. God bless you!

G. E. J.

LETTER 93.

[Fragment, ascribed to 1849.]

I begin to understand more and to judge less than formerly. Can you not come to us for a while? You shall be free here, and you know you can do what you will. It seems to me that it would be a first step towards remodelling your life, for you cannot go on as you are. I shall have my own room to work in—for work I must—and you can have the drawing room, and shall see me when you like, and be alone when you like, and nobody shall worry you. Consider me and my position in your hand, to use if you can. I say nothing of the good you would do me, nor the comfort you would be to me, because that is no motive for taking an extraordinary step such as leaving home just as you have returned; but if it would be an inducement, it is a fact that it would be a real blessing to me. We have been estranged so long that I want now to have some communion with you, and who knows how long we may live? Do not let us kill an opportunity. I think in the present state of matters coming here would be a wise thing. I am ill and I need you. Give any colour you like to give, if colour it need beyond your simple will; in fact, it matters not, only come. . . .

[Disconnected.]

Mr. Neuberg[1] has been here. I like that man immensely, there is such a well of loving-kindness in him. He called just now. But, instead of coming early, when I was alone and could have talked to him, he went to church, and called when I was in the midst of this letter, and —— was sitting by. I could say nothing, and it was a stiff visit. . . .

[Disconnected.]

Mr. Neuberg will call on you very soon. He will be in London 'en route' for Germany. I am quite annoyed at the idea of all the spiteful, running-down things he will hear of to-night. My hope is that —— went to Seaforth yesterday, and so did not get his note. —— is delighted at your letter. He has a very bad cold, which will nip his projects for this winter, I fancy ; but he is in a better fashion than he was. . . .

[Disconnected.]

LETTER 94.

[Fragment, date uncertain, 1848 or 1849.]

Friday.

Dearest Jane,—I want to talk to you, and writing is a very cumbrous process in place of that same. I was delighted to get a letter from you, which I was wanting more than enough ; and only to think, that

[1] An intimate friend of the Carlyle's.

the Queen giving a musical party should be the remote means of getting it for me! I cannot help thinking you are better, in spite of the headache. You are in a good atmosphere, and Lady —— is in every way just the person for you to be with. She always knows what she is about, seemingly, and has attained a wonderful degree of practical wisdom in arranging her daily life, and it must be very pleasant to sail in her current. What you say of her reminds me of Alfred Tennyson's lines—

> And the stately ship sails on
> To her haven under the hill.

But how thankfully we would all of us sail if we were under a hand strong enough to guide us. Women have so much docility, and yet we get no real teaching, no guidance, but what we make for ourselves. We are not, like men, in a position to know things, so we make a sort of 'cup and ball' and 'hit or miss' of our lives. I used to think that what was wise for men was the same for women. I had no notion of any difference between them, except in degree, but I am beginning to think I was mistaken. However, at this present we are neither one thing nor another, but I hope and believe that in a generation or two, women will be very different to what they have ever been yet. Instead of being born and educated, and having their manners and characters flavoured with certain qualities, or shadows of qualities, just to the point which may make them fancied as wives (for the tendency of all the training they get is just adapted to the prevailing fancy of men—a strong taste of housewifery in one generation, a dash of delicate 'feminine' stupidity in another, a gentle flavour of religion, as a sort of ornamental ring-fence to their virtue, and so on, not for the saving of their own souls, for they must not come it too strong)—to-day they may have a small, graceful tint of learning, and if married—the least touch in the world of abstract 'George Sandism,' but not to come within a mile of the practical. You understand! . . .

[Fragment.]

LETTER 95.

[Undated, beyond Wednesday night, 1849.]

Dearest Jane,—First to answer your questions. I have taught my servant to mend the table linen, and benevolent friends make my 'little things,' so I shall have leisure to see to my petticoats, and even those 'Mary Barton' has begged me out of charity to give her for one of her 'protégées' to make, whom she wants to find work for. So you see my good deeds are very vicarious! I think doing good to poor people is a somewhat questionable employment. Only this was such a spontaneous motion of pity for them that I did not like to quench my 'smoking flax,' and I actually went out on the spur of the moment, though it was raining genuine 'cats and dogs,' to stir up the clergyman's wife to make a sewing-meeting of two hours a week of the industrious members of the congregation. But that did not suit, so I was left to the exercise of my private benevolence and such help as I could get. I had a great bundle of print sent me the other day to make frocks and bed-gowns. I wish you were here to help me. Mr. —— sent me such a nice letter this morning, which I took very kind of him. —— is gone to meet ——, ——, and all the family, at the railway, and a precious cold he will catch for his pains. I wish they were staying away still longer. My head is somewhat better. I don't forget common care of myself so outrageously as I did some little while since. Still I am very good-for-nothing, though all has been set to rights, and I am, besides, very careful in my diet and so forth—this is all very stupid stuff to tell you, but I am up to nothing better. I had a letter from —— the other day, very kind and affectionate, but full of foreboding and misery. That man keeps taking fits of introspection, and, of course, like a true man, makes her bear the burden of his remorse. And when she quoted something you and I had said to her by way of trying to comfort her, he only rolled his eyes, and declared that we did not know right from wrong. I call that cool. What is to become of her? I feel as if a volcano must burst some day soon and blow her—where? He won't be any comfort to her in that ' dies iræ, dies illa.' The last time I saw him has given me a greater distaste to him than ever, in spite of all my efforts to be gracious and my penitence for having abused him. He left a bad taste in my mind. Mr. —— gives a very good account of you. Is it real or only what strangers see? I am dreadfully anxious about you, but I have great faith in my mesmeric sense, and I feel as if you were just now tolerably calm; only, it is but a lull, and the real cause of anxiety remains. I am hoping for a letter very soon. Dear child, the solution will come to you, never fear. You will not be abandoned nor left altogether in darkness. Light will come to you when you least expect it. Do let me hear from you. I don't like bothering you with questions, but you know all I want to hear. How do you go on? Only think what lies before me! A misguided cousin of mine has written a novel to illustrate the laws of ' entail and primogeniture ': and has sent to say she wants to visit me for a few days, and obtain my opinion, and that of some other competent person. She is going to publish it at her own expense. Have her I must, but it is a real penance. Doing good to poor people is nothing of a good deed, and yet it sounds like one. This costs twenty times the true virtue, and goes for nothing. So much for appearances and names of things. —— was here to-day. Did you get that scrap from one of his notes, in which he declares that if you will come here he will take lodgings in Greenheys to hear you talk? God bless you, dear love.

Your affectionate

G. E. J.

LETTER 96.

[Undated—1849?]

(About women and the Corn Law League.)

Sunday.

Dearest Jane,—I have been 'looking, and better looking'[1] for a letter from you all the week, and wondering what could have befallen you. This morning the postman came before I was out of bed, and brought your letter, which makes me fancy you are better, and that makes me more comfortable without any fancy at all! But, my dear, I am in a real fright; my eyes (confound them!) are threatening just as they began before. I can see to do nothing by candle-light, and not too much by daylight. I hope they will be stopped in time, but this damp weather is against me. I was so sick of my doctor last time, that I could not find either faith or patience to begin again with him, and I have a sort of Faust's revela-

[1] A Scotch expression, meaning 'looking and looking again.'—A. E. I.

tion, and on the strength of it set off to a lady, a very clever woman of my acquaintance who is wild after homœopathy. She has got a book and a medicine-chest, and doctors herself and her friends with great zeal. She looked at me, and read in her book, and finally brought out a little box the size and shape of a tiny tea-caddy, all full of miraculous-looking little bottles filled with what seemed pure water, but they were all deadly essences. She mixed me two drops of one in a phial of water; so now I am taking an infinitesimal dose of belladonna. Whether it is for good or harm I don't know, but it affects me very uncomfortably, and my eyes are rather worse to-day, but I do expect it will do me good. She promised to come and see me to-morrow, however. Meanwhile the medicine affects my head, and I am as limp, and washed out, and miserable to-day as anyone could wish me to be; it is a foggy, drizzling day, and I am neither dead nor alive. And I am vowed not to touch either tea or coffee, nor anything more comfortable than milk-and-water, which is very nasty, and I am cross. O ye gods! how cross!

—— was in dismay with me, thinking me gone mad, yesterday, and made a most touching admission that 'being a missis I might say what I pleased.' But only fancy, my dear, the vexation of being able to do nothing but shut my eyes the minute the candles come; but, *en revanche*, I sleep! Well, now, here I am, inflicting complaints on you as if you were my doctor, and God knows the poor man got plenty! But to talk of something else (now I have said my say). Well, perhaps, we are better off now than they used to be in old Greek times, when it was only slaves who were taught anything. God knows they are very uncomfortable, that's certain, but I believe we are touching on better days, when women will have a genuine, normal life of their own to lead. There, perhaps, will not be so many marriages, and women will be taught not to feel their destiny *manque* if they remain single. They will be able to be friends and companions in a way they cannot be now. All the strength of their feelings and thoughts will not run into love; they will be able to associate with men, and make friends of them, without being reduced by their position to see them as lovers or husbands. Instead of having appearances to attend to, they will be allowed to have their virtues, in any measure which it may please God to send, without being diluted down to the tepid 'rectified spirit' of 'feminine grace' and 'womanly timidity'—in short, they will make themselves women, as men are allowed to make themselves men. I think matters are tending to this, and I think that to this, in spite of that dreadful Mrs. ——, they will come before long; not in the present 'rising generation,' but in the one after. Except when my health is out of order, I do not feel that either you or I are to be called failures. We are indications of a development of womanhood which as yet is not recognised. It has, so far, no readymade channels to run in, but still we have looked, and tried, and found that the present rules for women will not hold us—that something better and stronger is needed. And as for us, individually, women a thousand times commoner, both in intellect and aspirations after doing right, may have made something apparently better out of their lives—still, I would prefer my own imperfect accomplishment. There are women to come after us, who will approach nearer the fulness of the measure of the stature of a woman's nature. I regard myself as a mere faint indication, a rudiment of the idea, of certain higher qualities and possibilities that lie in women, and all the eccentricities and mistakes and miseries and absurdities I have made are only the consequences of an imperfect formation, an immature growth. Where I am not wiser than the general run of women I am a much greater fool, and when I do not succeed in doing better than they, I do infinitely worse, and that is the general occurrence, *hélas!* But will you lay your hand on your heart, and say that, in your 'fifteen years' long illness,' as you call your life, you have not both felt and shown qualities infinitely higher and nobler than all the 'Mrs. Ellis-code' can dream of? You know you have. If you consider yourself as the 'be-all and the end-all' of what a superior woman can be, the balance of actual respectable facts might perchance be on the other side, but the power and possibility is with you, and it is that which is to be looked to. A 'Mrs. Ellis' woman is developed to the extreme of her little possibility; but I can see there is a precious mine of a species of womanhood yet undreamed of by the professors and essayists on female education, and I believe also that we belong to it. So there is a modest climax! I fear I shall never be available to any actual purposes except 'to point a moral and adorn a tale,' and even of that I feel dubious. I don't know what has possessed me to give you the benefit of this long 'settle,' except that your letter suggested it. Talking of practical matters, my bedroom is done (all but some of the hangings, for which the stuff has had to be made to match, and has not come home), and you must have yearned after a pretty bedroom all your life before you can understand the pleasure of getting it. I hope you will come and sleep in it some time. It will be such a nice room to write in. My visitor has not come. She is detained in Dublin, which will cut down her stay to a very short space. I must tell you a story. The other night the Lord-Lieutenant went in state to the theatre. Something had put the audience out of humour, or they were in an excited state, or something, but they began to give vent to their feelings by calling out for 'three cheers' to different people, pit and gallery taking it in turns. After three cheers for 'O'Connell,' the others insisted on three for 'Lord ——,' and then began a dreadful row, all the noises possible for *in*humanity to make. At last they grew more and more uproarious, and they were proceeding to tear up the benches when one fellow, seeing that he was likely in this way to lose his shilling's worth of the play, shouted at the top of his voice, during a momentary lull, 'Boys, three cheers for the Devil, entirely!' They were given, and peace was restored. That is quite true—gospel! By-the-way, talking of the Devil, do you remember ages ago that I wrote an article for ——, which he rejected with ignominious disdain. Well, then, I wrote it over again, and Carlyle was at the pains of sending it to 'Fraser,' as you told him to, who would not have it, but refused it in its amended state just as much. Well, it lay tossing about for a full twelvemonth, when I took it in hand once more, wrote it over again, and sent it to Douglas Jerrold, by way of calming down the little one that went with it. And lo! when the Magazine came yesterday, the first thing I saw was my poor little thing, flourishing in good legible print. I was quite pleased to see it. Whether it was that I had such trouble with it, or whether I was glad of my own way at last, I don't know; but I fancied it read very decently. I have

not heard from —— for a long while. She has been
to Manchester, but did not come near me. I spent
last Monday with the Smiths. He—Mr. J. B. Smith
—was one of the originators of the 'League.' He
brought the first resolution for repeal of the Corn
Laws, twenty years ago, before the Chamber of Commerce in Manchester, and could get no one to second
it, till at last one man did for the sake of discussion,
and was horrified when he found Mr. Smith was in
earnest. After a while Cobden joined, and about five
of them kept fighting to get a petition sent to Parlia-
ment; and there was such difficulty to get it agreed
to, and such little trembling resolutions proposed! I
think he said they were three years before they could
get the petition sent. My word, to hear him talk!
It gave me some notion of what perseverance means.
He afterwards was secretary to the League. He is a
little wizened, uninteresting-looking man; gives no
idea of any sort of what you call either greatness or
cleverness, but he was so in earnest. They all speak
of Cobden as a sort of martyr; they say he has ruined
his health, and made all sorts of sacrifices, injuring
his worldly affairs terribly. His house was doing infinitely more business ten years ago than it is now; it
has dwindled down, and everybody who knows him
speaks of his modesty and disinterestedness. There
was another man, Alderman ——, at dinner, remarkable
here for having been an 'ultra-Liberal' when Liberals

were only thought fit to send to prison. A very uninteresting man—tyrannical I am certain, for I felt as if sitting beside a thumb-screw. But he has done good work, and is now recognised as a respectable man; and it was curious to meet a man who could talk of Hone and Godwin, and all those people. He knew them, and he has spent money on his principles, so now he proses like a Patriarch. This is a letter and a-half. Write to me very soon.

Ever your own

G. E. J.

1850.

LETTER 97.

New Year's Day, January, 1850.

'Angry?' No! but uneasy. Yet, what is the matter? If it be your head, dear child, I wish you would do something besides bearing it. Your headaches signify more than pain, though that is bad enough. I wish you would consult Elliotson [1]—not to take his medicine, but to know what is the real matter with you. I believe he is the cleverest man in the world for seeing into the depth of people's ailments, though his treatment is too strong for human weakness. Anyway, there must be something that can be done for you. Do not write till you are quite able to do it without difficulty, least of all to me, who know so well what it is to try to write under such circumstances. I wish you would come down here for a spell. I have not been so well; I feel as if I were all falling to pieces—as if my body had no substance to oppose to the 'wear and tear' of life. How nice it must be to feel hard and firm and well! Only figure to yourself that I was out at

[1] Dr. Elliotson, the mesmerist.

two parties last night; one was a gathering at Mrs. Schwabe's for her 'Christmas Tree,' or rather, 'New Year's Eve Tree,' which was a superb affair, and, as your poor —— used to say, 'so expensive.' The guests were chiefly children and family connections; I was nearly the only alien. The presents were a show, and the whole room looked just like the dwelling of a 'good fairy,' while to see the delight of the children and the zeal with which, after seizing their gifts, they fell to plundering the tree of its gilt apples and bonbons, was charming. There were little tiny fairies, workboxes with gold fittings, ball-dresses, shawls, cloaks, brooches, &c., for the elder ones, and books, pictures, mats, puzzles, dolls, toys of every description, for the younger ones, but all so beautiful. The room was dazzling with light, and it was altogether the prettiest sight I ever saw. The tree bore for me a 'polka'-jacket to wear in the house—grey tweed, trimmed with blue, and lined with blue quilted silk —quite charming. Mrs. —— gave me an adorable châtelaine, full of everything that is possible or impossible in steel-work from a whistle down to a corkscrew. I go clanking about in it, like a ghost in a pantomime, and it is the envy of all beholders. After being at the 'Tree' I adjourned to ——'s, who was giving a grand ball in honour of Mr. and Mrs. ——; it was like a magic-lantern, all the people seemed bright phantoms . . . As to people who

have come to be of any importance and who keep a
court, I can fancy that Lady —— finds it a great comfort to have somebody who can stand on her own basis
and be a real person for her. By the way, I need
your feminine counsel on a most momentous point—
essential, indeed, not to my existence exactly, but to
my appearance, which is of the next consequence.
I want to know what sort of a dress you would
counsel me to get in case of evening parties. I am
pretty well off for heavy dresses, having a velvet and
two silk ones—one quite new and the other quite
good. But I have not forgotten all the plague you had
going with me to Howell & James's to choose a decent
gown for Mrs. ——'s party, and I don't want to have
any bother of that sort, and I am such a cold, shivering
wretch that I have a dread of light, elegant material.
So, my dear, please counsel me, for you always dress
yourself well without seeming to think of it, which, I
take it, is the *ne plus ultra* of success. It would be
such a comfort if anyone would just give me out
my dresses, and I might put them on without further
responsibility. Now, finally, good-bye. I have said
all I have the sense to say to-day, and I must go to
town. I hope 'Nero'[1] is quite well. My best regards
to him. He does not know me, but I had once a brief
interview with him in ——'s warehouse. —— is
very poorly, poor fellow, and when people are

[1] Mrs. Carlyle's little dog.

'poorly' I have got to think it is only another name for being worried.

Affectionately yours,
G. E. J.

P.S.—It was not the baby, as I supposed, that Lewes has lost, but a beautiful child beginning to walk, and which he used to rave about to me. What do you think of his paper? I am glad it is afloat ... When ordinary mortals are placed in that queen-like position,[1] it is a great deal if they can keep their human nature; they grow demoralised by living with courtiers who give way to them, and it is a great misfortune to lose the tread of the firm earth beneath their feet. Even on such high social levels there may be rough places and a great deal of unpleasant friction, and the attraction of gravitation, to contend against; and when I see people in her position or in yours—for you have one in your own way—I always feel a certain wonder at them for being so reasonable and keeping themselves together as they do. I know that I should be good for nothing but to be cast into the fire to be burned very soon. It is very easy for people to live moderately—easy, I mean, when they are knocked about and nobody cares whether they are vexed or pleased; in fact, when they are made of no consequence, and have to

---

[1] The allusion is probably to Lady Ashburton.

live on the daily bread of good-will and what good-nature they can excite. But it is very, very different —with you and with her! . . .

LETTER 98.

(Postmark, January 17, 1850.)

Dearest Jane,—I wrote you a note yesterday when I was so stunned that I hardly knew what I did. Only I wanted to speak to you at all events; so I don't know whether you would be able to make out anything. I am better this morning, only still my head feels like a jelly, and I am so trembling and weak I can hardly hold myself upright. But that is a very natural result of yesterday. It seemed as if the Devil kept sending people to see me whom I could not refuse to see, and every word I spoke sent the blood up and down like quicksilver. However, I got to bed soon after seven, have had a great deal of sleep, and am quite rational this morning, only shaken! I don't want to swindle you out of any sympathy. I don't think I need it. It seems to me that I have just now done what, if I had had the tenth part of a grain of sense, I ought to have done ten years ago. The more I reflect, the more satisfied I am. That is, all that is rational in me is satisfied; but then there is so much of one that is not rational, and it is that which suffers. During the interview of yesterday —— just showed all the qualities which have eaten into our connection. My brother Frank once had a magnificent hall-lamp, which had hung in great glory for many years. One Sunday morning it fell down with a crash when nobody was near it, and there was no earthly apparent reason why it should fall then, instead of the year before, or instead of hanging on to all eternity. But when they came to look into the matter, it was discovered that the chains which suspended it had been eaten into with rust, so, though they looked still to be all right, they were in reality as thin as brown paper, and fell because the little imperceptible, but too needful, links had been worn away.

I could not help thinking of this yesterday. In the first part of the interview —— seemed possessed by a devil. Every little thing I had ever told her or confided to her in the course of our intimacy she set up in battle array, to prove that it was all pure chance! I was not as she is. Then she showed me voluntarily how cruelly reckless she had been in her assertions about me to her own family, and the horrible meaning they had quite coolly and calmly attached to her statements, which they had repeated that very morning to her. She said, 'Oh, I only just said "so-and-so," and they went and thought all that. I never saw such people as those ——. It was no more than I have said about my own sister, but I have been battling for you only this morning.' I tried, but could not make her feel where she was wrong. She seems destitute of all faculty of apprehension. She stuck in little incidental details, and seemed to think that if she could excuse herself by a ' flaw in the indictment' she was neither morally wrong, nor was the mischief of the least consequence. Then again, when I told her that I had cleared —— to you about that speech imputed to him at ——, she said, 'Well, I did not exactly say that. It was he who said it. I only made a Jesuitical speech, and said that if he had said one thing he would say another, and that very likely it was he ; but then, of course, any woman has a right to clear her " Plato."' And all this without the least glimmering of an idea of the ultimate and natural effect of such conduct when persisted in. I was obliged, when pressed for a definite reason, to pronounce my detestation of ——, but that connection is only the fruit which the tree hath borne after its time. I might very likely have done better. I might and ought to have made more energetic efforts from the beginning against the rash and unscrupulous surmisings—reckless assertions never followed up by honest belief or disbelief, but left to hang in the wind like corpses on a gibbet, infecting the air. It has been weak, wrong, and foolish in me to stand by so long without awakening to a sense of what was right—commonly right, to say nothing of the stupidity of it. I am humiliated when I think how slow I have been to awaken to any moral perception. I have let myself be blinded by my liking for her, and by the pleasure I found in the place. When, however, it came to the last—when the coach came, and she had to go—then she showed herself very good and really noble. It took away all bitterness and anger from me. She showed that part of her character which had held me to her so long. She cried bitterly, and said everything she could think of, not to shake my resolution, but to prevent my feeling any remorse for it; and of her own accord she said, 'I think better of you than ever. I care for you more than ever. We have not quarrelled, we have only separated. I will never speak of you at all to those people, but I shall think of you as we have been for eighteen years.' Remember how mortifying to all feelings of human nature it must have been for me to leave her as I have done. All her *amour propre* she had to stifle down. When she went away her last words were, 'Some day you will feel how true a friend you have had in me!' As far as feeling an attachment to me goes, she is right, but something even higher than that is necessary if a friendship is to last. Attachment is a fine cement, but it is not the hewn stone and foundation of rock. You may fancy the state I was left in, but if it were to be done again, I should only regret that I had not taken the same course ten years earlier. I am very glad you took

the course you did in the —— affair. Explanations
would have been worse than useless; and besides,
after the specimen I had yesterday of the monstrous
growth of unfounded assertions, like the huge tropical fungi, I have no difficulty at all in seeing how
that horrible phantasmagoria arose to take all the
comfort out of my life for three years. But it would
be like dissecting a 'polypus' or a 'madrepore' to
enter into explanation with her. I have only one
additional trait to tell you, which is that last week,
when —— was with me, —— and 'little ——
came over from Stockport, where she has been
staying, to beg —— to go back with them express
to see ——, whom they both asserted to be 'now a
truly reformed character, —— behaved very properly and refused to go, saying it was they who first
opened her eyes to his character, and she could not
believe in his reform without some proof. Now, dear
child, do write to me; everything only makes me
more and more thankful that I have got you back.
Since Harriet Martineau went to live in the country,
I think she is much nicer than when she led the life
of a lion, and if you feel moved to write to
her cordially, do it by all means. I feel as if I
could get a great deal of good out of her, if
I saw her much; but with the limitation neces-
sarily imposed it is not feasible. But there is the
fine, honest, solid North-country element in her, and

she really loves you. If you had seen her face when she spoke of you, you would have loved her too. I can write no more to-day. God bless you, dear love, and let us hold very fast to each other.

G. E. J.

Do write to me.
January 17, 1850.

LETTER 99.

Saturday (Postmark, March 9, 1850).

Dearest Jane,—I send you a letter I have just received from ——. I am going to see —— this afternoon; I am very sorry for her, and it is not now that I can recollect all the discrepancies in her conduct. I shall not get mixed up again in a Seaforth quicksand, but this is a case where, even if it were certain pain, I must run the risk. I am very, very unwell, sick, and ill, and good for nothing; and this letter has upset me more than I can tell you; there is nothing but trouble going on. —— is in a bad way, but he is going on an expedition for some days, so that I can be spared. As to the 'tale,' I am dreadfully behindhand, but the last two chapters have been written in the midst of rows, and grievances, and family letter-writings of every description; all this, apparently, a good element for the 'tale'—but I am nearly dead myself. I cannot write any more, because I must do an hour's work at my chapter before I go; I will write and tell you how I go on with it. Dear —— is very poorly, worse than even I am; do write to him a nice letter; he is so good and noble I don't know what we would all do without him. By the way, I agree with you about that tale. But I had to answer the letter Dickens sent me, and I told him I would write him something suitable as soon as I had time; that, though I never kept my MS. on hand, yet I had written out a little tale which I believed was true; that it was in your hands, and, if he liked, he might have it; and that I would ask you to send it on to him, but that I did not think myself it had any recommendation beyond being a 'short story.' Anyway, let him see it, and the Devil may fly away with it for me! ——s wrote to —— to know if I would write a 'powerful tale' for them in twelve columns. Perhaps this would be more in his way, but, upon my honour, I am in such a state of reaction against all moral complications that I don't believe that I will meddle with the metaphysics of the Ten Commandments any time this side of the Millennium. I am bothered to death with that kind of thing in real life enough just now, and *there* these things are very great nuisances, whatever they may be in novels. Truly, when it comes to the reality, I find that I have just as much morality and cold-blooded common-sense as if I had never read a French novel in my life. I shall try to bring —— back with me. Oh! —— is a hypocritical scoundrel. He said to me he 'trembled to look at what ——'s future would be if she lost him,' and he was all the while only trying to get someone to break her fall. He will be very miserable, and if there be a Devil, he will go to him—by right of being the Devil's lawful due.

Ever your own
G. E. J.

P.S.—Dearest, I have not time to do my letter over again and not virtue enough to burn it, so read it, but read this afterwards as my final directions. I have read your note again when less in a hurry, and I think you are right about the story. So put it into the fire, and tell Dickens you did so by my directions. Just write him a line that he may not be expecting anything from me, and tell him that I am of your persuasion, and will not let myself be tempted, by the chance of its being accepted in some quarter and of being paid for, to publish what I should certainly have been sorry to invent. Do it! I am off now, and am very nervous at the thought of my errand. . . .

LETTER 100.

August 29, 1850.

Dearest Jane,—I might be —— you treat me so ill! Upon my honour, you are too bad for anything! When

I left you you were ill, and all your domestic concerns were in a most unsettled condition, and I don't know that they are any better yet. Do write me a line to say how you go on! I am alone, and enjoying an hour of quiet, which has not fallen to me since I came back. The ——s went to their lodgings on Monday. Poor Mrs. —— was hardly fit to be removed even there, but —— had been so intolerably disagreeable all week that I think she was glad to take him where she could—wife-like—conceal all his errors from the eyes of those who are not bound to put up with them. Upon my honour, it enlarged my idea of English husbands! He was put out of his way that he could not go to his lodgings the very day he fixed. His wife's illness made the house rather uncomfortable to him, because we had to attend to her, and so seemed less occupied about him; and —— one morning gave him strong coffee, and if it had been arsenic he could not have used more antidotes or made more fuss, and of course he vented his temper on his wife. I don't think he knew what an 'emancipated woman' he was showing off to. Was not I glad that I had no husband, whose ill-humours it was my duty to mind! He said once that a wife's illness made a man insignificant by occupying everybody in the house, and giving them something to do besides attending on himself. I am very poorly with a bad cold, which has fallen partly on my eyes, so you won't have much of a letter to-day, and you don't deserve one, either, for that matter!

On Saturday I got a parcel from London—'Alton Locke,' sent me by the 'Athenæum' to review. I had a precious letter to say it would be sent if I could say that I had not written it myself. So of course I could say 'No' with a clear conscience; but when I came to read it through from end to end I almost felt vain of the compliment, for it is the most striking book I ever read in my life, except your husband's. If you remember, I dipped into it and turned one or two leaves, and said how coarse it seemed, and we neither of us felt drawn to it. Well then, now I say, begin at the first page and read it through from end to end, don't skip one line, and see if you are not as much excited with it as I was. The style is here and there too much like Mr. ——, but that is a small flaw. It is written by Kingsley, of the 'Saints' Tragedy.' I have had my hands full. The article was wanted directly, and I felt ashamed of writing a critique on a work so infinitely superior to anything I could do myself. Do read it, if you have not done so.

Now good-bye, and God bless you. Regards to 'Nero.'

Your affectionate

G. E. J.

LETTER 101.

Wednesday night (Postmark, September 6, 1850).

Dearest Jane,—I begin a letter, though goodness knows if I shall be able to finish it, for I have been very poorly indeed with a feverish cold, and I am still in a queer way, unable to do anything. I went out yesterday in a coach, and to-day I have had a drive, but I am not yet strong enough to walk. I cannot imagine how two or three days could so pull me down. —— was very kind to me, and nursed me. I really like her! I think she is a good, sterling, sensible woman. What her genius may be I don't know at all, but I think she is a good woman in herself. The only thing is, that, living on her own basis, she has got a habit of taking care of herself, and making use of other people; that is the worst of women living in the world, and I don't know how they are to help it! I daresay I should get into the same sort of thing if I had to go about like men, and have nobody but myself to look to to help me. And —— is quite ready to help others, and to do kind things. But for all that, it is a problem that bothers me—viz., that when women get to be energetic, strong characters, with literary reputations of their own, and live in the world, with business to attend to, they all do get in the habit of making use of people, and of taking care of themselves in a way that is startling! And yet how are they to help it? If they are thrown into the world, they must swim for their life. And yet, again, one has a prejudice against anything that looks like personal calculation in a woman, though, as the Devil knows, they are the greatest schemers on earth. In short, whenever a woman gets to be a personage in any shape, it makes her hard and unwomanly in some point or other, and, as I tell you, I am bothered to explain how it is, or why it is, or how it should be otherwise. Because, if women chance to have genius, they have it, and must do something with it; and if there is any special saving grace in baptism, as the Bishop of Exeter teaches, then these women of genius ought to be baptised twice over! It is so hard for them not to fall into affectations of either virtue or vice, or into some 'devilment' worse still. When women are 'incomprise' they are miserable, but when they are recognised—their specialty spoils them as women, and I cannot at all reconcile the contradictions into anything like a theory. But one thing I must say, which is that —— has a good foundation of womanliness in her—a kind, motherly element about her, which is a deal better than all the books or reputation in the world! But it is odd that she should have been precisely the one to shake my ideas as to the desirableness of a 'distinguished reputation' for a woman—not by anything she has said, but by what I have seen. And yet, I

suppose I shall go on writing books, and all that, and
follow the profession of an author, as long as my brain
holds good for the work. I wish I had a good
husband and a dozen children! Only the difficulty
is that 'women of genius' require very special
husbands—men of noble character, not intellect, but
of a character and nature large enough, and strong
enough, and wise enough to take in them and their
genius too, without cutting it down to suit their own
crotchets, or reprobating half their qualities because
they don't understand what to do with them, or what
they are intended for. And so, as I shall never meet
with the special man who could manage me wisely,
it is lucky I have met with no one who has claimed
to do so. By the way, talking of 'special men,' ——
read me some of ——'s letters to her, and I like the
tone of them very much. He must be a very fine
man, as well as a very clever one, and I think it is
a highly fortunate connection for her, and it is reputable to death! She showed me also letters from
her brother and her sister, and they seem very nice
people; there is a strong family affection amongst
them, which made me think well of them all. I got
a note from Cairo yesterday, and another from ——.
All very kind and very nice, and highly as they
should be. But, my dear, hang me if I can understand anything about the actualities of life! I used
to think I did, but I am fairly bothered now, and

B B

have sat down on the ground, and will go to school
to anybody who will teach me to understand them!
I have some thought of going to church to see if
theology can throw any light on moral problems for
me. I am only certain of one thing, which is that I
know nothing about the matter. This is a most
rambling letter, but I cannot help it. I must go to
bed, being sleepy with having been so much in the
air, and not being strong yet. I had a most ridiculous
account to give you of an expedition Mrs. ——
and I made to some 'tea-gardens' here, and all we
saw was that those sort of places in broad daylight
have no shine in them. But I am too sleepy to tell
you to-night. I want very much to know how your
new maiden goes on, and whether you are yet
'delivered out of all your troubles.' Do write to me!
—— was here the other night, and inquired about
you. He seemed very pleased by my account of the
honour and glory of 'Nero.' When does Carlyle
come home? and how is ——? Do please write to
me, just to say how you are! I will write you a
better letter when I can. Now, good-night!

Ever your own
G. E. J.

P.S.—I forgot to tell you that —— is engaged to
——, and is to be married before long, and that ——
is much better. He is so kind to me—nothing could be

more thoughtful—and he has promised to take me abroad next year. I have not seen Mrs. —— since I came back. It is a fortnight to-night since I left you.

P.S.— —— was here the other day, and left his best respects for you and Mr. Carlyle. Any news of ——?

LETTER 102.

(Postmark, Manchester, October 22, 1850.)

Dearest Jane,—I was just going to write to you at Chelsea on the chance of your being there, as you said your visit would terminate on the 20th. But I am very glad you are stopping to see her Ladyship well through her cold, because it is a comfort to get some sort of a human hold over a person one likes, and who will keep herself bewitched in the enchanted circle of polite intercourse. Also I felt a grim satisfaction in thinking that Mr. Carlyle would have to be an uncomplaining victim, and go back alone and face his household destiny as best he might. He would feel the want of you without having the satisfaction of fancying himself ill-used, and —— for your substitute is altogether as good a Nemesis as one would wish to hear of. I hope her Ladyship will keep her cold a little while, and keep you along with it. As to Paris and Mr. Carlyle, you would have no comfort in that arrangement—going in that company, you would be worried and tantalised to death. You would have, at least, peace and comfort in your own room, as —— prophesied long ago, and as I firmly expect, allowing even more than the ordinary uncertainty of human affairs. I wish, indeed, that you would come down here. What is the expense? Not so much as a new bonnet or mantle. And why should you not spend money on comfort, as well as on visible results—tables, chairs, or carpets? I am sure it would do you good in every way, and the comfort to me would be beyond all price! My brother has said very often how he wished for you, declares that he feels inclined to write to beg you to come himself. —— also wants you, and we would do our best to make you well. Do let your impulse carry the day, and come to us. You need not even write an answer yourself. If you drove up in a cab, 'quite promiscuous,' you would find yourself expected, and all ready to receive you. And as to the fare, it really is so little that the diminution of the 'weekly bills' will more than cover it. So do not tremble on the brink, but come. Of course 'Nero' will come with you, and we have no cat to torment him. I was very poorly all last week, but I hope I am getting a little better now. We had sad news of poor Neukomm[1] the other day from Leipzig. He was descending the stairs, when, missing the first step, he rolled down to the bottom. Luckily he had on his hat, or he must have fractured his

[1] The Chevalier.

skull. As it was, he received a deep wound on his forehead, twisted his neck, and crushed his wrist —besides the terrible shock to his whole system. He is confined to bed, but dictated a letter to his mother, from whom the news came to us. Neukomm keeps his gaiety, and says that this scar will give him a martial look, and be equivalent to a decoration in these days! But I am very uneasy about him. At his age such a fall must, according to all the laws of gravitation, have serious, even permanent, results; and it is such a long time before we can get reports of his state, Leipzig being far off. Mr. —— has made me promise to go to London with him to see the Exhibition in May. He will be the best possible person to go through it with, and I have undertaken to go and see old Mr. —— the next time I am in town. But the secret motive of my wanting to go to London so soon is to see you! As to ——, she seems fast relapsing into a nebulous body. I answered her letter at once, for, as I have no cause against her, it had to be done, and I calculated that doing it soon would give an indifferent letter a virtue not its own! So I wrote, and kept it to 'still-life,' and made no inquiry after ——; not but what I should like to hear, but because I did not choose to be opening a channel of communication. Every day I feel more and more thankful to have got away from Seaforth. Instead of any relenting, I only feel wonder at my own want of instinct in not breaking away sooner, and I feel that —— is become so like a jelly-fish that one can keep no hold on her. The whole connection has come to an end by the natural law of dissolution, as opposed to the laws of cohesion. ——, however, wrote me an answer by return of post, and there our correspondence will remain 'high and dry' —not from any want of good-will, but just because she has got decomposed, and there is nothing left to lay hold of. My brother is reading me, at this moment, elaborate speculations on the 'nebular theory' and the formation of the solar system, and you may fancy what a confusion it makes in my ideas. I have to give my attention to 'satellites being detached from their primaries,' and I am writing by candle-light, and my eyes are complaining! I had many other things to say, but they must stand over. I will write again very soon. My brother sends his love. God bless you, dear child, and send you here!

Affectionately yours,
G. E. J.

I wrote to —— to tell him again about the papers being sent you. Mr. Scott[1] is elected Principal to the New College here.

---

[1] The late Principal Scott, once 'co-pastor,' or assistant-pastor, with Edward Irving, and, later on, one of the bright and shining lights of the Owens College, since named 'The Victoria University' of Manchester.'—A. E. I.

LETTER 103.

Tuesday (Postmark, October 30, 1850).

Dearest Jane,—I wrote you a letter on Sunday; but I was in a very bad way, and the letter was more than stupid, so I begin another. I was very anxious when I wrote, but things have cleared up. I want very much to know how you are now you are at home again, how your new maid 'shapes' to her work, but, above all, how you yourself are in every way. Do write to me, if it be only a line just to tell me. I think of you a great deal, and I am still hoping to see you arrive down here. As to me, I am not nearly so well as I was; I am again beginning to feel that weight in my head which condemns me to a state of oppressed stupidity. It is caused by these heavy fogs and damp days. When a bit of frost comes I am as brisk as a bee, but Mr. —— says Greenheys is too heavy for me, and I am sure it is too damp for my brother. I read a book the other day trying to prove that women live upon air—that is, that the air they breathe has much more influence over them than the food they eat. We are on the look-out for a new house, and we have seen one that I want very much. Whether I shall get it is another affair, and a question. I would almost sooner have your sickness than this constant oppression, which is as if somebody had put their hand on a spring and kept me down. The chief news I have to tell you is about myself, that I have found a good mantua-maker, and that she has made me a beautiful dress, which fits like one of yours. Also, I have been to see the fashions to-day, and bought myself a cloak which I think is a very good speculation. Is there not a certain satisfaction in the heart of every woman when she gets a successful bonnet, or cloak, or gown? I am almost ashamed of myself for being so pleased with this cloak—which, after all, is only of coarse brown cloth—but it has a hood, and hangs in the most beautiful folds. I got a note from —— the other day, which I send you. Surely people need not die of trouble unless they choose, for if anybody ever seemed obliged to hang themselves it was she, and yet she has pulled through, and it is always a comfort to see that. When people founder or make shipwreck, it frightens one for one's own prospects, and that, I fancy, is the secret of all human sympathy, and that is also why we are so anxious to prove that any sort of ill-luck comes from people's own fault—as we are prone to do, from the day of 'Job's friends' down to the present time. I was reading a book that pleased me much the other day; it was Legouvé's 'Histoire Morale des Femmes'—a sort of *résumé* of the actual position held by women in the social scale from feudal times down to to-day, their legal rights and disabilities, and it contains many sensible suggestions. As to the improvements that might be made in their position, it is out-and-out the best book about women I have yet read, being also free from the besetting sins of the French school. It is the tone in which it is written which pleases me. When I have time I intend to ease my mind by an article on this book and Mrs. ——, against whom I have a vicious spite that has not evaporated by keeping silence so long, and it will be a real comfort to 'say my say' about her. Has —— sent you the 'Ladies' Companion' yet? He wrote me word that he had been suffering under a severe affliction, which has made it difficult to remember many things. Do you know what it is? How is ——? I am very sorry for him, and yet his feeling for you is like a heavy piece of ordnance, with which he intends to blockade you, as if you were some strong place to be reduced by being bored into a surrender. Upon my honour, I am frightened when I recollect him. It is his military instinct which makes him 'manœuvre' his love, as if it were a detachment of heavy cavalry. Still, I am very sorry for him, and you can remember me to him. Do write me one line to tell me how you are, which is all the news I care to know. Where is Miss —— now? and how is Mazzini? If he has given you a copy of his book, I wish you would lend it to me. You can send it by post, and you shall have it back soon. Poor Neukomm is getting well. We have had a letter in his own handwriting which is reassuring, inasmuch as no very permanent effects will result from his accident.

Wednesday.—This is a day of unwearied rain, and I have had to do precisely the good-natured thing I detest most emphatically—viz., walking about in the rain. But then it was only to 'do as I would be done by'—and that is just the most subtly selfish maxim that has ever been brought into operation, though it is the distilled essence of Christianity notwithstanding. Since I came in, and before I was quite reposed from my fatigue and the ill-temper consequent on it, a parcel was brought purporting to come from Egypt. I opened it, and found two daguerreotype likenesses —one of —— himself, and the other of his little daughter ——, accompanied by a most affectionate letter thanking me most amiably. Now the letter I wrote some time ago might have been dictated by the Devil himself, it was so—what shall I say?—infernally disagreeable; in fact, I have had a great remorse ever since, and this is my reward. I laughed when I opened it. Everything in one's life seems such a mocking irony upon what one wishes, and what one tries to deserve, and what one gets precisely for not deserving. What possesses men to do things when it is too late, and which if done before would at that time have made one very happy, but about which one is now profoundly indifferent? By way of completing the thing, the glass which covers ———'s portrait is smashed all to pieces, so that I can hardly see the picture through it, and I expect the whole daguerreotype will have disappeared before I can get another taken, and I don't even feel vexed. I have even gone so far as to wonder what it will cost to get it replaced. I should fancy myself very hard and cold-hearted, feeling all this change, if I did not know that when I once care for people, my regard must be worn out by elaborate ill-behaviour before it is alienated. My inmost conscience tells me that I am not fickle, and so when change comes I cannot lament or abuse myself for being natural. Yet, even a lesson like this will not cure one of hoping and wishing to the end of the chapter about something or another; what a fool it makes one seem, or perhaps I only *seem* what I really *am*! God bless you; do write to me directly. I could not get this off yesterday. Do write and tell me about yourself.

       Yours,
        G. E. J.

LETTER 104.

Manchester, Sunday, November, 1850.

Dearest Jane,—I am very anxious to know how you are, and how the arnica answered. It is a most sovereign remedy for bruises of all kinds and wounds of every description. It is as wonderful as the herb which used to cause the spears and arrow-heads to fall out of the wounds of their own accord. I came home on Wednesday a great deal better, but have been getting worse ever since. For you may fancy the change from pure sea-air to the thickest and most continuous fogs you ever saw, even in London; and in the midst of these we are removing. We are in the most disorganised state you can conceive, even worse than your recent experiences. I have caught a cold such as I have not had for ages, and I am to-day very poorly. I do so hate these upsets. My brother wants to be in a new house for Christmas Day. He says there are too many 'ghosts' here for him to be happy in it, and as the house we have taken is on an altogether different 'beat,' there will be no associations, and no hindrance to his getting his soul and body quite well, both of them. The house we have taken is a very nice one, in a part of the town you don't know at all. It is called Ardwick. We are on the old London road, but quite out of the town, and opposite a very handsome house and garden. So we shall not be overlooked by opposite neighbours, which are my dread and detestation. There will be a nice room for you whenever you come, and I think you will like our new quarters better than these. It is a much handsomer and more commodious house, and we have a species of garden at the back. Old Peggy,[1] of course, goes with us. We might do many things if she were younger and stronger; but as we shall never part with her while she lives, we must arrange accordingly. She has softened very much, and is so good to my brother, and so much better to me, that I don't feel at all tempted to change. The cat will go with us too, whose history is remarkable. It came to us of its own accord, in deep distress, a homeless wanderer. We took it in, and it was so dirty and miserable that I ordered it to be drowned, bidding Peggy get plenty of water and a heavy brick, which she did—and I thought it despatched. The next morning, figure my horror! to hear a plaintive 'mew' outside my door. I thought the wretch had not been sufficiently drowned, and had escaped, brick and all. So it seemed, and she came, dripping and reproachful, to my door. I did not dare to look at her, but called wildly for someone to carry her away. It seemed she had not been drowned at all, for, as Peggy said indignantly, 'I had got the tub of water and the brick to tie round its neck quite nice and ready, and the cat ran away.' It came back again, and was again condemned, but escaped, and now, in my absence, it has thriven, and grown quite handsome and an ornament to feline society. I had a very kind note from —— the other day, saying that

[1] An attached maid-servant.—A. E. I.

—— seems disposed to take 'Marian Withers,' and bidding me send it up to be looked at, which I have done. I had such a shock the other day. Poor —— (that was) is dead, having died in her confinement, after suffering horrible agonies. I cannot tell you how sorry it has made me. She certainly enjoyed her life, and was fenced round and round, threefold, with self-complacency, which added much to her comfort; but she had good points, and then this dreadful death makes one forget all her sins. I did not think I felt half so kindly towards her : it has been a damp upon my mind ever since I heard it. And then to think what a dismal Christmas this will be to her husband! There was another thing I had to tell you, but it has slipped from me, though it was on the tip of my pen. Has —— sent that tale yet? I have not received my set, so I cannot send them. —— has been sitting for his picture to ——, who has made a beautiful likeness. I had a visit yesterday from ——, who married that cousin of mine, in spite of her dint of perseverance. They looked very happy, and he has grown so grand and so pompous I could hardly have sworn to his identity with his former self. . .

[Fragment.]

LETTER 105.

Sunday, December, 1850.

Dearest Jane,—I was very glad of your note, for I was getting just desperate to hear from you, and the postman came just in time to save me from the crisis of a great rage, which would have been a bad beginning of the New Year. I am very thankful you are better; and don't wait for 'convenient seasons' that never come, but just write when you can—at 5 A.M., if you will! Do let me have the 'diamond dust' *en attendant*: the jewel as large as a pigeon's egg will come all the same. I am writing on that principle now, for this is the chief thing I have to say, having a headache and being very sleepy. I send you another letter from ———. I had directed the letter wrong, and so sent another to inquire after the first. ——— got a mysterious letter from ———, wanting him to go over to see to his 'insurance,' and wishing to see me particularly before he spoke to anyone else. I fancy he will stop at home in peace. The people here are beginning mildly to be pained for Mr. 'Mary Barton.'[1] And one lady said to me the other day, 'I don't think authoresses ought ever to marry,' and then proceeded to eulogise Mr. Gaskell. I want to know how you got along with Mrs. Gaskell to-day? I have a notion that if one could get at the

[1] The late Rev. William Gaskell.

'Mary Barton' that is the kernel of Mrs. Gaskell one would like her, but I never have done so yet. Have you? I should have liked to have been at your dinner-parties. I have had two 'festivals of the season,' and dreadfully tired I was after them, for poor old Peggy is getting long past work, and of course I have to fetch out everything with my own hands and put it up again, clean the silver, and put it away, &c. When I had no nice things I used to wish for them, and think how delightful it would be to have them about me; but now I feel what a bother they are to keep in order and to keep together. Do you want to read a fascinating book (always supposing you don't know it already)? Get Ellis's 'Early English Metrical Romances.' I lighted on them quite by chance the other day, and found them charming, not in old-English jargon at all, but translated into intelligible prose, with here and there a special verse. My word! One's ancestors were not at all stupid. . . .

[Disconnected.]

What a lovely ribbon you sent me! I am so glad it was Lady —— who sent the velvet; you will enjoy your gown now.

G. E. J.

LETTER 100.

Tuesday, December, 1850.

Dearest Jane,—Only one word, to tell you how thankful your letter has made me. I was very unhappy about you, and if I seemed to speak very confidently and cheerfully about the 'arnica,' I was none the less anxious! If you only get well and keep well, it is all I ask. What will become of me if anything bad happens to you? Take care not to catch cold, and keep yourself warm, and then if you get better I don't care one straw whether you follow my small prescriptions or not. *Au reste*, I can quite sympathise with your contempt for all 'doctorings' from 'old women,' by which I mean all unauthorised practitioners. You feel towards them much as St. Paul did towards 'old wives' fables,' seeing he could write his own. I am also glad you have done with ——. There was a certain overbearingness and—what shall I say?—brutality in him, that has annoyed me when I have thought of it. He treated you like a town to be taken by storm. There was nothing either gentle or winning in him, and though women rather like to be tyrannised over by men they love, it is different when the love is all on one side; and, besides, the tyrannising, or rather worrying and domineering, has been carried on in quite a wrong fashion! I would almost sooner have had —— making love to me—and the force of comparison can no further go! And yet with all that I am sorry for him, for he had plenty of fine stuff in him, and the only comfort I have is in a moral reflection I once read about Poland and the Poles—viz., that when nations and people experienced such outrageous misfortunes, there was always some radical fault in themselves, and that, however sorry one might be, one could not help them till they helped themselves. But I have no time for moral reflections, or sympathy with anybody but myself. I am writing in the front parlour, full of packing-cases, and I am disorganised altogether! . . . But your letter this morning really did me good, and put me in good spirits, and I am only writing to tell you so. We go to our new house on Thursday, but I shall leave directions with the postman about my letters. And I am very malicious when I own to feeling excessively pleased that —— has come to me on compulsion. Any spite I had is amply gratified by that, and, besides, now I shall not have to use up any good-feeling on him. I wish you were going to see Macready in 'Richard II.' instead of that stupid play 'The Jealous Wife'—who, after all, is only a bad-tempered wife. Miss —— is married to-day, out of hand, and I am glad of it. Yesterday I packed up all my papers, letters, &c., burning many. Only to think of all the foolish hopes and fears one wastes, all the strength that goes for nothing! I burned up all Miss ——'s letters, all ——'s, and a heap of miscellaneous ones, but I did not feel any great sensibility on the occasion; those phases were over and done with. But I did feel very thankful that your letters were to me even more than they used to be ; and as I met with one or two that had been written during those three years, I felt glad that they meant really nothing except this—we were both miserable, and are now right, and that there had never been a reason for them. I always have burned at once, as soon as read, all private and confidential letters, and the rest are tied up in one packet, and if anything happened to me they would be sent to you, but I expect I am going to keep them a long while yet. My cold is nearly well, and the fog is gone, which is a blessing. I am so glad I need not feel it my duty to 'wash at home.' Now, good-bye ! and God bless you ! I must go out.

Ever your own
G. E. J.

[Last letter from the old house at Greenheys, December, 1850.]

1851.

LETTER 107.

Friday, February 6, 1851.

Dearest Jane,—I am so glad poor dear little 'Nero' is found. I always felt a secret faith in his good star, and that he would be able to come back to you; and I shall have faith in the strength of one's heart's desire another time, for if you had worked without that, I fear neither bills, nor rewards, nor friends, nor even 'Nero's' star would have brought him back. He is but a dog, and a sad dog too; but really I feel quite as much satisfaction as if it had been a stray Christian that had come back. I have been really happier since I knew he was safe with you. Do put a leather or brass collar round his neck, with his name, and your name and residence! As to his want of proper feeling on his return, my dear, I could find you a ream of sermons written to dogs' masters, reproaching them with caring so much more for the pleasures of sense, and the vanities of the world, instead of the things that concern their highest interests. If 'Nero' was allowed to eat as much as ever he chose (which vulgar people always let their dogs do), and never chastised for his faults—but encouraged in all his bad habits—how can you expect that the canine nature of a dog should not have become demoralised? Upon my word, I felt very touched with your account of him. It was so natural, that ¦I only felt all the more glad he had got back to you. I send you back ——'s letter, which charmed me very much. It is so clever and man-like. How can women have a chance when it comes to a regular hand-to-hand fight with a man? She may deceive him—she may overreach him—she may cut his claws, and draw his teeth by flattery and other Delilah-like means; but when it comes to a regular battle, she cannot succeed, and ought not so to do. I wish —— had been married to Mrs. ——. Perhaps in the world of retributive justice he will be obliged to take her, and then there would be nothing left for their worst enemies to desire! What is —— like? I am just enchanted with his letter, and I shall lay it up in my heart against the evil day, if Providence ever sends me a husband who is a bad one, and I can get no Chancellor to sympathise with me. Yet for all that I can understand poor Lady ——, sore and pestered with all her injuries, turning sick at the little hope, or indeed recognition, she receives, and the small chance of justice being obtained for her; and it is that sense of injustice, and the baffled fight to right oneself, that makes the difficulty of patience. The more I hear of her, the more sorry I feel for her. But can you not inoculate her with some of your own judgment and sense? Good gracious! where or what would you be now if you had gone on passionately protesting, and refusing to bear anything but what you thought you deserved? Do make her feel that she is not the only ill-used woman in the world. And if you could only make her more patient, and less bitter, it would be more to her benefit than any recognition of her wrongs or increase of income, or even any amount of justice or sympathy. As to Mrs. ——'s letter, it made me very sorry for a while, and then it struck me that it was all as false as a nightmare. Do not answer the letter (if that deed is still to do). It will do no good. The only hope for her is to be left alone, to meditate! You see, through the whole letter there is no recognition of her own fault, except perhaps some romantic blame she takes about her own conduct towards ——. All she says of her 'purgatory' is nothing but the effect of overstrained nerves, and has no genuine regret in it, nor any one wholesome sentiment. All that talk of 'a convent' to hide in is simply disgusting. She has no sense of the systematic and habitual heartlessness of her conduct. Her want of common humanity, saying what she does of ——'s death, is absurd—she does not really believe what she says. She wrote to me in London (the last letter I ever had from her), that she had been much shocked and pained by the report that, on the morning of his death, her husband was said to have seen the only person who could have told him certain things. . . .

LETTER 108.

Thursday (Postmark, April 1, 1851).

Dearest Jane,—Apparently you are tied to the 'mill-round' for some time to come, but your letter has only added to my anxiety about you. It does not arise from anything you say (for you tell me nothing), but from various symptoms in your letters of late. I fear I should be no great comfort to you even if I were with you, for I feel more helpless than ever as to 'doing good' to anybody every day of my life. But will you, dear, bear in mind that I myself, and all I have, or can do, is yours at any moment you want? If any sudden thought should strike you that you would like to come here, come on the instant. I shall not look surprised nor ask a single question. —— has sent an entreaty that you will come and see us, so you can feel no scruple about the 'master of the house.' If you were to walk in by return of post, you would fancy you had been certainly expected, and your room would be ready in a quarter of an hour. Will you bear this in mind? And recollect that I care a deal too much about you to feel any sort of curiosity! Whenever you feel that an escape somewhere—from all that worries you—is necessary, come here and recover strength, or do whatever it may please God to inspire. It may not be to-day, nor to-morrow, you will feel to wish to come to me: but whenever that thought strikes you, come! I am very poorly to-day, weak and anxious. My brother was called suddenly to Nottingham yesterday to see after a 'fire,' and I have had to calm and comfort the sensibilities of his little dog, which has been moaning and sobbing like a child, in spite of the most elaborate spoiling and petting. Poor Mrs. —— is very ill, and I feel very anxious about her. She is worse than when she left home. God bless you and keep you ever. Your own   G. E. J.

P.S.—I have been deep in Newman's sermons. Did I tell you of them in my last? They are wonderful, both for eloquence, and also as showing what is believed by a certain type of the Christian faith. To see those old doctrines all nakedly stated and boldly asserted without the least attempt to disguise them and soften them, is as astounding as if one of the old 'ichthyosauri' or 'mammoths' were to come stalking through the world. Then, as a

record of fearful struggles, and the mode in which
'reason' has been conquered by 'faith,' the work is a
spiritual revelation the most startling and tragical.
I have not read such a book in my whole life before.
It haunts me. Again, for mere beauty and eloquence
it beats any other book I know. I wish I had known
it had been published when I wrote my recent article,
but I must do another on 'Belief.' There is one
sermon, on the ' Mental Suffering of our Lord in His
Passion,' which is like a Greek tragedy. . . .

LETTER 109.

[Presumably late in the month of April.]

Friday, April, 1851.

Dearest Jane,—I cannot let ——'s letter go without
a line from me. I am stronger than when I wrote
the other day, and I suppose I am getting well, but
I cannot yet sit up, and I write this in bed, as it
fatigues me less. I have got into a bad way, and
can't 'go right' all at once. But I have no pain, or
nausea, or headache, only weakness; and as I eat
well, and sleep well, and am getting awfully cross, I
don't see that either body or soul could be in a better
line towards recovery! Poor dear —— has been
very anxious about me, and would have had me see
company all day long. He has been a most kind
nurse, and—for a sick person in some danger—I have
had a very comfortable time of it. I am very sorry

to be turned out of my bedroom to face all the worry of paying my bills, and seeing the house cleaned, and my clothes mended, to say nothing of the bore of finishing that 'tale' and the prospect of having to write others. I cannot tell you the blessedness of perfect idleness. You may fancy the pitch to which I was raised above sublunary concerns when I tell you that the kitchen chimney took to smoking in the most diabolical fashion, filling the house with the smell of brimstone (without treacle), and I could not get up any emotion about it. They have put up a chimney-pot now, which seems to answer, so I daresay these high winds will have a shy at it, and tumble it down. The only book I have been up to looking at is White's 'History of Selborne'—such a lovely book, and yet I don't know in what its fascination consists. I was offered a French novel, but I am not up to it. There is not a breath of fresh air in those French books. Do write to me, and tell me about yourself. You are far worse than I am, and your letters are always a comfort. God bless you, dear love.

Your own
G. E. J.

I would just give anything in the world to see you or have you within reach.

April, 1851, Manchester (after my dangerous illness).

LETTER 110.
Sea View House, Southport, Lancashire:
April 28, 1851.

Dearest Jane,—I want to know how you are, for the other day I was fidgeted with the idea that you were in one of your bad headaches, and in your last letter you have said nothing about your own health. I am very much better than I was—indeed, I suppose I ought to call myself well, only I can walk so little. Mrs. —— is much better, and able to sit up on the sofa and on the foot of the bed, but is still very weak. Her husband is going from home this week, so I have undertaken to remain until he returns; after which I must go home and finish my work, which is beginning to torture me worse than a nightmare. I went out to drink tea at the Rectory the other night. I was much amused at being amongst a set of people so different to those I am accustomed to; but the rooms, the house, the garden, might all of them have come out of an old book, they are the ideal of an English rectory. And this morning the brother was brought to call, a very clever man and a rabid anti-Protectionist, and he spent the whole call in trying to convince me that 'Protection' will be the ruin of the country, which he seems quite to believe. He is a landowner, and a magistrate, so I suppose he feels both as a man and a Briton. You cannot

think how strange it seems to be in a nest of
'Evangelicals,' who all write letters, and talk, as if
they were going to contribute to the happy life and
death of a religious magazine. How Mrs. ——
herself gets on amongst them I cannot imagine, she
is so superior to them all! But the Rectory people
are an exception : they are really nice, and Mrs. ——
actually read ' Zoe,' and made some extracts from it, in
spite of being so dreadfully shocked. So of course she
must have redeeming qualities ! I want to see Lady
——'s new novel. I see it is ' out.' Are you delivered
from her? and what is going to become of her? Poor
Mrs. —— has been dangerously ill again, and I am
very uneasy about her. My brother has bought a big
dog, that frightened him, and he is not its master by
any means. I hope it will be sold before I get back.
This letter is stupid to a degree, but I am left very
like a meadow that has been mowed ! . . . .

LETTER 111.

Sunday, May, 1851.

Dearest Jane,—I have looked for a letter from
you every day, but none has come, and I have grown
very uneasy. The more I have reflected upon that
last note of yours, written more than a fortnight
ago, the worse I feel; there was a ghastly calmness
about it which, combined with your long silence,

makes me fear that matters are very much amiss. At first I thought it was only an incidental attack of that sort of 'stagnation' to which I am very liable myself, but now I am become seriously uneasy. Another symptom has struck me also. It is, that I told you I was coming up to London very soon, and you have kept a total silence upon that piece of intelligence, which is not natural. When the postman this morning brought me no letter from you, all the anxiety about you that had been fermenting in my mind came to a crisis. Now —— goes up to London in a fortnight. What do you say to coming down here for as long as you can stay, whilst the house would be all to ourselves? I would either go back with you when you returned, or we would make any other excursion that we might take into our heads. Long ago we talked about an expedition together; let it come off now. I am not so good a walker as I was, but I am quite strong enough not to be tiresome. Do not you recollect how we settled that we 'go and seek our fortune,' that you were to defend me from all the cows we met in our way, and that we were to take a cottage in some place, either on a moor or on a mountain? What is to hinder our putting it in practice? I had rather do that, twenty times, than see the Exhibition and go through a course of 'amusement,' as I did last year. It would be a comfort to us all the remainder of our lives, and do us both a world of good, whilst you would get away from all the people and things which are worrying you. By the time —— goes off I shall have finally got rid of this cursed book, which, owing to my illness, has hung on hand till I feel quite frantic about it. Two more chapters will see the end of all that needs to be written, and then I shall feel free. I would far rather have you here than any other scheme of enjoyment that could be proposed to me. What do you say? Even if you do not feel tempted to make an expedition, you might come here to be quiet. It is a much more comfortable house for stopping in than the other was, and I cannot divest my mind of the impression that you are just now specially annoyed. A few weeks away from the people who are worrying you would be so much gained, and it would be a comfort to me beyond all I could tell you. Will you try and come? It may not be long that we shall have the chance of being together, and I think we should as much as possible strive after what we most desire, and I am sure your coming down here would be more to me than your remaining all the summer in London can be to all the heap of people who come to see you for their own amusement, and, ten to one, are the very people who make unkind speeches afterwards. You shall stop as long or as short a time as you will. You shall do anything and everything you like—only come! I shall suspend all purchase of the 'blue silk dress'; I had far rather spend the money in making a journey with you. I am so full of this scheme that I can write about nothing else, and I have a bad headache besides. My brother sends his love, and says he has been hoping to hear from you, and I am hoping too. God bless you, dear love!

Ever your affectionate
G. E. J.

P.S.—There was something else upon this sheet, which I have had to cut off, or else to re-write what is here, and that I am not up to.

LETTER 112.
Ardwick, Birchfield Terrace,
Monday night, May 14.

Dearest Jane,—If sympathy could do you any good, you have it in the most genuine form from me—that is to say, in the shape of fellow-feeling. For the last three weeks I have been blown upon by an east wind, and am as good-for-nothing and poor and cowardly as the Devil himself could desire; it is rather a comfort to know you are in the same way! I fancy everybody suffers more or less from these spiritual relapses—at least, I know that I never took up a religious biography without finding, on every other page lamentation over their 'deadness,' 'dulness,' and the impossibility of saying their prayers. I fancy it is only their way of complaining of what we feel. It is a nasty, miserable, sinful state, but I am waiting for an angel to come down and cause a reaction. It cannot go on long. As to your 'nightmare' of not being able to write letters, don't I know that? But then, I let them all go unwritten—and yet, not all. *You* have had letters and letters from me bearing 'the mark of that beast' upon them. Attempting to do anything when it is upon us, is like grinding in an empty coffee-mill—in fact, at this present time I am very wicked and uncomfortable, and all my skin, moral and physical, feels like the bark of a tree. But then, as to your physical health, I don't like your account of it at all, and it makes me very unhappy. I don't know what to say to you about it, nor what to think of it. I wish I could do you any good, but I cannot even make a suggestion for the sake of giving myself a hope it might open a door of relief to you. . . .

Now what is that about the 'enemies' who have made themselves manifest? What specially disagreeable thing have they been doing? I believe a real, practical enemy is as scarce as a true, thoroughgoing friend, but there are always people who make hateful speeches about one. Whether they mean them or not I don't know, but every now and then I wake up to the consciousness that I am being 'run down,' as —— used to call it, and, of course, by people I never did any harm to in all my life, and who can only detest me from some abstract sense of duty; and then, after a while, it subsides, to rise again like the wind in the East! It is very natural people should hate you, because, to the world without, your lot looks peculiarly enviable, and you seem to have every sort of prosperity the heart of a woman can desire, and they cannot see what you have done to deserve such good treatment. Talking of enemies, I was once transformed into one by a man whose name even was unknown to me! It happened in this way. I had to write an account of some play (for Douglas Jerrold, I think), and in the course of it I had occasion to remark that the man who enacted the lover made one wonder at the infatuation which had led the heroine to such a misplaced attachment, or something to that effect, and he got a friend to assist him to write a letter denouncing me as his 'enemy'!

I told you my brother had set up a big dog, and now he has set up an arbour as big as a cottage, and with the trunk of a tree for a table. So we shall have all manner of ruralities for you when you come to see us. But figure to yourself: this arbour, being far too big to get into the garden the lawful way, was obliged to be put over the palings, close by

Cæsar's kennel, and—would you believe it?—he allowed this phenomenon to be carried before his eyes, and did not even bark!

Wednesday.

This letter has not been despatched yet! I hoped to add something more witty, but the 'dead-level' of stupidity continues unbroken, and the fine May weather makes one feel as shabby in one's moral condition as in one's wardrobe. I shall make a dead push to go out and amuse myself to-day, for, since my illness, my spirits are strangely depressed—a thing I have not suffered from for years and years; and I am sure it is not for want of employing myself, which good books always declare to lie at the root of these clouds. I was out of doors this morning at five minutes past eight, which I take not to be bad, and then I have a cold bath every morning—but it is no good. I send you ——'s letter, and also one I have just received from Mrs. —— by way of balance. Do write me something, no matter what, but just say expressly what it is that is tormenting you.

LETTER 118.

Postmark, June 6, 1851.

Oh dear! Oh dear! Poor little Nero. But you are surely not going to lose heart about him, and leave him in the lion's den because he may be again stolen. 'Sufficient unto the day is the evil thereof,' and I have such faith in your powers of negotiation that I expect even 'dog-fanciers' will find a conscience. Nero must be got back: he was the only thing that did not torment you; he was a comfort, and must not be let go! I can sympathise more now than the last time, for I shall nearly break my heart if anything happens to Kennet,[1] and I have been pleasing myself with thinking what a friendship would spring up between Kennet and Nero when you brought him down here, though I fear there might be hostility. No! Nero must be got back, even at the risk of having his future liberty curtailed; he must henceforth walk in a string. I want very much to see you, and I daresay I shall come to town next Wednesday. I hope there will be no 'smash' for either your cousin or myself. —— went up the day before yesterday, and the next morning set off on a steamer to come and see you, but got on board a wrong one, which went the other way! He had a great quantity of tobacco for you, which —— sent by him. He is stopping at the ——s in Berners Street. I myself have had losses—as I lost my purse on Wednesday with 25s. in it. And I am more provoked than I can say, because not only I can't afford to lose money just now, but also I have been self-

[1] Miss Jewsbury's own pet dog.

denying, and done without a new shawl which the lost money would just have got, and, of course, if I had bought it, I should not have lost my money. I cannot even hope my pocket was picked, for everything else was safe. I must have dropped it myself, and I thought of you, who once lost just that sum in going to see after my affairs. As to ——, I am frightened of her. Never until I had got rid of her out of my home-life did I know how much cause I had to be thankful that I had done it, harsh as it was. Perhaps you will manage better, but I own I would as soon she were out of your road, too. I have had no relenting towards her; but, on the contrary, all that has come back to my memory of her former ways has been bad. I can recollect no single instance of common-sense or common principle, and her insinuations against everybody get into one's mind like dust. I shall always feel a difficulty in forgiving the bitter feelings and thoughts she has raised in me against numberless people. Nothing sterling or wholesome comes back to my thoughts as connected with her. The longer the time that elapses since our separation, the more decided is my repugnance to her. It was lately the anniversary of poor ——'s death, May 21, and I have thought of him and of her a great deal. That last letter of hers about him filled up the measure of my detestation. I hope she does suffer; but as she has no conscience, it will not be one-half what she deserves. So it is very lucky for our neighbours that we are none of us 'God Almighty,' to judge the world. I am expecting an old lady to dinner to whom I used to go to school when a very young girl. Poor soul, she has had a terribly hard life, of which a bad husband was one of the lightest ingredients—and now she is very solitary and poor, but keeps up her spirits and her courage in a way that makes me feel very much ashamed. God bless you, dear love! I feel always as if I had got you back from the ' shadow of death.' Don't let —— mention my name, for her tongue leaves ' a trail ' wherever it goes. Surely nothing and nobody will ever come between us again. Have you seen a wonderful book by Miss —— called ' Realities ' ? Oh good gracious ! good gracious ! that any woman should have ever been given over to such bad taste ! She has published it at her own expense, so that says much for her sincerity, but the book makes one feel 'trailed in the mud.' Nightmares are realities—but hardly real life. Yet the book is clever. Now, good-bye.

LETTER 114.

Higher Laver Rectory, near Ongar, Essex :
Monday, June 10, 1851.

Dearest Jane,—For the two last days anything like writing or reading has been out of all question. On Saturday we went out early in the morning to pay a visit for the day, and yesterday being Sunday, I had my hands full with going to church twice, which kept me till after post-time—to say nothing of the fact that I could not get off between the services. To be sure, I did console myself by taking a book to church with me (my dear old 'Thomas A-Kempis'), but Mr. —— somehow found out that I was not looking at my Prayer-book, and called me to order. To-day I am writing to you in bed with a heavy cold, which has been hanging on me for the last week, and I am now very feverish. So I have had to take it in time, and lying in bed has been from time immemorial the only discipline for my colds. Miss —— would fain make me lie without either reading or writing; but I am very anxious to hear how you are, and I suppose there is no hope of a letter from you until you have first had one from me. Do, please, send me a line, and tell me something about yourself, for indeed I feel quite in the dark about you, as all the time I was in London I never had one comfortable minute with you, and I know less about you than when I left home a few weeks ago. —— herself has a deal more of you than fell to my share, and it has made all my stay in London seem a failure to have had nothing of you. What would London be for me without you? I wonder if ever I should go there at all. Of course, I amused myself very well, but then it is because I have you in the background, to tell everything to and to make everything of some value; and I think you have behaved very shamefully to me in never writing me a single line all this last week! You seem as contented as possible whether you have me or not, and scarcely care a single straw whether you can speak to me or not. But it is no use going on in this way, for I am, I know, just now very irritable, and have been for several days. And so it is as well I am here with nobody but Miss ——, of whom I stand in a great deal of 'traditional' awe, and I must make haste and finish this scrawl before she comes and finds me in the act! The country looks lovely, all the trees in thicker leaf than ever I saw them. I had a long walk the other day with Mr. —— all through cornfields and bean-fields; and the hedges, not yet sacrificed to the 'improvements' in agriculture, were of wonderful beauty and luxuriance. To be sure, I tumbled once or twice into a ditch, the ground was so uneven: one stile fairly frightened me, and it was not until we had gone to the top of another field half a mile long and found no outlet, and had to retrace our steps, that I found necessity can conquer even impossibilities, and I did get over it! I have such a beautiful dog here, a retriever and pointer, quite a pet—though a good-sized dog; and I have undertaken his education, and bought a whip as a token of my affection. The brute will gnaw and bite everything that comes in his way, the flounces of our dresses especially. How is Nero? I hope quite safe; give my regards to him.

The dinner-party at Mrs. ——'s went off very pleasantly. It was like being translated into a novel. After I left you I found a very kind note from her, telling me she had made up a little party for me of people she thought I would like to meet. I called at a grand hairdresser's in Regent Street, and had my hair made decent for once in my life, but hardly knew my own face again with the hair brought low down on the cheeks. The muslin dress fitted very well and looked very nice, but it was high in the throat; and even Mrs. —— herself wore a low dress, with nothing but a pearl necklace round her throat. There was another young lady besides—her daughter —who was even thinner than myself, and she wore a very low dress; so I felt as if I had gone in a morning wrapper. Everything was very nice and in excellent taste. I knew some of the men, but I was put between two strangers at dinner—one, the Marquis of ——, and the other some young Guardsman, with a desperate pair of whiskers and moustaches to match, but they were both very conversable, and we got on very well. Lord —— is the most cold, calm, respectable-looking man I have seen for many a day, and I could scarcely believe in much I have heard of him. Mrs. —— talks very well indeed, and tells stories capitally. In fact, we all seemed like people and things out of a novel, and one wondered where the real life and human nature of the people had been stowed away, and whether any of them knew anything of the practical and economical difficulties of life. There was another chapter, too, just open for a glimpse—viz., of fashionable young ladies; but I cannot discuss that just now, and perhaps I had better wait till I have had an opportunity of seeing a few more. So I won't say what is on the tip of my pen, and perhaps someone else might say it more becomingly than I could do. Mrs. ―― sent me home, and was very kind. When you see Captain ――, will you tell him I intend to write him a note, as he always reproaches me with never replying to him; but to-day I am too tired and cannot hold up my head any longer. God bless you! Write soon.

Your affectionate
E. G. J.

LETTER 115.

Sunday, July 13, 1851.

Dearest Jane,—It seems as if we were to be always away from each other just at the time we might be of the most comfort and get the most good out of each other. What is the reason we can never be long together with those we most care for, and who make up the most of our lives? We see people we are indifferent about every day of our life, but the moment we begin to care for a person we are certain and sure to be carried away to the ends of the earth, or at least out of sight and hearing. Your letter made me very unhappy! If I had been with you I daresay I could have done no real good, but at least you would not have been left so lonely, to do your illness all by yourself. But it seems that it is only in novels that people live with those they most care for. I can better understand the mood you have so long been suffering from than perhaps you think, for some years ago I was in something very like it for a long while, but I did not understand it. I had no one to speak to, and I could not believe in it, and so tried to force myself out of it, which did me a great deal of harm. It was like living in one of those dreary, calm November days when there is but one cloud—but that one covers the whole heaven, and there is no believing in a sun whilst it lasts. I can only give you the sympathy of fellow-feeling! I hope and believe that it will clear off, but no effort of our own, nor any wisdom or maxim from without, can drive it away. I found one day a paper that I had written when I was suffering somewhat as you are now. I suppose I must have been getting better before I could have written it, but it made me shiver to read it, for I recollect writing it. I know it was a sullen 'daguerreotype' of what I felt, and written only because I had no soul then to speak to. It was the frightful absence of all feeling or energy, as if I were dead and yet alive under it all, that made it as horrible to me as being bricked up alive in a prison. I rather think I destroyed the paper, but if I can find it when I get home you shall have it. If I had given in to my wretchedness, and not tried to get up a feeling of some sort, it would have been better for me. I was reading to Miss —— the other day a chapter ('Ecclesiasticus,' in the 'Apocrypha'), and there was a verse that struck me much. It was, 'Make not haste in the time of clouds!' Now, I always have tried to 'make haste'—and struggled and plunged whenever I have been unhappy, and my testimony is, that it would have been much better if I had sat still and waited patiently for the clouds to pass over of themselves. But I think, too, that physical causes had a great deal to do with it! I shall never forget how aggravated I felt one day when I was in the blackest despair. One of the commonplace sensible women said to me, 'Ah, Miss Jewsbury, you have a charming flow of spirits, you have not learned what sorrow is yet.' It is just because one is becalmed in despair that one has one's wits about one, and can be very amusing for the benefit of such fools! This will reach you on your birthday. For my own sake, I shall write you a great many more letters on this day, for my life has been so much happier since I knew you (except that miserable time when I had been made to think ill of you, an error which brought its own punishment with it). I do not know what I should do if you were taken away from me!—not only for my own comfort's sake; but I should make all manner of mistakes, and get into scrapes innumerable, without you, especially if I am to go about at all amongst people. For though I have often taken my own way in spite of you, yet I have always had to own you were right at last. So, my dear love, please do not think about wanting to die, for you could be dreadfully ill-spared. When I am with you I often cannot say half a dozen words to you, not even when there is all the material, time, and space free before me. But when I am away I think of you constantly, and I refer all I see or do—to be told to you when I see you. I am very uneasy and anxious just now. You don't know my friend in Cairo, never saw him, and so you can't have much sympathy with me about him. You would have more if you knew how much I owe to him. Well, he has come back to France, as I think I told you, but I had a short note the other day from him. He is very ill; the change of climate has tried him severely, and he suffers from spasms, which grow more frequent every day, and I know this note was written to prepare me for the worst, though it may not come just yet. Loss of fortune is a great

thing, but what is it to losing one's friends? One seems so rich in them one minute, and then, perhaps, in a few months, they are gone away for ever! When one's money is done one has the chance of getting more, but one's friends, once lost, leave one in misery for ever. There is no replacing them, and yet I would rather they should die outright than live to turn to water and corruption, as the friendship between myself and —— has done. But do get well, dear child, and don't die; it makes me begin to cry if I even think of it. So what would the reality be? Do take care of yourself. This is not a letter worth anything, but I am not in good spirits, and there is no news here to tell you, except that I must close my letter and go to church again. —— is, I believe, in London, so you will most likely see him; he was to be up last Wednesday. As to that, —— will do better than I should. I hope you will have a fine day for East Sheen. I wish I were going, so send me an account of it. God bless you, my dear love! and
    Believe me always
      Your affectionate
        G. E. J.

LETTER 116.

London, Monday, July 28, 1851.

Dearest Jane,—I have engaged to spend next Wednesday with Mrs. ——, so the gleam of a chance of getting to you on Wednesday evening has closed up; but on Thursday I shall (if the Devil does not bewitch everything) be with you as early as possible. It is a great bother and provocation that I can get to see everybody else in perfect peace except you. You I have not seen, except in the midst of a worry and when you were tired to death. Not one word have I had with you, and I am in a state of protest against Providence for letting me leave home on a Friday, which I am sure is the cause of all my crosses. After leaving you on Saturday, I got two calls done successfully, but I lost my parasol and got no dinner. The parasol I left at the post-office, so I hope to recover it, and the lost dinner I have atoned for; so things might be worse. But what I have not got over is the seeing you so plagued as you were. If —— were not so frightened of doing wrong, he would oftener do right, and anyway be less of a bother. His services are like so many white elephants, of which nobody can make use, and yet that drain one's gratitude, if indeed one does not feel bankrupt. I have been to call on Madame ——, and I saw her, and not her husband, in spite of ——'s sarcasm, and I have a great notion that she is the better of the two. I was very much pleased with her. There is a look in her face, although she is neither young nor handsome, which I like. And she made me laugh at her account of all the 'lyrical' recognition which people have expected for all they ever did or had intended to do on behalf of her husband; and how they had all fallen ill—herself, husband, and children—the first thing, and been utterly incapable of making appropriate acknowledgments; and then her dismay at finding themselves set down as 'ungrateful' when they got about a little, and able to go abroad. She told it so nicely and naturally. And also how a whole host of 'refugees' had 'come in promiscuously' one Sunday to dine and sleep, and be put in the way of helping themselves—on Sunday, of all days, when the shops were shut—and all her difficulties in arranging their housekeeping and getting them lodgings! She must have a great deal of good in her. She seemed so helpful, for, besides having to interpret and see to the affairs of so many, she has to give lessons and earn the 'wherewithal' to keep her own house. I shall try and fire the train of Mrs. ———'s enthusiasm, which will be a good thing for her. God bless you! G. E. J.

Kind regards to ———.

P.S.—I went to hear Kingsley[1] preach last night.

[1] The late Canon Kingsley, author of 'Two Years Ago,' &c.

A very good, sensible sermon, something like what a sermon should be, but orthodox, as I thought, beyond reproach. And only fancy the dismay of the congregation when, after listening more than one hour and a half, and the whole was ended and the blessing given, the real clergyman of the Church started up in the reading-desk and told them that all they had heard was wrong, and dangerous, and false; and that if he had imagined what the sermon was to be the pulpit would never have been lent for the occasion. Kingsley sat like a stone, the congregation said 'Hush! hush!' to each other, and came out without making any observations. Was it not an odd conclusion? His sermon was on the text, ' One Lord, one faith, one baptism, one God and Father of all.'

LETTER 117.

[Fragment.]

London, August 9, 1851.

. . . I never felt so little interest in anything that concerned myself before. Mrs. —— is ordered abroad for the winter, and the doctor says it is the only chance for her. She leaves London next Sunday, and I am very sorry, for she is the only person I care for in Manchester, and I shall miss her very much. Her husband wants me to go along with her, but that I cannot do. I have been so interrupted with people talking that I hardly know what I write—only know that I have not told you one-half of what I intended.

I went to call on Mrs. Procter [1]—I thought it only polite—and found her at home. Her black dog tried to fly at me, and was consequently sent away in disgrace. She talked of Harriet Martineau, who has been to one of her 'swarrys' lately, and all her old friends cut her because of her 'Atheism.' 'But, *en revanche*, "Miss Adelaide," who had not known her previously, begged to be presented to her, and sat a long time conversing with her.' I could hardly help laughing. I also called on Mrs. Browning, but I only saw the 'baby,'[2] which is the most lovely, noble-looking child I ever saw. I think I shall make another attempt to see her—Mrs. Browning.[3] As to the 'Romance,' just let it take its chance till the spirit moves you, which it will in due time. As to John Carlyle, he has not been near me, and I don't feel at all tempted to earn either the 'epitaph' or the 'teapot.' Do write to me again soon.

Your affectionate
G. E. J.

[1] Wife, and afterwards widow, of B. W. Procter (Barry Cornwall), and mother of Adelaide Procter, the poetess.
[2] Robert Barrett Browning.
[3] Elizabeth Barrett Browning.

LETTER 118.

London, Monday night, August 18, 1851.

(We go home on Thursday.)[1]

Dearest Jane,—I ought to go upstairs and begin packing, but the Devil may run riot with my trunks until I have written to you. I think he must have been in me that I have not got a single line written to you, and when I fail to write to you, you may always conclude that something desperate is the matter. My dear, it is the ' necessity,' which affects the gods themselves—too strong for mortals—which has stood in the way, and intercepted your letters, and hindered those I *thought* to you from getting written! I hardly know whether my head is the right side before, and the provoking part is that I have written plenty of the sanest letters to other people! Let me begin at the beginning, and tell you as much as I can. I have been doing that poor artist of Miss ——'s for one thing, though little did I think of taking up a *protégé* when you left—but if one begins to stir, one must move on to the end. It is like getting on the treadmill—one step obliges another; one cannot leave a thing half-finished. But I am quite sure I have no general benevolence in me—it is nothing but the innate necessity of finishing up a thing to the end. It began by my thinking I

[1] Mrs. Carlyle was at Great Malvern.—A. E. I.

could get him into the Hahnneman Hospital. I wrote to Neukomm, and he stirred up Madame ——, and, as there was no place in the hospital, he wrote and sent a guinea and a recommendation for a nurse. That meant a day's journey to go into the City to see the matron, and I am sure I could write a tale about all the things I have seen. But, really, the spontaneous kindness people have shown, and the trouble people have given themselves—not in a sickly and sentimental benevolent way, but in a quiet, matter-of-fact, effectual way—has impressed me very much, and such help and assistance as each could give has been given without grudging. . . . In all this development of mutual virtues in all the world, the most wonderful remains to be told. What do you think I have done?—come to the inheritance of all Miss Farrer's finery. She brought me this morning a box of the most lovely French flowers, very little the worse for wear, a large bundle of gauze and lace, a ball-dress and trimmings, and satin shoes—till it was quite exciting to any female mind to contemplate them. And she has promised me a quantity more! It was a bright idea that came to me one morning to beg the wrecks of the season from her. All the difficulties of finding Miss —— in stage dresses will fall on the mother, and I knew Miss Farrer would have plenty of articles to bring away—rubbish to her, but treasures for stage costumes!

So I told her that a young girl in whom I took some interest had gone on the stage, and told her what I wanted, and, really, since I was a child and had a parcel of dolls'-clothes given me, I never experienced such an entrancing sensation as when I contemplated all these sundries this morning. I all but danced round the bandbox—and they will be so useful, and save the mother so much worry. I suppose it is the innate vanity of the female mind which makes me feel so much more amused at getting this cast-off finery for Miss —— than I did in trying to get the poor man into the hospital. And Miss Farrer seemed to be amused too, and to like giving them for that purpose. . . .

[Fragment.]

LETTER 119.

Tuesday (Postmark, August 26, 1851).

Dearest Jane,—Will I? Can I? What ridiculous questions! As if you could come at any time when I wouldn't be only too thankful to get hold of you. Only, don't talk about going away. You must stop here as long as possible; and, instead of going on to Liverpool, why not come on direct to me? Separate from Mr. Carlyle at Birmingham, and come down here afterwards. We will go together to Liverpool for a day, if anybody is at home there. The house is in its first gloss of cleanness, for —— has spent her time polishing it up during our absence, and she is very glad at the prospect of seeing you again. Kennet writes by this post to Nero to assure him of his friendship. I have a great heap of things to tell, and was just going to write when yours came, and now the prospect of seeing you so soon has made them all look not worth writing. I fear from your letter that you are but little better for your sojourn. How jealous I feel of those two women who have had you so long all to themselves! I am in the midst of shirt-mending. Now that I have got that book off my mind, I see how shamefully dilapidated I have let ——'s shirts become, and am mending them accordingly. Manchester looks very dingy after London, but that is my fault. There was plenty of excuse for ——'s neglect of both of us. He was arranging his sister's marriage, and it is settled now, and it seems to me something very like sacrilege. No man on earth is worthy to touch the tip of her finger, and I never felt so tempted as I did to shut her up in a convent, and let nobody so much as look at her. She is a perfect type of woman before any sort of system had been invented for her—just as Nature intended a woman to be; there is something so noble and primæval about her. It is her brother's intimate friend who is elected. I used to like him, and he is well enough for a man, and would have been quite good enough for ninety-nine women, but this hundredth is too good for anybody I ever saw. This half-Oriental, half-practical mode of marrying, strange as it seems to us, is the custom they all hold to most religiously; and it answers in practice, for unhappy and ill-assorted unions are rare! Poor Mrs. —— has lost one of her children; it was from disease of the brain, I fancy. Now, God bless you! I must keep all I have to say till we meet, which, D.V., will be next Saturday—not Monday. But don't bother to write. I shall have your room all ready, so come, like an angel, when you will. God bless you!

Your affectionate
G. E. J.

You don't say you have got my long letter all safe.

LETTER 120.

[After Miss Jewsbury's last visit to Manchester, October 2, 1851.]

You dear Child!—I don't like your symptoms at all. It is the worst sort of nervousness. I have suffered from it much, and when that 'flying' feeling comes I always am in a bad way. I wish to Heaven you would see after yourself a little, and then we should know if that headache here was only an ordinary one! What can your headaches be? I am very unhappy about you. I wish you were

here, that I might see after you. I don't like the way
you are in; I am getting very frightened about you,
and I don't get frightened for nothing. Will you
take some advice? I don't think John [1] (kind as he
is) realises your case or knows how ill you are ; he
has no faith in his profession, and he has, besides,
got used to seeing you suffer, and does not know how
serious the case is. You are wearing yourself away.
As to ———, I am very thankful that he is good to
you. You would miss him if he were away, and it
is being so sure of him that enables you to feel no
sort of anxiety, for there is no friction. Harriet
Martineau is here—has been here three days—and I
have seen a great deal of her. I like her exceedingly;
she has been good to me, and I think my good-will is
the reaction of all my prejudice, and her good-will
to me ditto. She is genial, and cordial, and natural
—not the 'pagoda' manner I expected. We went
together to see some industrial schools, and she was
very agreeable and gentle. She only mentioned you
incidentally, and made no allusion to anything that
had passed until this morning, and then I said, 'I
heard from Jane yesterday, and she is very poorly.'
The tears came into her eyes, and she spoke very
tenderly of you and very nicely. In the end she said,
'Jane has misjudged, but we are all right again now,'
and then she went on to say more. She loves you, I

[1] Dr. John Carlyle.

think, better than anyone else, but regrets that you are a very long way off, and wishes you could be nearer to each other.

LETTER 121.

Monday, October 6, 1851.

Good heavens! those —— have come again. Read the enclosed advertisement, read the enclosed letters, and see if you think I have done right. I could not feel comfortable to let people go and fall into the same 'Slough of Despond' as we did, and I feel, besides, 'called' to put a stop to their lying career. I don't know whether to write to any of the other people or not. If you don't like the letters, send them back to me, and tell me how to alter them. I want very much to know how you are; I thought I should have had a letter yesterday. I am pretty well, but, having missed my morning walk yesterday and to-day, I am all the worse for it; you cannot think the difference it makes to me. I am going up to my old friend's to-night; he is, I am sorry to say, very poorly, and looks wretched. I wish you would fulfil your promise of writing to him. He was very much hurt at our not calling to say 'good-bye,' and had to comfort himself with reading a book of 'Hindoo Proverbs,' and it says much for the extremity to which a man is reduced by his friends when he has to extract consolation from such candied and petrified sweets of wisdom as proverbs in use before the Christian Era—it is worse than receiving a lock of hair from off a mummy by way of souvenir! Do write to him—it will be only common good-nature! I hope and trust you are writing your tale. I have been thinking of you a great deal, and I am very anxious you should have some employment more stimulating than mending old clothes, something that will really employ your energy. Writing, as an occupation, has most excellent properties; it not only blunts one's *amour propre*—or, as we politely term it, our sensibilities—so that we not only feel less acutely things that would otherwise irritate beyond endurance, but these things are transformed for us into artistic studies, instructions, experiences, and this goes a long way towards softening their intensely personal application to ourselves. Besides which, one's work is an 'ark of refuge,' into which one flings oneself on all occasions of provocation. When I am much annoyed, or have done anything foolish (which is a reflection that stings worse than remorse, as I can testify, though you don't know it so well as I do), my first impulse is always to cut my throat, and the next, to set to work savagely, and it is surprising how soon one gets into a state of indifference! It is not, however, altogether for your own sake that I am anxious you should set to work upon a story or a book of any kind that you are moved to do. You have more sense and stronger judgment than any other woman I ever knew, or expect to know; also, you have had such singular life-experiences that it is in your power to say both strengthening and comforting things to other women, who, when the Devil assists them, are apt to think, as poor —— used to say, that 'never was a person placed in such a situation before'; and it takes the shine wonderfully out of 'situations' to meet with them recorded in their simple principles, and stripped of all the halo of self-love, vanity, and fancy. If you had had daughters, they would have been educated as few women have the luck to be, and I think you might have enough maternal feeling, sisterly affection, *esprit de corps*, or what you will, to wish to help other women in their very complicated duties and difficulties. Do not go to Mr. Carlyle for sympathy, do not let him dash you with cold water. You must respect your own work and your own motives; if people only did what others thought good and useful, half the work in the world would be left undone. 'She hath done what she could' is all that the best can expect or desire. Now, do set to work resolutely. I am just now open to any sort of arrangement you like to make. I will give the staple of my time to this mutual tale if you will begin, for I am needing a regular work on hand; this desultory writing for the 'Athenæum' does not employ all my time, nor is it likely to last. So begin, begin! half your loneliness comes from having no outlet for your energies, and no engrossing employment. As to ——, your doing anything in 'pique' is quite unworthy of you, and it only recoils on yourself; the harder we strike, whether in revenge or justice, it comes back upon ourselves with far more pain than we have wished to inflict. You ought to have had a dozen daughters—and I am sure they exist somewhere, either 'in the body or out of the body,' or else in some charming 'spiritual translucent element,' as Origen calls it. So let your work be dedicated to your 'unknown daughters.' I am one of your children, after a fashion; I am sure you care for me more as if I were a daughter than as a woman cares for her friend, and the real sympathy between us is when you forget all the usual 'punctilios' between grown-up people, and think of me as of a child, to be taken care of and not be allowed to get into mischief. If ever I am good for you, it is in the way a daughter would be to her mother, for the practical fact that I am nearly as old as you are never interferes with the sentiment. So, finally, my dear love, begin to work; but first write to our poor dear friend. And now good-bye! My head is very weak to-day. —— sends his best love. —— is in London; I don't know whether he has his wife along with him. Let me hear from you very soon.

Your loving
G. E. J.

P.S.—Has Mr. Carlyle returned? If you do not think the letters 'judgmatical,' send them back to me, and suggest a better course.

LETTER 122.
[Fragment.]

November 4, 1851.

. . . I have read 'Sterling'[1] through. If Mr. Carlyle were to write a tragedy, he would produce one far beyond the 'Œdipus,' or even 'Prometheus.' I never felt so profoundly miserable after finishing a book in my life. It left me far below all attempts to express either criticism or admiration. I could not even cry, which one generally is up to doing when one can say nothing. I was just crushed down under the sense of the misery of all the world, from which seemingly there is neither help nor escape till death. As a biography it is the most exquisite life-picture I ever read. No other that I know is to be compared with it. One feels as if one had at once gained and lost a personal friend. But, oh! the weight of hopelessness that lies on one when one has finally shut the

---

[1] Carlyle's 'Life of Sterling.'

book! I was thankful to be obliged to rush out down to town to pay some bills, and to forget it for a little. There is a review of it in the *Times* by somebody who does not understand it. Of course, one would never have the wild expectation that Mr. Carlyle will ever approve or admire any human effort. But then he does better: he rouses one to desire to do right, and we can work without caring for his praise. And, moreover, as our best doings are only very pitiful shortcomings, worth little or nothing, it is just as good for us that the consciousness of our unprofitableness should be kept constantly before us, instead of the serene self-complacency of doing wonders, over which we should fall asleep, certainly neither in blessedness nor the odour of sanctity! Now dinner is here, and I must go. God bless you!

Ever affectionately,

G.

P.S.—I forgot to tell you that the moral of this letter is to be that you are to do what you can—which is, write your tale! I am looking out for it.

LETTER 123.

Last Tuesday night in this Year of Grace, 1851.

Dearest Jane,—I hope you will like the apron. I have had two made, one for you, and one for me, and I send the one that I think you will like best; if, on seeing mine, you prefer it, we can change. I intended you to get this on New Year's Day, but as you won't be at home it will be waiting for you; and I think it is always pleasant to find letters or parcels waiting for one when one gets home after an absence. There is something very blank in coming back into a house that has been chilled by emptiness. My brother wishes you many Happy New Years, which I do, too, only the newness so soon wears off, and the 'copper' shines through one's attempt at hoping. I hope you will come back without cold, which is a hope so practicable and moderate that a disappointment would justify complaint—if that would do any good either, or if there were any 'Providence' appointed to listen to that sort of thing! I have not been at all well of late, but that is not very remarkable. What troubles me is that I have had from time to time a threatening of the return of those old fits of blackness and depression which make me feel sick when I look back to them, years ago! I hoped they were passed away for ever! Of course, I shall fight against them with all my might, but there are so many more years on my head now than there were then, that if they once fairly come on me there will be no deliverance. It was like being suddenly shut up, as one is in a nightmare, or a black cloud dropping down upon one. I

don't know what I shall do if it really comes in full
tide. I suppose people who have been put to the
torture once are more afraid of it the second time
than they were the first. You will write to me as
often as you can? A good letter from you does me
more good than anything else, and is, besides, the
only thing I care much about now. Don't send me
any more witty, polite letters. I cannot stand them
just now, and I don't think it can be much pleasure
to you to write them. How is 'Nero,' the good little
dog? 'Kennet' is not much of a comfort to me,
and will have to be sent away. I must tell you a
well-authenticated ghost story, which I hope will give
you the thrill of horror it gave me; the person who
told it me had it from the cousin of the young ladies
in question. In a village near Newcastle-on-Tyne—
the name I was told, but forget—there stands a house
which was built in 1800 on the ruins of an old building which had enjoyed a reputation for having had
all manner of unutterable crimes committed in it. The
new house soon had the reputation of being haunted.
Two young ladies, who were sisters, went on a visit
to the family who owned the house, and who naturally
would not listen to such reports: thus the visitors were
put to sleep in the room most haunted, without being
told anything about the matter. In this room there
was a species of large press, full of drawers, and the
door shut close against them, so that it was a physical

impossibility for anyone to be concealed in it. Towards morning one of the sisters was lying awake, and, looking towards the press, she saw the head and upper part of a female figure, dressed in grey, leaning out; the face was turned towards her, and had no eyes, only the hollows where the eyes ought to have been. The figure uttered a dreadful wail, and the poor girl fainted with fright. Her sister was awakened by her falling back on the bed, and on finding her insensible rang the bell and roused the whole house, very much alarmed, as you may fancy, but without any suspicion of what had caused it. Whilst the people who came running to see what was the matter were going about looking for 'eau de Cologne' and 'smelling-salts,' and all the things in requisition at such times, the sister who had been asleep chanced to look towards the press, and saw the head of a woman, without eyes, grinning and nodding at her; she was clothed in grey. Both the sisters were ill in consequence of the shock, and left the house that very day. The inhabitants of the village declare they have often seen a figure in a grey mantle walking up the side of the house, as if she were mounting a flight of stairs, and some have seen her head looking in at their windows. The house is still standing, but has long been uninhabited. . . . .

1852.

LETTER 124.

Dated Good Friday, 1852.

My dear Jane,—I was glad to get your letter. I hope by this time something definite has come out of that domestic chaos of servants and servants' illnesses. I am sorry, very sorry, to hear of poor ——, but I am more provoked by a great deal else that you tell me. I don't see why you are to be tormented for everlasting by other people's incompetency. It is small encouragement to be up to doing things oneself; but I suppose, in this world, those who *can* do, *must* do—for themselves and their neighbours too. I remember, as a very little girl, how I used to cry to be carried; indeed, I have had a great taste for it all my life, only I have been made to find my own feet. And, if I might recommend, I should say, let your people do the like. You have plenty to do in keeping yourself up and going without an armful of other people and their children to look after; so I hope you will let them drop, the first soft place you meet with. Servants, even the best of them, seem to have an idiosyncrasy of morality peculiar to themselves. I had a letter the other day from Mrs. ——, whom you have heard me mention. She went with her husband on a scientific expedition to Africa. Well, her letter came along with yours, and, oddly enough, contained the details of the departure of a servant who had lived with her for thirty years. I never read anything so outrageous in a woman not insane. If you will fancy the ill-conduct of that old servant of your own, exaggerated and magnified in the proportion of length of years, you may have some notion. This woman had not been always a servant, but was much better born and educated than is usual among that class; and Mrs. —— had tried to save her feelings in every way—bearing with her temper, which was a very bad one, and treating her more as a friend than a servant. When her daughters married this woman expected to be retained as 'companion,' and because she was not she came up the other day, when her mistress was ill (with an attack of the heart complaint, under which she labours), and in a great domestic sorrow besides, and, after exploding into violent abuse, flung herself down on the floor, and kicked, and screamed; and when peremptorily ordered to get up and go out, lay down on the stairs at the drawing-room door, groaning and sobbing, for two hours, and the next day ordered a coach, sent word by the housemaid that she was going, took her wages sullenly, and departed without a word of softening or remorse. She has behaved much as —— did to you after her departure. I always like to hear of other people's misfortunes; it prevents one thinking one is ill-used oneself. I don't care for troubles when they are the rule, and not an exception on my behalf! I want to know how your parties went off at Lady ——'s, and what you wore, and how you looked, &c. So do not forget, when you write, to tell me. I set up a very beautiful dress the other day, and such a bargain that, although we were not in communication with each other just then, my first instinct was to wish I could turn it over to you. It is one of those rich brocaded silks that almost stand on end, a beautiful pink colour, and I got it at ——'s for 3*l*. 5*s*., and there was no earthly reason that I could see why it should not have been charged its original price, nine guineas; but they said it was because broad stripes were not fashionable. Ah! I suppose it is only angels that improve with eternity; everything else is only good when new! And, talking of bargains, only fancy my feelings! At a sale of books the other day 'Marian Withers' fetched nine-pence a volume, though a bookseller whom —— asked to bid for him said that he was prepared to go as high as a shilling for it!

LETTER 125.

Tuesday, May 11, 1852.

Your letter just come.

Dearest Jane,—Just one line to ask you how you are after that precious expedition to the dentist's. I have always felt some complacency on the matter of that sort of fortitude, but I could not have gone like you in an omnibus, with my mind made up to the prospect of losing a tooth. I might have acquiesced in the supreme moment of desperation, but to go after realising the event, I don't think I could. And then I know all the after-wretchedness and 'shatteredness' that follows the violent loss of a tooth. So let me know, please, how you are, and whether you have come to your natural sleep again. When I was a young girl I had a weariful experience with a dentist not only pulling out teeth, but pulling one straight that grew crooked. It was a horrid time, but the man was a Scotchman. I forget what his name was. And on the table in the waiting-room there were wonderful books to beguile the time. It was there and then I read the first volume of 'La Nouvelle Heloise.' Only fancy! that on a dentist's table!

But I want to know how you are. Has that sickness and headache at all slackened? Is it sickness in the course of nature, or worry from some Satanic entrance? As to your servant, what you say about her virtues makes me think it is quite time to get rid of her. If they took fire or boiled over, they would be vices directly! They say expression spoils the symmetry of beauty, so I suppose the same rule applies to virtue. —— is still very poorly indeed, and has only been to the office twice or three times, and been always much worse for it. He cannot talk at all, and I don't at all like the way he is in. What is that your cousin says about your going away to Germany for a year? I have heard nothing beyond the possibility of a month with Lady ——. Whatever is it? You may as well tell me, so that . . .

Wednesday, May 12.

Heaven only recollects what the end of that sentence was to have been! I was called off on the moment to do something or other, or go somewhere, for my brother, and I had not time to finish, and since then I have been ill in bed, with sore-throat, and pains in the limbs, and all sorts of devilments. I am not well yet, and can eat nothing but bread-and-water. . . .

Friday, May 14.

Until to-day, that is, for now I am quite well again, and have made a dinner that would not disgrace a dragoon, and by the blessing of Providence I will finish this letter. I only send the previous disjointed fragments that I may get the credit of my good intentions, which were that you should receive an answer by return. I suppose if one were very resolute, and had the miraculous gift of 'loaves and fishes' with respect to one's time—I mean if one could really employ to the uttermost every moment one has, that the result would be as wonderful as the 'twelve baskets full' of scraps, and this letter which I wanted to write would have got achieved somehow. But then, that sort of industry does not lie in me, and one's moments of idleness are as indispensable as the air one has to breathe. Whilst I have been lying in bed I have been tormented by the notion of your going out of the country for a year. What does it all mean? Do write and tell me, even if you say nothing else, and have your time even more 'hashed up' than mine has been of late, which would be difficult.

I have had further communication with Messrs. —— and —— who are quite content to give me sixty guineas for 'The Adopted Child,' and I want to write it. It is to be a small volume. But I must get quiet first, and a convalescent man in the house, who is not only a man but literally a 'brother,' seems to come before all the tales in the world, except such as are already printed and good for reading; such dissipation of mind is produced thereby. I did not know till I tried it how the mere fact of being always at hand to be talked to makes work at composition impossible, but, *en revanche*, I have done a deal of sewing, for I have been permitted to re-garnish the linen-chest, which was getting empty. There are still three pairs of sheets and a couple of tablecloths to be done, but I have stitched my way through half a piece of linen. I was in the midst of workpeople when I last wrote to you, for I had been having clean summer curtains put up, and a new bed for myself— such a beauty! After mature deliberation I chose a peach-coloured chintz, all dotted with roses, to see what 'sleeping in roses was like,' and the wretched woman who made it up scrimped the curtains (which was a deal worse than doubling the rose-leaves), and I have been waiting ever since to have them properly done. The clean blinds and muslin curtains were scarcely up when that blessed kitchen-chimney began to smoke and fill the house with its abomination— and it had behaved itself for all the year before! And now something has entered the heart of our landlady to send to know what 'painting and whitewashing we would like to have done?'—an offer not to be refused. So my brother goes to Southport to-morrow, and the house is upset with a vengeance, and my darling curtains will be—where? I am going, the moment I have finished this, to move all my household gods out of the drawing-room, and prepare for the inroad of the 'Goths and Vandals.' I wish you were here to advise me and help me; I should not feel so helpless over it. How is Nero? Kennet is getting most fat and lazy. He invites one to kick him to express one's abhorrence of laziness.

—— was here on Monday. He inquired after you. He has been made churchwarden! I had a quantity to tell you that I have been nursing up; but these things must be like the 'manna of the Israelites'—fresh, and fresh, or they are not worth writing. My brother has just awoke, and sends his love. How is Mazzini? Dr. Smith said he had been ill. Do write soon to

Affectionately yours,

G. E. J.

P.S.—You had better read the end of this letter first, because the first part was written so long ago!

LETTER 126.

Tuesday, August 3, 1852.

Dearest Jane,—I send you by this post—(at least Frank[1] has taken it to town to send you)—the chapters of the MS. up to chapter eleven inclusive! I have altered all the others, and cut them very much shorter, which I hope will be an improvement. You sent me three leaves of the third chapter, and as I suppose you sent them to be mended I tried to do so, and have compressed them considerably. So I hope you will be better satisfied with them on the whole. As I am somewhat after time, will you forward them as soon as you can, and put the three leaves in the right place? In the condition of your household I had some qualms of bothering you with this batch of MS.,

[1] Mr. Frank Jewsbury, referred to so often as 'my brother.' The brother and sister were very deeply attached to each other.—A. E. I.

but as you have the other portion, it will be as little trouble to send all as half, and very much more satisfactory to me if you have time to look them over and say how you find them. But don't feel obliged to read them unless 'time and the hour' are propitious, and in conjunction with your own inclination. I feel very much obliged to you for making me re-write those chapters. And now—so much for business—you have told me what you are doing at the house, but I want to know why you are doing all this, and not building a new house at once, rather; in fact, you have told me so little about yourself and your doings, that I feel to be plunging about in the midst of things, striving in vain to find bottom or top. What are you after? And why is your old servant gone away, just when she was bound by all the laws of gratitude to stop and take the house on her shoulders, and help you and keep you from all vexations? I am beginning to think gratitude is an entirely fictitious paper issue from the bank of virtue, and that there is no sort of specie to answer to it. It is perfectly absurd how often one hears of it, and how seldom one sees it. Finally, I want to know how you are in the midst of this wreck. Did you go down to Sherborne? and how did you find poor Mrs. Macready? With regard to that little servant of yours—I would not keep her if I were you; such a development of curiosity will surely be fatal to any mistress under the sun. It will not confine itself to inspecting letters, and all that, but it will show itself in listening to private conversations, and in prying into all your comings and goings; and servants are so coarse in all their thoughts that they can understand nothing they see, but put the most abominable construction on all that passes. The best of them are uneducated in all their ideas, and those who are professedly curious and prying will not be bound by any laws of gratitude for kindness they may receive, or any respect they ought to feel. That girl will do you a mischief if she stays with you, and me, too, if she gets hold of this letter and reads it. At first I was inclined to laugh at your way of describing her—but it has come back to me several times, and has much disturbed me. You will get no good out of my letters until that tale is finished; it gets into a sort of insanity, the anxiety attending the end of a book. Frank is engaged just now in flying from one end of a railway to the other to inspect all the sheds and buildings. He tries to make himself out a martyr, but it is a fine 'lark' for him—at least, it would be to me, I know. We are overrun with mice, which Kennet barks at, but he does nothing more; and my servant, in despair, introduced the other day a little sprite of a kitten, such a morsel! and the problem was to make it stay, and for Kennet to leave it in peace. Poor little thing! If he had mistaken it for a rat it would have been all over with it, but the little brute has actually cowed him by facing

her enemy, and swearing like a trooper. Kennet
actually runs away when he sees her! 'Ah!' said
——, ' she is like a woman, she can use her tongue ! '
If one could hope for the same success it would be
an inducement to do the like. How is poor dear little
'Nero' in the midst of all this turmoil? How does
he like it? You have never said a word about him
this long time. Did I ever tell you how Kennet was
nearly dying, and how I had to send him to the
veterinary surgeon's to be poisoned? For I fancied
the poor wretch was dying, and he had been in such
agony for three days that I could stand it no longer,
and he looked so pitiful, just like a sick child—so,
with tears in my eyes, I set off. But the man (a
Scotchman) said he would try to cure him, and sent
him back, at the end of ten days, quite well—though
with a long bill. This is some little time ago, but I
have always forgotten to tell you, and all the fun that
was made of me by my brother for my humanity. I
am sure if Christians were measured by their doctors'
bills, there is not one in a hundred that would be
found really worth what it costs to cure them! I
have no news. I want to hear from you very much.
Try not to kill yourself!

Yours always,

G. E. J.

A CATALOGUE OF WORKS

IN

GENERAL LITERATURE

PUBLISHED BY

MESSRS. LONGMANS, GREEN, & CO.

39 PATERNOSTER ROW, LONDON, E.C.

MESSRS. LONGMANS, GREEN, & CO.

Issue the undermentioned Lists of their Publications, which may be had post free on application:—

1. MONTHLY LIST OF NEW WORKS AND NEW EDITIONS.

2. QUARTERLY LIST OF ANNOUNCEMENTS AND NEW WORKS.

3. NOTES ON BOOKS; BEING AN ANALYSIS OF THE WORKS PUBLISHED DURING EACH QUARTER.

4. CATALOGUE OF SCIENTIFIC WORKS.

5. CATALOGUE OF MEDICAL AND SURGICAL WORKS.

6. CATALOGUE OF SCHOOL BOOKS AND EDUCATIONAL WORKS.

7. CATALOGUE OF BOOKS FOR ELEMENTARY SCHOOLS AND PUPIL TEACHERS.

8. CATALOGUE OF THEOLOGICAL WORKS BY DIVINES AND MEMBERS OF THE CHURCH OF ENGLAND.

9. CATALOGUE OF WORKS IN GENERAL LITERATURE.

BBEY and OVERTON.—**The English Church in the Eighteenth Century.** By CHARLES J. ABBEY and JOHN H. OVERTON. Cr. 8vo. 7s. 6d.

BBOTT (Evelyn, M.A., LL.D.)—WORKS BY.

A Skeleton Outline of Greek History. Chronologically Arranged. Crown 8vo. 2s. 6d.

A History of Greece.
Part I.—From the Earliest Times to the Ionian Revolt. Crown 8vo. 10s. 6d.
Part II.—500-445 B.C. 10s. 6d.

Hellenica. A Collection of Essays on Greek Poetry, Philosophy, History, and Religion. Edited by EVELYN ABBOTT, M.A., LL.D. 8vo. 16s.

ACLAND and RANSOME.—**A Handbook in Outline of the Political History of England to 1890.** Chronologically Arranged. By A. H. DYKE ACLAND, M.P., and CYRIL RANSOME, M.A. Crown 8vo. 6s.

ACTON.—**Modern Cookery.** By ELIZA ACTON. With 150 Woodcuts. Fcp. 8vo. 4s. 6d.

A. K. H. B.—WORKS BY THE VERY REVEREND A. K. H. BOYD, D.D.

Twenty-five Years of St. Andrews. 1865-1890. 2 vols. 8vo. Vol. I. 8vo. 12s. [*Ready*]. Vol. II. [*In Preparation*].

Autumn Holidays of a Country Parson. 3s. 6d.

Changed Aspects of Unchanged Truths. 3s. 6d.

Commonplace Philosopher. 3s. 6d.

[*Continued on next page.*

A. K. H. B.—THE ESSAYS AND CONTRIBUTIONS OF—continued.

Counsel and Comfort from a City Pulpit. 3s. 6d.
Critical Essays of a Country Parson. 3s. 6d.
East Coast Days and Memories. 3s. 6d.
Graver Thoughts of a Country Parson. Three Series. 3s. 6d. each.
Landscapes, Churches, and Moralities. 3s. 6d.
Leisure Hours in Town. 3s. 6d.
Lessons of Middle Age. 3s. 6d.
Our Little Life. Two Series. 3s. 6d. each.
Our Homely Comedy; and Tragedy. 3s.6d.
Present Day Thoughts. 3s. 6d.
Recreations of a Country Parson. Three Series. 3s. 6d. each. Also 1st series, 6d.
Seaside Musings. 3s. 6d.
Sunday Afternoons in the Parish Church of a Scottish University City. 3s. 6d.
'To Meet the Day' through the Christian year: being a Text of Scripture, with an Original Meditation and a Short Selection in Verse for Every Day. 4s. 6d.

AMOS.—**A Primer of the English Constitution and Government.** By SHELDON AMOS. Crown 8vo. 6s.

Annual Register (The). A Review of Public Events at Home and Abroad, for the year 1891. 8vo. 18s.

*** Volumes of the 'Annual Register' for the years 1863-1890 can still be had.

ANSTEY (F.)—WORKS BY.

The Black Poodle, and other Stories. Crown 8vo. 2s. bds.; 2s. 6d. cl.

Voces Populi. Reprinted from *Punch.* 1st Series. With 20 Illustrations by J. BERNARD PARTRIDGE. Fcp. 4to. 5s. 2nd Series. [*In the Press.*

The Travelling Companions. Reprinted from *Punch.* With Illustrations by J. BERNARD PARTRIDGE. Post 4to. 5s.

ARISTOTLE.—THE WORKS OF.

The Politics: G. Bekker's Greek Text of Books I. III. IV. (VII.), with an English Translation by W. E. BOLLAND, M.A.; and short Introductory Essays by A. LANG, M.A. Crown 8vo. 7s. 6d.

The Politics: Introductory Essays. By ANDREW LANG. (From Bolland and Lang's 'Politics'.) Crown 8vo. 2s. 6d.

The Ethics: Greek Text, Illustrated with Essays and Notes. By Sir ALEXANDER GRANT, Bart. 2 vols. 8vo. 32s.

The Nicomachean Ethics: Newly Translated into English. By ROBERT WILLIAMS. Crown 8vo. 7s. 6d.

ARMSTRONG (G. F. Savage-)—WORKS BY.

Poems: Lyrical and Dramatic. Fcp. 8vo. 6s.

King Saul. (The Tragedy of Israel, Part I.) Fcp. 8vo. 5s.

King David. (The Tragedy of Israel, Part II.) Fcp. 8vo. 6s.

King Solomon. (The Tragedy of Israel, Part III.) Fcp. 8vo. 6s.

Ugone: A Tragedy. Fcp. 8vo. 6s.

A Garland from Greece; Poems. Fcp. 8vo. 7s. 6d.

Stories of Wicklow; Poems. Fcp. 8vo. 7s. 6d.

Mephistopheles in Broadcloth: a Satire. Fcp. 8vo. 4s.

One in the Infinite; a Poem. Crown 8vo. 7s. 6d.

The Life and Letters of Edmund J. Armstrong. Fcp. 8vo. 7s. 6d.

ARMSTRONG (E. J.)—WORKS BY.

Poetical Works. Fcp. 8vo. 5s.

Essays and Sketches. Fcp. 8vo. 5s.

ARMSTRONG. — **Elizabeth Farnese:** the Termagant of Spain. By EDWARD ARMSTRONG, Queen's College, Oxford. 8vo. 16s.

ARNOLD (Sir Edwin, K.C.I.E.)—WORKS BY.

The Light of the World; or, the Great Consummation. A Poem. Crown 8vo. 7s. 6d. net.

Seas and Lands. Reprinted letters from the 'Daily Telegraph'. With 71 Illustrations. Crown 8vo. 7s. 6d.

Potiphar's Wife, and other Poems. Crown 8vo. 5s. net.

ARNOLD (Dr. T.)—WORKS BY.

Introductory Lectures on Modern History. 8vo. 7s. 6d.

Miscellaneous Works. 8vo. 7s.6d.

ASHLEY.—**English Economic History and Theory.** By W. J. ASHLEY, M.A. Part I. The Middle Ages. 5s.

Atelier (The) du Lys; or, An Art Student in the Reign of Terror. By the Author of 'Mademoiselle Mori'. Crown 8vo. 2s. 6d.

BY THE SAME AUTHOR.

Mademoiselle Mori: a Tale of Modern Rome. Crown 8vo. 2s. 6d.

That Child. Illustrated by GORDON BROWNE. Crown 8vo. 2s. 6d.

[*Continued on next page.*

Atelier (The) du Lys—*WORKS BY THE AUTHOR OF—continued.*

Under a Cloud. Cr. 8vo. 2s. 6d.

The Fiddler of Lugau. With Illustrations by W. RALSTON. Crown 8vo. 2s. 6d.

A Child of the Revolution. With Illustrations by C. J. STANILAND. Crown 8vo. 2s. 6d.

Hester's Venture: a Novel. Cr. 8vo. 2s. 6d.

In the Olden Time: a Tale of the Peasant War in Germany. Cr. 8vo. 2s. 6d.

The Younger Sister: a Tale. Crown 8vo. 6s.

BACON.—*THE WORKS AND LIFE OF.*

Complete Works. Edited by R. L. ELLIS, J. SPEDDING, and D. D. HEATH. 7 vols. 8vo. £3 13s. 6d.

Letters and Life, including all his Occasional Works. Edited by J. SPEDDING. 7 vols. 8vo. £4 4s.

The Essays; with Annotations. By RICHARD WHATELY, D.D., 8vo. 10s. 6d.

The Essays; with Introduction, Notes, and Index. By E. A. ABBOTT, D.D. 2 vols. fcp. 8vo. price 6s. Text and Index only, without Introduction and Notes, in 1 vol. Fcp. 8vo. 2s. 6d.

The BADMINTON LIBRARY, Edited by the DUKE OF BEAUFORT, K.G., assisted by ALFRED E. T. WATSON.

Hunting. By the DUKE OF BEAUFORT, K.G., and MOWBRAY MORRIS. With 53 Illus. by J. Sturgess, J. Charlton, and A. M. Biddulph. Cr. 8vo. 10s. 6d.

Fishing. By H. CHOLMONDELEY-PENNELL.
Vol. I. Salmon, Trout, and Grayling. With 158 Illustrations. Cr. 8vo. 10s. 6d.
Vol. II. Pike and other Coarse Fish. With 132 Illustrations. Cr. 8vo. 10s. 6d.

Racing and Steeplechasing. By the EARL OF SUFFOLK AND BERKSHIRE, W. G. CRAVEN, &c. With 56 Illustrations by J. Sturgess. Cr. 8vo. 10s. 6d.

Shooting. By LORD WALSINGHAM and Sir RALPH PAYNE-GALLWEY, Bart.
Vol. I. Field and Covert. With 105 Illustrations. Cr. 8vo. 10s. 6d.
Vol. II. Moor and Marsh. With 65 Illustrations. Cr. 8vo. 10s. 6d.

Cycling. By VISCOUNT BURY (Earl of Albemarle), K.C.M.G., and G. LACY HILLIER. With 19 Plates and 70 Woodcuts, &c., by Viscount Bury, Joseph Pennell, &c. Crown 8vo. 10s. 6d.

The BADMINTON LIBRARY—*continued.*

Athletics and Football. By MONTAGUE SHEARMAN. With 6 full-page Illustrations and 45 Woodcuts, &c., by Stanley Berkeley, and from Photographs by G. Mitchell. Crown 8vo. 10s. 6d.

Boating. By W. B. WOODGATE. With 10 full-page Illustrations and 39 woodcuts, &c., in the Text. Cr. 8vo. 10s. 6d.

Cricket. By A. G. STEEL and the Hon. R. H. LYTTELTON, With 11 full-page Illustrations and 52 Woodcuts, &c., in the Text, by Lucien Davis. Cr. 8vo. 10s. 6d.

Driving. By the DUKE OF BEAUFORT. With 11 Plates and 54 Woodcuts, &c., by J. Sturgess and G. D. Giles. Crown 8vo. 10s. 6d.

Fencing, Boxing, and Wrestling. By WALTER H. POLLOCK, F. C. GROVE. C. PREVOST, E. B. MICHELL, and WALTER ARMSTRONG. With 18 Plates and 24 Woodcuts, &c. Crown 8vo. 10s. 6d.

Golf. By HORACE HUTCHINSON, the Rt. Hon. A. J. BALFOUR, M.P., ANDREW LANG, Sir W. G. SIMPSON, Bart., &c. With 19 Plates and 69 Woodcuts, &c. Crown 8vo. 10s. 6d.

Tennis, Lawn Tennis, Rackets, and Fives. By J. M. and C. G. HEATHCOTE, E. O. PLEYDELL-BOUVERIE, and A. C. AINGER. With 12 Plates and 67 Woodcuts, &c. Crown 8vo. 10s. 6d.

Riding and Polo. By Captain ROBERT WEIR, Riding Master, R.H.G., and J. MORAY BROWN, the DUKE OF BEAUFORT, K.G., the EARL of SUFFOLK and BERKSHIRE, &c. With 18 Plates and 41 Woodcuts, &c. Crown 8vo. 10s. 6d.

Skating, Curling, Tobogganing, and other Ice Sports. By J. M. HEATHCOTE, C. G. TEBBUTT, T. MAXWELL WITHAM, the Rev. JOHN KERR, ORMOND HAKE, and Colonel BUCK. With 12 Plates and 272 Woodcuts. Cr. 8vo. 10s. 6d.

Mountaineering. By C. T. DENT, Sir F. POLLOCK, Bart., W. M. CONWAY, DOUGLAS FRESHFIELD, C. E. MATHEWS, C. PILKINGTON, and other Writers. With Illustrations by H. G. WILLINK.

BAGEHOT (*Walter*).—*WORKS BY.*
Biographical Studies. 8vo. 12s.
Economic Studies. 8vo. 10s. 6d.
Literary Studies. 2 vols. 8vo. 28s.
The Postulates of English Political Economy. Cr. 8vo. 2s. 6d.

BAGWELL.—Ireland under the Tudors. By RICHARD BAGWELL. (3 vols.) Vols. I. and II. From the first invasion of the Northmen to the year 1578. 8vo. 32s. Vol. III. 1578-1603. 8vo. 18s.

BAIN (Alexander).—WORKS BY.
Mental and Moral Science. Cr. 8vo. 10s. 6d.
Senses and the Intellect. 8vo. 15s.
Emotions and the Will. 8vo. 15s.
Logic, Deductive, and Inductive. PART I., 4s. PART II., 6s. 6d.
Practical Essays. Cr. 8vo. 2s.

BAKER (Sir S. W.).—WORKS BY.
Eight Years in Ceylon. With 6 Illustrations. Crown 8vo. 3s. 6d.
The Rifle and the Hound in Ceylon. 6 Illustrations. Cr. 8vo. 3s. 6d.

BALDWIN.—Where Town and Country Meet; a Novel. By Mrs. ALFRED BALDWIN. Crown 8vo. 6s.

BALL (The Rt. Hon. J. T.).—WORKS.
The Reformed Church of Ireland. (1537-1889). 8vo. 7s. 6d.
Historical Review of the Legislative Systems Operative in Ireland, from the Invasion of Henry the Second to the Union (1172-1800). 8vo. 6s.

BARING-GOULD (Rev. S.).—WORKS BY.
Curious Myths of the Middle Ages. Crown 8vo. 3s. 6d.
Origin and Development of Religious Belief. 2 vols. 7s.

BEACONSFIELD (The Earl of).—WORKS BY.
Novels and Tales. The Hughenden Edition. With 2 Portraits and 11 Vignettes. 11 vols. Crown 8vo. 42s.
Endymion. Henrietta Temple.
Lothair. Contarini, Fleming, &c.
Coningsby. Alroy, Ixion, &c.
Tancred. Sybil. The Young Duke, &c.
Venetia. Vivian Grey.
Novels and Tales. Cheap Edition. Complete in 11 vols. Crown 8vo. 1s. each, boards; 1s. 6d. each, cloth.

BECKER (Professor).—WORKS BY.
Gallus; or, Roman Scenes in the Time of Augustus. Post 8vo. 7s. 6d.
Charicles; or, Illustrations of the Private Life of the Ancient Greeks. Post 8vo. 7s. 6d.

BELL (Mrs. Hugh).—WORKS BY.
Chamber Comedies: a Collection of Plays and Monologues for the Drawing Room. Crown 8vo. 6s.
Nursery Comedies: Twelve Tiny Plays for Children. Fcap. 8vo. 1s. 6d.

BLAKE.—Tables for the Conversion of 5 per Cent. Interest from $\frac{1}{16}$ to 7 per Cent. By J. BLAKE, of the London Joint Stock Bank, Limited. 8vo. 12s. 6d.

Book (The) of Wedding Days. Arranged on the Plan of a Birthday Book. With 96 Illustrated Borders, Frontispiece, and Title-page by WALTER CRANE; and Quotations for each Day. Compiled and Arranged by K. E. J. REID, MAY ROSS, and MABEL BAMFIELD. 4to. 21s.

BRASSEY (Lady).—WORKS BY.
A Voyage in the 'Sunbeam,' our Home on the Ocean for Eleven Months.
Library Edition. With 8 Maps and Charts, and 118 Illustrations, 8vo. 21s.
Cabinet Edition. With Map and 66 Illustrations, Crown 8vo. 7s. 6d.
'Silver Library' Edition. With 66 Illustrations. Crown 8vo. 3s. 6d.
Popular Edition. With 60 Illustrations, 4to. 6d. sewed, 1s. cloth.
School Edition. With 37 Illustrations, Fcp. 2s. cloth, or 3s. white parchment.

Sunshine and Storm in the East.
Library Edition. With 2 Maps and 114 Illustrations, 8vo. 21s.
Cabinet Edition. With 2 Maps and 114 Illustrations, Crown 8vo. 7s. 6d.
Popular Edition. With 103 Illustrations, 4to. 6d. sewed, 1s. cloth.

In the Trades, the Tropics, and the 'Roaring Forties'.
Cabinet Edition. With Map and 220 Illustrations, Crown 8vo. 7s. 6d.
Popular Edition. With 183 Illustrations, 4to. 6d. sewed, 1s. cloth.

The Last Voyage to India and Australia in the 'Sunbeam'. With Charts and Maps, and 40 Illustrations in Monotone (20 full-page), and nearly 200 Illustrations in the Text from Drawings by R. T. PRITCHETT. 8vo. 21s.

Three Voyages in the 'Sunbeam'. Popular Edition. With 346 Illustrations, 4to. 2s. 6d.

BRAY.—The Philosophy of Necessity; or, Law in Mind as in Matter. By CHARLES BRAY. Crown 8vo. 5s.

BRIGHT.—**A History of England.**
By the Rev. J. FRANCK BRIGHT, D.D., Master of University College, Oxford. 4 vols. Crown 8vo.
Period I.—Mediæval Monarchy: The Departure of the Romans to Richard III. From A.D. 449 to 1485. 4s. 6d.
Period II.—Personal Monarchy: Henry VII. to James II. From 1485 to 1688. 5s.
Period III. — Constitutional Monarchy: William and Mary to William IV. From 1689 to 1837. 7s. 6d.
Period IV.—The Growth of Democracy: Victoria. From 1837 to 1880. 6s.

BRYDEN.—**Kloof and Karroo:** Sport, Legend, and Natural History in Cape Colony. By H. A. BRYDEN. With 17 Illustrations. 8vo. 10s. 6d.

BUCKLE.—**History of Civilisation in England and France, Spain and Scotland.** By HENRY THOMAS BUCKLE. 3 vols. Cr. 8vo. 24s.

BULL (Thomas).—*WORKS BY.*
Hints to Mothers on the Management of their Health during the Period of Pregnancy. Fcp. 8vo. 1s. 6d.
The Maternal Management of Children in Health and Disease. Fcp. 8vo. 1s. 6d.

BUTLER (Samuel).—*WORKS BY.*
Op. 1. **Erewhon.** Crown 8vo. 5s.
Op. 2. **The Fair Haven.** A Work in defence of the Miraculous Element in our Lord's Ministry. Crown 8vo. 7s. 6d.
Op. 3. **Life and Habit.** An Essay after a Completer View of Evolution. Crown 8vo. 7s. 6d.
Op. 4. **Evolution, Old and New.** Crown 8vo. 10s. 6d.
Op. 5. **Unconscious Memory.** Crown 8vo. 7s. 6d.
Op. 6. **Alps and Sanctuaries of Piedmont and Canton Ticino.** Illustrated. Pott 4to. 10s. 6d.
Op. 7. **Selections from Ops. 1-6.** With Remarks on Mr. ROMANES' 'Mental Evolution in Animals'. Cr. 8vo. 7s. 6d.
Op. 8. **Luck, or Cunning, as the Main Means of Organic Modification?** Cr. 8vo. 7s. 6d.
Op. 9. **Ex Voto.** An Account of the Sacro Monte or New Jerusalem at Varallo-Sesia. 10s. 6d.
Holbein's 'La Danse'. A Note on a Drawing called 'La Danse'. 3s.

CARLYLE.—**Thomas Carlyle: a History of His Life.** By J. A. FROUDE. 1795-1835, 2 vols. Crown 8vo. 7s. 1834-1881, 2 vols. Crown 8vo. 7s.
Last Words of Thomas Carlyle —Wotton Reinfred—Excursion (Futile enough) to Paris—Letters to Varnhagen von Ense, &c. Crown 8vo. 6s. 6d. net.

CASE.—**Physical Realism:** being an Analytical Philosophy from the Physical Objects of Science to the Physical Data of Sense. By THOMAS CASE, M.A., Fellow and Senior Tutor, C.C.C. 8vo. 15s.

CHETWYND.—**Racing Reminiscences and Experiences of the Turf.** By Sir GEORGE CHETWYND, Bart. 2 vols. 8vo. 21s.

CHETWYND-STAPYLTON.—**Chetwynds of Ingestre (The):** being a History of that Family from a very early Date. By H. E. CHETWYND-STAPYLTON. With numerous Portraits and Illustrations. 8vo. 14s.

CHILD.—**Church and State under the Tudors.** By GILBERT W. CHILD, M.A. 8vo. 15s.

CHILTON.—**The History of a Failure, and other Tales.** By E. CHILTON. Fcp. 8vo. 3s. 6d.

CHISHOLM.—**Handbook of Commercial Geography.** By G. G. CHISHOLM. New edition. With 29 Maps. 8vo. 10s. net.

CHURCH.—**Sir Richard Church,** C.B., G.C.H. Commander-in-Chief of the Greeks in the War of Independence: a Memoir. By STANLEY LANE-POOLE. With 2 Plans. 8vo. 5s.

CLERKE.—**Familiar Studies in Homer.** By AGNES M. CLERKE. Crown 8vo. 7s. 6d.

CLODD.—**The Story of Creation:** a Plain Account of Evolution. By EDWARD CLODD. With 77 Illustrations. Crown 8vo. 3s. 6d.

CLUTTERBUCK (W. J.).—*WORKS BY.*
The Skipper in Arctic Seas. With 39 Illustrations. Cr. 8vo. 10s. 6d.
About Ceylon and Borneo: being an Account of Two Visits to Ceylon, one to Borneo, and How we Fell Out on our Homeward Journey. With 47 Illustrations. Crown 8vo. 10s. 6d.

COLENSO.—**The Pentateuch and Book of Joshua Critically Examined.** By J. W. COLENSO, D.D., late Bishop of Natal. Cr. 8vo. 6s.

COMYN.—**Atherstone Priory:** a Tale. By L. N. COMYN. Cr. 8vo. 2s. 6d.

CONINGTON (*John*).—*WORKS BY.*

The Æneid of Virgil. Translated into English Verse. Crown 8vo. 6s.

The Poems of Virgil. Translated into English Prose. Crown 8vo. 6s.

COX.— **A General History of Greece,** from the Earliest Period to the Death of Alexander the Great; with a sketch of the subsequent History to the Present Time. By the Rev. Sir G. W. COX, Bart., M.A. With 11 Maps and Plans. Crown 8vo. 7s. 6d.

CRAKE (*Rev. A. D.*).—*WORKS BY.*

Historical Tales. Crown 8vo. 5 vols. 2s. 6d. each.

Edwy the Fair; or, The First Chronicle of Æscendune.

Alfgar the Dane; or, the Second Chronicle of Æscendune.

The Rival Heirs : being the Third and Last Chronicle of Æscendune.

The House of Walderne. A Tale of the Cloister and the Forest in the Days of the Barons' Wars.

Brian Fitz-Count. A Story of Wallingford Castle and Dorchester Abbey.

History of the Church under the Roman Empire, A.D. 30-476. Crown 8vo. 7s. 6d.

CREALOCK. — **Deer-Stalking in the Highlands of Scotland.** By the late Lieutenant-General H. H. CREALOCK. Edited by his brother, Major-General JOHN NORTH CREALOCK. With 36 full-page Plates reproduced in autotype, and numerous Illustrations in the Text. Royal 4to. Six guineas net.

CREIGHTON. — **History of the Papacy during the Reformation.** BY MANDELL CREIGHTON, D.D., LL.D., Bishop of Peterborough. 8vo. Vols. I. and II., 1378-1464, 32s. ; Vols. III. and IV., 1464-1518, 24s.

CRUMP (A.).—*WORKS BY.*

A Short Enquiry into the Formation of Political Opinion, from the reign of the Great Families to the Advent of Democracy. 8vo. 7s. 6d.

CRUMP (A.).—*WORKS BY.—cont.*

An Investigation into the Causes of the Great Fall in Prices which took place coincidently with the Demonetisation of Silver by Germany. 8vo. 6s.

CUDWORTH.—**An Introduction to Cudworth's Treatise concerning Eternal and Immutable Morality.** By W. R. SCOTT. Crown 8vo. 3s.

CURZON.—**Persia and the Persian Question.** By the Hon. GEORGE N. CURZON, M.P., late Fellow of All Souls College, Oxford, Author of 'Russia in Central Asia'. With 9 Maps, 96 Illustrations, Appendices, and an Index. 2 vols. 8vo. 42s.

DANTE.—**La Commedia di Dante.** A New Text, carefully Revised with the aid of the most recent Editions and Collations. Small 8vo. 6s.

DAVIDSON (*W. L.*).—*WORKS BY.*

The Logic of Definition Explained and Applied. Cr. 8vo. 6s.

Leading and Important English Words Explained and Exemplified. Fcp. 8vo. 3s. 6d.

Dead Shot (The) ; or, Sportman's Complete Guide. Being a Treatise on the Use of the Gun, with Rudimentary and Finishing Lessons on the Art of Shooting Game of all kinds, also Game Driving, Wild - Fowl and Pigeon Shooting, Dog Breaking, &c. By MARKSMAN. Sixth Edition, Revised and Enlarged. Crown 8vo. 10s. 6d.

DELAND (*Mrs.*).—*WORKS BY.*

John Ward, Preacher: a Story. Crown 8vo. 2s. boards, 2s. 6d. cloth.

Sidney: a Novel. Crown 8vo. 6s.

The Old Garden, and other Verses. Fcp. 8vo. 5s.

DE LA SAUSSAYE.—**A Manual of the Science of Religion.** By Professor CHANTEPIE DE LA SAUSSAYE. Translated by Mrs. COLYER FERGUSSON (*née* MAX MÜLLER). Revised by the Author. Crown 8vo. 12s. 6d.

DE REDCLIFFE.—**The Life of the Right Hon. Stratford Canning: Viscount Stratford De Redcliffe.** By STANLEY LANE-POOLE. Crown 8vo. 7s. 6d.

DE SALIS (Mrs.).—WORKS BY.

Cakes and Confections à la Mode. Fcp. 8vo. *1s. 6d.*

Dressed Game and Poultry à la Mode. Fcp. 8vo. *1s. 6d.*

Dressed Vegetables à la Mode. Fcp. 8vo. *1s. 6d.*

Drinks à la Mode. Fcp. 8vo. *1s.6d.*

Entrées à la Mode. Fcp. 8vo. *1s. 6d.*

Floral Decorations. Suggestions and Descriptions. Fcap. 8vo. *1s. 6d.*

New-Laid Eggs: Hints for Amateur Poultry Rearers. Fcp. 8vo. *1s. 6d.*

Oysters à la Mode. Fcp. 8vo. *1s. 6d.*

Puddings and Pastry à la Mode. Fcp. 8vo. *1s. 6d.*

Savouries à la Mode. Fcp. 8vo. *1s. 6d.*

Soups and Dressed Fish à la Mode. Fcp. 8vo. *1s. 6d.*

Sweets and Supper Dishes à la Mode. Fcp. 8vo. *1s. 6d.*

Tempting Dishes for Small Incomes. Fcp. 8vo. *1s. 6d.*

Wrinkles and Notions for every Household. Crown 8vo. *1s. 6d.*

DE TOCQUEVILLE.—**Democracy in America.** By ALEXIS DE TOCQUEVILLE. 2 vols. Crown 8vo. 16s.

Dorothy Wallis: an Autobiography. With Preface by WALTER BESANT. Crown 8vo. 6s.

DOUGALL.—**Beggars All: a Novel.** By L. DOUGALL. Crown 8vo. 3s. 6d.

DOWELL.—**A History of Taxation and Taxes in England** from the Earliest Times to the Year 1885. By STEPHEN DOWELL. (4 vols. 8vo.) Vols. I. and II. The History of Taxation, 21s. Vols. III. and IV. The History of Taxes, 21s.

DOYLE (A. Conan).—WORKS BY.

Micah Clarke. A tale of Monmouth's Rebellion. With Frontispiece and Vignette. Crown 8vo. 3s. 6d.

The Captain of the Polestar; and other Tales. Crown 8vo. 3s. 6d.

DRANE.—**The History of St. Dominic.** By AUGUSTA THEODORA DRANE. 32 Illustrations. 8vo. 15s.

Dublin University Press Series (The): a Series of Works undertaken by the Provost and Senior Fellows of Trinity College, Dublin.

Abbott's (T. K.) Codex Rescriptus Dublinensis of St. Matthew. 4to. 21s.

—— Evangeliorum Versio Antehieronymiana ex Codice Usseriano (Dublinensi). 2 vols. Crown 8vo. 21s.

—— Short Notes on St. Paul's Epistles to the Romans, Corinthians, Galatians, Ephesians, and Philippians. Fcp. 8vo. 4s.

Allman's (G. J.) Greek Geometry from Thales to Euclid. 8vo. 10s. 6d.

Burnside (W. S.) and Panton's (A. W.) Theory of Equations. 8vo. 12s. 6d.

Casey's (John) Sequel to Euclid's Elements. Crown 8vo. 3s. 6d.

—— Analytical Geometry of the Conic Sections. Crown 8vo. 7s. 6d.

Davies' (J. F.) Eumenides of Æschylus. With Metrical English Translation. 8vo. 7s.

Dublin Translations into Greek and Latin Verse. Edited by R. Y. Tyrrell. 8vo. 6s.

Graves' (R. P.) Life of Sir William Hamilton. 3 vols. 15s. each.

—— Addendum to the Life of Sir William Rowan Hamilton, LL.D., D.C.L. 8vo. 6d. sewed.

Griffin (R. W.) on Parabola, Ellipse, and Hyperbola. Crown 8vo. 6s.

Hobart's (W. K.) Medical Language of St. Luke. 8vo. 16s.

Leslie's (T. E. Cliffe) Essays in Political Economy. 8vo. 10s. 6d.

Macalister's (A.) Zoology and Morphology of Vertebrata. 8vo. 10s. 6d.

MacCullagh's (James) Mathematical and other Tracts. 8vo. 15s.

Maguire's (T.) Parmenides of Plato, Text, with Introduction, Analysis, &c. 8vo. 7s. 6d.

Monck's (W. H. S.) Introduction to Logic. Crown 8vo. 5s.

Roberts' (R. A.) Examples on the Analytic Geometry of Plane Conics. Cr. 8vo. 5s.

Southey's (R.) Correspondence with Caroline Bowles. Edited by E. Dowden. 8vo. 14s.

[Continued on next page.

Dublin University Press Series (The).—*continued.*

Stubbs' (J. W.) History of the University of Dublin, from its Foundation to the End of the Eighteenth Century. 8vo. 12s. 6d.

Thornhill's (W. J.) The Æneid of Virgil, freely translated into English Blank Verse. Crown 8vo. 7s. 6d.

Tyrrell's (R. Y.) Cicero's Correspondence. Vols. I. II, III. 8vo. each 12s.

—————— **The Acharnians of Aristophanes**, translated into English Verse. Crown 8vo. 1s.

Webb's (T. E.) Goethe's Faust, Translation and Notes. 8vo. 12s. 6d.

—————— **The Veil of Isis:** a Series of Essays on Idealism. 8vo. 10s. 6d.

Wilkins' (G.) The Growth of the Homeric Poems. 8vo. 6s.

Epochs of Modern History.
Edited by C. COLBECK, M.A. 19 vols. Fcp. 8vo. with Maps, 2s. 6d. each.
*** *List will be sent on application.*

Epochs of Church History. Edited by MANDELL CREIGHTON, D.D., Bishop of Peterborough. 15 vols. Fcp. 8vo. 2s. 6d. each.
*** *List will be sent on application.*

Epochs of Ancient History.
Edited by the Rev. Sir G. W. COX, Bart., M.A., and by C. SANKEY, M.A. 10 volumes, Fcp. 8vo. with Maps, 2s. 6d. each.
*** *List will be sent on application.*

Epochs of American History.
Edited by Dr. ALBERT BUSHNELL HART, Assistant Professor of History in Harvard College.

THWAITES (R. G.).—The Colonies (1492-1763). Fcp. 8vo. 3s. 6d.
*** *Others in preparation.*

Epochs of English History.
Complete in One Volume, with 27 Tables and Pedigrees, and 23 Maps. Fcp. 8vo. 5s.
*** For details of Parts *see* Longmans & Co.'s Catalogue of School Books.

EWALD (Heinrich).—WORKS BY.

The Antiquities of Israel. Translated from the German by H. S. SOLLY, M.A. 8vo. 12s. 6d.

The History of Israel. Translated from the German. 8 vols. 8vo. Vols. I. and II. 24s. Vols. III. and IV. 21s. Vol. V. 18s. Vol. VI. 16s. Vol. VII. 21s. Vol. VIII., with Index to the Complete Work, 18s.

FALKENER. — Games, Ancient and Oriental, and how to play them. Being the Games of the Ancient Egyptians, the Hiera Gramme of the Greeks, the Ludus Latrunculorum of the Romans, and the Oriental Games of Chess, Draughts, Backgammon, and Magic Squares. By EDWARD FALKENER. With numerous Photographs, Diagrams, &c. 8vo. 21s.

FARNELL.—Greek Lyric Poetry: a Complete Collection of the Surviving Passages from the Greek Song-Writers. Arranged with Prefatory Articles, Introductory Matter, and Commentary. By GEORGE S. FARNELL, M.A. With 5 Plates. 8vo. 16s.

FARRAR (Ven. Archdeacon).—WORKS BY.

Darkness and Dawn; or, Scenes in the Days of Nero. An Historic Tale. Crown 8vo. 7s. 6d.

Language and Languages. A Revised Edition of *Chapters on Language and Families of Speech.* Crown 8vo. 6s.

FITZPATRICK. — Secret Service under Pitt. By W. J. FITZPATRICK, F.S.A., Author of 'Correspondence of Daniel O'Connell'. 8vo. 14s.

FITZWYGRAM. — Horses and Stables. By Major-General Sir F. FITZWYGRAM, Bart. With 19 pages of Illustrations. 8vo. 5s.

FORD.—The Theory and Practice of Archery. By the late HORACE FORD. New Edition, thoroughly Revised and Re-written by W. BUTT, M.A. With a Preface by C. J. LONGMAN, M.A., F.S.A. 8vo. 14s.

FOUARD.—The Christ the Son of God: a Life of our Lord and Saviour Jesus Christ. By the Abbé CONSTANT FOUARD. With an Introduction by Cardinal MANNING. 2 vols. Crown 8vo. 14s.

FOX. — The Early History of Charles James Fox. By the Right Hon. Sir G. O. TREVELYAN, Bart. Library Edition, 8vo. 18s. Cabinet Edition, Crown 8vo. 6s.

FRANCIS.—A Book on Angling; or, Treatise on the Art of Fishing in every branch; including full Illustrated List of Salmon Flies. By FRANCIS FRANCIS. With Portrait and Coloured Plates. Crown 8vo. 15s.

FREEMAN.—**The Historical Geography of Europe.** By E. A FREEMAN. With 65 Maps. 2 vols. 8vo. 31s. 6d.

FROUDE (James A.).—*WORKS BY.*

The History of England, from the Fall of Wolsey to the Defeat of the Spanish Armada. 12 vols. Crown 8vo. 3s. 6d. each.

The Divorce of Catherine of Aragon; the Story as told by the Imperial Ambassadors resident at the Court of Henry VIII. *In usum Laicorum.* 8vo. 16s.

Short Studies on Great Subjects. Cabinet Edition, 4 vols. Crown 8vo. 24s. Cheap Edition, 4 vols. Crown 8vo. 3s. 6d. each.

Cæsar: a Sketch. Crown 8vo. 3s. 6d.

The English in Ireland in the Eighteenth Century. 3 vols. Crown 8vo. 18s.

Oceana; or, England and her Colonies. With 9 Illustrations Crown 8vo. 2s. boards, 2s. 6d. cloth.

The English in the West Indies; or, the Bow of Ulysses. With 9 Illustrations. Crown 8vo. 2s. boards, 2s. 6d. cloth.

The Two Chiefs of Dunboy; an Irish Romance of the Last Century. Crown 8vo. 3s. 6d.

Thomas Carlyle, a History of his Life. 1795 to 1835. 2 vols. Crown 8vo. 7s. 1834 to 1881. 2 vols. Crown 8vo. 7s.

The Spanish Story of the Armada, and other Essays, Historical and Descriptive. Crown 8vo. 6s.

GALLWEY.—**Letters to Young Shooters.** (First Series.) On the Choice and Use of a Gun. By Sir RALPH PAYNE-GALLWEY, Bart. With Illustrations. Crown 8vo. 7s. 6d.

GARDINER (Samuel Rawson).—*WORKS BY.*

History of England, from the Accession of James I. to the Outbreak of the Civil War, 1603-1642. 10 vols. Crown 8vo. price 6s. each.

A History of the Great Civil War, 1642-1649. (3 vols.) Vol. I. 1642-1644. With 24 Maps. 8vo. (*out of print*). Vol. II. 1644-1647. With 21 Maps. 8vo. 24s. Vol. III. 1647-1649. With 8 Maps. 8vo. 28s.

GARDINER (Samuel Rawson).—*WORKS BY.—continued.*

The Student's History of England. Vol. I. B.C. 55—A.D. 1509, with 173 Illustrations. Crown 8vo. 4s. Vol. II. 1509-1689, with 96 Illustrations. Crown 8vo. 4s. Vol. III. (1689-1865). With 109 Illustrations. Crown 8vo. 4s. Complete in 1 vol. With 378 Illustrations. Crown 8vo. 12s.

A School Atlas of English History. With 66 Maps and 22 Plans of Battles, &c. Fcap. 4to. 5s.

GIBERNE.—**Nigel Browning.** By AGNES GIBERNE. Crown 8vo. 5s.

GOETHE.—**Faust.** A New Translation chiefly in Blank Verse; with Introduction and Notes. By JAMES ADEY BIRDS. Crown 8vo. 6s.

Faust. The Second Part. A New Translation in Verse. By JAMES ADEY BIRDS. Crown 8vo. 6s.

GREEN.—**The Works of Thomas Hill Green.** Edited by R. L. NETTLESHIP. (3 vols.) Vols. I. and II.—Philosophical Works. 8vo. 16s. each. Vol. III.—Miscellanies. With Index to the three Volumes and Memoir. 8vo. 21s.

The Witness of God and Faith: Two Lay Sermons. By T. H. GREEN. Fcp. 8vo. 2s.

GREVILLE.—**A Journal of the Reigns of King George IV., King William IV., and Queen Victoria.** By C. C. F. GREVILLE. 8 vols. Crown 8vo. 6s. each.

GWILT.—**An Encyclopædia of Architecture.** By JOSEPH GWILT, F.S.A. Illustrated with more than 1700 Engravings on Wood. 8vo. 52s. 6d.

HAGGARD.—**Life and its Author:** an Essay in Verse. By ELLA HAGGARD. With a Memoir by H. RIDER HAGGARD, and Portrait. Fcp. 8vo. 3s. 6d.

HAGGARD (H. Rider).—*WORKS BY.*

She. With 32 Illustrations by M. GREIFFENHAGEN and C. H. M. KERR. Crown 8vo. 3s. 6d.

Allan Quatermain. With 31 Illustrations by C. H. M. KERR. Crown 8vo. 3s. 6d.

Maiwa's Revenge; or, The War of the Little Hand. Crown 8vo. 1s. boards; 1s. 6d. cloth.

Colonel Quaritch, V.C. A Novel. Crown 8vo. 3s. 6d.

[*Continued on next page.*

HAGGARD (H. Rider.)—WORKS BY.
—*continued.*

Cleopatra. With 29 Full-page Illustrations by M. Greiffenhagen and R. Caton Woodville. Crown 8vo. 3s. 6d.

Beatrice. A Novel. Cr. 8vo. 3s. 6d.

Eric Brighteyes. With 17 Plates and 34 Illustrations in the Text by LANCELOT SPEED. Crown 8vo. 6s.

Nada the Lily. With 23 Illustrations by C. H. M. KERR. Crown 8vo. 6s.

HAGGARD and LANG.—The World's Desire. By H. RIDER HAGGARD and ANDREW LANG. Crown 8vo. 6s.

HALLIWELL-PHILLIPPS.—A Calendar of the Halliwell-Phillipps' collection of Shakespearean Rarities. Enlarged by ERNEST E. BAKER, F.S.A. 8vo. 10s. 6d.

HARRISON.—Myths of the Odyssey in Art and Literature. Illustrated with Outline Drawings. By JANE E. HARRISON. 8vo. 18s.

HARRISON.—The Contemporary History of the French Revolution, compiled from the 'Annual Register'. By F. BAYFORD HARRISON. Crown 8vo. 3s. 6d.

HARRISON.—Cookery for Busy Lives and Small Incomes. By MARY HARRISON. Fcp. 8vo. 1s.

HARTE (Bret).—WORKS BY.
In the Carquinez Woods. Fcp. 8vo. 1s. boards; 1s. 6d. cloth.
On the Frontier. 16mo. 1s.
By Shore and Sedge. 16mo. 1s.

HARTWIG (Dr.).—WORKS BY.
The Sea and its Living Wonders. With 12 Plates and 303 Woodcuts. 8vo. 7s. net.
The Tropical World. With 8 Plates and 172 Woodcuts. 8vo. 7s. net.
The Polar World. With 3 Maps, 8 Plates and 85 Woodcuts. 8vo. 7s. net.
The Subterranean World. With 3 Maps and 80 Woodcuts. 8vo. 7s. net.
The Aerial World. With Map, 8 Plates and 60 Woodcuts. 8vo. 7s. net.

HAVELOCK.—Memoirs of Sir Henry Havelock, K.C.B. By JOHN CLARK MARSHMAN. Crown 8vo. 3s. 6d.

HEARN (W. Edward).—WORKS BY.
The Government of England: its Structure and its Development. 8vo. 16s.
The Aryan Household: its Structure and its Development. An Introduction to Comparative Jurisprudence. 8vo. 16s.

HISTORIC TOWNS. Edited by E. A. FREEMAN, D.C.L., and Rev. WILLIAM HUNT, M.A. With Maps and Plans. Crown 8vo. 3s. 6d. each.

Bristol. By Rev. W. HUNT.
Carlisle. By Rev. MANDELL CREIGHTON.
Cinque Ports. By MONTAGU BURROWS.
Colchester. By Rev. E. L. CUTTS.
Exeter. By E. A. FREEMAN.
London. By Rev. W. J. LOFTIE.
Oxford. By Rev. C. W. BOASE.
Winchester. By Rev. G. W. KITCHIN, D.D.
New York. By THEODORE ROOSEVELT.
Boston (U.S.). By HENRY CABOT LODGE.
York. By Rev. JAMES RAINE.

HODGSON (Shadworth H.).—WORKS BY.
Time and Space: a Metaphysical Essay. 8vo. 16s.
The Theory of Practice: an Ethical Enquiry. 2 vols. 8vo. 24s.
The Philosophy of Reflection: 2 vols. 8vo. 21s.
Outcast Essays and Verse Translations. Essays: The Genius of De Quincey—De Quincey as Political Economist—The Supernatural in English Poetry; with Note on the True Symbol of Christian Union—English Verse. Verse Translations: Nineteen Passages from Lucretius, Horace, Homer, &c. Crown 8vo. 8s. 6d.

HOOPER.—Abraham Fabert: Governor of Sedan, Marshall of France. His Life and Times, 1599-1662. By GEORGE HOOPER. With a Portrait. 8vo. 10s. 6d.

HOWITT.—Visits to Remarkable Places, Old Halls, Battle-Fields, Scenes, illustrative of Striking Passages in English History and Poetry. By WILLIAM HOWITT. With 80 Illustrations. Crown 8vo. 3s. 6d.

HULLAH (John).—WORKS BY.

Course of Lectures on the History of Modern Music. 8vo. 8s. 6d.

Course of Lectures on the Transition Period of Musical History. 8vo. 10s. 6d.

HUME.--**The Philosophical Works of David Hume.** Edited by T. H. GREEN and T. H. GROSE. 4 vols. 8vo. 56s. Or Separately, Essays, 2 vols. 28s. Treatise of Human Nature. 2 vols. 28s.

HUTCHINSON. — **Famous Golf Links.** By HORACE G. HUTCHINSON, ANDREW LANG, H. S. C. EVERARD, T. RUTHERFORD CLARK, &c. With numerous Illustrations by F. P. HOPKINS, T. HODGES, H. S. KING, and from Photographs. Crown 8vo. 6s.

HUTH.—**The Marriage of Near Kin,** considered with respect to the Law of Nations, the Result of Experience, and the Teachings of Biology. By ALFRED H. HUTH. Royal 8vo. 21s.

INGELOW (Jean).— WORKS BY.

Poetical Works. Vols. I. and II. Fcp. 8vo. 12s. Vol. III. Fcp. 8vo. 5s.

Lyrical and other Poems. Selected from the Writings of JEAN INGELOW. Fcp. 8vo. 2s. 6d. cloth plain; 3s. cloth gilt.

Very Young and Quite Another Story: Two Stories. Cr. 8vo. 6s.

Investors' Review (The) (Quarterly). Edited by A. J. WILSON. Royal 8vo. 5s.

JAMESON (Mrs.).— WORKS BY.

Sacred and Legendary Art. With 19 Etchings and 187 Woodcuts. 2 vols. 8vo. 20s. net.

Legends of the Madonna. The Virgin Mary as represented in Sacred and Legendary Art. With 27 Etchings and 165 Woodcuts. 1 vol. 8vo. 10s. net.

Legends of the Monastic Orders. With 11 Etchings and 88 Woodcuts. 1 vol. 8vo. 10s. net.

History of Our Lord. His Types and Precursors. Completed by Lady EASTLAKE. With 31 Etchings and 281 Woodcuts. 2 vols. 8vo. 20s. net.

JEFFERIES (Richard).— WORKS BY.

Field and Hedgerow: last Essays. With Portrait. Crown 8vo. 3s. 6d.

The Story of My Heart: my Autobiography. With Portrait and new Preface by C. J. LONGMAN. Crown 8vo. 3s. 6d.

Red Deer. With 17 Illustrations by J. CHARLTON and H. TUNALY. Crown 8vo. 3s. 6d.

Wiltshire Labourers. With autotype reproduction of bust of Richard Jefferies. Crown 8vo.

JENNINGS.--**Ecclesia Anglicana.** A History of the Church of Christ in England, from the Earliest to the Present Times. By the Rev. ARTHUR CHARLES JENNINGS, M.A. Crown 8vo. 7s. 6d.

JOHNSON.—**The Patentee's Manual;** a Treatise on the Law and Practice of Letters Patent. By J. JOHNSON and J. H. JOHNSON. 8vo. 10s. 6d.

JORDAN (William Leighton).—**The Standard of Value.** By WILLIAM LEIGHTON JORDAN. 8vo. 6s.

JUSTINIAN.—**The Institutes of Justinian;** Latin Text, chiefly that of Huschke, with English Introduction, Translation, Notes, and Summary. By THOMAS C. SANDARS, M.A. 8vo. 18s.

KALISCH (M. M.).— WORKS BY.

Bible Studies. Part I. The Prophecies of Balaam. 8vo. 10s. 6d. Part II. The Book of Jonah. 8vo. 10s. 6d.

Commentary on the Old Testament; with a New Translation. Vol. I. Genesis, 8vo. 18s. or adapted for the General Reader, 12s. Vol. II. Exodus, 15s. or adapted for the General Reader, 12s. Vol. III. Leviticus, Part I. 15s. or adapted for the General Reader, 8s. Vol. IV. Leviticus, Part II. 15s. or adapted for the General Reader, 8s.

KANT (Immanuel).— WORKS BY.

Critique of Practical Reason, and other Works on the Theory of Ethics. Translated by T. K. Abbott, B.D. With Memoir. 8vo. 12s. 6d.

Introduction to Logic, and his Essay on the Mistaken Subtilty of the Four Figures. Translated by T. K. Abbott. Notes by S. T. Coleridge. 8vo. 6s.

KILLICK.—**Handbook to Mill's System of Logic.** By the Rev. A. H. KILLICK, M.A. Crown 8vo. 3s. 6d.

KNIGHT (E. F.).—WORKS BY.
The Cruise of the 'Alerte,'; the Narrative of a Search for Treasure on the Desert Island of Trinidad. With 2 Maps and 23 Illustrations. Crown 8vo. 3s. 6d.
Save Me from my Friends: a Novel. Crown 8vo. 6s.

LADD (George T.).—WORKS BY.
Elements of Physiological Psychology. 8vo. 21s.
Outlines of Physiological Psychology. A Text-book of Mental Science for Academies and Colleges. 8vo. 12s.

LANG (Andrew).—WORKS BY.
Custom and Myth: Studies of Early Usage and Belief. With 15 Illustrations. Crown 8vo. 7s. 6d.
Ballads of Books. Edited by ANDREW LANG. Fcp. 8vo. 6s.
Letters to Dead Authors. Fcp. 8vo. 2s. 6d. net.
Books and Bookmen. With 2 Coloured Plates and 17 Illustrations. Fcp. 8vo. 2s. 6d. net.
Old Friends. Fcp. 8vo. 2s. 6d. net.
Letters on Literature. Fcp. 8vo. 2s. 6d. net.
Grass of Parnassus. Fcp. 8vo. 2s. 6d. net.
Angling Sketches. With 20 Illustrations by W. G. Brown Murdoch. Crown 8vo. 7s. 6d.
The Blue Fairy Book. Edited by ANDREW LANG. With 8 Plates and 130 Illustrations in the Text by H. J. Ford and G. P. Jacomb Hood. Cr. 8vo. 6s.
The Red Fairy Book. Edited by ANDREW LANG. With 4 Plates and 96 Illustrations in the Text by H. J. Ford and Lancelot Speed. Crown 8vo. 6s.
The Blue Poetry Book. Edited by ANDREW LANG. With 12 Plates and 88 Illustrations in the Text by H. J. Ford and Lancelot Speed. Crown 8vo. 6s.
The Blue Poetry Book. School Edition, without Illustrations. Fcp. 8vo. 2s. 6d.
The Green Fairy Book. Edited by ANDREW LANG. With Illustrations by H. J. Ford. Crown 8vo.

*LAVISSE.—***General View of the Political History of Europe.** By ERNEST LAVISSE, Professor at the Sorbonne. Translated by CHARLES GROSS, Ph.D. Crown 8vo. 5s.

LECKY (W. E. H.).—WORKS BY.
History of England in the Eighteenth Century. Library Edition. 8vo. vols. I. & II. 1700-1760. 36s. Vols. III. & IV. 1760-1784. 36s. Vols. V. & VI. 1784-1793. 36s. Vols. VII. & VIII. 1793-1800. 36s.
Cabinet Edition. England. 7 vols. Crown 8vo. 6s. each. Ireland. 5 vols. Crown 8vo. 6s. each. [*In Monthly Volumes from January,* 1892.
The History of European Morals from Augustus to Charlemagne. 2 vols. Crown 8vo. 16s.
History of the Rise and Influence of the Spirit of Rationalism in Europe. 2 vols. Crown 8vo. 16s.
Poems. Fcp. 8vo. 5s.

LEES and CLUTTERBUCK.—B. C. 1887, **A Ramble in British Columbia.** By J. A. LEES and W. J. CLUTTERBUCK. With Map and 75 Illustrations. Crown 8vo. 3s. 6d.

*LEGER.—***A History of Austro-Hungary.** From the Earliest Time to the year 1889. By LOUIS LEGER. With a Preface by E. A. FREEMAN, D.C.L. Crown 8vo. 10s. 6d.

*LEWES.—***The History of Philosophy,** from Thales to Comte. By GEORGE HENRY LEWES. 2 vols. 8vo. 32s.

*LIDDELL.—***The Memoirs of the Tenth Royal Hussars (Prince of Wales' Own)**: Historical and Social. Collected and Arranged by Colonel R. S. LIDDELL, late Commanding Tenth Royal Hussars. With Portraits and Coloured Illustration. Imperial 8vo. 63s.

*LLOYD.—***The Science of Agriculture.** By F. J. LLOYD. 8vo. 12s.

LONGMAN (Frederick W.).—WORKS BY.
Chess Openings. Fcp. 8vo. 2s. 6d.
Frederick the Great and the Seven Years' War. Fcp. 8vo. 2s. 6d.

Longman's Magazine. Published Monthly. Price Sixpence.
Vols, 1-19. 8vo. price 5s. each.

Longmans' New Atlas. Political and Physical. For the Use of Schools and Private Persons. Consisting of 40 Quarto and 16 Octavo Maps and Diagrams, and 16 Plates of Views. Edited by GEO. G. CHISHOLM, M.A., B.Sc. Imp. 4to. or Imp. 8vo. 12s. 6d.

LONGMORE.—**Richard Wiseman,** Surgeon and Sergeant-Surgeon to Charles II.: a Biographical Study. By Surgeon General Sir T. LONGMORE, C.B., F.R.C.S., &c. With Portrait and Illustrations. 8vo. 10s. 6d.

LOUDON (J. C.).—WORKS BY.

Encyclopædia of Gardening. With 1000 Woodcuts. 8vo. 21s.

Encyclopædia of Agriculture; the Laying-out, Improvement, and Management of Landed Property. With 1100 Woodcuts. 8vo. 21s.

Encyclopædia of Plants; the Specific Character, &c., of all Plants found in Great Britain. With 12,000 Woodcuts. 8vo. 42s.

LUBBOCK.—**The Origin of Civilisation** and the Primitive Condition of Man. By Sir J. LUBBOCK, Bart., M.P. With 5 Plates and 20 Illustrations in the Text. 8vo. 18s.

LYALL.—**The Autobiography of a Slander.** By EDNA LYALL, Author of 'Donovan,' &c. Fcp. 8vo. 1s. sewed.

LYDEKKER.—**Phases of Animal Life, Past and Present.** By R. LYDEKKER, B.A. With 82 Illustrations. Crown 8vo. 6s.

LYDE.—**An Introduction to Ancient History:** being a Sketch of the History of Egypt, Mesopotamia, Greece, and Rome. With a Chapter on the Development of the Roman Empire into the Powers of Modern Europe. By LIONEL W. LYDE, M.A. With 3 Coloured Maps. Crown 8vo. 3s.

LYONS.—**Christianity and Infallibility**—Both or Neither. By the Rev. DANIEL LYONS. Crown 8vo. 5s.

LYTTON.—**Marah.** By OWEN MEREDITH (the late Earl of Lytton). Fcp. 8vo. 6s. 6d.

MACAULAY (Lord).—WORKS OF.

Complete Works of Lord Macaulay:
Library Edition, 8 vols. 8vo. £5 5s.
Cabinet Edition, 16 vols. Post 8vo. £4 16s.

MACAULAY (Lord).—WORKS OF.—continued.

History of England from the Accession of James the Second:
Popular Edition, 2 vols. Crown 8vo. 5s.
Student's Edition, 2 vols. Crown 8vo. 12s.
People's Edition, 4 vols. Crown 8vo. 16s.
Cabinet Edition, 8 vols. Post 8vo. 48s.
Library Edition, 5 vols. 8vo. £4.

Critical and Historical Essays, with Lays of Ancient Rome, in 1 volume:
Popular Edition, Crown 8vo. 2s. 6d.
Authorised Edition, Crown 8vo. 2s. 6d. or 3s. 6d. gilt edges.
Silver Library Edition, Crown 8vo. 3s. 6d.

Critical and Historical Essays:
Student's Edition, 1 vol. Crown 8vo. 6s.
People's Edition, 2 vols. Crown 8vo. 8s.
Trevelyan Edition, 2 vols. Crown 8vo. 9s.
Cabinet Edition, 4 vols. Post 8vo. 24s.
Library Edition, 3 vols. 8vo. 36s.

Essays which may be had separately price 6d. each sewed, 1s. each cloth:
Addison and Walpole.
Frederick the Great.
Croker's Boswell's Johnson.
Hallam's Constitutional History.
Warren Hastings. (3d. sewed, 6d cloth.)
The Earl of Chatham (Two Essays).
Ranke and Gladstone.
Milton and Machiavelli.
Lord Bacon.
Lord Clive.
Lord Byron, and The Comic Dramatists of the Restoration.

The Essay on Warren Hastings annotated by S. HALES, 1s. 6d.
The Essay on Lord Clive annotated by H. COURTHOPE BOWEN, M.A., 2s. 6d.

Speeches:
People's Edition, Crown 8vo. 3s. 6d.

Lays of Ancient Rome, &c.:
Illustrated by G. Scharf, Fcp. 4to. 10s. 6d.
——— Bijou Edition, 18mo. 2s. 6d. gilt top.
——— Popular Edition, Fcp. 4to. 6d. sewed, 1s. cloth.
Illustrated by J. R. Weguelin, Crown 8vo. 3s. 6d. cloth extra, gilt edges.
Cabinet Edition, Post 8vo. 3s. 6d.
Annotated Edition, Fcp. 8vo. 1s. sewed, 1s. 6d. cloth.

Miscellaneous Writings:
People's Edition, 1 vol. Crown 8vo. 4s. 6d.
Library Edition, 2 vols. 8vo. 21s.

[*Continued on next page.*

***MACAULAY** (Lord).—WORKS OF.—continued.*

Miscellaneous Writings and Speeches:
Popular Edition, 1 vol. Crown 8vo. 2s. 6d.
Student's Edition, in 1 vol. Crown 8vo. 6s.
Cabinet Edition, including Indian Penal Code, Lays of Ancient Rome, and Miscellaneous Poems, 4 vols. Post 8vo. 24s.

Selections from the Writings of Lord Macaulay. Edited, with Occasional Notes, by the Right Hon. Sir G. O. TREVELYAN, Bart. Cr. 8vo. 6s.

The Life and Letters of Lord Macaulay. By the Right Hon. Sir G. O. TREVELYAN, Bart.:
Popular Edition, 1 vol. Crown 8vo. 2s. 6d.
Student's Edition, 1 vol. Crown 8vo. 6s.
Cabinet Edition, 2 vols. Post 8vo. 12s.
Library Edition, 2 vols. 8vo. 36s.

***MACDONALD** (Geo.).—WORKS BY.*
Unspoken Sermons. Three Series. Crown 8vo. 3s. 6d. each.
The Miracles of Our Lord. Crown 8vo. 3s. 6d.
A Book of Strife, in the Form of the Diary of an Old Soul: Poems. 12mo. 6s.

***MACFARREN** (Sir G. A.).—WORKS BY.*
Lectures on Harmony. 8vo. 12s.

***MACKAIL.*—SelectEpigrams from the Greek Anthology.** Edited, with a Revised Text, Introduction, Translation, and Notes, by J. W. MACKAIL, M.A. 8vo. 16s.

***MACLEOD** (Henry D.).—WORKS BY.*
The Elements of Banking. Crown 8vo. 3s. 6d.
The Theory and Practice of Banking. Vol. I. 8vo. 12s. Vol. II. 14s.
The Theory of Credit. 8vo. Vol. I. 7s. 6d.; Vol. II. Part I. 4s. 6d.; Vol. II. Part II. 10s. 6d.

***M^cCULLOCH.*—The Dictionary of Commerce** and Commercial Navigation of the late J. R. MCCULLOCH. 8vo. with 11 Maps and 30 Charts, 63s.

***MACVINE.* — Sixty-Three Years' Angling,** from the Mountain Streamlet to the Mighty Tay. By JOHN MACVINE. Crown 8vo. 10s. 6d.

***MALMESBURY.*—Memoirs of an Ex-Minister.** By the Earl of MALMESBURY. Crown 8vo. 7s. 6d.

***MANNERING.*—With Axe and Rope in the New Zealand Alps.** By GEORGE EDWARD MANNERING. With 18 Illustrations. 8vo. 12s. 6d.

MANUALS OF CATHOLIC PHILOSOPHY (*Stonyhurst Series*) :
Logic. By RICHARD F. CLARKE, S.J. Crown 8vo. 5s.
First Principles of Knowledge. By JOHN RICKABY, S.J. Crown 8vo. 5s.
Moral Philosophy (Ethics and Natural Law). By JOSEPH RICKABY, S.J. Crown 8vo. 5s.
General Metaphysics. By JOHN RICKABY, S.J. Crown 8vo. 5s.
Psychology. By MICHAEL MAHER, S.J. Crown 8vo. 6s. 6d.
Natural Theology. By BERNARD BOEDDER, S.J. Crown 8vo. 6s. 6d.
Political Economy. By CHARLES S. DEVAS. Crown 8vo. 6s. 6d.

***MARBOT.*—The Memoirs of the Baron de Marbot.** Translated from the French. 2 vols. 8vo. 32s.

***MARTINEAU** (James).—WORKS BY.*
Hours of Thought on Sacred Things. Two Volumes of Sermons. 2 vols. Crown 8vo. 7s. 6d. each.
Endeavours after the Christian Life. Discourses. Cr. 8vo. 7s. 6d.
The Seat of Authority in Religion. 8vo. 14s.
Essays, Reviews, and Addresses. 4 vols. Cr. 8vo. 7s. 6d. each.
I. Personal : Political.
II. Ecclesiastical : Historical.
III. Theological : Philosophical.
IV. Academical : Religious.
Home Prayers, with Two Services for Public Worship. Crown 8vo. 3s. 6d.

***MATTHEWS** (Brander).—WORKS BY.*
A Family Tree, and other Stories. Crown 8vo. 6s.
Pen and Ink: Papers on Subjects of more or less Importance. Cr. 8vo. 5s.
With My Friends: Tales told in Partnership. With an Introductory Essay on the Art and Mystery of Collaboration. Crown 8vo. 6s.

MAUNDER'S TREASURIES.

Biographical Treasury. With Supplement brought down to 1889, by Rev. JAS. WOOD. Fcp. 8vo. 6s.

Treasury of Natural History; or, Popular Dictionary of Zoology. Fcp. 8vo. with 900 Woodcuts, 6s.

Treasury of Geography, Physical, Historical, Descriptive, and Political. With 7 Maps and 16 Plates. Fcp. 8vo. 9s.

Scientific and Literary Treasury. Fcp. 8vo. 6s.

Historical Treasury: Outlines of Universal History, Separate Histories of all Nations. Fcp. 8vo. 6s.

Treasury of Knowledge and Library of Reference. Comprising an English Dictionary and Grammar, Universal Gazetteer, Classical Dictionary, Chronology, Law Dictionary, &c. Fcp. 8vo. 6s.

The Treasury of Bible Knowledge. By the Rev. J. AYRE, M.A. With 5 Maps, 15 Plates, and 300 Woodcuts. Fcp. 8vo. 6s.

The Treasury of Botany. Edited by J. LINDLEY, F.R.S., and T. MOORE, F.L.S. With 274 Woodcuts and 20 Steel Plates. 2 vols. Fcp. 8vo. 12s.

MAX MULLER (F.).—WORKS BY.

Selected Essays on Language, Mythology and Religion. 2 vols. Crown 8vo. 16s.

The Science of Language, Founded on Lectures delivered at the Royal Institution in 1861 and 1863. 2 vols. Crown 8vo. 21s.

Three Lectures on the Science of Language and its Place in General Education, delivered at the Oxford University Extension Meeting, 1889. Crown 8vo. 3s.

Hibbert Lectures on the Origin and Growth of Religion, as illustrated by the Religions of India. Crown 8vo. 7s. 6d.

Introduction to the Science of Religion; Four Lectures delivered at the Royal Institution. Crown 8vo. 7s. 6d.

Natural Religion. The Gifford Lectures, delivered before the University of Glasgow in 1888. Crown 8vo. 10s. 6d.

Physical Religion. The Gifford Lectures, delivered before the University of Glasgow in 1890. Crown 8vo. 10s. 6d.

MAX MÜLLER (F.).—WORKS BY.— continued.

Anthropological Religion: The Gifford Lectures delivered before the University of Glasgow in 1891. Cr.8vo. 10s.6d.

The Science of Thought. 8vo. 21s.

Three Introductory Lectures on the Science of Thought. 8vo. 2s. 6d.

Biographies of Words, and the Home of the Aryas. Crown 8vo. 7s. 6d.

India, what can it teach us? Crown 8vo. 3s. 6d.

A Sanskrit Grammar for Beginners. Abridged Edition. By A. A. MACDONELL. Cr. 8vo. 6s.

MAY.—The Constitutional History of England since the Accession of George III. 1760-1870. By the Right Hon. Sir THOMAS ERSKINE MAY, K.C.B. 3 vols. Crown 8vo. 18s.

MEADE (L. T.).—WORKS BY.

Daddy's Boy. With Illustrations. Crown 8vo. 3s. 6d.

Deb and the Duchess. With Illustrations by M. E. EDWARDS. Crown 8vo. 3s. 6d.

The Beresford Prize. With Illustrations by M. E. EDWARDS. Crown 8vo. 5s.

MEATH (The Earl of).—WORKS BY.

Social Arrows: Reprinted Articles on various Social Subjects. Cr. 8vo. 5s.

Prosperity or Pauperism? Physical, Industrial, and Technical Training. (Edited by the EARL OF MEATH.) 8vo. 5s.

MELVILLE (G. J. Whyte).—NOVELS BY. Crown 8vo. 1s. each, boards; 1s. 6d. each, cloth.

The Gladiators.	Holmby House.
The Interpreter.	Kate Coventry.
Good for Nothing.	Digby Grand.
The Queen's Maries.	General Bounce.

MENDELSSOHN.—The Letters of Felix Mendelssohn. Translated by Lady WALLACE. 2 vols. Crown 8vo. 10s.

MERIVALE (*The Very Rev. Chas.*).— WORKS BY.
History of the Romans under the Empire. Cabinet Edition, 8 vols. Crown 8vo. 48s.
Popular Edition, 8 vols. Cr. 8vo. 3s. 6d. each.
The Fall of the Roman Republic: a Short History of the Last Century of the Commonwealth. 12mo. 7s. 6d.
General History of Rome from B.C. 753 to A.D. 476. Cr. 8vo. 7s. 6d.
The Roman Triumvirates. With Maps. Fcp. 8vo. 2s. 6d.

MILES.—**The Correspondence of William Augustus Miles on the French Revolution, 1789-1817.** Edited by the Rev. CHARLES POPHAM MILES, M.A. 2 vols. 8vo. 32s.

MILL.—**Analysis of the Phenomena of the Human Mind.** By JAMES MILL. 2 vols. 8vo. 28s.

MILL (*John Stuart*).— WORKS BY.
Principles of Political Economy. Library Edition, 2 vols. 8vo. 30s.
People's Edition, 1 vol. Crown 8vo. 3s. 6d.
A System of Logic. Cr. 8vo. 3s. 6d.
On Liberty. Crown 8vo. 1s. 4d.
On Representative Government. Crown 8vo. 2s.
Utilitarianism. 8vo. 5s.
Examination of Sir William Hamilton's Philosophy. 8vo. 16s.
Nature, the Utility of Religion, and Theism. Three Essays. 8vo. 5s.

MOLESWORTH (*Mrs.*).—*WORKS BY.*
Marrying and Giving in Marriage: a Novel. Illustrated. Fcp. 8vo. 2s. 6d.
Silverthorns. Illustrated. Crown 8vo. 5s.
The Palace in the Garden. Illustrated. Crown 8vo. 5s.
The Third Miss St. Quentin. Crown 8vo. 6s.
Neighbours. Illustrated. Crown 8vo. 6s.
The Story of a Spring Morning, &c. Illustrated. Crown 8vo. 5s.
Stories of the Saints for Children: the Black Letter Saints. With Illustrations. Royal 16mo. 5s.

MOORE.—**Dante and his Early Biographers.** By EDWARD MOORE, D.D., Principal of St. Edmund Hall, Oxford. Crown 8vo. 4s. 6d.

MULHALL.—**History of Prices since the Year 1850.** By MICHAEL G. MULHALL. Cr. 8vo. 6s.

NANSEN.—**The First Crossing of Greenland.** By Dr. FRIDTJOF NANSEN. With 5 Maps, 12 Plates, and 150 Illustrations in the Text. 2 vols. 8vo. 36s. Cheaper Edition, abridged. With numerous Illustrations and a Map. In 1 vol. crown 8vo. 7s. 6d.

NAPIER.—**The Life of Sir Joseph Napier, Bart., Ex-Lord Chancellor of Ireland.** By ALEX. CHARLES EWALD, F.S.A. With Portrait. 8vo. 15s.

NAPIER.—**The Lectures, Essays, and Letters of the Right Hon. Sir Joseph Napier, Bart.,** late Lord Chancellor of Ireland. 8vo. 12s. 6d.

NESBIT.—**Leaves of Life:** Verses. By E. NESBIT. Crown 8vo. 5s.
Lays and Legends. By E. NESBIT (Mrs. HUBERT BLAND). FIRST Series. New and Cheaper Edition. Crown 8vo. 3s. 6d. SECOND Series. With Portrait. Crown 8vo. 5s.

NEWMAN.—**The Letters and Correspondence of John Henry Newman** during his Life in the English Church. With a brief Autobiographical Memoir. Arranged and Edited by ANNE MOZLEY. With Portraits. 2 vols. 8vo. 30s. net.

NEWMAN (*Cardinal*).—*WORKS BY.*
Apologia pro Vitâ Sua. Cabinet Edition, Crown 8vo. 6s. Cheap Edition, Crown 8vo. 3s. 6d.
Discourses to Mixed Congregations. Cabinet Edition, Crown 8vo. 6s. Cheap Edition, Cr. 8vo. 3s. 6d.
Sermons on Various Occasions. Cabinet Edition. Crown 8vo. 6s. Cheap Edition. 3s. 6d.
The Idea of a University defined and illustrated. Cabinet Edition, Crown 8vo. 7s. Cheap Edition, Crown 8vo. 3s. 6d.

[*Continued on next page.*

NEWMAN (Cardinal).—WORKS BY.
—*continued.*

Historical Sketches. 3 vols. Cabinet Edition. Crown 8vo. 6s. each. Cheap Edition, 3 vols. 3s. 6d. each.

The Arians of the Fourth Century. Cabinet Edition, Crown 8vo. 6s. Cheap Edition, Cr. 8vo. 3s. 6d.

Select Treatises of St. Athanasius in Controversy with the Arians. Freely Translated. 2 vols. Cr. 8vo. 15s.

Discussions and Arguments on Various Subjects. Cabinet Edition, Crown 8vo. 6s. Cheap Edition, Crown 8vo. 3s. 6d.

An Essay on the Development of Christian Doctrine. Cabinet Edition, Crown 8vo. 6s. Cheap Edition, Crown 8vo. 3s. 6d.

Certain Difficulties felt by Anglicans in Catholic Teaching Considered. Cabinet Edition, Vol. I., Crown 8vo. 7s. 6d. ; Vol. II., Cr. 8vo. 5s. 6d. Cheap Edition, 2 vols. Cr. 8vo. 3s. 6d. each.

The Via Media of the Anglican Church, illustrated in Lectures, &c. 2 vols. Cabinet Edition. Cr. 8vo. 6s. each. Cheap Edition, 2 vols. 3s. 6d. each.

Essays, Critical and Historical. Cabinet Edition, 2 vols. Crown 8vo. 12s. Cheap Edition, 2 vols. Crown 8vo. 7s.

Essays on Biblical and on Ecclesiastical Miracles. Cabinet Edition, Crown 8vo. 6s. Cheap Edition, Crown 8vo. 3s. 6d.

Tracts. 1. Dissertatiunculæ. 2. On the Text of the Seven Epistles of St. Ignatius. 3. Doctrinal Causes of Arianism. 4. Apollinarianism. 5. St. Cyril's Formula. 6. Ordo de Tempore. 7. Douay Version of Scripture. Crown 8vo. 8s.

An Essay in Aid of a Grammar of Assent. Cabinet Edition, Crown 8vo. 7s. 6d. Cheap Edition, Crown 8vo. 3s. 6d.

Present Position of Catholics in England. Cabinet Edition, Cr. 8vo. 7s. 6d. Cheap Edition, Cr. 8vo. 3s 6d.

Callista: a Tale of the Third Century. Cabinet Edition, Crown 8vo. 6s. Cheap Edition, Crown 8vo. 3s. 6d.

NEWMAN (Cardinal).—WORKS OF.—continued.

Loss and Gain: a Tale. Cabinet Edition, Crown 8vo. 6s. Cheap Edition, Crown 8vo. 3s. 6d.

The Dream of Gerontius. 16mo. 6d. sewed. 1s. cloth.

Verses on Various Occasions. Cabinet Edition, Crown 8vo. 6s. Cheap Edition, Crown 8vo. 3s. 6d.

Fabulae Quaedam ex Terentio et Plauto ad usum Puerorum accommodatae. With English Notes and Translations to assist the representation. Cardinal Newman's Edition, Crown 8vo. 6s.

*** For Cardinal Newman's other Works see Messrs. Longmans & Co.'s *Catalogue of Church of England Theological Works.*

NORTON (Charles L.).—WORKS BY.

Political Americanisms: a Glossary of Terms and Phrases Current at Different Periods in American Politics. Fcp. 8vo. 2s. 6d.

A Handbook of Florida. With 49 Maps and Plans. Fcp. 8vo. 5s.

O'BRIEN.—**When we were Boys:** a Novel. By WILLIAM O'BRIEN, M.P. Crown 8vo. 2s. 6d.

OLIPHANT (Mrs.).—NOVELS BY.

Madam. Cr. 8vo. 1s. bds. ; 1s. 6d. cl.

In Trust. Cr. 8vo. 1s. bds.; 1s. 6d. cl.

OMAN.—**A History of Greece from the Earliest Times to the Macedonian Conquest.** By C. W. C. OMAN, M.A., F.S.A. With Maps and Plans. Crown 8vo. 4s. 6d.

O'REILLY.—**Hurstleigh Dene:** a Tale. By Mrs. O'REILLY. Illustrated by M. ELLEN EDWARDS. Cr. 8vo. 5s.

PAUL.—**Principles of the History of Language.** By HERMANN PAUL. Translated by H. A. STRONG. 8vo. 10s. 6d.

PAYN (James).—NOVELS BY.

The Luck of the Darrells. Cr. 8vo. 1s. boards ; 1s. 6d. cloth.

Thicker than Water. Crown 8vo. 1s. boards; 1s. 6d. cloth.

PERRING (Sir Philip).—WORKS BY.
Hard Knots in Shakespeare.
8vo. 7s. 6d.

The 'Works and Days' of Moses.
Crown 8vo. 3s. 6d.

PHILLIPPS-WOLLEY.—**Snap**: a Legend of the Lone Mountain. By C. PHILLIPPS-WOLLEY. With 13 Illustrations by H. G. WILLINK. Cr. 8vo. 3s. 6d.

POLE.—**The Theory of the Modern Scientific Game of Whist.** By W. POLE, F.R.S. Fcp. 8vo. 2s. 6d.

POLLOCK.—**The Seal of Fate**: a Novel. By Lady POLLOCK and W. H. POLLOCK. Crown 8vo. 6s.

POOLE.—**Cookery for the Diabetic.** By W. H. and Mrs. POOLE. With Preface by Dr. PAVY. Fcp. 8vo. 2s. 6d.

PRAEGER.—**Wagner as I knew him.** By FERDINAND PRAEGER. Crown 8vo. 7s. 6d.

PRATT.—**To the Snows of Tibet through China.** By A. E. PRATT, F.R.G.S. With 33 Illustrations and a Map. 8vo. 18s.

PRENDERGAST.—**Ireland, from the Restoration to the Revolution, 1660-1690.** By JOHN P. PRENDERGAST. 8vo. 5s.

PROCTOR (R. A.).—WORKS BY.
Old and New Astronomy. 12 Parts, 2s. 6d. each. Supplementary Section, 1s. Complete in 1 vol. 4to. 36s.
[*In course of publication.*]

The Orbs Around Us; a Series of Essays on the Moon and Planets, Meteors and Comets. With Chart and Diagrams. Crown 8vo. 5s.

Other Worlds than Ours; The Plurality of Worlds Studied under the Light of Recent Scientific Researches. With 14 Illustrations. Crown 8vo. 5s.

The Moon; her Motions, Aspects Scenery, and Physical Condition. With Plates, Charts, Woodcuts, &c. Cr. 8vo. 5s.

Universe of Stars; Presenting Researches into and New Views respecting the Constitution of the Heavens. With 22 Charts and 22 Diagrams. 8vo. 10s. 6d.

PROCTOR (R. A.).—WORKS BY. —continued.

Larger Star Atlas for the Library, in 12 Circular Maps, with Introduction and 2 Index Pages. Folio, 15s. or Maps only, 12s. 6d.

The Student's Atlas. In Twelve Circular Maps on a Uniform Projection and one Scale. 8vo. 5s.

New Star Atlas for the Library, the School, and the Observatory, in 12 Circular Maps. Crown 8vo. 5s.

Light Science for Leisure Hours. Familiar Essays on Scientific Subjects. 3 vols. Crown 8vo. 5s. each.

Chance and Luck; a Discussion of the Laws of Luck, Coincidences, Wagers, Lotteries, and the Fallacies of Gambling, &c. Crown 8vo. 2s. boards; 2s. 6d. cloth.

Studies of Venus-Transits. With 7 Diagrams and 10 Plates. 8vo. 5s.

How to Play Whist: with the Laws and Etiquette of Whist. Crown 8vo. 3s. 6d.

Home Whist: an Easy Guide to Correct Play. 16mo. 1s.

The Stars in their Seasons. An Easy Guide to a Knowledge of the Star Groups, in 12 Maps. Roy. 8vo. 5s.

Star Primer. Showing the Starry Sky Week by Week, in 24 Hourly Maps. Crown 4to. 2s. 6d.

The Seasons pictured in 48 Sun-Views of the Earth, and 24 Zodiacal Maps, &c. Demy 4to. 5s.

Strength and Happiness. With 9 Illustrations. Crown 8vo. 5s.

Strength: How to get Strong and keep Strong, with Chapters on Rowing and Swimming, Fat, Age, and the Waist. With 9 Illustrations. Crown 8vo. 2s.

Rough Ways Made Smooth. Familiar Essays on Scientific Subjects. Crown 8vo. 5s.

Our Place Among Infinities. A Series of Essays contrasting our Little Abode in Space and Time with the Infinities around us. Crown 8vo. 5s.

[*Continued on next page.*]

PROCTOR (R. A.).—WORKS BY.— continued.

The Expanse of Heaven. Essays on the Wonders of the Firmament. Cr. 8vo. 5s.

The Great Pyramid, Observatory, Tomb, and Temple. With Illustrations. Crown 8vo. 5s.

Pleasant Ways in Science. Cr. 8vo. 5s.

Myths and Marvels of Astronomy. Crown 8vo. 5s.

Nature Studies. By GRANT ALLEN, A. WILSON, T. FOSTER, E. CLODD, and R. A. PROCTOR. Crown 8vo. 5s.

Leisure Readings. By E. CLODD, A. WILSON, T. FOSTER, A. C. RANYARD, and R. A. PROCTOR. Crown 8vo. 5s.

PRYCE.—**The Ancient British Church**: an Historical Essay. By JOHN PRYCE, M.A. Crown 8vo. 6s.

RANSOME.—**The Rise of Constitutional Government in England**: being a Series of Twenty Lectures on the History of the English Constitution delivered to a Popular Audience. By CYRIL RANSOME, M.A. Crown 8vo. 6s.

RAWLINSON.—**The History of Phœnicia.** By GEORGE RAWLINSON, M.A., Canon of Canterbury, &c. With numerous Illustrations. 8vo. 24s.

RIBOT.—**The Psychology of Attention.** By TH. RIBOT. Crown 8vo. 3s.

RICH.—**A Dictionary of Roman and Greek Antiquities.** With 2000 Woodcuts. By A. RICH. Crown 8vo. 7s. 6d.

RICHARDSON.—**National Health.** Abridged from 'The Health of Nations'. A Review of the Works of Sir Edwin Chadwick, K.C.B. By Dr. B. W. RICHARDSON. Crown, 4s. 6d.

RILEY.—**Athos**; or, the Mountain of the Monks. By ATHELSTAN RILEY, M.A., F.R.G.S. With Map and 29 Illustrations. 8vo. 21s.

RILEY.—**Old-Fashioned Roses**: Poems. By JAMES WHITCOMB RILEY. 12mo. 5s.

RIVERS.—**The Miniature Fruit Garden**; or, The Culture of Pyramidal and Bush Fruit Trees. By THOMAS and T. F. RIVERS. With 32 Illustrations. Crown 8vo. 4s.

RIVERS.—**The Rose Amateur's Guide.** By THOMAS RIVERS. Fcp. 8vo. 4s. 6d.

ROBERTSON.—**The Kidnapped Squatter,** and other Australian Tales. By A. ROBERTSON. Cr. 8vo. 6s.

ROCKHILL.—**The Land of the Lamas**: Notes of a Journey through China, Mongolia and Tibet. With 2 Maps and 6 Illustrations. By W. W. ROCKHILL. 8vo. 15s.

ROGET.—**A History of the 'Old Water-Colour' Society** (now the Royal Society of Painters in Water-Colours). With Biographical Notices of its Older and all its Deceased Members and Associates. By JOHN LEWIS ROGET, M.A. 2 vols. Royal 8vo. 42s.

ROGET.—**Thesaurus of English Words and Phrases.** Classified and Arranged so as to facilitate the Expression of Ideas. By PETER M. ROGET. Crown 8vo. 10s. 6d.

ROMANES. — **Darwin, and after Darwin**: an Exposition of the Darwinian Theory and a Discussion of Post-Darwinian Questions. By GEORGE JOHN ROMANES, M.A., LL.D., F.R.S., Author of 'Mental Evolution in Man,' &c. Part I.—The Darwinian Theory. With Portrait of Darwin and 125 Illustrations. Crown 8vo. 10s. 6d.

RONALDS. — **The Fly-Fisher's Entomology.** By A. RONALDS. With 20 Coloured Plates. 8vo. 14s.

ROSSETTI.—**A Shadow of Dante**: being an Essay towards studying Himself, his World, and his Pilgrimage. By MARIA FRANCESCA ROSSETTI. With Illustrations. Crown 8vo. 10s. 6d.

ROUND. — **Geoffrey de Mandeville**: a Study of the Anarchy. By J. H. ROUND, M.A., Author of 'The Early Life of Anne Boleyn: a Critical Essay'. 8vo. 16s.

RUSSELL.—**A Life of Lord John Russell (Earl Russell, K.G.).** By SPENCER WALPOLE. With 2 Portraits. 2 vols. 8vo. 36s. Cabinet Edition, 2 vols. Crown 8vo. 12s.

SEEBOHM (*Frederic*).—*WORKS BY*.
The Oxford Reformers—John Colet, Erasmus, and Thomas More; a History of their Fellow-Work. 8vo. 14*s*.

The English Village Community Examined in its Relations to the Manorial and Tribal Systems, &c. 13 Maps and Plates. 8vo. 16*s*.

The Era of the Protestant Revolution. With Map. Fcp. 8vo. 2*s*. 6*d*.

SEWELL.—Stories and Tales. By Elizabeth M. Sewell. Crown 8vo. 1*s*. 6*d*. each, cloth plain; 2*s*. 6*d*. each, cloth extra, gilt edges:—

Amy Herbert.	Laneton Parsonage.
The Earl's Daughter.	Ursula.
The Experience of Life.	Gertrude.
A Glimpse of the World.	Ivors.
Cleve Hall.	Home Life.
Katharine Ashton.	After Life.
Margaret Percival.	

SHAKESPEARE. — Bowdler's Family Shakespeare. 1 Vol. 8vo. With 36 Woodcuts, 14*s*. or in 6 vols. Fcp. 8vo. 21*s*.

Outlines of the Life of Shakespeare. By J. O. Halliwell-Phillipps. With numerous Illustrations and Fac-similes. 2 vols. Royal 8vo. £1 1*s*.

A Calendar of the Halliwell-Phillipps' Collection of Shakespearean Rarities Formerly Preserved at Hollingbury Copse, Brighton. Enlarged by Ernest E. Baker, F.S.A. 8vo. 10*s*. 6*d*.

Shakespeare's True Life. By James Walter. With 500 Illustrations. Imp. 8vo. 21*s*.

The Shakespeare Birthday Book. By Mary F. Dunbar. 32mo. 1*s*. 6*d*. cloth. With Photographs, 32mo. 5*s*. Drawing-Room Edition, with Photographs, Fcp. 8vo. 10*s*. 6*d*.

SIDGWICK.—Distinction: and the Criticism of Belief. By Alfred Sidgwick. Crown 8vo. 6*s*.

SILVER LIBRARY (The). — Crown 8vo. 3*s*. 6*d*. each volume.

Baker's (Sir S. W.) Eight Years in Ceylon. With 6 Illustrations. 3*s*. 6*d*.

Baker's (Sir S. W.) Rifle and Hound in Ceylon. With 6 Illustrations. 3*s*. 6*d*.

Baring-Gould's Curious Myths of the Middle Ages. 3*s*. 6*d*.

SILVER LIBRARY (The).—*continued.*

Baring-Gould's (Rev. S.) Origin and Development of Religious Belief. 2 vols. 7*s*.

Brassey's (Lady) A Voyage in the 'Sunbeam'. With 66 Illustrations. 3*s*. 6*d*.

Clodd's (E.) Story of Creation: a Plain Account of Evolution. With 77 Illustrations. 3*s*. 6*d*.

Conybeare (Rev. W. J.) and Howson's (Very Rev. J. S.) Life and Epistles of St. Paul. 46 Illustrations. Crown 8vo. 3*s*. 6*d*.

Dougall's (L.) Beggars All: a Novel. Crown 8vo. 3*s*. 6*d*.

Doyle's (A. Conan) Micah Clarke. A Tale of Monmouth's Rebellion. 3*s*. 6*d*.

Doyle's (A. Conan) The Captain of the Polestar, and other Tales. Crown 8vo. 3*s*. 6*d*.

Froude's (J. A.) Short Studies on Great Subjects. 4 vols. 3*s*. 6*d*. each.

Froude's (J. A.) Cæsar: a Sketch. 3*s*. 6*d*.

Froude's (J. A.) Thomas Carlyle: a History of his Life. 1795-1835. 2 vols. 1834-1881. 2 vols. 7*s*. each.

Froude's (J. A.) The Two Chiefs of Dunboy: an Irish Romance of the Last Century. 3*s*. 6*d*.

Gleig's (Rev. G. R.) Life of the Duke of Wellington. With Portrait. 3*s*. 6*d*.

Haggard's (H. R.) She: A History of Adventure. 32 Illustrations. 3*s*. 6*d*.

Haggard's (H. R.) Allan Quatermain. With 20 Illustrations. 3*s*. 6*d*.

Haggard's (H. R.) Colonel Quaritch, V.C.: a Tale of Country Life. 3*s*. 6*d*.

Haggard's (H. R.) Cleopatra. With 29 Full-page Illustrations. 3*s*. 6*d*.

Haggard's (H. R.) Beatrice. 3*s*. 6*d*.

Howitt's (W.) Visits to Remarkable Places. 80 Illustrations. 3*s*. 6*d*.

Jefferies' (R.) The Story of My Heart: My Autobiography. With Portrait. 3*s*. 6*d*.

Jefferies' (R.) Field and Hedgerow. Last Essays of. With Portrait. 3*s*. 6*d*.

Jefferies' (R.) Red Deer. With 17 Illustrations by J. Charlton and H. Tunaly. Crown 8vo. 3*s*. 6*d*.

Knight's (E. F.) The Cruise of the 'Alerte:' the Narrative of a Search for Treasure on the Desert Island of Trinidad. With 2 Maps and 23 Illustrations. Crown 8vo. 3*s*. 6*d*.

Lees (J. A.) and Clutterbuck's (W. J.), B. C. 1887, A Ramble in British Columbia. With Maps and 75 Illustrations. 3*s*. 6*d*.

[*Continued on next page.*

SILVER LIBRARY (The).—continued.

Macaulay's (Lord) Essays and Lays. With Portrait and Illustration. 3s. 6d.

Macleod's (H. D.) The Elements of Banking. 3s. 6d.

Marshman's (J. C.) Memoirs of Sir Henry Havelock. 3s. 6d.

Max Müller's (F.) India, what can it teach us? Crown 8vo. 3s. 6d.

Merivale's (Dean) History of the Romans under the Empire. 8 vols. 3s. 6d. each.

Mill's (J. S.) Principles of Political Economy. 3s. 6d.

Mill's (J. S.) System of Logic 3s. 6d.

Newman's (Cardinal) Historical Sketches. 3 vols. 3s. 6d. each.

Newman's (Cardinal) Apologia Pro Vitâ Suâ. 3s. 6d.

Newman's (Cardinal) Callista: a Tale of the Third Century. 3s. 6d.

Newman's (Cardinal) Loss and Gain: a Tale. 3s. 6d.

Newman's (Cardinal) Essays, Critical and Historical. 2 vols. 7s.

Newman's (Cardinal) An Essay on the Development of Christian Doctrine. 3s. 6d.

Newman's (Cardinal) The Arians of the Fourth Century. 3s. 6d.

Newman's (Cardinal) Verses on Various Occasions. 3s. 6d.

Newman's (Cardinal) The Present Position of Catholics in England. 3s. 6d.

Newman's (Cardinal) Parochial and Plain Sermons. 8 vols. 3s. 6d. each.

Newman's (Cardinal) Selection, adapted to the Seasons of the Ecclesiastical Year, from the 'Parochial and Plain Sermons'. 3s. 6d.

Newman's (Cardinal) Sermons bearing upon Subjects of the Day. Edited by the Rev. W. J. Copeland, B.D., late Rector of Farnham, Essex. 3s. 6d.

Newman's (Cardinal) Difficulties felt by Anglicans in Catholic Teaching Considered. 2 vols. 3s. 6d. each.

Newman's (Cardinal) The Idea of a University Defined and Illustrated. 3s. 6d.

Newman's (Cardinal) Biblical and Ecclesiastical Miracles. 3s. 6d.

Newman's (Cardinal) Discussions and Arguments on Various Subjects. 3s. 6d.

Newman's (Cardinal) Grammar of Assent. 3s. 6d.

Newman's (Cardinal) Fifteen Sermons Preached before the University of Oxford. Crown 8vo. 3s. 6d.

SILVER LIBRARY (The).—continued.

Newman's (Cardinal) Lectures on the Doctrine of Justification. Crown 8vo. 3s. 6d.

Newman's (Cardinal) Sermons on Various Occasions. Crown 8vo. 3s. 6d.

Newman's (Cardinal) The Via Media of the Anglican Church, illustrated in Lectures, &c. 2 vols. 3s. 6d. each.

Newman's (Cardinal) Discourses to Mixed Congregations. 3s. 6d.

Phillipps-Wolley's (C.) Snap: a Legend of the Lone Mountain. With 13 Illustrations. 3s. 6d.

Stanley's (Bishop) Familiar History of Birds. 160 Illustrations. 3s. 6d.

Stevenson (R. L.) and Osbourne's (Ll.) The Wrong Box. Crown 8vo. 3s. 6d.

Weyman's (Stanley J.) The House of the Wolf: a Romance. Cr. 8vo. 3s. 6d.

Wood's (Rev. J. G.) Petland Revisited. With 33 Illustrations. 3s. 6d.

Wood's (Rev. J. G.) Strange Dwellings: With 60 Illustrations. 3s. 6d.

Wood's (Rev. J. G.) Out of Doors. 11 Illustrations. 3s. 6d.

SMITH (R. Bosworth).—Carthage and the Carthagenians. By R. BOSWORTH SMITH, M.A. Maps, Plans, &c. Crown 8vo. 6s.

Sophocles. Translated into English Verse. By ROBERT WHITELAW, M.A. Assistant-Master in Rugby School; late Fellow of Trinity College, Cambridge. Crown 8vo. 8s. 6d.

STEEL (J. H.).—WORKS BY.

A Treatise on the Diseases of the Dog; being a Manual of Canine Pathology. 88 Illustrations. 8vo. 10s. 6d.

A Treatise on the Diseases of the Ox; being a Manual of Bovine Pathology. 2 Plates and 117 Woodcuts. 8vo. 15s.

A Treatise on the Diseases of the Sheep; being a Manual of Ovine Pathology. With Coloured Plate and 99 Woodcuts. 8vo. 12s.

STEPHEN.—Essays in Ecclesiastical Biography. By the Right Hon. Sir J. STEPHEN. Crown 8vo. 7s. 6d.

STEPHENS.—A History of the French Revolution. By H. MORSE STEPHENS, Balliol College, Oxford. 3 vols. 8vo. Vols. I. and II. 18s. each.

STEVENSON (Robt. Louis).—WORKS BY.

A Child's Garden of Verses. Small Fcp. 8vo. 5s.

A Child's Garland of Songs, Gathered from 'A Child's Garden of Verses'. By ROBERT LOUIS STEVENSON, and set to Music by C. VILLIERS STANFORD, Mus. Doc. 4to. 2s. sewed, 3s. 6d. cloth gilt.

The Dynamiter. Fcp. 8vo. 1s. sewed ; 1s. 6d. cloth.

Strange Case of Dr. Jekyll and Mr. Hyde. Fcp. 8vo. 1s. swd.; 1s. 6d. cloth.

STEVENSON and OSBOURNE.—
The Wrong Box. By ROBERT LOUIS STEVENSON and LLOYD OSBOURNE. Crown 8vo. 3s. 6d.

STOCK.—**Deductive Logic.** By ST. GEORGE STOCK. Fcp. 8vo. 3s. 6d.

'STONEHENGE'.—**The Dog in Health and Disease.** By 'STONEHENGE'. With 84 Wood Engravings. Square Crown 8vo. 7s. 6d.

STRONG, LOGEMAN, and WHEELER.—**Introduction to the Study of the History of Language.** By HERBERT A. STRONG, M.A., LL.D. ; WILLEM S. LOGEMAN ; and BENJAMIN IDE WHEELER. 8vo. 10s. 6d.

SULLY (James).— WORKS BY.

The Human Mind : a Text-Book of Psychology. 2 vols. 8vo. 21s.

Outlines of Psychology. With Special Reference to the Theory of Education. 8vo. 10s.

The Teacher's Handbook of Psychology, on the Basis of 'Outlines of Psychology'. Cr. 8vo. 5s.

Supernatural Religion; an Inquiry into the Reality of Divine Revelation. 3 vols. 8vo. 36s.

Reply (A) to Dr. Lightfoot's Essays. By the Author of 'Supernatural Religion'. 8vo. 6s.

SWINBURNE.—**Picture Logic ;** an Attempt to Popularise the Science of Reasoning. By A. J. SWINBURNE, B.A. Post 8vo. 5s.

SYMES (J. E.).— WORKS BY.

Prelude to Modern History: being a Brief Sketch of the World's History from the Third to the Ninth Century. With 5 Maps. Crown 8vo. 2s. 6d.

A Companion to School Histories of England. Crown 8vo. 2s. 6d.

Political Economy. With Problems for Solution, and Hints for Supplementary Reading. Crown 8vo. 2s. 6d.

TAYLOR.—**A Student's Manual of the History of India.** By Colonel MEADOWS TAYLOR, C.S.I., &c. Crown 8vo. 7s. 6d.

THOMPSON (D. Greenleaf).— WORKS BY.

The Problem of Evil : an Introduction to the Practical Sciences. 8vo. 10s. 6d.

A System of Psychology. 2 vols. 8vo. 36s.

The Religious Sentiments of the Human Mind. 8vo. 7s. 6d.

Social Progress : an Essay. 8vo. 7s. 6d.

The Philosophy of Fiction in Literature : an Essay. Cr. 8vo. 6s.

Three in Norway. By Two of THEM. With a Map and 59 Illustrations. Cr. 8vo. 2s. boards ; 2s. 6d. cloth.

THOMSON. — **Outlines of the Necessary Laws of Thought :** a Treatise on Pure and Applied Logic. By the Most Rev. WILLIAM THOMSON, D.D., late Lord Archbishop of York. Post 8vo. 6s.

TIREBUCK.—**Dorrie :** a Novel. By WILLIAM TIREBUCK. Crown 8vo. 6s.

TOYNBEE.—**Lectures on the Industrial Revolution of the 18th Century in England.** By ARNOLD TOYNBEE. 8vo. 10s. 6d.

TREVELYAN (Sir G. O., Bart.).— WORKS BY.

The Life and Letters of Lord Macaulay.
POPULAR EDITION, Crown 8vo. 2s. 6d.
STUDENT'S EDITION, Crown 8vo. 6s.
CABINET EDITION, 2 vols. Cr. 8vo. 12s.
LIBRARY EDITION, 2 vols. 8vo. 36s.

[Continued on next page.

TREVELYAN (Sir G. O., Bart.).—WORKS BY.—continued.

The Early History of Charles James Fox. Library Edition, 8vo. 18s. Cabinet Edition, Cr. 8vo. 6s.

TROLLOPE (Anthony).—NOVELS BY.

The Warden. Crown 8vo. 1s. boards; 1s. 6d. cloth.

Barchester Towers. Crown 8vo. 1s. boards; 1s. 6d. cloth.

VERNEY.—**Memoirs of the Verney Family during the Civil War.** Compiled from the Letters and Illustrated by the Portraits at Claydon House, Bucks. By FRANCES PARTHENOPE VERNEY. With a Preface by S. R. GARDINER, M.A., LL.D. With 38 Portraits, Woodcuts and Facsimile. 2 vols. Royal 8vo. 42s.

VILLE.—**The Perplexed Farmer:** How is he to meet Alien Competition? By GEORGE VILLE. Translated from the French by WILLIAM CROOKES, F.R.S., V.P.C.S., &c. Crown 8vo. 5s.

VIRGIL.—**Publi Vergili Maronis Bucolica, Georgica, Æneis;** The Works of VIRGIL, Latin Text, with English Commentary and Index. By B. H. KENNEDY, D.D. Cr. 8vo. 10s. 6d.

The Æneid of Virgil. Translated into English Verse. By JOHN CONINGTON, M.A. Crown 8vo. 6s.

The Poems of Virgil. Translated into English Prose. By JOHN CONINGTON, M.A. Crown 8vo. 6s.

The Eclogues and Georgics of Virgil. Translated from the Latin by J. W. MACKAIL, M.A., Fellow of Balliol College, Oxford. Printed on Dutch Hand-made Paper. Royal 16mo. 5s.

WAKEMAN and HASSALL.—**Essays Introductory to the Study of English Constitutional History.** By Resident Members of the University of Oxford. Edited by HENRY OFFLEY WAKEMAN, M.A., and ARTHUR HASSALL, M.A. Crown 8vo. 6s.

WALFORD.—**The Mischief of Monica:** a Novel. By L. B. WALFORD. Crown 8vo. 6s.

WALKER.—**The Correct Card;** or How to Play at Whist; a Whist Catechism. By Major A. CAMPBELL-WALKER, F.R.G.S. Fcp. 8vo. 2s. 6d.

WALPOLE.—**History of England from the Conclusion of the Great War in 1815 to 1858.** By SPENCER WALPOLE. Library Edition. 5 vols. 8vo. £4 10s. Cabinet Edition. 6 vols. Crown 8vo. 6s. each.

WELLINGTON.—**Life of the Duke of Wellington.** By the Rev. G. R. GLEIG, M.A. Crown 8vo. 3s. 6d.

WELLS. — **Recent Economic Changes** and their Effect on the Production and Distribution of Wealth and the Well-being of Society. By DAVID A. WELLS. Crown 8vo. 10s. 6d.

WENDT.—**Papers on Maritime Legislation,** with a Translation of the German Mercantile Laws relating to Maritime Commerce. By ERNEST EMIL WENDT. Royal 8vo. £1 11s. 6d.

WEST.—**Half-hours with the Millionaires:** Showing how much harder it is to spend a million than to make it. Edited by B. B. WEST. Crown 8vo. 6s.

WEYMAN.—**The House of the Wolf:** a Romance. By STANLEY J. WEYMAN. Crown 8vo. 3s. 6d.

WHATELY (E. Jane).—WORKS BY.

English Synonyms. Edited by R. WHATELY, D.D. Fcp. 8vo. 3s.

Life and Correspondence of Richard Whately, D.D., late Archbishop of Dublin. With Portrait. Crown 8vo. 10s. 6d.

WHATELY (Archbishop). — WORKS BY.

Elements of Logic. Crown 8vo. 4s. 6d.

Elements of Rhetoric. Crown 8vo. 4s. 6d.

Lessons on Reasoning. Fcp. 8vo. 1s. 6d.

Bacon's Essays, with Annotations. 8vo. 10s. 6d.

Whist in Diagrams: a Supplement to American Whist, Illustrated; being a Series of Hands played through, Illustrating the American leads, the new play, the forms of Finesse, and celebrated coups of Masters. With Explanation and Analysis. By G. W. P. Fcp. 8vo. 6s. 6d.

WILCOCKS.—The Sea Fisherman, Comprising the Chief Methods of Hook and Line Fishing in the British and other Seas, and Remarks on Nets, Boats, and Boating. By J. C. WILCOCKS. Profusely Illustrated. Crown 8vo. 6s.

WILLICH.—Popular Tables for giving Information for ascertaining the value of Lifehold, Leasehold, and Church Property, the Public Funds, &c. By CHARLES M. WILLICH. Edited by H. BENCE JONES. Crown 8vo. 10s. 6d.

WILLOUGHBY.—East Africa and its Big Game. By Capt. Sir JOHN C. WILLOUGHBY, Bart. Illustrated by G. D. Giles and Mrs. Gordon Hake. Royal 8vo. 21s.

WITT (*Prof.*).—WORKS BY. Translated by FRANCES YOUNGHUSBAND.

The Trojan War. Crown 8vo. 2s.

Myths of Hellas; or, Greek Tales. Crown 8vo. 3s. 6d.

The Wanderings of Ulysses. Crown 8vo. 3s. 6d.

The Retreat of the Ten Thousand; being the story of Xenophon's 'Anabasis'. With Illustrations. Crown 8vo. 3s. 6d.

WOLFF (*Henry W.*).—WORKS BY.

Rambles in the Black Forest. Crown 8vo. 7s. 6d.

The Watering Places of the Vosges. Crown 8vo. 4s. 6d.

The Country of the Vosges. With a Map. 8vo. 12s.

WOOD (*Rev. J. G.*).—WORKS BY.

Homes Without Hands; a Description of the Habitations of Animals, classed according to the Principle of Construction. With 140 Illustrations. 8vo. 7s. net.

Insects at Home; a Popular Account of British Insects, their Structure, Habits, and Transformations. With 700 Illustrations. 8vo. 7s. net.

Insects Abroad; a Popular Account of Foreign Insects, their Structure, Habits, and Transformations. With 600 Illustrations. 8vo. 7s. net.

WOOD (*Rev. J G.*).—WORKS BY,—continued.

Bible Animals; a Description of every Living Creature mentioned in the Scriptures. With 112 Illustrations. 8vo. 7s. net.

Strange Dwellings; a Description of the Habitations of Animals, abridged from 'Homes without Hands'. With 60 Illustrations. Crown 8vo. 3s. 6d.

Out of Doors; a Selection of Original Articles on Practical Natural History. With 11 Illustrations. Crown 8vo. 3s. 6d.

Petland Revisited. With 33 Illustrations. Crown 8vo. 3s. 6d.

WORDSWORTH.—Annals of My Early Life, 1806-46. By CHARLES WORDSWORTH, D.C.L., Bishop of St. Andrews. 8vo. 15s.

WYLIE.—History of England under Henry IV. By JAMES HAMILTON WYLIE. 2 vols. Vol. I., 1399-1404. Crown 8vo. 10s. 6d. Vol. II. [*In the Press.*]

YOUATT (*William*).—WORKS BY:

The Horse. Revised and enlarged. 8vo. Woodcuts, 7s. 6d.

The Dog. Revised and enlarged. 8vo. Woodcuts, 6s.

ZELLER (*Dr. E.*).—WORKS BY.

History of Eclecticism in Greek Philosophy. Translated by SARAH F. ALLEYNE. Cr. 8vo. 10s. 6d.

The Stoics, Epicureans, and Sceptics. Translated by the Rev. O. J. REICHEL, M.A. Crown 8vo. 15s.

Socrates and the Socratic Schools. Translated by the Rev. O. J. REICHEL, M.A. Cr. 8vo. 10s. 6d.

Plato and the Older Academy. Translated by SARAH F. ALLEYNE and ALFRED GOODWIN, B.A. Crown 8vo. 18s.

The Pre-Socratic Schools: a History of Greek Philosophy from the Earliest Period to the time of Socrates. Translated by SARAH F. ALLEYNE. 2 vols. Crown 8vo. 30s.

Outlines of the History of Greek Philosophy. Translated by SARAH F. ALLEYNE and EVELYN ABBOTT. Crown 8vo. 10s. 6d.

10,000/6/92. THE ABERDEEN UNIVERSITY PRESS.

www.ingramcontent.com/pod-product-compliance
Lightning Source LLC
Chambersburg PA
CBHW051235300426
44114CB00011B/748